# Russian Discourses on International Law



A number of recent events in the last decade have renewed interest in Russian discourses on international law. This book evaluates and presents a contemporary analysis of Russian discourses on international law from various perspectives, including sociological, theoretical, political, and philosophical. The aim is to identify how Russia interacts with international law, the reasons behind such interactions, and how such interactions compare with the general practice of international law. It also examines whether legal culture and other phenomena can justify Russia's interaction in international law.

*Russian Discourses on International Law* explains Russia's interpretation of international law through the lens of both leading western scholars and contemporary western-based Russian scholars. It will be of value to international law scholars looking for a better understanding of Russia's behavior in international legal relations, law and society, foreign policy, and domestic application of international law. Further, those in fields such as sociology, politics, philosophy, or general graduate students, lawyers, think tanks, government departments, and specialized Russian studies programs will find the book helpful.

**P. Sean Morris** teaches international economic law at the University of Helsinki, Finland.

## Routledge Research in International Law

For a full list of titles in this series, visit www.routledge.com/Routledge-Research-in-International-Law/book-series/INTNLLAW

**Available:**

**Demilitarization and International Law in Context**
The Åland Islands
*Sia Spiliopoulou Åkermark, Saila Heinikoski and Pirjo Kleemola-Juntunen*

**International Criminal Law and Sexual Violence against Women**
The Interpretation of Gender in the Contemporary International Criminal Trial
*Daniela Nadj*

**Unilateral Acts**
A History of a Legal Doctrine
*Betina Appel Kuzmarov*

**Regional Developmentalism through Law**
Establishing an African Economic Community
*Jonathan Bashi Rudahindwa*

**China's One Belt One Road Initiative and Private International Law**
*Edited by Poomintr Sooksripaisarnkit and Sai Ramani Garimella*

**Transnational Terrorist Groups and International Criminal Law**
*Anna Marie Brennan*

**The Rule of Unwritten International Law**
Customary Law, General Principles, and World Order
*Peter G. Staubach*

**Confronting Cyberespionage Under International Law**
*Oğuz Kaan Pehlivan*

**Russian Discourses on International Law**
Sociological and Philosophical Phenomenon
*Edited by P. Sean Morris*

# Russian Discourses on International Law

## Sociological and Philosophical Phenomenon

**Edited by**
**P. Sean Morris**

Routledge
Taylor & Francis Group
NEW YORK AND LONDON

First published 2019
by Routledge
52 Vanderbilt Avenue, New York, NY 10017, USA

and by Routledge
2 Park Square, Milton Park, Abingdon, Oxon OX14 4RN

First issued in paperback 2020

*Routledge is an imprint of the Taylor & Francis Group, an informa business*



*Library of Congress Cataloging in Publication Data*
Names: Morris, P. Sean, editor.
Title: Russian discourses on international law : sociological and philosophical phenomenon / edited by P. Sean Morris.
Description: Abingdon, Oxon [UK] ; New York, NY : Routledge, 2018. | Series: Routledge research in international law | Includes bibliographical references and index.
Identifiers: LCCN 2018020860 | ISBN 9781138566705 (hbk)
Subjects: LCSH: International law--Russia (Federation) | International and municipal law--Russia (Federation) | International law--Social aspects--Russia (Federation) | International law--Russia (Federation)--Philosophy. | International law and human rights--Russia (Federation) | Law--Russia (Federation)
Classification: LCC KLB2325 .R87 2018 | DDC 341--dc23
LC record available at https://lccn.loc.gov/2018020860

ISBN 13: 978-0-367-58602-7 (pbk)
ISBN 13: 978-1-138-56670-5 (hbk)

Typeset in Galliard
by Taylor & Francis Books

# Contents

# Contributors

**Bill Bowring** is professor of law at Birkbeck, University of London, a practicing barrister at Field Court Chambers, Gray's Inn, and an expert in the law of Russia and the former Soviet Union. He is currently a fellow of the Human Rights Centre at the University of Essex, a senior research fellow at the Institute of Advanced Legal Studies, and a visiting professor at the University of Northampton. Professor Bowring has many publications on topics of international law, human rights, and the law of Russia and other former Soviet Union countries. He frequently acts as a court expert. His most recent book is *Law, Rights and Ideology in Russia: Landmarks in the Destiny of a Great Power* (Routledge, 2013).

**W. E. Butler** is the John Edward Fowler Distinguished Professor of Law, Dickinson Law, Pennsylvania State University; Emeritus Professor of Comparative Law, University of London (University College London); Foreign Member, National Academy of Sciences of Ukraine and National Academy of Legal Sciences of Ukraine, and of the Russian Academy of Natural Sciences. He was the founding editor of *Sudebnik* (1995–2007), *Russian Law: Theory and Practice* (2004–2009), *East European and Russian Yearbook of International and Comparative Law* (2007–2016), and is a founding co-editor of the *Journal of Comparative Law* (2005–) and founding editor of *Jus Gentium: Journal of the History of International Law* (2016–). He serves on the editorial boards of numerous journals in Belarus, Latvia, Russia, Ukraine, western Europe, and the United States. He is as a member of the Kazakhstan International Commercial Arbitrage and the International Commercial Arbitration courts of Russia and Ukraine. Recent books include *Russian Law and Legal Institutions* (2014; 2nd edn, 2018); *Russian Family Law* (2014); *Russian Inheritance Law* (2015); and a translation in six volumes of *Ukrainian Legal Doctrine* (2015–2018).

**Tuomas Forsberg** is Director of the Helsinki Collegium for Advanced Studies and Professor of International of International Relations at the University of Tampere (on leave of absence 2018–2023). He is also a member of the board for Aleksanteri Institute at the University of Helsinki. Forsberg has authored a number of articles in leading journals discussing foreign policy and/or Russian politics. His latest book is *The European Union and Russia* (Palgrave, 2016) (co-authored with Hiski Haukkala).

**Anna Isaeva** teaches comparative jurisprudence at the University of Florence and is a researcher on the International Cold War Project. She is a member of the department of legal theory at University of Florence, where she obtained a PhD in the theory and history of human rights. From September 2015 to June 2016 she worked as an assistant editor of the *European Journal of International Law*.

**Anna Lukina** is a member of Hertford College, University of Oxford, reading jurisprudence (law). She has a particular interest in Soviet and Russian law and legal theory. Her previous work has been published in the *Review of Central and East European Law* ('The Semenchuk Case of 1936: Storytelling and Propaganda above the Law in the Soviet Criminal Trial').

**Tero Lundstedt** is a doctoral candidate in international law at the University of Helsinki and an affiliate fellow of the Erik Castrén Institute of International Law and Human Rights. He is co-author 'The Role of International Law in the Foreign Policy of the Russian Federation: Especially Concerning State Sovereignty, the Prohibition of the Use of Force and the People's Right to Self-Determination' (2016) a research report for the Finnish Ministry of Defense. Since October 2015, Lundstedt has been an associate editor of the *Finnish Yearbook of International Law*.

**P. Sean Morris** teaches international economic law at the Faculty of Law University of Helsinki. He obtained his LLB in international law (jurisprudence) at the Faculty of Law, Russian Peoples' Friendship University, Moscow (1998–2003), and since then has been based at the University of Helsinki.

**Christer Pursiainen** is Professor of Societal Safety and Environment at the Arctic University of Norway, Tromsø. He is also Adjunct Professor (docent) of International Relations at the University of Helsinki and holds a doctorate in political science from the same university. His many Russia-related publications include the edited volume *At the Crossroads of Post-Communist Modernisation: Russia and China in Comparative Perspective* (Palgrave Macmillan, 2012); the co-edited *Russia as a Great Power: Dimensions of Security Under Putin* (Routledge, 2005); and the monograph *Russian Foreign Policy and International Relations Theory* (Ashgate, 2000).

**Sebastian Rimestad** studied politics, international relations and religious studies in Aberdeen, Tartu, and Erfurt. He finished his PhD in religious studies at the University of Erfurt in 2012 and works there as a postdoctoral scholar with a project on Orthodox Christianity in western Europe. His publications include *The Challenges of Modernity to the Orthodox Church in Estonia and Latvia, 1917–1940* (Peter Lang, 2012), and numerous articles in peer-reviewed journals and collective volumes.

**Maria Smirnova** joined the School of Law, University of Manchester in September 2014 as a member of an international team of researchers working on Professor Christopher Thornhill's research project on the sociology of transnational constitution. She completed an LLM in international human rights law at the University of Exeter, and her PhD dissertation (Moscow, 2006) focused on the constitutional right to education and the guarantees of its realization in private educational institutions. Previously she worked as a researcher in the Moscow-based Federal Centre for Educational Legislation focusing on Russian and international education law and policy.

**Chris Thornhill** is professor in law at the University of Manchester, and a former professor of European political thought and head of politics at the University of Glasgow, where his research focused both on the relations between legal and political theory and legal and political sociology, and on processes of state formation and constitution writing in different European societies.

**Vladislav L. Tolstykh** is a professor of law at the Novosibirsk State University, Faculty of Law and head of the department of International Law. In addition to his academic appointments, Professor Tolstykh is a senior researcher of the Institute of Philosophy and Law of the Siberian Branch of the Russian Academy of Sciences. He has held visiting professorships with universities in Germany, Ukraine, France, and China and sits on the editorial board of several of Russia's leading law journals.

**Alexander A. Vishnevskiy** is a professor in the department of civil and business law at the National Research University, Higher School of Economics (Moscow), lecturing on comparative business law, comparative banking law, comparative canon law, and religious legal systems. He is also a lecturer on modern (comparative) banking law in the University of Helsinki. Professor Vishnevskiy is the author of numerous articles and books on banking law and canon law, including *The Banking Law of England* (Moscow: Statut, 2000); *The Banking Law of the European Union* (Moscow: Statut, 2000); and *Modern Banking Law: The Banker–Customer Relationship* (Moscow: Statut, 2013).

# Acknowledgments

The editor would like to thank the contributors for their time and effort in writing their respective chapters for this volume. Furthermore, the editor extends his deepest gratitude to two anonymous peer reviewers for comments on the initial draft abstracts and later for their feedback on the completed chapters. The team at Routledge, former and present (Briana Ascher), on the international law lists, and those on the production and editorial desks, Nicola Sharpe and Veronica Morgan are also owed thanks for their help in navigating the publishing process. Finally, thanks to Martin Barr for excellent copyediting.

# Introduction

This volume is intended to provide a balance narrative on the growth and development of international law from the perspective of other discourses. As such, it brings together contemporary writers who have a specialist knowledge of Russian perspectives on international law, or, are based in Russia, and can provide a unique insight on the practice and development of international law in Russia. This is not to say, that the volume is a comprehensive work that examine all aspects of international law in the Russian tradition. Actually, it is not. What this volume does, is to present phenomological, sociological and economic narratives that drives Russia in the international legal order. The contributions elevate those interests by addressing complex questions on how socio-philosophico systems account for constitutional developments in Russia that shapes its role in international law. The contributions explore specifically questions ranging from religious issues, human rights, ideology, and financial soft law. The volume helps to shape some of the arguments required for the specialized understanding of international that is not necessarily a purely western-based narrative, but systematically engaged or explained how Russia exerts its influence in the global legal order using the language of international. In other words, the volume opens a discussion and provides the necessary streams to further understand some of the nuances or theoretical insights on Russian discourses on international law.

Divided into five parts, the first provides a survey which examines contradictions in the international legal discourses on Russia, and also how the philosophical foundations of human rights are rooted in Russia's past. Part II explores the systemic sociological factors that have given rise to ideology and how Russia's living constitutional character adapts to realism in the international legal order. Part III introduces some "outside" questions such as the role of the Orthodox Church in shaping how Russia adapts in the international legal order, and also questions whether Russia has a transplanted legal regime. Part IV engages some of the foreign policy issues that shape Russian international law discourses and how those policies interact with questions on self-determination and/or the territorial integrity of states. The final part examines a more concrete question: to what extent does Russia rely on international soft law to shape economic reform, in particular in the banking sector.

The book will be of interest to international law scholars looking for a better understanding of Russia's behavior in international legal relations, law, and society; social science scholars in fields such as sociology and politics, philosophers; graduate students, lawyers, think tanks, government departments, and specialized Russian studies programs.

P. Sean Morris

# Part I

# Russia and the Theoretical Struggles on International Law

# 1 The Nature of Russian Discourses on International Law

## A Contemporary Survey

*Vladislav L. Tolstykh*[*]

## 1 Russian Doctrine of International Law before 1991

The science of international law started to develop in Russia in the second half of the nineteenth century and from its very beginning followed European patterns. According to one of Russia's nineteenth-century international legal scholars, Dmitry Kachenovsky (1827–1872), "The science of international law came to us from the West, first in the form of a foreign theory."[1] The same idea was expressed by Yuri Klyuchnikov (1886–1938): "The idea of law was combined with the idea of the West in the mind of Russian liberals of the forties and the fifties … They loved the West for the incarnation of the life ideal in the law."[2] In 1847 Tikhon Stepanov (1795–1847) from Kharkiv wrote the first Russian textbook on international law, which was never published ('International Law in Conjunction with Diplomacy'); in 1856 and 1859 Mikhail Kapustin from Moscow (1828–1899) published his short *Survey of Subjects of International Law*; in 1863 Dmitry Kachenovsky from Kharkiv published his short course on international law; and, in 1882–1883, Fedor Martens (1845–1909) published his famous work *International law of Civilised Nations.* A number of young authors of the day defended various dissertations on the emerging school of international law such as: Mechislav Zaremba, *Historical Development of the Notion of Military Contraband* (1849); Peter Bibikov, *Essay on International Law in Greece* (1852); Ivan Andreevsky (1831–1991), *On the Rights of Foreigners in Russia* (1854); Alexander Lokhvitsky (1830–1884), *On the status of prisoners in ancient Russian law* (1855); and Dmitry Kachenovsky, *On Privateers and Prize-winning Legal Proceedings in Relation to Neutral Trade* (1855). Russian scientists visited foreign universities, presented their reports, and translated works of Johan Kaspar Bluntschli, Franz von Liszt, and other foreign authors into Russian.[3]

* The author is grateful to Elena Vaina for assistance with the translation.

1 *Course of International Law* (Kharkov, 1863) xii.

2 *At the Great Historical Crossroads* (Berlin, 1922) 157.

3 For a detailed exposition of the early history of the Russian science of international law, see Vladimir Grabar, *Materials on the History of the Literature of International Law in Russia (1647–1917)* (Publishing House of the Academy of Sciences of the USSR, 1958).

Russian scientists did not limit themselves to didactic activity: they also put forward projects of international reforms. For example, D. Kachenovsky called for the joint work of scientists from different countries and codification of international law (report of the London Law Society, 1861); Leonid Kamarovsky (1846–1912) carried out a thorough analysis of the idea of international courts and proposed a design for a future court;[4] and F. Martens prepared a number of texts for the Hague Peace Conferences, including the famous Martens Clause, and acted as an arbiter in several interstate disputes. The second half of the twentieth century was a period of transition from classicism to positivism. As their western colleagues, Russian scientists did not follow a single theoretical path: L. Kamarovsky and D. Kachenovsky advanced naturalist concepts; F. Martens paid much attention to the facts of state life, but, on the other hand, put forward the idea of international communication, which had inherently natural character; Nikolai Korkunov (1853–1904) believed that the main function of international law is to protect rights related to civil, criminal, administrative, and other branches of internal law; and Vladimir Ulyanitsky (1855–1917) tried to systematize the existing ideas and present them in an accessible format.

International law was originally taught at non-specialized departments, for example, at the Department of Natural, Political and Popular Law of the Moscow University; lectures were often given by specialists in the field of state law and history. The University charter of 1835 provided for a common public law department, thereby giving an incentive for specialization. In 1880, the Russian Society of International Law was established in St. Petersburg. Thus, for several decades the Russian doctrine managed to catch up with European schools, master the existing array of knowledge, and develop its own traditions.[5] This development of Russian doctrine in the general line of western patterns was interrupted in 1917.

The Russian Revolution of 1917 differed from other revolutions. First, it was the first revolution caused not by an internal political or economic crisis but by a

4 According to Kamarovsky, the World Court should be guided by the following principles: independence, collegiality, oral process, competitiveness, publicity, existence of two instances, division into departments (diplomacy, military and maritime affairs, private international law, social international law). The Court is formed by the states, each appointing two members. Over time, the appointment of judges should be delegated to international congresses. The Court is permanent, but sits as necessary. Its jurisdiction is voluntary and extends only to the states of Europe and America. The Court not only applies the existing law but also drafts new laws and forwards them for consideration of governments. The Court sits in Brussels and uses French. In case of non-execution of its decisions, the interested party may enforce them, while other states may impose sanctions (cessation of diplomatic relations, termination of contracts, closure of markets, and even resort to war) (Leonid Kamarovsky, *On the International Court* (Malinsky, 1881)).

5 In 1863 Kachenovsky (n. 1) pointed out:

> It is not difficult for a Russian to grasp the latest results of knowledge and transmit them in a lively, clear, expressive language … A Russian man is very capable of understanding international issues and, if he wants, he will find the calmness necessary for their thorough solution.
>
> (xxxvi, xliv)

global crisis (World War I). In this regard its strategic goal was to change the world order in its entirety (and not only the internal order). Second, it was the first anti-capitalist revolution (all the preceding revolutions were anti-feudal). Eventually, this goal was not achieved but the very fact of its formation demonstrated the transient nature of capitalism. Third, it was the first revolution based on scientific methods: its plan and instruments were defined by political and economic theory; and it was not done spontaneously.

Immediately after the Revolution, the Soviet government attempted to translate Marxist ideas into practice. First, it took steps to organize a world revolution. In the Decree on Peace (October 26, 1917), it proposed that the belligerent peoples and governments begin peace negotiations and declared the abolition of secret diplomacy;[6] in 1919 it established the Third Comintern, which aims to "create a World union of Soviet republics."[7] Second, it introduced the policy of military communism and nationalized large enterprises and banks, centralized production management, established a monopoly on foreign trade, and introduced obligatory labor service and mandatory food withdrawal system. Third, it established a new governance system, based on the Soviets (assemblies) of people's deputies; and the exploiters (bourgeoise) were deprived of the right to vote.

Yet most of these measures failed before Lenin's death. The Decree on the Peace was not implemented by workers of other countries; Russia withdrew from the war only thanks to the humiliating Brest Peace Treaty (Treaty of Brest-Litovsk, February 9, 1918). The Rappal Treaty with Germany of 1922 marked the beginning of Russia's gradual accession to the existing international system.[8] The policy of war during communism led to a sharp reduction in production, caused famine and riots: as a result, the government abandoned it and introduced the New Economic Policy.[9] The system of Soviets was preserved until the Soviet Union collapsed, but the real power passed to the bureaucratic elite composed of party functionaries and members of executive committees, which formed a new privileged class which separated itself from the majority of the population. Thus,

6 Hélène Carrère d'Encausse noted:

> This text is particularly interesting because it is addressed not to governments but to the people, against governments. Thus, Lenin rejects the classical concept of international relations and declares his desire to create a new political order … The Decree on Peace is a worldwide call for revolution.
>
> (*Nicholas II: The Interrupted Transition* (Olma Press, 2006) 351–2)

7 Program and Charter of the Communist International (LenPartizdat, 1933).

8 Leon Lipson noted: "For strategic reasons it proved necessary to coexist temporarily with other states that remained opposed to the Bolshevik revolution; for economic reasons it was necessary for the young, ravaged, and very poor Soviet state to establish commercial relations abroad" 'The Soviet View on International Law' in R. B. Lillich and J. Norton Moore (eds), 61 *Role of International Law and Evolving Ocean Law* (Naval War College Press, 1980) 101–2.

9 In 1921 Lenin said: "The new economic policy … means to a large extent a transition to restoration of capitalism" (Vladimir Lenin, 'New Economic Policy and Problems of Political Education' in 44 *Complete Works (Political Literature 1970*) 159–60).

before the threat of revolt and economic catastrophe, the Soviet government carried out a counter-revolution of its own. Subsequently, the policy of the USSR was changed several more times. However, none of these changes were accompanied by a return to the original Marxist project.

In general, the USSR cannot be considered as an implementation of the Marxist project. It implemented some of the Marxist objectives: eliminated the capitalist class, nationalized the instruments of production, ensured a broad social protection of citizens, and gave them equal access to all areas of public life.[10] These objectives, however, were implemented by the means of creating new imbalances. Instead of the capitalist class, a powerful state bureaucracy grew up; the *socialization* of the instruments of production took place in the form of their nationalization (thus, a worker did not become their master); the high level of social protection did not solve the problem of food and housing shortages; and democratization was formal and not accompanied by the provision of real opportunities for participation in politics.

Some points of the Marxist program were completely ignored. The problem of alienation was not solved: Soviet citizens were alienated from labor and politics no less than their western colleagues. Not only did they fail to overcome the stage of Hobbesian man, who is striving for security and accumulation of property – on the contrary, they were thrown back to the more archaic stage of the ancient Eastern state slave. For a time, the USSR existed at the expense of the initial impulse and internal centuries-old traditions of statehood. By the end of the 1980s, however, economic problems became chronic, the Marxist rhetoric lost its heat, people ceased to believe in communist ideals, and came under the influence of bourgeois values. Thus, the collapse of the USSR in 1991 became the necessary result of a protracted illness.

Perhaps the most accurate characteristic of the evolution of the Soviet system was given by Leon Trotsky (1879–1940), who defined Stalin's policy as a "thermidor." The material precondition for communism is a high level of economic development, while Russia was the weakest link in the capitalist system. For this reason, many economic contradictions arose in the USSR, generating social antagonisms. These antagonisms caused a social demand for bureaucracy. As a result, the Soviet state did not wither away but grew and de facto became a "bourgeois state, albeit without a bourgeoisie."[11]

Immediately after the Revolution, the Soviet doctrine was divided by a very important dispute. Some authors denied any legal form; the most consistent among them was Evgeny Pashukanis (1891–1937). He saw the source of the legal relationship in the economic attitude of equal persons who own goods. The legal subject is "abstract commodity owner elevated to the heavens," who wants to exchange and conclude contracts. Among two equal owners, no one can act as a power regulator; this requires a third person, i.e. the state. The withering away of

10 Michael Head notes that the Russian Revolution marked the first attempt (apart from the short-lived and localized Paris Commune) to fundamentally reorganize economic, social, and legal life along egalitarian lines ('The Passionate Legal Debates of the Early Years of the Russian Revolution' (2001) 14 *Canadian Journal of Law and Jurisprudence* 3).

11 Leon Trotsky, *The Revolution Betrayed: What Is the Soviet Union and Where Is It Going?* (T8 Rugram, 2017).

the law and state will occur, only when labor ceases to be a means for life and becomes its first need, i.e. when any form of equivalent relation will be obsolete. The withering away of the bourgeois law does not mean replacing it by the proletarian law, but means a withering away of the law in general.[12]

Other authors insisted on the special nature of the Soviet state and law. Thus, recognizing the inevitability of the withering away of the state, Peter Stuchka (1865–1932) emphasized the continuance of the proletarian revolution and the need to suppress the class enemy, and warned against the "bias towards the too hasty expectations of withering away of the state."[13] Andrey Vyshinsky (1883–1954) took a more radical position: in 1938, he called Pashukanis a "grief-scientist" and "traitor" and said that his book had "no gram of Marxism." Seeing the inevitability of the withering away of the law and the state, the Marxism sets for the proletariat, who had seized power, goals, and objectives relating to the use of the law and state and, consequently, to the need to maximize their strengthening. If a new economy is being created, a new law is being created too. This law is fundamentally different from the bourgeois one.[14] Eventually, supporters of the latter approach, enjoying the support of Stalin, gained the upper hand, and the supporters of the former were purged (Pashukanis was executed in 1937).

The Vyshinsky approach determined the future of the Soviet legal science in general and the Soviet science of international law in particular. First, although this science was positioned as a Marxist one, its adoption of the Marxist ideas was formal and selective.[15] Second, it was positivistic, i.e. justified a strong state, the rule of law, and the willful nature of law. Third, it identified the law with the command economy and, as a result, was scholastic and isolated from philosophy, history, and economics.[16] Fourth, it proceeded from the special nature of the Soviet state and law, manifested in the non-adversarial nature of society, genuine democracy, reduction of coercion, transfer of many functions to public organizations, and scientific nature of governance.[17]

12 Eugene Pashukanis, *General Theory of Law and Marxism* (3rd edn, Publishing House of the Communist Academy, 1929).

13 Petr Stuchka, *Doctrine of the Soviet State and Its Constitution: The USSR and the RSFSR* (State Publishing House, 1929) 49–50, 311.

14 Andrei Vyshinsky, 'Main Objectives of the Science of the Soviet Socialist Law: Report at the First Meeting on the Science of the Soviet State and Law (July 16–19, 1938), Beginning' (2009) 1 *Questions of Jurisprudence* 191.

15 Rett Ludwikowski notes:

> Everyday contact with Marxism has a very peculiar impact on the mentality of a socialist lawyer. On the one hand, he is well trained in how to decorate his speeches and works with phrases taken from the 'sacred books' on classical Marxism; on the other hand, he does not take Marxist rhetoric very seriously.
>
> ('Socialistic Legal Theory in the Post-Pashukanis Era' (1987) 10 *Boston College International and Comparative Law Review* 323–4)

16 In the cited report Andrei Vyshinsky defined the law as "a set of rules of behavior expressing the will of the ruling class" (Vyshinsky (n. 14) 233–4).

17 Similar assessments can be found among western authors. Thus, Leon Lipson considers that the Soviet doctrine of international law was official, i.e. obliged to justify

In order to disguise the departure from Marxism, Soviet authors used several techniques. First, while not denying the thesis of the withering away of the state, they discussed it incidentally, as a distant perspective which did not affect the existence and value of the Soviet system.[18] Second, they used Stalin's "dialectic" thesis, that without a strong state it is impossible to build communism. Third, they argued that by creating a new type of basis, socialism created a new type of superstructure: the Soviet law, fundamentally different from the bourgeois law and not subject to withering away. Thus, the issue of abrogation of the law was replaced by the issue of abolishing the old principles of law: thereby the form was artificially separated from the content. These distortions have caused the weakness of Soviet jurisprudence, both in the field of general theoretical developments and in the field of sectoral regulation.

In the postwar period, the Soviet doctrine of international law, represented by Fedor Kozhevnikov (1903–1998), Vladimir Koretsky (1890–1984), Evgeny Korovin (1892–1964), Sergey Krylov (1888–1958), Grigory Tunkin (1906–1993), Nikolay Ushakov (1918–2001), David Feldman (1922–1924) et al., developed the following ideas: (1) the world is divided into antagonistic systems, which, however, can coexist peacefully and obey common international law; (2) socialist states, unlike capitalist states, express national interests and promote progressive development of international law; (3) international law has a conciliatory nature and regulates specific relations and not issues of ideology; (4) relations between socialist countries are regulated by socialist international law, which refers to general law as *lex specialis*; (5) the main means of resolving international disputes are negotiating; and (6) international law does not have a direct effect in the internal order and needs to be transformed. Thus, it borrowed the concept of voluntarism (positive law) from the West but sought to give it an ideological coloring of its own. In relation to classical Marxism, which calls for a world revolution and a withering away of the state, it was of a revisionist nature.

## 2 Rhetorical Structure of Russian Doctrine

In 1991, the USSR disintegrated. Its legal successor was the Russian Federation, which, having embarked on a capitalist path, joined the IMF and the WTO, recognized the ECHR jurisdiction, concluded new bilateral investment treaties, etc. Several integration associations were created on the post-Soviet space: the Commonwealth of Independent States (CIS), the Union State of Russia and Belarus, and the Eurasian Economic Union (EAEU). The Russian doctrine abandoned the Soviet ideology and borrowed the ideology of its former adversaries and thereby lost its relative independence. This resulted in a number of adverse

actions of the state; moralistic, i.e. perceived the USSR as a progressive actor; projective, i.e. attributed to others insidious ideas and intentions; offensive, i.e. put forward counter accusations against any kind of criticism; and intellectually underdeveloped. Lipson (n. 8) 104–8.

18 For instance, Stuchka in the *Doctrine of the Soviet State and Its Constitution* devoted 300 pages to the description of the Soviet state and only four pages (308–11) to the withering away of the state. Stuchka (n. 13).

consequences. First, the new ideas came into conflict with the surviving elements of the old ideology: as a result, the Russian theory of international law became internally contradictory. Second, the new ideas were not borrowed in their entirety: some were simplified to the level of slogans, others were ignored, and some were simply distorted; as a result, they were unable to provide a high level of legal rhetoric. Third, the Russian doctrine never became a full participant in the western discourse and did not affect its content, sometimes conflicting with Russia's national interests.

The "hard-line" arguments of the modern Russian doctrine are relatively homogeneous: they mainly reflect postulates of voluntarism formulated at the end of the nineteenth and the beginning of the twentieth century by Georg Jellinek, Dionisio Anzilotti, and others. These postulates were creatively restyled by the Soviet doctrine, primarily by G. Tunkin.[19] The key voluntaristic idea is the derivation of international law from an individual state will; the source is the main criteria of the existence of legal provisions. Voluntarism can effectively operate in an international community where states play a major role: the Cold War era was exactly that. The modern community however is different: besides states, its active subjects are supranational and nongovernmental institutions, whose influence is constantly growing whereas the influence of states is weakening. This new reality is based on new approaches such as normativism (Hans Kelsen), analytical school (Herbert Hart), legal realism (Hans Morgenthau), the concept of global governance (James Rosenau), structuralism (David Kennedy, Martti Koskenniemi), neo-naturalism (Philip Allot), etc. All these approaches are mainly unfamiliar to the Russian doctrine and are not discussed by Russian international law academics. The negative consequences of the monopoly of voluntarism are, first, a dogmatic weakness of the doctrine and its inability to controversy with non-voluntaristic concepts; and, second, an isolation of the doctrine from the social reality and, as a result, its practical inefficiency.

A big problem of the Russian doctrine is the neglect of fundamental theoretical issues related to the history of international law, lawmaking, statehood, and so on. These questions are rarely considered in dissertations and monographs and are described very superficially in general courses, usually with reference to the Soviet concepts. These concepts, in turn, hardly correspond to the needs of the modern science. For example, the often-cited work by Yury Baskin and David Feldman on the history of international law is quite good but very brief (205 pages) and does not reflect problematic issues and discussions in the field.[20] Another example: the monograph of G. Tunkin, *The Theory of International Law*, considered by many scientists as an example of a high theory, reflects only one radical voluntaristic concept. This, however, does not mean that the Russian doctrine does not involve theoretical disputes. These disputes exist but concern very abstract and scholastic issues: for example, whether an individual is a subject of international law, whether

19 George Tunkin, *Theory of International Law* (International Relations, 1970).

20 Yury Baskin and David Feldman, *History of International Law* (International Relations, 1990).

provisions of international law shall be applied directly, whether international law restricts the sovereignty of a state, and so forth. The point is not even that these issues are not of practical importance but that they are discussed in isolation from practice and these discussions never affect the policies of the state. This imbalance is partly due to the inertia that has been preserved since Soviet times and assumes confidence in the already existing ideological paradigm, and partly is caused by the weak theoretical skills of Russian scientists and their non-participation in theoretical debates, which their western colleagues are happily participating in. In the absence of a solid theoretical basis, the sectoral researches have acquired a purely reflective nature and do not influence the development of international law.

The level of argumentation of the Russian doctrine is rather low. It is characterized by the underdevelopment of techniques of intentional, linguistic, and teleological interpretation; inability to establish links between the elements of legal system (interpretation, displacement, supplementation, hierarchy, etc.); the inability to work with basic terms (such as "will," "subject," "act," etc.); subordination of legal discourse to political conjuncture; and ignorance of historical, political, and cultural aspects. A legal argument is often formulated as a direct and obvious deduction from the norm, not developing its content, or, as a speculative statement, not based on a solid foundation. A good example is the practice of post-Soviet international courts: while the decisions of the Economic Court of the CIS are characterized by the first extreme (they are obvious), the decisions of the EAUC Court are characterized by the second extreme (they are often unfounded). The same can be said about the Russian textbooks, whose content is more referential than analytical: the problem is at best ascertained but never disclosed and solved. Being devoid of the necessary rhetorical tools, the Russian doctrine, first, is incapable of comprehending theoretical patterns and developing its position in theoretical and practical disputes; second, Russian legal doctrine seeks to go beyond legal discourse and use non-legal arguments (appeal to history, political conflict, opponent's bias, etc.); third, Russian legal doctrine turns into a ritual detached from reality, a method of psychological unloading, justifying its own impotence in an avoided rhetorical duel.

The Russian specialists in the field of international law can be divided into four groups. The first group includes scientists who use the dogmatic method; they see their task in construction of definitions and classifications, looking for solutions of abstract problems, formulation of general conclusions, etc. They refuse to analyze judicial decisions, considering this an unworthy work, or to use philosophy and political science, considering it a task inappropriate for a lawyer. This group is the most numerous and is mainly represented by scientists of the older Soviet generation and their pupils. The second group includes scientists who use the practical method; they actively work with the latest western concepts, give comments on judicial practice, collaborate with foreign colleagues, and participate in foreign scientific events. These are mostly young scientists working in universities in Moscow and St. Petersburg (Alexey Ispolinov, Vera Rusinova, Anait Smbatyan, Vladislav Starzhenetsky, etc.). The third group includes several scientists who try to use the critical method, i.e. assess international law from an external standpoint (for example, from the standpoint of natural law) and describe its internal contradictions. Among them there are Alexander Mezyayev, Vladislav Tolstykh, and several constitutionalists who oppose activist practices of the ECHR. Finally, the fourth group includes scientists who are poorly versed in international law but formally are part of the legal community; their activity consists of compilations of official texts or empty apologetics of international projects.

Like their foreign colleagues, Russian scientists publish textbooks and monographs. Textbooks, as a rule, are written by a collective of authors, under the auspices of a university and under the guidance of a famous scientist; many of them run to several editions. The textbook edited by Gennady Ignatenko (UrGUU),[21] Alexander Vylegzhanin (MGIMO), Alexander Kovalev and Stanyslav Chernichenko (Diplomatic Academy), Kamil Bekyashev (MGUU) are some examples. Several textbooks were written by individual authors (Ilya Lukashuk, Nikolay Ushakov, Vladislav Tolstykh).[22] The number of monographs on international law has dropped sharply in recent years: this is due to the fact that universities direct their staff to write articles and to the fact that publishers do not have a commercial interest (the book market in Russia is in crisis, as everywhere in the world). There are many law journals published in Russia. Some of them are specialized, others are general; some are published by independent publishers, others by universities. Specialized journals are the *Moscow Journal of International Law* (MGIMO, four issues/year); *International Private Law* (Publishing House Russia-Neva, four issues/year); *International Public and Private Law* (the publishing group "Lawyer," six issues/year); and *International Justice* (Institute of Law and Public Policy, four issues/year). All of them have quite a small audience and, as a rule, a theoretical focus. The exception is "International Justice," which is focused on the analysis of the jurisprudence. Among the journals on general

21 Hereafter, the following abbreviations of official names of Russian academic institutions are used in Russian transliteration: MGIMO – Moscow State Institute of International Relations; MGUU – Kutafin Moscow State Law University; UrGUU – Ural State Law University; SGUA – Saratov State Law Academy; RUDN – Peoples' Friendship University of Russia; MGU – Moscow State University; NGU – Novosibirsk State University; SPGU – Saint Petersburg; KGU – Kazan State University; RUP – Russian University of Justice; VShE – Higher School of Economics; IGPAN – Institute of State and Law (ISL) of the Russian Academy of Sciences; IZISP – Institute of Legislation and Comparative Law under the Russian Federation Government.

22 Международное право / Под ред. Г. Игнатенко и О. Тиунова. М.: Норма, 2005 (Gennady Ignatenko and Oleg Tiunov (eds), *International Law* (Moscow: Norma, 2005)); Международное право / под ред. А. Ковалева и С. Черниченко. М.: Омега-Л, 2006 (Alexander Kovalev and Stanislav Cherniechenko (eds), *International Law* (Moscow, Omega-L, 2006)); Международное право / под ред. А. Вылегжанина, М.: Юрайт, 2011 (Alexander Vylegzhanin (ed.), *International Law* (Moscow: Yurayt, 2011)); Лукашук И. Международное право. М.: Волтерс Клувер 2005 (Iilya Lukashuk, *International Law* (Moscow: Kluwer, 2005)); Международное публичное право / под ред. К.А. Бекяшева. М.: Проспект 2009 (Kamil Bekyashev (ed), Public International Law (Moscow: Prospect, 2009)); Толстых В. Курс международного права. М.: Проспект 2018 (Vladislav Tolstykh, *A General Course on International Law* (Moscow: Prospect, 2018)).

legal topics, the *Russian Law Journal* (*RUJ*)[23] and *Eurasian Law Journal*, which regularly publish articles on international law, stand out. The quality of articles is not uniform. Most of them pursue a purely pragmatic goal: to fulfill the indices necessary to present a dissertation or fulfill an effective contract, and do not cause any particular interest. Some of the articles often deserve attention, however, they do not always cause a resonance. Articles, as a rule, are isolated works and tend to be very short: journals rarely organize discussions *pro* and *contra*, compose thematic issues, publish critical reviews, etc. (*RUJ* is an exception). Recently journals have started to publish translated articles (*International Justice* and *RUJ*). A number of Russian authors are also publishing their works in foreign journals.

Despite a certain number of good works, the quality of scientific texts as a whole is low. They have the following typical shortcomings: reciting official documents (the amount of such borrowings is sometimes greater than the amount of the author's material); statement of obvious facts under the guise of discoveries; promotion of questionable, often utopian, proposals; obtrusive anti-western rhetoric; frequent quoting of political figures and finding a deep meaning in their words; non-use of modern scientific instruments; abuse of stereotypes, in particular, an almost ritual reference to human rights; absence of serious economic, sociological, and historical calculations; non-use of foreign doctrine and judicial practice; excessive scholasticism (a taste for construction of definitions and classifications); language defects (confusion of styles, use of cumbersome formulations, and inconsistency of presentation); and ignorance of the fundamental problems and inability to identify and solve them. The situation is aggravated by the fact that with the introduction of the new requirements to employment contracts and dissertations (theses), publishing of scientific works has become an obligation for university professors, including those who do not have a taste or talent for this. In this situation, some Russian scientists have switched to using western works; their usage however raises certain problems such as inability to participate fully in the discussion, generation of intellectual passivity, degradation of legal language, fragmentation of knowledge, etc.

Russian scientists do actively participate in various conferences, round tables, and other scientific events. As a rule, each major university holds one general conference annually, as well as several thematic events. General conferences ubiquitously include sections on international law. The most famous and mass general conferences are the Kutafin Readings (MGUU), the Eurasian Law Congress (UrGUU), the most famous conferences on international law are the Tunkin Readings (MGU), the Blishenko Readings (Peoples' Friendship University of Russia), and the annual meetings of the Russian Association of International Law (RAIL). A Russian conference consists of a series of reports and speeches, during which selected speakers present theses not intended for verification in the course of a scientific dialogue. The audience, as a rule, is deprived of an opportunity to ask questions, while the speaker is deprived of an opportunity to get the audience's feedback. Participation in such events may be attempted out of idle

23 This is not to be confused with the English-language *Russian Law Journal.*

curiosity, or driven by a desire to establish scientific contacts, prepare a scientific report, spend budgetary funds, engage in academic tourism – anything but not the first and primary goal of direct scientific communication. Many scientists whose opinion might be of interest, being presented both in the form of a report and in the form of a question, avoid participation in such events, rightly seeing them as a profanation.

The ineffectiveness of scientific events is determined not only by their format but also by a new university policy aimed at increasing quantitative indicators. Each university seeks to organize as many events as possible: it is presumed that in this way it can enhance its status. Instead of intensifying scientific communication, this politics disintegrates it: none of the hundreds of events provides the level of representation necessary for setting common goals and developing common positions. Another problem is that the Russian forums try to avoid discussions of actual problems (such as the *Yukos* affair, the reunification of Crimea with Russia, the war in Syria, etc.) and controversial political issues (such as the centennial anniversary of the Russian Revolution). This has nothing to do with the state policy; rather Russian international law academics feel more comfortable when limiting their discussions to abstract issues.

## 3 Thematic Structure of Russian Doctrine

The thematic structure of the Russian doctrine is characterized by serious imbalances. As already noted, the issues related to statehood (sovereignty, jurisdiction, succession, recognition, and self-determination) are not explored on a serious level; as a result, scholasticism, false theories, and incompetence arise. Among the most significant works, there are a review book of N. Ushakov and an analytical work of P. Kremnev, related to succession.[24] Apparently, this state of affairs stems from the inertia of a fundamental refusal of the Soviet doctrine to resolve the dispute about the withering away of the state. Even the problem of Crimea and Russia's reunification did not change the situation: most of the experts did not discuss this issue and the articles by A. Kapustin and V. Tolstykh did not provoke any real resonance.[25] Modern works on the history of international law and its doctrine are practically absent; this gap is partially compensated by the efforts of scientists specializing in history, primarily L. Kofanov, and several scientists from the post-Soviet countries.[26] Russian research and scholarship also pays little

24 Nicolay Ushakov, *State in the System of International Legal Regulation* (Institute of State and Law, 1997); Peter Kremnev, *Collapse of the USSR and Succession of States* (Yurlitinform, 2012).

25 Anatoly Kapustin, 'Crimea's Self-Determination in the Light of Contemporary International Law' (2015) 75 *Heidelberg JIL*, 101; Vladislav Tolstykh, 'Right to Self-determination as a Legal Basis for the Reunification of Crimea with Russia' (2014) 102 *Comparative Constitutional Review* 73; Vladimir Tomsinov, 'Unification of Crimea with Russia from the Point of View of International Law' (2014) 6 *Legislation* 10.

26 Leonid Kofanov, *External System of Roman Law: Law of Nature, Law of Peoples and Commercial Law in the Legal Thought of Antiquity* (Statute, 2015); Olga Butkevich,

attention to territorial issues: for example, most textbooks do not engage with the theory of occupation, notion of *res nullius*, and principle of *uti possidetis juris*. In the Soviet period, issues of the population were dealt with by S. Chernichenko and Yu. Boyars; at present they are mainly engaged by constitutionalists.[27] Diplomatic and consular law is set out in several works of didactic orientation and, as a whole, is on the periphery of research.[28]

The situation related to the law of international organizations looks paradoxical. In 1996, MGIMO and, in 1998, MGUA established departments of European law. Their collaborators wrote a number of monographs and articles, translated official texts, organized a number of conferences, etc.[29] Some universities included a course of European law in their curriculum, and the academic specialty "international law" (12.00.10) has become a two-part module (international law, European law). Problems of post-Soviet integration, on the contrary, were hardly analyzed or analyzed very narrowly; in many respects, this was due to the imperfection of the CIS legal framework. The situation changed with the launch of the EAEU (2009–2012); the EAEU Court, unlike the Economic Court of the CIS, was entitled to render binding decisions. Another factor was the cooling of relations with the West and the irritated reaction of the Constitutional Court to the activist decisions of the ECHR. The European law departments partially switched to Eurasian studies, some universities opened corresponding specializations, and several authors have begun to systematically comment on decisions of the EAEU Court (Alexey Ispolinov, Tatyana Neshataeva systematically, Anait Smbatyan, Vladislav Tolstykh). The Eurasian studies have become a priority for some journals, most of the articles, however, contain an unfounded apologetics of integration. Among works on general topics, there are collective monographs published under the editorship of S. Kashkin and T. Neshataeva.[30] Despite some institutional modifications and statements about a special path, the Eurasian integration follows the European model: the EAEU Commission uses the EU commodity nomenclature and the EAEU Court refers to the decisions of the EU Court in almost every decision.

The Eurasian studies are hampered by a number of problems. The problems of the first group are related to the imperfection of the regulatory base of the EAEU:

*At the Root of International Law* (Legal Center-Press, 2008) (the work mainly deals with the medieval international law); Lauri Mälksoo, *Russian Approaches to International Law* (OUP, 2015).

27 See, for example, Oleg Kutafin, *Russian Citizenship* (Prospekt, 2014).

28 Igor Blishchenko, *Diplomatic Law* (Higher School, 1990); Tatyana Matveeva, *Diplomatic and Consular Law* (RAGS, 2009); V. Meshcherikov, E. Pavelieva et al., *Diplomatic and Consular Law* (Prospekt, 2015); Olga Plotnikova and Olga Dubrovina, *Consular Relations and Consular Law* (Norma, 2018).

29 Lev Entin, *European Law: Law of the European Union and Legal Protection of Human Rights* (Norma, 2007); Lev Entin, *Law of the European Union: A New Stage of Evolution: 2009–2017* (Axiom, 2009); Sergey Kashkin (ed.), *Law of the European Union* (Yurayt, 2010).

30 Sergey Kashkin (ed.), *Fundamentals of Legal Regulation of Integration Processes in the Post-Soviet Space* (Norma 2015); Tatyana Neshataeva (ed.), *Eurasian Integration: Role of the Court* (Statute, 2015).

the basic documents contain contradictions, gaps, and inaccuracies, or are simply written in bad language. The defects in the primary law result in defects in the secondary law (decisions of the EAEU Commission and the Court), which is extremely difficult to analyze. The problems of the second group are due to the imperfection of the institutional structure of the Union, whose architects seem to have failed to form a holistic vision of its nature: whether it is an improved version of the CIS or a truly supranational entity. The problems of the third group are determined by the activity of the EAEU Court, whose first steps were rather unsuccessful: the Court rendered several activist and unjustified decisions, and, as a result, in 2013 the member states canceled some of the most important powers of it (incl. preliminary ruling competence).

The general theory of international organizations is represented by a three-volume referential *Encyclopedia of International Organizations* and a monograph of T. Neshataeva, who seems to support the position of F. Seyersted on the independent character of the law of international organizations.[31] UN activities are examined by several monographs of political content, as well as in articles by Yury Maleev (UN reform issues) and V. Kartashkin (human rights protection).[32] Russian scientists are not in the habit of giving an article-by-article analysis of the UN Charter or comment on particular resolutions of the UN Security Council, at best limiting themselves to reproaching the west vis-à-vis for deviating from the principles of the Yalta–Potsdam system.

The analysis of sources of international law is uneven. Voluntarism involves increased attention to the law of treaties; among the authors of the older generation, A. Talalayev and I. Lukashuk published several detailed monographs on this; among young authors, N. Simonova and A. Ispolinov did the same.[33] Customary international law, which in the Soviet period was explored by G. Tunkin and G. Danilenko, practically ceased to be of interest to the Russian scientists; one of the few exceptions is a review article by A. Vylegzhanin and R. Kalamkaryan.[34] Some Russian authors mistakenly perceive custom as an auxiliary source of international law, whose meaning is close to the meaning of commercial custom. The situation with general principles of law is even more problematic: most often they are incorrectly identified with the principles of

31 Ludmila Galenskaya and Sergey Malinin (eds), *Encyclopedia of International Organizations* (St Petersburg State University, 2003); Tatyana Neshataeva, *International Organizations and Law: New Trends in International Legal Regulation* (Business, 1998); Finn Seyersted, *Common Law of International Organizations* (Brill, 2008).

32 Vladimir Zaemsky, *New History of the UN Reform* (MGIMO, 2008); Vladimir Zaemsky, *Theory and Practice of UN Peacekeeping* (MGIMO, 2008); David Harutyunyan, *Secretary-General of the United Nations and International Law* (ITOUR, 2010); Anatoly Gromyko (ed.), *UN in the Beginning of the Twenty-first Century* (Institute of Africa, 2008).

33 Anatoly Talalaev, *Vienna Convention on the Law of Treaties: Commentary* (Legal Literature, 1997); Anatoly Talalaev, *Law of International Treaties* (Zertsalo, 2009); Ilya Lukashuk, *Modern Law of International Treaties* (Kluwer, 2006).

34 Alexandre Vylegzhanin and Ruben Kalamkaryan, 'International Custom as the Main Source of International Law' (2012) 6 *State and Law* 78.

international law;[35] and sometimes with the *jus cogens.* [36] Judicial decisions for a long time caused deep mistrust; it continues to be ignored in the vast majority of monographs and textbooks. In recent years, however, qualitative changes have occurred (primarily thanks to the efforts of A. Smbatyan, A. Ispolinov, I. Rachkov, V. Tolstykh, and the authors associated with the journal *International Justice*). The phenomenon of soft law is recognized; its studies however rarely go beyond statements on the very fact of its existence.[37] This selective attitude results in poor analysis of situations not covered by treaties;[38] passivity with respect to the formation of noncontractual sources and inability to use appropriate technologies;[39] and incomplete analysis of treaty's sources.

The basis of the Russian approach to the relationship between international law and national law is the classical dualism of H. Triepel and D. Anzilotti, supplemented by the thesis on the automatic transformation of international law, carried out even in the case of reference (renvoi). Distinguished Russian dualists are S. Chernichenko, L. Anufrieva, V. Gavrilov, B. Zimnenko, and E. Usenko.[40] Some authors however defend postulates of monism (G. Ignatenko and I. Blyshchenko),[41] while others do not identify themselves with any school, offering to focus on practical aspects of application of international law.[42] Some positions in

35 This approach was expressed by V. Koretsky:

> If we interpret the expression "general principles of law" in the sense that they give a generalisation of the principles of internal law, we will have to admit that the international court should not take into account the basic principles of international law, for article 38 does not mention – among possible sources of international law – other principles, except "general principles of law".
>
> ('General Principles of Law in International Law' 2 *Selected Works* (Naukova dumka, 1989) 194–5)

36 See Resolution of the Plenum of the Supreme Court of October 10, 2003 "On the application by the courts of general jurisdiction of universally recognised principles and norms of international law and international treaties of the Russian Federation."

37 Among the existing works there is a monograph of Sergey Bakhin on the *lex mercatoria* (*Sublaw* (Legal Press Center, 2002)).

38 An example is the reunification of Crimea and Russia, which was ignored by most experts.

39 There are six unrecognized states in the post-Soviet area, all of which are to some extent supported by Russia. The legal regime of these entities has many lacunae related to recognition of documents, crossing borders, responsibility, *locus standi*, etc. However, neither Russian authorities, nor individual scientists have attempted to find certain customs in this area and propose relevant draft articles.

40 Ludmila Anufrieva, *Relationship between the International Public Law and Private International Law: Legal Categories* (Spark, 2002); Vyacheslav Gavrilov, *Concept and Relationship between International and National Legal Systems* (DSU Publishing House, 2005); Bogdan Zimnenko, *International Law and Legal System of the Russian Federation* (Statute, 2006); Eugene Usenko, *Essays on the Theory of International Law* (Norma, 2008); Stanislav Chernichenko, *International Law: Modern Theoretical Problems* (International Relations, 1993).

41 Gennady Ignatenko and Oleg Tiunov (eds), *International Law* (Norma, 2013).

42 Sergey Marochkin, *Application and Implementation of the Norms of International Law in the Legal System of the Russian Federation* (Norma, 2017).

the field are formulated by constitutionalists who lack sufficient experience in the area of international law.[43] Academic dualism has little effect on the position of the legislator. Article 15 of the Constitution and some other norms speak in favor of monism; for example, Russia is one of the few states which recognizes the direct effect of WTO rules – allowing for legal provisions which are in conflict with WTO rules to be challenged directly in domestic courts and the EAEU Court.[44] At the same time, the Constitutional Court pursues a consistent dualistic line and seeks to approve the priority of the Constitution before the treaties and its right to control the implementation of the ECHR decisions.[45] Such a tension between the three levels of discourse does not help to clarify the situation.

Despite Russia's involvement in the conflict in Syria and several other conflicts on the territories of the former USSR (primarily the conflict in the southeast of Ukraine), there is no serious analysis of the regime of use of force and current trends in the field. Russian authors usually share the governmental position, advocate for consistent compliance with the UN Charter, and condemn manifestations of "humanitarian intervention."[46] Among works on this topic there are monographs of N. Ushakov and V. Kotlyar[47] and a number of articles (I. Farkhutdinov and L. Scotnikov). Issues on state responsibility are also on the periphery of the research; some textbooks still contain obsolete terminology that does not correspond to the Articles on Responsibility of States of 2001. A detailed account of the Commission's work however is presented in a monograph by I. Lukashuk.[48] Unfortunately, there are almost no other works on this issue.

The research on peaceful settlement of disputes has shown great progress. The Soviet doctrine explored this institution superficially and denied the very

43 The first example is the following. In the Decree dated October 10, 2003, the Supreme Court of the Russian Federation identified the notion of "universally recognised principles and norms of international law" contained in Art. 15 of the Constitution with *jus cogens*. Thus, international customs were virtually excluded from the scope of this article and therefore from the sphere of internal order as a whole. The second example: in the Decree of July 14, 2015, the Constitutional Court declared its right to control compliance of ECHR decisions with Art. 31 of the Convention on the Law of Treaties of 1969 and indicated that according to Art. 46 of this Convention, a state may refuse to carry out a treaty which violates important constitutional provisions.

44 See Report of the Working Party on Russia's Accession to the WTO paras 151, 163, 186, as well as Art. 1 of the Treaty on the Functioning of the Customs Union in the framework of the multilateral trading system (2011).

45 See Decisions of the Constitutional Court: on the constitutionality of the Art. 1 of the Federal Law On Ratification of the Convention on Human Rights dated July 14, 2015; on the possibility of enforcing the ECHR judgment in the case *Anchugov and Gladkov* v. *Russia* dated April 19, 2016; on the possibility of enforcing the ECHR judgment in the case of *Yukos* v. *Russia* dated January 19, 2017.

46 A certain exception is the position of Igor Blischenko, expressed in the early 1990s. Igor Blischenko and Maya Solntseva, *World Politics and International Law* (International Relations, 1991) 132.

47 Nicolay Ushakov, *Legal Regulation of Use of Force in International Relations* (IGPAN, 1997); Vladimir Kotlyar, *International Law and Modern Strategic Concepts of the United States and the NATO* (Scientific Books, 2007).

48 *Law of International Responsibility* (Kluwer, 2004).

possibility of an adequate judicial settlement of disputes between states representing different social systems. Following the governmental approach, the Russian doctrine rejected this point of view and joined the discussion on international justice and its particular aspects (precedent character of decisions, proliferation of international courts, appropriateness of dissenting opinions, etc.). Among authors working in the field there are L. Anufrieva, G. Velyaminov, A. Ispolinov, R. Kalamkaryan, T. Neshataeva, A. Smbatyan, and V. Tolstykh.[49] Many of them are not limited to theoretical research and regularly comment on specific decisions: V. Tolstykh on decisions of the ICJ, the PCA, and the EAEU Court; A. Ispolinov on decisions of the EAEU Court and the ECJ; A. Smbatyan on decisions of the EAEU Court and decisions rendered under the aegis of the WTO; I. Rachkov on decisions of investment arbitration; and A. Kovler on decisions of the ECHR. Authors who monitor the activities of the EAEU Court often reproach the Court for bias, activism, ignorance of international law, weak arguments, etc. The Court (represented by individual judges) objects to this critique, but, on the other hand, takes it into account. It should be noted that criticisms of the ECHR by the Russian Constitutional Court had little effect on the general rational attitude toward international courts. In 2016, several interesting articles on this problem were published in the journal/edited volume *Comparative Constitutional Review* and the journal/edited volume *International Justice*, setting out arguments *pro* and *contra* (Konstantin Aranovsky, Grigory Vaipan, Sergey Knyazev, Dmitry Krasikov, and Tatiana Morshchakova).[50]

The Russian doctrine pays close attention to human rights law, humanitarian law, and criminal law, with a number of works appearing in recent years examining the main trends and problems in relevant areas (V. Rusinova, V. Kartashkin, A. Abashidze,

49 Anait Smbatyan, *International Trade Disputes in GATT/WTO* (Kluwer, 2006), her doctoral thesis is 'Decisions of the organs of international justice and their role in strengthening the international legal order' (RUDN, 2013); Aslan Abashidze and Alexandre Solntsev, *Peaceful Resolution of International Disputes: Modern Problems* (RUDN, 2011); Ruben Kalamkaryan, *International Court of Justice in the World Order Based on the Rule of Law* (Science, 2012); Vladislav Tolstykh (ed.), *Institutes of International Justice* (International Relations, 2014); Vladislav Tolstykh, *International Courts and Their Practice* (International Relations, 2015); Gennady Velyaminov, Ninel Voznesenskaya et al., *Mechanism for Resolving Disputes in Regional Integration Groups as Exemplified by European Union, EAEU, ASEAN, MERCOSUR, NAFTA and GATT/WTO* (International Relations, 2018).

50 Konstantin Aranovskiy and Sergey Knyazev, 'Correlation between Constitutional Principles and International Standards in the Context of Russian Criminal Justice' (2016) 4 *Sravnitel'noe konstitutsionnoe obozrenie* 41; Grigory Vaypan, 'Hard to Be a God: The Russian Constitutional Court and Its First Case on Enforceability of a Judgment of the European Court of Human Rights' (2016) 4 *Sravnitel'noe konstitutsionnoe obozrenie* 107; Dmitry Krasikov, 'Collisions and Illusions amid the Convention and the Constitution: What Underlies the Russian Constitutional Court's Objection to the European Court of Human Rights?' (2016) 3 *Mezhdunarodnoe Pravosudie* 101; Tatiana Morshchakova, 'Constitutional and Judicial Implementation of the European Convention on Human Rights' 2 *Sravnitel'noe konstitutsionnoe obozrenie*, 182.

G. Bogush, et al.).[51] Many works contain apologetics of relevant institutions and a thorough positivist analysis but lack a critical component. The exception is the thesis of A. Mezyaev, containing deep criticism of the criminal justice system, and the article by V. Tolstykh about the Renaissance grounds of human rights.[52]

Having access to three oceans, Russia has a developed doctrine of maritime law; among reputed authors there are K. Bekyashev, A. Vylegzhanin, A. Kovalev, and A. Kolodkin.[53]A thorough level of research is not accompanied by diplomatic success: Russia failed to achieve a profitable settlement of the border dispute with Norway in the Barents Sea and the border dispute with the US in the Bering Sea, lost the *Arctic Sunrise* case against the Netherlands[54] and couldn't justify its special rights in the Arctic. Air law is represented by V. Bordunov and Yury Maleev;[55] space law by Gennady Zhukov;[56] environmental law by A. Vylegzhanin, M. Kopilov, N. Sokolova, A. Solntsev, and others.[57] Works in this area usually have a rather didactic character.

After the collapse of the Soviet Union, Russia, like the other post-Soviet states, joined the capitalist system. This entailed the conclusion of investment and taxation treaties, accession to the IMF and the WTO, establishment of the EAEU, and

51 Vladimir Kartashkin, *Human Rights: International Protection in the Context of Globalization* (Norma, 2011); Anatoly Kapustin (ed.), *International Humanitarian Law* (Yurayt, 2011); Vera Rusinova, *Human Rights in Armed Conflicts: Problems of the Relationship between International Humanitarian Law and International Human Rights Law* (Statute, 2015); Gleb Bogush, Gennady Esakov and Vera Rusinova, *International Crimes: A Model of Implementation in the Russian Criminal Law* (Prospekt, 2017); Aslan Abashidze, *Human Rights Treaty Bodies* (RUDN, 2012).

52 Vladislav Tolstykh, 'Renaissance Understanding of Dignity and Its Influence on Modern Concept of Human Rights' (2016) 325 *Jurisprudence* 48.

53 Victor Sidorchenko, *Legal Regulation of Maritime Disputes* (Legal Center, 2001); Anatoly Kolodkin, Vasily Gutsulyak and Yulia Bobrova, *World Ocean: International Legal Regime: Main Problems* (Statute, 2007); Alexandre Kovalev, *Modern International Maritime Law and Practice of Its Application* (Scientific Book, 2003); Damir Bekiashev, *International Legal Problems of Fisheries Management* (Prospekt, 2017); Alexandre Vylegzhanin, *Decisions of the International Court of Justice on Disputes on the Delimitation of Maritime Spaces* (Legal Literature, 2004).

54 Arctic Sunrise arbitration (Netherlands and Russia), Award of August 14, 2015 (merits), PCA Case N° 2014-02.

55 Vitaly Bordunov, *International Air Law* (Scientific Books, 2006). In a short essay published in 2013, the same author marks the decline of the Russian science of air law after the collapse of the USSR and uncertainty of its future ('Russian Science of Air Law' (2013) *Aviation EXplorer*www.aex.ru/docs/2/2013/12/10/1945 (accessed January 30, 2018); Yury Maleev and Vladimir Podberezny, *Flight without Landing* (MNIMP, 1996).

56 Gennady Zhukov and Yury Kolosov (eds), *International Space Law* (International Relations, 1999); Aslan Abashidze and Gennady Zhukov (eds), *International Space Law* (RUDN, 2014).

57 Alexandre Vylegzhanin, *Marine Natural Resources (International Legal Regime)* (SOPS, 2001); M. Kopilov, *Introduction in International Environmental Law* (RUDN, 2007); Natalya Sokolova, *International Legal Problems of Management in the Field of Environmental Protection* (Prospekt, 2010); Revol Valeev (ed.), *International Environmental Law* (Statute, 2012).

helped to reshape modern international economic law. Currently, Russia's participation in international economic law is examined by several reputed authors: Ludmila Anufrieva, Georgy Velyaminov, Alexey Ispolinov, Vladimir Kanashevsky, Anayt Smbatyan, Yuri Yumashev, et al., whose works mainly reproduce western concepts.[58]

## 4 Sociological and Institutional Structure of Russian Doctrine

The academic community in the field of international law is not homogeneous. Most of it consists of professional professors who achieved a law degree at public universities and successfully presented dissertations. Since the Soviet education did not presuppose a narrow specialization, these professors, as a rule, have a knowledge of not only international law but also domestic law. The downside of this is a poor command of foreign languages, political doctrines, and social philosophy. The exception is made by MGIMO graduates, who are still trained according to special standards; they are competent in international law and fluent in foreign languages, but are poorly trained in the general theory of law. In the 1990s, most graduates of law departments sought to find work in the private sector and neglected teaching work; at the same time, new law departments have been opened. As a result, many professor vacancies were occupied by persons with no legal education (graduates of police and military academies; and pedagogical, historical, and economic departments). Since these people brought with them knowledge and skills inherent in their main profession, the general level of law education has significantly decreased. This process has been recently stopped; moreover, the state now requires that persons who aim at teaching law but lack special education shall undergo retraining. The integrity of the academic community, however, is already broken. The young generation of scientists, as a rule, has legal education but its quality is much inferior to the quality of the Soviet education. This is due to several reasons: mass nature of legal education,[59] lack of qualified professors, orientation toward scientometric indicators (neglecting substantial results), intensive bureaucratization, etc.

The career of a Russian scientist presupposes the presentation of two theses: PhD (lower doctorate or candidate) and a higher doctorate (doctor). Work on the first is conducted for three to four years and ends with public presentation at specialized dissertational councils, consisting of specialists in the field. The

58 Ludmila Anufrieva (ed.), *WTO Law: Theory and Practice* (Norma, 2016); Georgy Velyaminov, *International Economic Law and Process* (Kluwer, 2004); Vladimir Kanashevsky, *Legal Regime of Offshore Companies and Trusts* (International Relations, 2015); Anait Smbatyan, *Interpretation and Application of WTO Rules* (Infra-M, 2017); Insur Farkhutdinov, *International Investment Law and Process* (Prospekt, 2010); Yury Yumashev and Elena Postnikova, *Economic Law of the EU* (Norma, 2015).

59 According to the President of the Federal Chamber of Advocates Y. Pilipenko, 150,000 diplomas on legal education are issued annually in Russia (October 6, 2017), http://rapsinews.ru/incident_news/20171006/280408218.html (accessed January 30, 2018).

candidate's thesis is a text of 180–220 pages, that contains "solution of a scientific problem relevant to the development of a relevant branch of knowledge or new science-based technical, technological or other results which are essential for the development of the state." A doctoral thesis, as a rule, is presented several years after the presentation of the candidate thesis; its minimal volume is 300 pages and should contain:

> theoretical provisions that can be altogether qualified as a scientific achievement, or solution of a scientific problem having a political, socio-economic, cultural or economic significance, or new science-based technical, technological or other results whose implementation supposes significant contribution to the development of the state.[60]

In recent years, some post-Soviet states (for example, Kazakhstan) have switched to a one-level system of dissertations (PhD). The same is currently considered in Russia. Resistance of the academic community however is strong; in addition, it is not entirely clear what practical benefits such a reform could provide.

This system generates several serious problems. First, presentation of a thesis is not only a symbol of scientific advances but also opens access to administrative positions of heads of departments, deans, and rectors, or (if the author is engaged in legal practice) increases the author's social status. Accordingly, after the presentation of a thesis, many authors cease scientific activity or reduce it to cite their previous works. Second, since the criteria of scientific value are blurring, many theses contain compilations, purely scholastic ideas, and (at worst) plagiarism. The Higher Attestation Commission (VAK), responsible for awarding academic degrees, tries to combat plagiarism[61] but is not able to solve the quality problem. Third, although the procedure of presentation is rarely accompanied by facts of direct corruption, it often assumes a system of mutual guarantee, which makes the success of a thesis presentation dependent on the authority of its supervisor.

Currently, there are nine scientific councils on the specialty 12.00.10 (international law, European law), eight of which sit in Moscow and one of which sits in Kazan State University.[62] In the last five years (2013–2017), 127 theses were presented:[63] 117 of them were candidate and ten were doctoral.[64] One thesis was

60 Regulation on the Award of Academic Degrees, approved by Resolution of the Government of the Russian Federation of September 24, 2013, n. 842, para. 9.

61 Wide public resonance was caused by checks for plagiarism conducted by the "Dissernet" – an independent internet community.

62 List of councils considering dissertations for undergraduate and postgraduate programs, January 26, 2018, http://vak.ed.gov.ru/89 (accessed January 30, 2018).

63 In 2013, 23 dissertations were presented; in 2014, 19; in 2015, 30; in 2016, 42; in 2017, 23.

64 Alexandre Mezyayev, 'Rights of the Accused in the Modern International Criminal Trial (Theory and Practice Issues)'; Olga Tolochko, 'International Economic Law and Implementation of Its Norms in the National Legal Order (on the Example of the Republic of Belarus)'; Valentine Talimonchik, 'International Legal Regulation of Relations in the Field of Information'; Natalya Tyurina, 'Public Interest in

on the history of international law,[65] three on its provisions and sources, one on law of treaties, four on the relationship between international law and domestic law, none (!) on statehood, recognition, or succession,[66] two on issues of population, four on international organizations, 19 on EU law; three on diplomatic law, eight on international security issues, four on state responsibility, 23 on human rights, three on humanitarian law, 25 on criminal law, 13 on maritime law, five on air law, four on space law, 16 on environmental law, 11 on general issues of economic law, eight on WTO law, three on financial law, three on investment law, and two on other issues. Thus, the topic of dissertations reflects the general imbalance inherent in the Russian doctrine: priority of narrow special studies and neglect of fundamental theoretical issues.

The problem of poor quality of theses is no less serious. Many theses contain conclusions that are difficult to recognize as new and scientific. They state obvious facts, propose new definitions of old concepts, introduce questionable terminology, etc. The novelty of some theses consists exclusively in transferring of western theories to the domestic soil. The scientific value of such theses requires an additional discussion: on the one hand, it often exceeds the value of theses based on domestic material; on the other hand, they don't contain creative authors' contributions.

Most Russian international scholars are engaged exclusively in science and teaching and don't participate in litigation. Some, however, have a civil law practice, prepare applications to the ECHR and the Constitutional Court, or act as arbitrators. The Ministry of Foreign Affairs, the Ministry of Economy and other state bodies prefer to employ foreign lawyers to protect Russia's interests in international courts. Thus, the interests of Russia in the *Yukos* case were defended by Cleary Gottlieb Steen and Hamilton LLP and Baker Botts LLP and in the *Ukraine* v. *Russia* case by S. Wordsworth, A. Zimmermann, and M. Forteau. Some bodies establish advisory councils consisting of scientists (the Advisory Council under the Russian Supreme Court) but their influence on current practice is insignificant.

The community of Russian specialists in international law is united by the RAIL.[67] At present the Association is headed by Anatoly Kapustin, the first deputy director of the Institute of Legislation and Comparative Law (IZISP). The

International Trade Law'; Rustem Davletgildeev, 'International Legal Regulation of Labor at the Regional Level'; Vera Rusinova, 'Human Rights in Armed Conflicts: The Relationship between International Humanitarian Law and International Human Rights Law'; Andrey Danelyan, 'International Legal Regime of Foreign Investment'; Darya Boklan, 'Interaction of International Environmental Law and International Economic Law'; Alfiya Kayumova, 'Criminal Jurisdiction in International Law: Theory and Practice'; Inna Khavanova, 'Avoidance of Double Taxation and Prevention of Tax Evasion in Conditions of Interaction of National and International Law'.

65 Some theses related to two branches, for example, the thesis 'Legal regulation of police cooperation in the EU' (Igor Nikishkin) related to criminal law and EU law.

66 In 2018 Satenic Aleksanyan presented the thesis 'The Principle of Equality and Self-determination of Peoples in Modern International Law'.

67 The official site of the Association is www.ilarb.ru (accessed January 30, 2018).

Association has its own Secretariat and Executive Committee. Its general meetings are held every year and are attended by several hundred scientists from all over the country. They last for several days and are devoted to one, rather general, theme. For example, the 61st meeting held in Moscow on January 29–31, 2018 was devoted to the topic "Global Challenges of the Present and Enhancement of the Effectiveness of International Law."

The main centers of Russian international legal doctrine are research institutes and universities. The former are engaged exclusively in research and do not participate in any educational activities (except for preparation of postgraduates). They include the Institute of State and Law of the Russian Academy of Sciences and the Institute of Legislation and Comparative Law under the Government of Russia. Universities, whose number exceeds 1,000, are engaged in both education and research. The law is taught, first, at all classical state universities, which function in all subjects of the Russian Federation; second, at specialized law schools (MGU, UGUU, SGUA); third, at departmental universities subordinated not to the Ministry of Education but to other ministries (RUP, MGIMO, Academy of Foreign Trade under the Ministry of Economic Development, Customs Academy under the Federal Customs Service); fourth, at some unspecialized universities (technical, economic, pedagogical, agricultural, etc.); fifth, at private universities, whose number is gradually decreasing. The top level is formed by the law departments of Moscow universities: MGU, MGUU, VShE, as well as SPGU and UGUU.

Much like everywhere else in the world, Russian universities are undergoing a radical transformation. One of its aspects is the introduction of so-called effective contracts, requiring professors to fulfill certain standards of scientific work: to write a fixed number of articles, participate in conferences, direct student researches, etc. This system is focused exclusively on quantitative and financial indicators, involves a lot of bureaucratic formalities, and seriously threatens academic freedoms. One of its results is a sharp increase in the number of publications, directly proportional to an overall decline in their quality.

Departments of international law are opened in almost all metropolitan universities and major regional universities (for example, in Kazan and Novosibirsk universities). Generally, they consist of six to ten people engaged in teaching general courses of international public law and international private law, several special courses, and sometimes comparative law, Roman law, etc. At other universities, international law is taught at the departments of constitutional (state) law. Most departments specialize in certain areas, often depending on scientific interests of their head. For example, the department of MGU specializes in commercial law and international justice, the department of VShE in commercial law and human rights, and the department of the RUP in commercial law and international justice.

A general course of international law usually takes a small number of hours (usually 72, which is one semester), half for lectures and half for practical classes. Some universities however devote more hours to international law (for example, Novosibirsk University allocates about 200 hours). Sometimes classes on international law are taught by specializing professors, sometimes they present an additional burden for professors of constitutional law. Some universities opened special subdepartments where an in-depth study of international law is carried out; as a rule, they specialize in commercial law and regional integration.

## 5 Some Conclusions

The Russian doctrine has abandoned the Soviet ideology, but could not overcome methodological flaws inherent in the Soviet doctrine such as scholasticism, isolation, etc.; some of them were exacerbated by the general crisis of culture in the country. Many authors try to change the situation and call for reform of legal discourse; their efforts, however, are not always fruitful.[68] The Russian doctrine continues to stand on rather voluntaristic positions and remains indifferent to alternative concepts. This isolation however is not "brilliant" and does not meet interests of the state. As for the specific fields of scientific research, many Russian authors follow western models and see their task in adapting them on the domestic soil. Thematic structure of the Russian doctrine is quite diverse and characterized by a focus on issues of regional law, human rights, international justice, criminal, and commercial law. Issues related to statehood, norm formation, etc., on the contrary, are almost never analyzed. Some studies have a critical focus. Russian doctrine remains passive with respect to landmark events, for example, trials and conflicts involving Russia, but sensitive to ECHR decisions. This passivity has a positive side: Russian international law academics can defend an independent position and are not obliged to take into account changes in the political course.[69] The institutional environment of Russian doctrine is in crisis; symptoms of degradation are numerous and diverse: over-bureaucratization, cessation of scientific development, interruption of academic relations, sharp deterioration in the quality of education, outflow of talented scientists, etc. In general, all of this is recognized by the scientific community; this, however, does not imply an immediate treatment. Thus, the Russian doctrine of international law is on the verge of radical changes. These changes can consist in further degradation, gradual ascension to the level of the western doctrine, and, finally, transition to a fundamentally different scientific paradigm. Time will tell.

68 See Alexander Mezyaev, 'Proposals on Some Issues of Organization of Work of the Russian Association of International Law' (2007) 1 *Kazan Journal of International Law* 153; Anait Smbatyan, 'Decisions of the EurAsEC Court Don't Generate a Scientific Interest?' (2014) 73 *Eurasian Law Journal* 63; Vladislav Tolstykh, 'An Outline of the Current State of the Russian Doctrine of International Law (2016) 3 (electronic annex to) *Russian Law Journal* 50.

69 For example, despite widespread opinion, there has been no structural changes in the Russian doctrine after the events of 2014.

# 2 Contradictions and Incompleteness in Russian Legal Discourses

*Anna Isaeva*

## 1 Introduction

The historical and theoretical development and historical systemic construction of law offers an insight into the important tendencies and phenomena of modern legal understanding. Delving into Soviet legal doctrine and observing its formation helps illuminate the patterns of modern Russian legal understanding which are not entirely obvious, especially when considering the importance of Soviet law during the period of democratic reconstruction and transition in post-communist Russia. The narrative of Soviet legal history started on October 25, 1917 with the proclamation of Soviet rule. On this day, to culminate the October Revolution, Soviet rebels seized the Winter Palace in Saint Petersburg and hoisted upon it Soviet flags. By ordinances and decrees a new Soviet power was formally legislated into the status of the main state body – the Soviet Commission of the Peoples' Deputies. Since the new Soviet state established its power over an immense territory, it faced all the realities that the former Russian Empire suffered, namely famine due to problems with the supply of provisions, danger of a new war against a state weakened after the revolution, instability because of counter-revolutionary movements inside the country, internal political fight, etc. The measures taken by the new power were mostly reactive and aimed at survival and consolidating power in very difficult conditions. Very soon after, idealistic expectations about establishing a ruling power of the working class according to Marxist doctrine, as opposed to the style of the old monarchy, resulted in inconsistencies and the need for laws and legislative provisions emerged. However, despite the clear necessity, there was a lack of resources to formulate a new legal doctrine and form a state which could fully function in its new reality. To compound this, the lack of any gradual or profound study failed to tackle any of the problems the new legislation created.

## 2 The Quest for a Soviet Formula of Law and Order

The decision was made during the first few years of Soviet rule to abolish all laws and legal norms from the previous tsarist regime and consider the old laws of the former Russian Empire valid, on the proviso that they did not contravene the decrees of Soviet power and revolutionary consciousness. This provision was set forth in the first acts of the new Soviet power and stated that the courts should sustain the decisions on the basis of the revolutionary consciousness and the revolutionary sense of justice.[1] Accordingly, the initial Soviet judicial system, dating from the October Revolution to 1922–3 was characterized by extreme judicial fluidity which meant the absence of determinate legal norms and a legal basis for taking decisions, since the legislation of the Russian Empire was abolished but still enforceable in conditions of formation of Soviet normative replacement. This led to creative lawmaking with a strong orientation toward the contingent political situation on the part of judges. The judiciary constituted the state organ that was authorized to determine which norms should be abolished, and the main criterion for the application of laws was the lack of contravention of revolutionary consciousness. While they were given very broad discretion with respect to judicial authority, the Soviet government nonetheless never aimed at institutionalizing the independence of judges, granting more power to state organs administered by the judicial authority. Through this mechanism, judicial power expressed itself as a direct arm of the state.[2]

Revolutionary "creativeness" in decision-making was welcomed, and found its expression in many legislative and normative acts of that period as a declaration of new principles of a young Soviet state.[3] The new power stated that any decision could be justified by the revolutionary consciousness of the judges and the conditions for the dependence of power became a political instrument of control. The first Soviet prosecutor and head of the Soviet Institute of Law Dmitry Kursky (1874–1932) in a 1918 speech stated that revolutionary consciousness should be considered a primary source for decision-making in the courts. He highlighted that in the newly founded people's courts it would not be possible to ascertain in advance a transgressor's duration of sentence. The decisions were based on the circumstances, and Kursky saw in this phenomenon an unconditional freedom from any limits of Soviet justice.[4] At the same time he claimed, being holders of unlimited power and based only on the revolutionary consciousness, the judges should be available to guarantee state authority. Moreover, Kursky claimed that no particular reason or decree was required, the termination of the judges' status

1 Decree on Courts adopted by the Council of People's Commissars of the Russian Soviet Federated Socialist Republic, November 22, 1917.

2 R. Schlesinger, *La teoria del diritto nell'Unione Sovietica* [*The theory of the law in the Soviet Union*] (Einaudi, 1952) 14.

3 Such as, for instance, the Ordinance on temporary revolutionary courts in the Novgorodskaya region, of 1917, which stated that

> a person found to be guilty is subject to the punishment which the court decides. The court shouldn't limit itself with any existing legislative prescriptions, as a non-obligatory source it may use Criminal Code and Code on punishments [of the Russian Empire].
>
> (from *Положение о временных революционных судах Новгородской губернии* [*The ordinance on temporary revolutionary courts of Novgorodskaya region*], December 30, 1917, cited in D. V. Kursky, Избранные статьи и речи [Selected articles and speeches] (Ministry of Justice of USSR, 1948) 17)

4 Ibid., 30.

at any moment for any reason was required by exceptional absolutism of their power in order to preserve the dictatorship of the proletariat which should not be limited.[5]

It was also prescribed that the judges should not be professional in the sense that they were not supposed to have any legal qualification, but Kursky claimed that professional judges were more likely to provide the ready formulas from the Codes of Imperial Russia and not provide a place for revolutionary consciousness. For the same reason it was prescribed that together with the judges, two people's assessors should be elected for the same period, and neither candidate should be required to have any educational background. As Kursky claimed, this would allow the direct involvement of the poorest peasants and workers in the judicial process and create a people's court in a true sense.[6]

Such a formula very soon showed its ineffectiveness, since non-professional judges without any educational qualifications were not able to cope with all the complexities of the post-revolutionary situation. The crucial conflict came in the failure of the institution to meet the expectations which came after the revolution. Marxian doctrine did not provide solutions on how to run a post-revolution state. Following the provisions of Marx, such as abolishing bourgeois legal norms and all other structures of the old state, led to dangerous levels of chaos and criminality. In Moscow for example, from March to August 1917 in comparison to the same period in 1916, the level of criminal acts increased substantially; murders increased by 1,075.0 percent (from 8 to 86), robberies 1,196.9 percent (from 27 to 323), thefts 546.5 percent (from 3,618 to 19,773).[7]

The year of 1922 marked the end of the transition period from Imperial Russian legislation to that of the Soviet Republic, further individualization of the new Soviet laws fueled an adoption of the new Soviet Penal Code of 1922 and a proclamation of the judicial reform of 1923 and other fundamental legal acts. A feature of Soviet legal doctrine notable from this early period was a strong orientation toward the defense of the new political order. This created the possibility of using the law as a weapon against counter-revolutionary elements. One of the methods of fighting counter-revolutionaries became the revolutionary courts and another, the adoption of new laws, were designed mainly to strengthen the positions of the Bolsheviks. These measures were a reaction to the rise in the number of counter-revolutionary crimes that made up 4,000 of 7,000 decisions made by the People's Courts in Moscow alone. More than half of the sentences handed down were aimed at maintaining social order with the criminal People's Courts playing a central revolutionary role.[8]

5 Ibid., 38.
6 Ibid., 14–15.
7 Central State Archive of the October Revolution, F.393, Op.6.7.124, p 17, cited in AA Abramovsky, 'Становление института Советского суда на Урале в 1917–1918 годах (на примере Оренбургской губернии)' ['Formation of the Soviet courts in the Urals in 1917–198 (the case of the Orenbug region)'] (2004) 1 *Vestnik of Chelyabinsk State University* 4, 29.
8 Kursky (n. 3) 43.

Law itself began to take the form of an instrument in the fight to defend the new political power of the Bolsheviks against all social classes with the exception of workers and peasants. This was exercised by establishing such discriminatory laws that countered even potentially counter-revolutionary elements in a bond together with the creation of an ideology and political orientation. Article 7 of the new Constitution of 1918 proclaimed the inevitable abolition of all anti-Soviet elements, or those which might be potentially counter-revolutionary, deferring all the power exclusively to the working people and soviet representatives of workers, soldiers, and peasants.[9] Following this ideological arrangement, rights and freedoms guaranteed by the Soviet Constitution were legally proclaimed but not for all Soviet citizens. Article 23 of the Constitution 1918 foresaw the deprivation of rights from individuals in order to make the socialist revolution more effective and successful.

These legal provisions were in accordance with Engels's theory which considered the state as an expression of class contradictions:

> so that these opposed classes with antagonistic economic interests did not devour one another and society in hopeless struggle, for this a power became necessary, a power seemingly standing above society, a power which moderated the conflict, and held it within the limits of "order." And this power arising from society but placing itself above it, and more and more alienating itself from it, is the state.[10]

From this passage we can see how Engels specifies the meaning of the state and the fact that state power naturally evolves in the hands of the strongest class, which uses the state machine to assert its dominance. So, the young Soviet state made a tool and an instrument to fight the counter-revolutionary elements which potentially were dangerous for the new Soviet order. This tendency continued in the adjudication of criminal law.

The Criminal Code of 1922, article 6, defined a crime as an act that threatens the fundamentals of the Soviet state and legal order. Notably, such a definition did not engage whatsoever with the moral nature of criminality and was concerned exclusively with the Soviet legal and state order.

Hence, the severity of punishment was also contingent on the personality of the transgressor and their potential risk to the Soviet state, or which class they belonged to. Background checks, in accordance with article 24 of the Criminal Code, afforded a judge the possibility of calibrating the level of punishment against an evaluation of the transgressor's danger to the Soviet state. This feature was also highlighted by legal doctrine, but it was seen as orienting toward the collective good as much as against the egoistic and individualistic approach of bourgeois law.[11]

9 Constitution of RSFSR adopted by the Fifth All-Russia Congress of Soviets, July 10, 1918.

10 F. Engels, *The Origin of the Family, Private Property and the State* (1884).

11 M Cossuta, *Formalismo Sovietico delle teorie giuridiche di Vyshinskij, Stucka e Pasukanis* [*Soviet formalism of the legal theories of Vyshinskij, Stuchka and Pashukanis*] (Edizione Scientifiche Italiane, 1992) 1126.

Following the development of the Soviet state after the transition in 1922, once again the urgency to reform Soviet legislation became readily apparent. The 1924 Constitution[12] established new Soviet institutions of power: article 37 of the Constitution set up the Council of People's Commissars which exercised the general management of the affairs of the Russian Socialist Federative Soviet Republic. This state organ was represented in every Soviet republic (article 67 of the Constitution). Article 37 also formed the Supreme Court, and granted it competence to monitor revolutionary legislation throughout the Soviet Union. Article 46 created the role of the general procurator, who was not only entitled to prosecute crimes in the court, but also to provide his opinion on any question put forward by the court.

## 3 Shaping Law as Ideology

Alongside the institutionalization of governmental organs and bodies, it became evident that interpretation and adaptation of the Marxian ideology for the new state was required which was not to be found in the writings of Marx or Engels. Instead, there were only two possible sources available which could form the basis of an established legal system: Soviet political government or academic socialist scholars. For both, by far the greatest difficulty was in interpreting classical Marxian texts which did not contain direct prescriptions on how the state and legislation ought to be organized.

Soviet legal scholars had a very complicated position vis-à-vis the law in general, since classical Marxian theory treated the law as a weapon in the struggle of socialism against capitalism and held that the state, and indeed, the law itself, should eventually wither away. Moreover, key to Marxian theory was the division of society into two social classes: workers and capitalists (bourgeois), with antagonistic interests.[13] Law itself was considered as an instrument of oppression of one social class by another, and the state established by law existed for the same reason. Hans Kelsen (1881–1973) wrote that Friedrich Engels (1820–1895) conceived of the state as a "coercive machinery"[14] aimed at continuing suppression of one social class by the other, and the whole state structure kept alive the conflict and ensured the exploitation of workers and peasants by the dominant class. The views of Engels were to have a significant impact on the chief instigator of the Soviet Union.

In 1917 Vladimir Lenin (1870–1924) published his work on the interpretation of communist theory. His work *State and Revolution* is considered the basic and first work on Soviet legal theory. In this seminal work Lenin laid the foundation for the interpretation of key issues on Marxian doctrine which became the basis for future scholars and an inevitable part of the study of historical materialism. Due to

12 Constitution of RSFSR adopted at II All-Russia Congress of Soviets, January 31, 1924.

13 F. Engels and K. Marx, 'Manifesto of the Communist Party' *Marx/Engels Selected Works*, vol. I, 99–137 (Progress, 1969) [first published February 1848].

14 H. Kelsen, *The Communist Theory of Law* (Praeger, 1955) Ch. 1.

its significance, the contribution to the whole concept took Lenin's name; the communists of the Soviet Union already followed the teaching of what they called Marxism-Leninism. The fundamental theoretical assertion in *State and Revolution* on law and state was developed by Lenin in order to execute the prime task of "[reestablishing] what Marx really thought on the subject of the state."[15] Therefore, following Marx's theory, Lenin admitted that the state acts to conserve and maintain class conflicts and antagonisms, so too does law.

It was Lenin who developed the thesis that law would not wither away with the overthrowing of the bourgeois state. In his *State and Revolution* Lenin argued that the process of the withering away of the state should not be rapid since the collective communist mentality needs time to form. The state machinery of social control and law had to exist in the transition period. It was, however, the machinery of control over individuals, not over classes, which was to disappear gradually. According to Lenin, the process of the withering away of the state would create the situation where a substantial part of private law will be incorporated into public law. After the revolution, bourgeois law would begin to gradually disappear as long as economic progress was steady.[16] This made future contributions on law and legislation from other scholars possible, which due to Lenin's writings were no longer considered "counter-revolutionary." But still the definition of law was not accepted wholly or without suspicion.

Crucially, a fundamental issue was resolved: law in the Soviet Union existed subject to the necessities of the state. A further question followed, which disappointed many: what form of law will it be? Alongside the institutionalization of governmental organs and bodies, there had to be a parallel and functioning adaptation of Marxian ideology. Legal scholars of that period gave different, uncertain hypotheses about the interplay of law and Marxian doctrine.

One such example is that of "octroyed" rights[17] by Aleksandr Malitsky (1874–1930), according to which the rights and freedoms of an individual were a privilege granted to them by the state. Since rights were seen as a "gift," it was logical that privilege from the state required exercising some obligations in exchange for them. It may be striking that this theory of rights was seen as a bond with the state and depended on the state's will with no recognition of inalienable human rights. Though the concept of "octroyed rights" was harshly criticized for contradicting Marxian theory, it reflected two very important features of legal understanding at the time. First, that rights were seen as a privilege granted by the state, and this privilege was directly influenced by the state's will. Second, an individual was supposed to follow all prescriptions by the state, since public interest was a priority provided by the public necessity of the construction of communism.

15 V. I. Lenin, 'The State and Revolution' *Collected Works*, Vol. XXV, pt I (Political Literature, 1965).

16 Ibid., 326.

17 A. Malitsky, 'Советская Конституция' ['Soviet Constitution'] (People's Commissariat of Justice of Ukrainian SSR, 1925).

Malitsky adhered to the dictatorship of the proletariat, and the rights of Soviet citizens he saw as "octroyed" privilege, handed down to them from the state in return for fulfilment of obligations. He saw the Soviet Union as a lawful state and took the view that the activity of any governmental body was prescribed by law. He said:

> subordination of all governmental bodies to the rule of law is called "legal regime" and the state itself, functioning in the legal regime is called "lawful state," here we can admit that Soviet republic is a lawful state which functions according to its laws.[18]

Malitsky continued such a legalistic view of law claiming that it was the state that created law, as well as defining the rights, freedoms, and obligations of individuals. Following this logic, Malitsky came to the conclusion that since it was the state that defined the rights of individuals, it could not be correct for individuals to sacrifice a part of their rights to the state in return for safety and order. Conversely, it was the state that "octroys" rights and freedoms to the individual but with a reservation, that the individual should exercise their rights in the interests of the whole of society and for the sake of development of "industrial forces." Explaining his theory of "octroyed" rights, Malitsky stated that the state endows rights to the individual not because they are born human, but individuals receive them from the ruling class in the interest of society as a whole because their possession of rights is the guarantee that they will keep carrying out their wider obligations to society. Malitsky also provided a very interesting correlation between rights and duties:

> In the Soviet Republic civil rights as well as public rights should be seen as a way of the citizen to carry out his social obligations, his official functions. This means that the rights that an individual enjoys is not solely about their freedom, but their social duty. Rights as duty, this is a main difference between the socialist view on the subjective rights of the individual and the bourgeois doctrine of the West.[19]

Continuing his theory of dictatorship of the proletariat and "octroyed rights," Malitsky stated that during socialism the legislative and executive branches of power in the activity of governmental bodies would be merged since management of the state would reunite with the legislative bodies.[20]

Malitsky came under severe criticism from his contemporaries, the harshest coming from Lazar Kaganovich (1893–1991), a communist party leader and one of the closest associates of Joseph Stalin (1878–1953). It should be noted that

18 Ibid., 27–8.
19 Ibid., 49.
20 Ibid., 35.

Kaganovich's interpretation of Marxism corresponded much more to the Marxian legacy than Malitsky's scholarship.

In his article "Twelve Years Constructing the Soviet State," Kaganovich claimed that many scholars still used bourgeois methodology. As an example, he claimed that Malitsky in his analysis of the Soviet Constitution uses only bourgeois legal methods. Malitsky stated that due to the Soviet Constitution, the state itself and government organ function due to the rule of law. Kaganovich criticized Malitsky's approach, citing Lenin, who explained the essence of a dictatorship founded on unlimited force and not on law.[21]

Interpreting the dictatorship of the working class as the main force unlimited by law, Kaganovich conceded that law still exists. As far as law and legal order were concerned, Kaganovich wrote that the existence of law should not give the wrong impression, laws were to be determined by revolutionary necessity and could be abolished at any moment.[22] Kaganovich also highlighted the necessity to abolish all forms of bourgeois law and orient the working class toward dictatorship. This position was very close to the works of D. Kursky, and both he and Kaganovich followed the writings of Marx and Lenin.

Evgeny Pashukanis (1891–1937), a prominent representative of Soviet legal theory, whose juridical mentor was another Soviet legal scholar Piotr Stuchka (1865–1932), was an orthodox follower of Marx and his writings, as were many at the time. One of his major works *The General Theory of Law and Marxism*[23] was first published in Moscow in 1924 and subsequently translated into French, German, Japanese, Serbo-Croat, and English. Pashukanis in this work was among many Bolsheviks who claimed there was a necessity to abolish the state due to orthodox Marxism stating that the withering away of legal and political institutions should have happened immediately after the victory of the revolution. Expectations were based on the creation of a new revolutionary consciousness of justice which should be developed by revolutionary jurists and should replace the formal bourgeois legal heritage. This is despite the contradiction between Pashukanis's writings and Lenin's position on the necessity of law during a transition period of gradual transformation of society to socialism. But, formally, Pashukanis was right to claim that Marx stated that law in its early stages of a communist society would be bourgeois in nature.

Another alternative representative of legal scholarship was Leon Petrajitsky (1867–1931). Being an academic of Saint Petersburg University from 1898 to 1918, Petrajitsky was a representative of Imperial Russian scholarship. Owing to this, after the revolution of 1917, he was forced to immigrate to Poland in order to protect himself from the new communist authorities. His psychological concept

21 L. Kaganovich, 'Двенадцать лет строительства Советского государства' ['12 years constructing the Soviet state'] (1930) 1 *Journal of Soviet State and Revolution of Law* 9.
22 Ibid.
23 E. B. Pashukanis, *The General Theory of Law and Marxism* (3rd edn, Communist Academy, 1929).

of law[24] represents a complex philosophical legal theory centered around the individual perception of law and conscious origins of legal understating. This concept was adopted by Mikhail Reisner (1868–1962) who put it on "Marxian foundations" and with it provided a new paradigm of psychology in Soviet legal scholarship.[25]

Mechislav Kozlovsky (1876–1921), Bolshevik and People's Commissar of Justice, claimed after the revolution that a special type of Soviet law existed highlighting its "otherness." Kozlovsky stated that due to the global transition from capitalism to socialism which the Bolsheviks had heralded in, the world was witnessing the creation of a new unprecedented type of Soviet proletarian law which was not exactly bourgeois in essence.[26] Though this conception of "proletarian law" contradicted Marxian predictions about residual bourgeois law after the revolution during the first stages of socialism, Marxian theorists highlighted the unity of the proletarian-class approach to law and state of Soviet legal theory and Marxian theory rather than its contradictions.[27] Conceptions of "proletarian law" were further developed by Kursky who saw proletarian law as a system of norms which guaranteed the interests and power of the whole proletarian class, which only became possible under a dictatorship of the proletariat.[28] To that end, Kursky claimed, law should reflect the interests of the whole class and there is no place for the enshrined rights of individuals in the form of *habeas corpus* or any other legal prescription of individual rights. Kursky drew a lot from "revolutionary law" and believed by abolishing *habeas corpus*, it would aid the fight against counter-revolutionary elements. These norms, which protected individual rights, could limit the proletariat in the fight for its interests.[29] Kursky called his conception a "proletarian communist law" which can be seen as a revolutionary type of legal theory, which also largely reflected another tendency in Soviet legal scholarship: the elaboration of the existence of a particular new type of Soviet law altogether different from the bourgeois legal order.

However, even while managing the contradictions of Marxian theory, Lenin's ideas about the necessity of law, and then the accompanying political discourse, there was still scope to develop these concepts into what would become the basis of Soviet legal doctrine. As described by Vladik Nersesyants (1938–2005), such a variety of legal concepts had enough in common with Marxism-Leninism and its approach to law, such as the justification of dictatorship and its dictatorial norms,

24 L.I. Petrazhitsky, *Теория государства и права в связи с теорией нравственности* [*Theory of state and law in correlation with theory of morality*] (1909).

25 M. Reisner, Теория Л.И.Петражицкого, *марксизм и социальная идеология* [*Theory of LI Petrajutsky, Marxism and social ideology*] (1908).

26 M. Kozlovsky, 'Пролетарская революция и уголовное право' ['Proletarian revolution and criminal law'], *Пролетарская революция и право* [*Proletarian revolution and law*] 1, 1918, 24, cited in V. S. Nersesyants, *Общая теория государства и права* [*General theory of state and law*] (INFRA-M, 1999).

27 Nersesyants (n. 26) 155.

28 Kursky (n. 3) 38.

29 Ibid., 40.

that by shunning bourgeois law, its precepts and its legal logic, the Soviet Union was able to establish the proletarian communist dictatorship.[30] It reconciled Marxian thought with the legal project of establishing a ruling class made up of the proletariat with unlimited prescriptions and frames. With such a foundation, when Marxian theory in its deep essence prescribes the withering away of law and the state, while seeing them both as only a transitional necessity, the elaboration of consistent and logical legal theories often found its contradiction. The full expression of proletarian law was an attempt to illustrate a different Soviet reality that meant that legality and law were something different to Soviet scholars than their classical scientific meaning. This was explained by the appearance of a new type of Soviet law and complimented by the difference in notions and definitions.

The resulting dilemma about what law should be and which elements it should contain was anticipated by careful study of Stalin's policy. Evgeny Pashukanis was criticized and repressed for his academic views that equated all law with bourgeois law and his predictions on the withering away of the state. In early 1937, Pashukanis was avowed a "traitor and wrecker" and soon afterwards he was arrested and liquidated on Stalin's orders.

Thereafter, the Soviet General Procurator Andrey Vyshinsky (1883–1954), who was also a director of the Soviet Academy of Sciences Institute of State and Law, took a new line in the development of Soviet legal doctrine: the state was to establish law with the sole function of being an expression of state will through sanctions and coercion. Vyshinsky further developed this view, stating that:

> The dictatorship of the proletariat is a power unlimited without any law, but creating its own law and using it – it punishes those who violate the established political order. The dictatorship cannot stand the anarchy and disorder, on the contrary, it strictly follows the laws and principles established in the Fundamental Law of the proletarian State in the Soviet Constitution.[31]

That was a drastic turnaround from the legally nihilist character which defined the beginning of Soviet legal development and resulted in legal idealism when the law became a weapon for managing the rebels of the counter-revolutionaries inside the country and the remaining defeated bourgeoisie, as well as external attacks from the capitalist world. At this stage Soviet law took a strict course on forming the most flexible instrument to express the political interests more effectively, as P. Stuchka wrote in *The Revolutionary Function of Soviet State and Law*: "we don't need stable laws … we need a Constitution which gives us the possibility to change the laws in twenty-four hours."[32]

30 Nersesyants (n. 26) 155.
31 A. J. Vyshinsky, *Вопросы теории государства и права* [*Issues of theory of state and law*] (1949).
32 P. Stuchka, *Избранные произведения по марксистско-ленинской теории права* [*Selected writings on Marxian-Lenin's theory of law*] (1964).

At the beginning of the communist revolution many Bolsheviks combated the state believing that the withering away of legal and political institutions would happen immediately after the victory of the revolution. Since classical Marxian theory treated the law as a weapon in the struggle of socialism against capitalism, they held that the state, and indeed, the law itself, should eventually wither away. Expectations were based on the creation of a new revolutionary consciousness of justice which should be developed by revolutionary jurists and should replace the formal bourgeois legal heritage.

Extremely "liquid" judicial norms matched organically well with the conception of the law as an instrument to fight against all risks for a new state, rather than establishing the rights and guarantees for individuals (as an inevitable characteristic of classical definition of law). Moreover, political "course" determined that individual protection was not considered a priority. As Malitsky stated, the essence of capitalist law is abstract since it is based on the conception of "natural rights," it places the individual at the center of the system, and Soviet law places the interests of the collective as a priority. Soviet law defended the class interests and that is why it was more efficient.[33]

The emphasis of Soviet legal scholars was based on the thesis of the collective which established that only collectively by all citizens is it possible to provide for the interests of individuals. Segregation of personal rights in favor of the big idea was the leitmotif of development of Soviet legal thought. It was presumed that the State "knows" better about the needs of its citizens, since individuals did not possess the status of independent actors.

The idea of challenging the authorities by taking responsibility for defending the state's laws against violation from the state itself was first formulated by the dissident and mathematician Aleksandr Esenin-Volpin (1924–2016). He firmly stated ideas that a legalist approach is much more effective and better than violent revolution. Together with other dissidents in 1965, Volpin organized the "Demonstration of *glasnost* (transparency)" in the center of Moscow which was the first public protest in postwar Soviet Union. The "Demonstration of *glasnost*" was organized in support of Andrei Siniavskii (1925–1997) and Iulii Daniel (1925–1988), two poets who were arrested for publishing anti-Soviet pieces, and demanded to make the judicial procedures against them public.

Volpin was an author of various "Civil appeal" pamphlets which aimed to attract participants to demonstrations, he asked for an open judicial hearing and claimed violations by the state.[34] Volpin was arrested during the protest and was taken directly to the KGB for interrogation. Nevertheless, Volpin's arrest failed to prevent his legal ideas spreading among the Russian dissident intelligentsia. As another dissident Vladimir Bukovsky (born 1942) put it, "So let us defend our

33 Cited in T. E. Towe, 'Fundamental Rights in the Soviet Union: A Comparative Approach' (1967) 115 *University of Pennsylvania Law Review* 1264.

34 A. Ginsburg, *Белая книга: Сб. документов по делу А. Синявского и Ю. Даниэля* [*White paper: collection of the documents on the case of A Siniavskii and I Daniel*] (Posev, 1967).

laws from being encroached upon by the authorities. We are on the side of the law. They are against it."[35] Bukovsky liked the idea of public expression of the protest as a way of informing larger numbers of people about violations.

In 1976 the Moscow Helsinki Group was founded, nowadays the oldest existing human rights organization in Russia. Initially, its main purpose was to monitor the Soviet Union's compliance with the Final Act of the Conference on Security and Cooperation in Europe signed in Helsinki in 1975, embodying A. Esenin-Volpin's idea about a legal approach to fight violations of the authorities. Ludmila Alekseeva (a founding member) recalled the conversation with Volpin:

> He would explain to anyone who cared to listen a simple but unfamiliar idea: all laws ought to be understood in exactly the way they are written and not as they are interpreted by the government and the government ought to fulfil those laws to the letter.[36]

As this section has shown, Soviet legal scholarship, in general lacked consistency since changes in political situation required changes in all spheres of law, and theoretical inclinations were supposed to follow those political changes. As Hans Kelsen wrote, one of the claims of Marxian doctrine about anti-ideological science was widely violated since Soviet theory of law was dominated by ideology and state pressure.[37]

## 4 Law: High Hopes, Transitions, and the Soviet Shadow

Perestroika and the political course of Mikhail Gorbachev (born 1931) in the years before the collapse of USSR (1985–1991) exposed the increasing tendency in the weakening of communism. The end of the Cold War and communism losing its position meant that the world was bipolar no more. The western model of capitalism remained absolute since there was no other force to oppose it. The most extreme interpretation was extended by Francis Fukuyama explaining that "the triumph idea is evident first of all in the total exhaustion of viable alternatives to Western liberalism."[38] Though, this view was criticized broadly, many moderate evaluations of the end of global ideological opposition agreed that it was a matter of time before post-communist countries would construct democracies following the western model.[39]

35 P. Boobbyer, 'Vladimir Bukovsky and Soviet Communism' (2009) 87(3) *Slavonic and East European Review* 452–87.
36 L. Alekseeva, *Soviet Dissent: Contemporary Movements for National, Religious and Human Rights* (Wesleyan UP, 1987) 276.
37 Kelsen (n. 14) 193.
38 Ibid., 3.
39 J. Gray, 'Post-totalitarianism, Civil Society, and the Limits of the Western Model' in Z. Rau (ed.), *The Reemergence of Civil Society in Eastern Europe and the Soviet Union* (Westview Press, 1991) 145.

Still the western capitalist model is full of its own contradictions and there is no perfect model to be found in western democracies in terms of respecting human rights. Mutua Makau responds to this claim: the fact that human rights are violated in liberal democracies, just confirms that fact that "human rights and democracy are both works in progress."[40]

The claim about the triumph of western liberalism refers to the whole corpus of human rights, and democratic traditions coming out of the West which have been diffused globally. Mutua W. Makau in his "Ideology of Human Rights" argues that rights are the product of western culture since its main promoters have always been western elements, whether they were academic, activists, or human rights organizations. Though rights are usually presented as non-ideological, this claim was broadly contested. It is hard to deny the influence of political deliberation on the human rights corpus. As Mutua W. Makao wrote, human rights are not only a set of normative principles and provisions, they also concern routine politics and political choices. He takes the premise that human rights and liberal democracy are both western products, which seem to be different, but in reality are unified since one is a universalized notion of the other.[41] One of the arguments which Mutua W. Makao uses in support of his claim about the European roots of both liberalism and human rights is that the major part of the elements, which formulated the corpus of human rights, was European. Mutua Makao gradually proves that existing systems of human rights could hardly be called "universal." He argues that due to the fact that main actors in providing or exercising human rights – the activists of the biggest human rights NGOs – are western, they influence the legal concept of human rights adding it to their own values.[42] The UN Declaration of Human Rights has a significantly western view on human rights.[43]

And, still, could we claim peremptorily that after the dissolution of the Soviet Union and the overthrowing of communist ideology, post-Soviet countries adopted the western model of liberalism and construction of democracy in conditions of the absence of any other relevant ideological alternative? Is it correct to claim that after the end of the Cold War and bipolar global political opposition, democratic reconstruction of post-communist countries has proved the enduring success of the western model?

Karl Klare has criticized such a view about the triumph of western liberalism as the one and only remaining global ideology. After the dissolution of the Soviet Union and the end of the Cold War, the western model of capitalism strengthened its position but still, the claim about its absolutism should still be taken with a pinch of salt. Klare wrote that it is mistaken to believe that "1989 reflects the

40 M. Mutua, 'The Ideology of Human Rights' (1996) *Virginia Journal of International Law Association* 593.

41 Ibid.

42 Mutua (n. 40).

43 A. Cassese, 'The General Assembly: Historical Perspective 1945–1989' in P. Alston (ed.), *The United Nations and Human Rights: A Critical Appraisal* (OUP, 1992) 31.

definitive triumph of liberalism in politics and capitalism in economics."[44] The first reason for Karl Klare's criticism of the "triumphalist view" on the western concepts was the existence of that discursive domestic contest which made all new democracies different due to the special economic and political condition found in each of them.[45]

New democracies in post-communist countries faced such an enormous variety of complex problems that it is evidently problematic to claim a mere legal transplant of other juridical constructions which copies a foreign legal concept is the solution. Another reason to contest the triumph of the western model is that "there is no single form of eastern liberal democracy to be exported eastwards."[46]

It is dubious to claim that a foreign legal model could be transplanted as a "franchise" to post-Soviet countries due to the historical, ideological, economic contest since legal transplants always require contextual study. A domestic discursive contest about any legal transplant is still inevitable. And a very special case is the Russian one. It cannot be denied that Russian modern legal thinking still has traces of its Soviet heritage, which is why the democratic reconstruction after the dissolution of the Soviet regime was not linear and did not merely copy the western tradition.

After the collapse of the Soviet Union, Vladik Nersesyants, Soviet and later Russian legal scholar, elaborated the original concept of libertarianism,[47] on the basis of the initial premises where he detailed the path from socialism to a new democratic legal order. The core premise on which the legal conception of libertarianism is based is the division of law in a strictly positivist sense and legality as a legal order. Nersesyants wrote that it is absolutely wrong to agree with the claim that the existence of Soviet socialistic legislation necessarily creates Soviet socialistic law. He insisted that legislation (or law in a positive sense as written norms and ordinances) existed in the Soviet Union but this in fact did not create law itself since law in terms of legality prescribes the necessary conditions of individual freedom and equality under the law. Nersesyants went on to call Soviet socialistic legislation as the "illusion … when totalitarian illegal legislation is interpreted as 'socialistic law.'"[48] Nersesyants explained that this misunderstanding and perception of totalitarian legislation as law became possible because of the absence of a clear specific description of what law in a classical sense really meant and implied.

44 K. E. Klare, 'Legal Theory and Democratic Reconstruction: Reflections on 1989' (1991) *UBC Law Review* 70.

45 Ibid.

46 Ibid.

47 Initially he formulated his theory in the 1970s in his article 'Law and Legislature: Defining and Correlation' which was refused publication in the leading legal journal *Soviet State and Law* due to criticism about the shallow relation of his theory to the acknowledged classical Marxian provisions. However, Nersesyants's views on the problems of redefining law were still included for publication due to his participation in the Soviet Academy of Science's symposium on the institute of state and law.

48 V. Nersesyants, *Философия права* [*Philosophy of law*] (Russian Academy of Sciences and Law, 1998) 321.

As such, it became impossible to specify the illegal character of some official legal acts and legislation.

Therefore, for a period of time the Soviet government saw the idea of justice as being merely about what appeared to be universal on the surface. The judiciary, for instance, in the Soviet system was seen as one of the "instruments of the state" which was necessary to submit to and be managed by the ruling communist party. It had lost its primary fundamental principle of independence. It remains a very complicated task for lawyers to consider how this structure and Russian "civilizational" values will be affected by any legal transitions and reforms. The state has a necessity to take into the account the unique cultural patterns in the endless series of socially significant choices. This is the difficulty facing post-Soviet countries to orient themselves toward their national identity and certain social needs due to their historic context. As Gray put it: "post-communist countries should avoid both the lawless legality of the communist past and the politicized legality of the western present."[49]

The conclusion of this research is that Russian understanding of law is special, and it has a peculiar legal culture which is not exactly western in its essence. Soviet legal doctrine, while extremely interesting for those researching the history of legal thought, goes to the heart of the peculiarities of modern Russian legal thinking.

The adoption of legal concepts of western liberalism and democracy after the collapse of the USSR did not lead to mere use of legal transplants. Due to an obvious national context, and less obvious but perhaps even more important, a historical dimension to the development of legal scholarships, western concepts were significantly transformed. The universality of human rights is widely contested in international legal scholarship, and this fact confirms the necessity of looking at national contexts and studying deep layers of legal thinking in order to understand the real nature of legal theory. Soviet legal doctrine has a very original dimension. It was officially stated and widely proclaimed that Soviet legal doctrine and the whole political as well as social and economic systems are based on Marxian theory of communism. But, in fact, even at first sight, which is confirmed through more accurate study, the Soviet formation of communist theory contains numerous contradictions despite making claims about following the theory literally. Those contradictions were inevitable since complex social problems were not premised by the theory outlined by Engels and Marx, and situations often demanded ad hoc decisions.

Though the whole structure of Soviet theory was firmly rooted in Marxism-Leninism, the doctrine was not purely Marxian.[50] That is why it is interesting to study the concepts of alternative lawyers who were not mainstream during Soviet rule. Their works were still influenced by the political will and due to their non-mainstream position, they were more liberal in elaborating concepts which reflected the immediate conditions more precisely rather than adjusted to mainstream

49 Gray (n. 39) 159.
50 See e.g. I Scobbie, 'Some Common Heresies about International Law: Sundry Theoretical Perspectives' in M Evans (ed.), *International Law* (2nd edn, OUP, 2006) 83.

doctrine. Arguably, their less prominent position gave jurists more freedom to disentangle their conception of law and ideology. Different theories formulated by Soviet scholars, the claim of P. Stuchka about the formation of the new type of special Soviet law, contradicted the provision of Marxian doctrine about the overcoming of law on a global scale. Marxian theory did not contain a theoretical notion of law itself due to the social, historical, and practical impossibility of its existence in the contest of the Marxian concept of proletarian communist socialism.[51]

The contradictions in legal theory were not only due to the lack of provisions in Marxian theory about complex social demands which faced a new, post-revolutionary state, but were also conditioned by the need to constantly adapt to the necessities of Soviet political power.[52] Soviet legal scholarship had to face the same complexities as political power did, but it had a secondary role and had to always correlate it and justify its political choices ideologically.

Soviet politics was specifically aimed at and demanded legal justification. Soviet Procurator A. Vyshinsky during trials used highly elaborated legal rhetoric mixed with personal insults aimed at the defendant. Of course, legal rhetoric was only literal during the political process, but it had the desired effect of superficial justice.[53] Language was used as a substitute for legality and justice.

Soviet power widely used legal justifications for many of its activities, but sometimes avoided creating legal acts on politically significant issues in order to not be bound to them in the Communist Party of the Soviet Union (CPSU) through legislative acts.

Though the role of the Communist Party could hardly be overemphasized – it was a core institution in almost all spheres of Soviet society – it became a "vanguard" and oriented the political course as well as public morality for the whole population. In a strictly legal sense the CPSU was a social organization, but the Constitution of the USSR of 1977 emphasized the Party's "leading role" for the whole political system (art. 6). The guiding role of the CPSU as well as directing foreign and internal policy makes its status rather disappointing. This is relevant for the main argument of the present research as an example of contradictory and peculiar juridical constructions which are conditioned by a special historic context and which could be traced in the national legal consciousness in terms of understanding modern legal practices. Martin Krygier argues that disrespect toward legality in Eastern and Central European regimes has its roots in the view of the "law's role as subordinate to social forces and as a mask for ruling class interests."[54] This tendency exists due to the Marxian doctrine provision on the withering away of law in future and as a consequence its unimportant function: "It was necessary, not that law fulfils any mythical essence … but it

51 Nersesyants (n. 48) 175.

52 Kelsen (n. 14).

53 See e.g. A. Shikman, *Деятели отечественной истории. Биографический справочник* [*Activists of national history. Biographical encyclopedia*] (AST, 1997).

54 'Marxism and the Rule of Law: Reflections after the Collapse of Communism' (1990) 15 *Law and Social Inquiry* 633.

disappears along with the state, and with the civil society which supported them and which they supported."[55]

As Lauri Mälksoo noted, Russian international legal scholarship has been "a world apart from Western scholarship."[56] This tendency has old roots from the Soviet legal scholarship, claims about a new type of special Soviet law or Soviet "socialistic" law, did not prescribe the necessity of knowledge of western legal academic studies. Soviet legal scholarship highlighted its self-sufficiency, and used citations from foreign lawyers for one purpose: to demonstrate the falseness of bourgeois legal concepts. Mälksoo notices the same tendency in Russian international legal scholarship, claiming that Russian authors tend to have a limited knowledge of western sources, usually fragmentary. One of the reasons he gives for this is the language barrier. A lot of Russian legal scholars do not read or write in languages other than Russian.[57] Another reason for this phenomenon is the historical tendency in the development of Russian scholarship, and the image of "self-sufficiency" of Soviet academia which still has its traces in self-determination of Russian lawyers and their academic traditions.

## 5 Concluding Observations

After the collapse of the USSR a very widespread opinion was that the Russian Federation had no choice other than to adopt western values. Russia was constrained to transplant western models of democracy and liberalism, absent other viable alternatives. The expectations of post-communist countries merely joining the western liberal tradition could not come to fruition. The complex situation and rich historical background made it impossible in real life to make any claims about the pure adoption of legal and political transplants in post-Soviet countries. As Mälksoo put it:

> Russia did not, politically or ideologically speaking, become like Poland or the Czech Republic. It became a member of the OSCE and the Council of Europe but not of the EU and NATO. Quite soon, efforts to "Westernize" Russia were confronted by serious backlashes and it became obvious that rather than becoming "Western," Russia was choosing its own way, also ideologically.[58]

Another explanation of the special character of Russian legal thinking is that since the universality of rights is widely contested, this is inevitable. Every country has its own way of understanding the law: "the human rights regime has serious and dramatic implications for questions of cultural diversity, the sovereignty of states,

55 R. B. Roth, 'Marxian Insights for the Human Rights Project' in S. Marks (ed.), *International Law on the Left* (CUP, 2010) 222.
56 *Russian Approaches to International Law* (OUP, 2015).
57 Ibid.
58 Mälksoo (n. 56) 9.

and ultimately the 'universality' of human rights."[59] Moreover, this is true of countries with a Soviet background, which has a special impact on any legal construction.

Additionally, usually very elastic and indeterminate legal concept requires wide interpretation, as well as detailed elaboration. The most important and principled human rights concepts are formulated with extremely high levels of abstraction.[60] This elastic and open-ended character of legal concepts requires setting up a lot of special provisions which depend on the context and reality of the relevant country. Moreover, in post-communist societies lawyers and drafters of new laws had a wholly different legal thinking process, which was developed during Soviet rule. It is rather unrealistic to expect them to be synchronized with western-leaning conceptual jurisdictions.

Post-communist Russia experienced the return of arguments on different cultural and civilizational issues on the features of Marxist-Leninist ideology. This view is opposed by the alternative position that it is always people and institutions to blame for violations of legality.[61] Nonetheless, the main argument of the present research is based on a historiographical method, for which it is necessity to reconstruct the bonds between past and the present in order to grasp the essence of the object of the study and the premise that history should not be undervalued.

Similarly, in the research, a view which is completely different from such westernized position was presented. John Gray argues that is it profoundly defective to measure the reconstruction of democracy in post-communist societies against the accomplishment of western liberal institutions. Post-communist countries in general would reach deadlock if they had simply copied western democracies. Gradually, most post-Soviet states that built up a civil society were as a result of adapting particular institutional needs and circumstances of the society. Such a vision of the development of civil society on the democratic transformations in post-communist countries touches deeper layers of social consciousness rather than measure the technical approach to the establishment of democratic institutions. The category of civil society is strictly bound to the social legal thought and overall culture of a certain community. It reflects more clearly the real situation regarding democratic changes rather than the institutional approach.

Post-communist legal reconstruction revealed complex risks to achieving democracy and the responsibility of lawyers' democratic input. The role of Soviet heritage should not be neglected during any meaningful and complex study of the peculiarities of Russian understanding and use of law. The current political and legislative situation, reforms aimed at establishing new democratic authorities, and the judicial system should be explained from a historical perspective in order to have a complex understanding of the processes. An examination of the complex

59 Mutua (n. 40) 595.
60 Klare (n. 44) 99.
61 See e.g. for some aspects of this position A. Etkind, 'Decay of Public Sphere in Russia' (2015) *Current History*, available at: www.academia.edu/16261875/_Decay_of_Public_Sphere_in_Russia_published_in_Current_History_ (accessed June 3, 2018).

historical events in the Soviet Union and its post-communist democratic reconstruction is necessary to analyze the current Russian understanding of law. Historiographical study of legal theory forms the basis for academics and political thinkers to establish links between the past and the present situation in order to achieve a deeper understanding of modern events as well as the essence of institutions and doctrines.

# 3 Russia and International Human Rights Law

## A View from the Past

*Anna Lukina*[1]

## I Socioeconomic Rights in Russia: An Overview, 1917–2017

This section will focus on the evolution of socioeconomic rights in Soviet and then Russian understanding of both domestic and international law. The overview will identify certain themes/motives central to the concept of human rights adopted in Soviet Russia and retained in the modern world. This view of human rights was characterized by emphasis on economic and social rights as opposed to personal and political rights in the West. Moreover, positive rights (cf. more traditional negative rights) were more prevalent in this model. Finally, specific collective rights – rights of collective agents, in Leslie Green's terminology,[2] were given preference over Green's rights to collective goods and individual rights.

### *1 Marxist Origins and the New View of Human Rights*

Marxist thought was instrumental in Soviet state-building,[3] especially in the earlier stages. From the very start, Marxism opposed the (at that time) mainstream, individualistic conception of human rights as expressed in national human rights documents such as the 1791 Declaration of the Rights of Man and Citizen.[4] The criticism was made on two levels. First, Marx did not believe in the possibility of creating a universal framework of rights and freedoms (the cornerstone of the natural rights theory), as rights, to him, represented relationships of economic

1 An abridged version of this chapter was published as 'Soviet Union and the Universal Declaration of Human Rights' Max Planck Institute for European Legal History Research Paper Series No. 2017-01 (April 12, 2017). I thank Dr. Jarna Petman whose lecture at the 5th Martens Summer School on International Law has inspired the subject matter, and Ewan Smith for his insightful comments on the first draft.

2 'Two Views of Collective Rights' [1991] 4(2) *Canadian Journal of Law and Jurisprudence* 315.

3 It is debatable whether all tenets of Marxism were followed by the Soviet state at its different stages (see, for instance, Bernard Rudden, 'Law and Ideology in the Soviet Union' [1978] 31(1) *Current Legal Problems* 189); however, the fact that Marxism had at least some significant influence on Soviet legal theories is obvious.

4 The Declaration of the Rights of Man and of the Citizen (Déclaration des droits de l'homme et du citoyen) 1791.

production in a certain given time frame. Second, and more importantly, he condemned the 1791 Declaration as promoting the rights of an egoistic man separated from and opposed to society.[5] Lenin, on the other hand, did not devote even such limited attention to the question of human rights as individual rights. However, the subject of collective rights fascinated him (as rights of collective agents per Green).[6] His work on the rights of nations to self-determination recognized the coexistence of political task of defeating nationalism with more far-reaching respect for the individual states' secession.[7] While the notion of self-determination is not alien to modern legal thought, it is rarely considered alongside personal human rights, and hence this approach appears to be unusual for an orthodox understanding of rights. Later on, as will be shown, these rights will be further connected via social and economic rights that are, essentially, collective rights of "toiling classes."[8] Hence, it can be argued that both Marx and Lenin presented an unusual vision of human rights from the very start.

## *2 The People's Constitutions*

The 1918 Constitution of the Russian Soviet Federative Socialist Republic (RSFSR) contained a provision (art. 1) entitled 'Declaration of Rights of the Laboring and Exploited People.' This continued the trend of Soviet view deviating from the orthodox conception of individual liberties. It was hardly a statement of fundamental rights universality, an assumption placed in the center of the former canon, confirmed by Vyshinsky's later admission that "[the Constitution] frankly and openly declared that [these rights were] granted only to the toilers."[9] Moreover, the named article contained no "classic" rights ("*habeas corpus*, methods of trial and punishment, and the rights of private property" as "familiar Western civil liberties"),[10] with a large part of it (ch. 2) focusing on urgent economic and social matters: land ownership, emancipation of workers through arming them, abolition of private property, and an obligation to work. Moreover, other guarantees like gender and race equality, traditional by current standards yet revolutionary by past standards, were also embedded in the Constitution, yet stated separately[11] (for example, principles regarding the equality between the man and the woman were implied in all provisions regarding the status of the citizens, and article 64 specifically emphasized the right to universal suffrage), elevating the Soviet level of protection of these rights above those of Soviet Russia's western counterparts. This very brief review of the 1918 Constitution does not only highlight its focus on the economic and social matters, but

5 Karl Marx, 'On the Jewish Question' (1843).
6 Green (n. 2).
7 Vladimir Lenin, 'The Right of Nations to Self-Determination' (1914).
8 See later in this subsection.
9 Andrey Vyshinsky, *The Law of the Soviet State* (Macmillan, 1948) 557.
10 Frederic Ogg, 'The Russian Soviet Constitution' [1919] 13(1) *American Political Science Review* 293.
11 Oleg Chistiakov, *Konstitutsia RSFSR 1918 Goda* (Zertsalo, 2015) 47.

demonstrates collectivism as opposed to individualism: rights were granted on the basis of one's membership of a class (or an ethnic/gender minority group). Both trends clearly go back to the philosophical origins noted above; while the class struggle overshadowed intricate legal matters of individual rights, collective rights were still highly respected. This was not surprising considering their role in supporting the class philosophy rather than acting against it (what individualist values inevitably do).

The 1924 Constitution of the USSR contained no provisions on rights. However, according to Towe, it could be because they were already enshrined in the Constitutions of the individual republics.[12] Still, the very fact that these values were not taken up at the federal level could mean that they were not regarded as the key priority, unlike the other provisions concerning the structure of the state and federalism guarantees (since the Treaty on the Creation of the USSR was signed two years earlier). Moreover, if we were to take the 1925 Constitution of the RSFSR as an example of a more local constitutional instrument, that constitution still contained no mention of fundamental rights of individuals whatsoever. It focused, for instance, on rights of individual republics to secede instead (art. 13) and a few political guarantees such as the freedom of association (art. 6, which, however, limited the scope of application of such a right to demonstrations furthering the Soviet ideological agenda). The universal draft, surprisingly, was also characterized as an "honorary right" (*pochetnoe pravo*) to serve one's country in times of war despite being compulsory. It proves that the language of rights presented more of a rhetorical tool than tangible guarantees of actual rights as known to the West. Despite the rather empty language of both Constitutions, Vyshinsky, reflecting on the 1924 Constitution later, characterized it as providing a guarantee of "legal equality of citizens" via granting more autonomy to the individual republics.[13] Therefore, even if rights were not separated from the rest of the provisions, they might have been supported by rules, which, at first sight, were purely administrative and had nothing to do with freedoms. Hence, if this explanation is plausible, one can argue that substitution of individual rights with the autonomy of the republics as a seemingly equal, if not superior, value continued the trend of a strong emphasis on collectivism and collective rights as such.

### *3 Stalin's Human Rights Legacy?*

Surprisingly, "Stalin's Constitution" of 1936 was a significant development of human or fundamental rights doctrine within Soviet constitutionalism. This effect of Stalin's reforms was rather unusual against the overall backdrop of that era: being less satisfactory in terms of individual rights and freedoms than what the Constitution officially stated. The Great Terror showed numerous violations of,

12 Thomas Towe, 'Fundamental Rights in the Soviet Union: A Comparative Approach' [1967] 115 *University of Pennsylvania Law Review* 1251.

13 Vyshynsky (n. 9) 559.

for instance, the right to due process and other related rights. Still, the document demonstrated an inspired discussion about rights in both the leadership and the academic circles and further development of the Soviet view on these fundamental rights. Unlike the 1918 Constitution, Stalin's Constitution placed fundamental rights (and duties) of Soviet citizens at the very end, chapter 10, thus symbolically retaining the 1924 philosophy of putting the state first and the citizens second. The chapter was structured in the following way (although this was not identified by any subheadings or other markers): socioeconomic rights (right to work, right to leisure, right to social services, right to education); equality guarantees (for women specifically and for citizens in general); political and personal freedoms (freedom of conscience, freedom of speech, freedom of association, and personal inviolability); and duties (to abide by the law, to respect *public* property, and to defend their fatherland in the event of war). On the subject of duties, one should note that the fusion of rights and duties proposed by the Soviet state's vision of rights would render one's rights (including economic and social rights) depending on the individual's execution of their own duties: hence, for example, access to certain jobs was regularly denied on political grounds, which furthers this idea of link between obligations and rights.[14] Therefore, while the new Constitution was more balanced than the previous ones, socioeconomic rights still remained the top priority and were placed before everything else. Moreover, the Constitution did not only proclaim the rights, but provided specific guarantees – the duties conferred on both the citizens and the state (the latter expanded in the individual articles, e.g., "universal, compulsory elementary education" in article 121) – in order to facilitate them. The Constitution was therefore a policy tool as much as a propaganda document. As for the latter purpose, according to Towe,[15] the defined provisions were aimed to convince three groups of people – Soviet citizens, the rest of the world, and future generations – that Stalin's legal order effectively preserves and protects fundamental rights. This narrative, in my view, explained the inclusion (or, rather, "transplantation") of certain individualistic political rights in the Constitution, contrary to the stance of Marxism-Leninism. Therefore, one can say that only socioeconomic promises represented something substantial and tangible (even though they were not always supported in practice),[16] with political and personal freedoms sidelined. The Great Terror has demonstrated that these types of freedoms were fragile and subject to violations by the state – unlike socioeconomic guarantees which were abused less.

14 Jack Donnelly, 'Human Rights and Human Dignity: An Analytic Critique of Non-Western Conceptions of Human Rights' [1982] 76(2) *American Political Science Review* 310.

15 Towe (n. 12).

16 A thorough discussion of whether socioeconomic rights were protected in practice can be found in Mark Smith, 'Social Rights in the Soviet Dictatorship: The Constitutional Right to Welfare from Stalin to Brezhnev' [2012] 3(3) *Humanity: An International Journal of Human Rights, Humanitarianism, and Development* 385, 392.

## *4 Human Rights after the War*

The new human rights framework developed after World War II introduced the new, revised concept of human rights on an international stage. Therefore, the Soviet approach to international law by that time should be relevant to mapping the understanding of human rights in the Soviet period. In 1946, Sergey Krylov, the Soviet member of the International Court of Justice, defined it as a body of norms regulating relationships between states and expressing the will of the states' dominant classes.[17] Thus, he simply transplanted the Marxist-Leninist concept of law as a representation of class struggle onto the international plane. Other than that, the understanding of international law seems to be not different from the approach adopted by most western states. More interestingly, in this definition Krylov expressed the view (along with previous Soviet scholars, like Korovin, who stated that only states and international organizations of states should be subjects of international law)[18] that international law should be concerned solely with states, which can be seen as problematic in relation to human rights: matters that involve individuals as well as states. According to Kelsen, this "implies that there can be no effective protection of the rights of individuals against violations of these rights by their own state,"[19] because the Soviet international law doctrine, and in particular the understanding of state sovereignty does not allow this to happen. Therefore, while the notion of fundamental rights was not alien to the Soviet Union, enforcement of these rights through international law mechanisms proved a novelty and caused understandable confusion and even distrust of new framework from the Soviet side. For instance, Soviet writers argued that, in Kelsen's restatement, offering individuals access an international court would "aggravate international relations" and damage peace.[20] However, the Soviet Union, in practice, played a major role in introducing individual responsibility on the international law stage, both in humanitarian law developments (as seen in the Soviet enthusiasm and innovation during the Nuremberg trials)[21] and human rights developments.[22]

## *5 The Universal Declaration of Human Rights: Clash of Cultures?*

The Soviet delegation (and Vyshinsky as its representative) offered a robust critique of the western proposal of the Universal Declaration of Human Rights. Rather than commenting on the Declaration generally, Vyshinsky addressed specific provisions of the Declaration, touching on a wide variety of rights, including: "life,

17 Sergey Krylov, 'Les notions principales du droit des gens' [1947] I(70) *Recueil des Cours de l'Academie de Droit International* 420.
18 Evgeny Korovin, *Mezhdunarodnoe Pravo Perekhodnogo Perioda* (1924).
19 Hans Kelsen, *The Communist Theory of Law* (Praeger, 1955) 179.
20 Ibid.
21 Francine Hirsch, 'The Soviets at Nuremburg: International Law, Propaganda, and the Making of the Postwar Order' [2008] 113(3) *American Historical Review* 701.
22 See Lori Damroch, 'International Human Rights Law in Soviet and American Courts' [1991] 100 *Yale Law Journal* 2315.

liberty and security of person" (art. 3);[23] "social security" (art. 22);[24] "freedom of opinion and expression" (art. 19);[25] "freedom of peaceful assembly and association" (art. 20);[26] "national culture and identity" (not included in the Declaration);[27] equality in the enjoyment of rights (art. 2);[28] "self-determination of nations" (not included in the Declaration).[29] This, in turn, can be split into three thematic categories: the content of human rights, human rights guarantees, and human rights limitations.

### *(a) The Content of Human Rights*

Vyshinsky, following the "collective rights" thread, tried to introduce the rights to "national culture and identity" and "self-determination of nations" into the Declaration.[30] The former appeared in Vyshinsky's reference to the right of every person to "[their] national culture" (such as the ability to learn their national language or use it in court).[31] Interestingly enough, as he notes, a comparable provision was contained in the initial project of the Declaration – the so-called Geneva project, but that article was rejected in the later stages of the drafting process. The emphasis put on this right by the Soviet delegation can be explained by the importance of Stalin's nationalities policy, or rather the narrative aimed to promote it. For example, in his book *The Law of the Soviet State*, Vyshinsky referenced Stalin's *Marxism and the National Question*,[32] where rights to national culture were described as a "necessary point" in resolving tensions between different ethnic groups. Meanwhile, "self-determination of nations" resembled rights of the Soviet republics, the foundation of the federal system as laid down by the 1924 Soviet Constitution (the two interests, however, were considered to be linked, unlike in other "bourgeois" societies).[33] The self-determination question was therefore, like in the Soviet legal order, considered "essential" for the Declaration.[34] While, traditionally, the question of self-determination can hardly be seen as a matter of human rights law, Vyshinsky successfully linked it to the notion of equality as seen in article 2 of the Declaration. These proposals, while not being consistent with real-life Soviet practices (mistreatment of national

23 Andrey Vyshinsky, *Voprosy Mezhdunarodnovo Prava i Mezhdunarodnoi Politiki* (Gosjurizdat, 1951) 368.
24 Ibid.
25 Ibid., 370.
26 Ibid., 373.
27 Ibid., 376.
28 Ibid., 377.
29 Ibid., 383.
30 This claim, however, was not distinctly Soviet – countries of the Soviet bloc and non-aligned powers made similar suggestions regarding the content of human rights. This section, concerned with the Soviet approach, will, however, focus primarily on it.
31 Vyshinsky (n. 23) 376.
32 Vyshinsky (n. 9) 599.
33 Ibid., 598.
34 Vyshinsky (n. 23) 385.

minorities and expansionist attitudes toward the satellite state), still reflected the importance of collectivity to the Soviet understanding of human rights. Moreover, propagandistic moves can also reflect internal attitudes since they need to be consistent with other foundations of the ideology in question and appeal to the citizens' and decision-makers' beliefs.

### *(b) Human Rights Guarantees*

The most striking feature of the Soviet proposal was the introduction of positive socioeconomic rights to the Declaration. First, the Declaration should have promoted respect for the universal rights and freedoms for everyone regardless of their characteristics (such as, as already noted, nationality or religion). Second, the Declaration should have not only stated (or declared) rights, but also *guarantee their implementation*. The latter notion was inseparable from the former: each right promoted should have been backed up by certain practical measures – or positive obligations on behalf of the state (of course with a caveat that "economic, social, and national features" of individual countries should be taken into account), as was already noted in the analysis of fundamental rights in Soviet constitutionalism. While the western concept emphasized "negative rights" – individuals' claims against the government impinging on their life, dignity, and privacy, the Soviet system focused on "positive rights" – rights that could only be granted by the government.[35] Therefore, Soviet criticism largely centered on the absence of such practical, tangible guarantees in the actual project of the Declaration, which were at the forefront of the USSR's strong understanding of and commitment to socioeconomic positive rights. There were two relevant examples in Vyshinsky's speech: "life, liberty and security of person"[36] and "social security."[37] While the first right can be regarded as a more personal right and the second – as social right, the criticism leveled at both provisions was strikingly similar. For the first right, the Soviet delegation tried to pass an amendment saying that the state "should provide every human with protection against crimes, make sure that the risk of death out of hunger is prevented, and etc."[38] Therefore, the Soviets argued that the original personal right should have been supported by additional positive guarantees from the state, which, by themselves, could be regarded as separate social rights analogous to right to nutrition (in case of the guarantees related to natural causes of death). The second right was initially a social right – entitlement of everyone to realize their own, personal rights through the measures provided by social security. However, the Soviet delegation intended to take it further with more specific measures, and, most importantly,

35 Bertrand Patenaude, 'Regional Perspectives on Human Rights: the USSR and Russia, Part One – The USSR' SPICE Stanford Working Papers (2012).

36 Vyshinsky (n. 23) 368.

37 Ibid.

38 Ibid.

recognizing the obligation the state and society have regarding the development of the discussed social security mechanisms.[39] Thus, these rights and associated guarantees were considered central to the notion of human rights as such, which went against the position expressed, for instance, by Eleanor Roosevelt, who said that the US government did not think that socioeconomic rights "imply an obligation on governments to assure the enjoyment of these rights by direct governmental action."[40] This emphasized the distinction between the USSR and the West: while the former considered the state's duty to provide, for instance, job security and nutrition, the latter saw its duty only extending to non-intervention in one's private affairs.

### *(c) Human Rights Limitations*

The Soviet delegation proposed two potential limitations to rights in question: state sovereignty and public interest. Vyshinsky devoted a whole section of his speech to condemning the "attempts to use the Declaration [against] state sovereignty."[41] However, he did not provide any specific examples from the Declaration, preferring to refer to the philosophy underpinning it, specific to the western understanding of sovereignty. He rebutted the proposition attacking the primacy of human rights over the "absolute" sovereignty of the state, showing a rather distinct understanding of this concept: to him, human rights were inseparable from the state, since it was the state which protects human rights and stops them from becoming an "illusion."[42] This "sovereignty" analysis, however, evidently did not apply to socioeconomic guarantees, since Vyshinsky argued, as manifested above, that they were supposed to be imposed on states, potentially against their will; this can be rather seen as an attack on personal rights. Moreover, attracting much controversy, Vyshinsky argued that certain rights should be curtailed because of a prevailing public interest. Most importantly, he attacked unlimited freedom of expression, stating that it should have provided exceptions for wrong, "harmful" ideas such as fascism, "warmongering," and creation of hostility between the nations.[43] These two developments, contrary to previously noted positive attitudes toward socioeconomic rights, expressed hostility and caution in relation to personal and political freedoms. One might criticize these arguments for curbing the very nature of human rights – being determined by the will of the state and the right-holder's political affiliation they would not be as powerful and, most importantly, *universal*. Vyshinsky hence presented a rather authoritarian and statist vision of human rights, which, while having certain benefits for the state, could be detrimental to individuals.

39 Ibid., 369.
40 Eleanor Roosevelt, 'On the Adoption of the Universal Declaration of Human Rights' (1948).
41 Vyshinsky (n. 23) 379.
42 Ibid., 380.
43 Ibid., 371.

### *6 The 1977 Constitution*

The 1977 "Brezhnev" Constitution, unlike its predecessors, moved the human rights provisions to the front of the document – chapter 2, aptly titled "The state and the individual" (which is rather unusual considering the collectivist tendencies indicated above). Article 36, however, placed "socioeconomic freedoms" before all other freedoms, which indicated their remaining exceptional status. In practice, these freedoms were also promoted in a better way than before, with welfare being at the forefront of the government policy.[44] The rights and freedoms themselves, both political and economic, mostly mirrored the ones listed in the 1936 Constitution. Interestingly, a fair proportion of the Constitution was devoted to the concept of equality: on the basis of gender (arts. 34 and 35), race and nationality (arts. 34 and 36), and citizenship status (arts. 34, 37, and 38). This, as it can be argued, supported the trend of collectivity – equality between individuals achieved via parity established between different social and legal groups. All in all, the 1977 Constitution represented the most "advanced" and "evolved" picture of rights in the Soviet constitutional history.

### *7 The International Covenant on Economic, Social, and Cultural Rights: Winning the Debate?*

This human rights treaty was signed by the USSR in 1968 and ratified in 1973. However, even though it finally introduced socioeconomic rights into the mainstream legal devices, its history – and the Soviet response throughout – was far from being smooth. In particular, at the early stages of negotiation on the Covenant, the Soviet representatives rejected the French approach (which was at the foundation of the Covenant) as being incorrect in separating socioeconomic rights and political rights[45] by proposing two different covenants. This exposed the ideological differences – with the West still seeing personal and social rights as "first generation" and "second generation" and the Soviet Union demanding parity between personal and social rights in terms of protection from the start. The Soviet bloc later on stated that, in line with Marxist philosophy that prioritized economic matters (the "basis") over everything else, socioeconomic rights, similarly, were only a foundation for other (personal and political) rights, the absence of former guarantees rendering the latter impossible to exist.[46] This, in turn, demonstrated and reaffirmed the origins of the Soviet position – the Soviets viewed the socioeconomic matters, according to Marxist philosophy, as a basis for all other relations – and this hierarchy should have applied to rights as well, therefore reversing the western model and conceptualizing the socioeconomic rights of being "first generation." However, it shows a flaw in Soviet thinking – it

44 Smith (n. 16) 397.
45 Michael Dennis and David Stewart, 'Justiciability of Economic, Social, and Cultural Rights: Should There Be an International Complaints Mechanism to Adjudicate the Rights to Food, Water, Housing, and Health?' [2004] 98 *AJIL* 462, 478.
46 Ibid., 481.

is impossible to advocate the parity between rights and, at the same time, argue for a clear hierarchy. Therefore the Soviet position shifted between opposing fusion of rights and opposing the creation of two separate covenants. Moreover, there was another problem with the Covenant – the western countries intended to conceptualize it as merely advisory in terms of development goals and exclude any possibility of these rights being practically enforced against states, despite the working Committee's "revisionist" developments in this area. The Polish proposal arguing for a right of redress in case of violation of such rights – as transplanted from the International Covenant on Civil and Political Rights – was rejected by the overall vote, even though it was obviously supported by the Soviets. The western states were willing to create an international court for the purposes of supervising implementation of personal and political rights, but did not wish to extend this level of protection to socioeconomic rights, while the Soviet bloc demanded the opposite.[47] Therefore, while the Covenant supplemented the Declaration in terms of the sheer list of rights in question, it did not address the enforceability point that has always been advocated for by the Soviets. Overall, the Covenant has certainly not been a symbol of total Soviet success; its counterpart focusing on political rights, however, has provided a robust defense of freedoms in question. Once again, history repeated itself – the western vision, more watered down in terms of socioeconomic rights, prevailed over the Soviet vision that placed them above more conventional personal and political freedoms.

### *8 The Helsinki Declaration*

In 1975, the Helsinki Declaration,[48] aiming to improve relations between the communist bloc and the western states, was signed. The Declaration included an article on "respect for human rights and fundamental freedoms, including the freedom of thought, conscience, religion or belief." It encouraged the signatory states to promote "the effective exercise of civil, political, economic, social, cultural and other rights and freedoms." Therefore, the Declaration recognized both types of rights as worthy of protection. Moreover, it emphasized the significance of some collective rights such as rights of ethnic minorities and self-determination rights (in a separate section). The Declaration referred to the Charter of the United Nations, the Universal Declaration of Human Rights, and both human rights covenants, as well as any other agreements as sources of said human rights. Hence, they emphasized the significance of a multitude of rights, including economic and social rights. This document was crucial for diplomacy, but its legal impact is debated. The strongest position is that the Declaration was not a legal document at all. The opposite view sees it as a source of customary international

47 Matthew Craven, 'The UN Committee on Economic, Social and Cultural Rights' in Asbjorn Eide, Catarina Krause, and Allan Rosas (eds), *Economic, Social and Cultural Rights* (Martinus Nijhoff, 2001) 456.

48 The Final Act of the Conference on Security and Cooperation in Europe, August 1, 1975, 14 *ILM* 1292 (Helsinki Declaration).

law.[49] Gottlieb expressed a middle-ground position, emphasizing political and moral obligations imposed by the Declaration that appeared to be as strong as legal ones.[50] This last thesis might explain that while the Declaration did not introduce anything new in terms of the list of rights, they could still have affected nations' commitment to promoting such rights, including socioeconomic ones.

## *9 The 1993 Constitution and Its View on Human Rights*

The 1993 Constitution, similarly to the 1977 Constitution, puts human rights at the front of the document: chapter 2 is entitled "Rights and freedoms of persons and citizens." The chapter contains a fair mix of both personal (for instance, art. 19, part 1 – equality before the law), and social (e.g., art. 40 – right to shelter). Some of the "social" rights, however, are naturally stripped of their prior context rooted in communist ideology. For example, article 37 states that "[w]ork is free, and [e]veryone should be able to freely dispose of their talents," which turns the Soviet notion of an obligation to work around. Part 2 of the article explicitly reiterates that forced labor is prohibited. Still, even though some of the changes reflected the shift in economic setup, some public goods remain constitutionally provided by the state, such as healthcare (art. 41) and education (art. 43). Thus, one can say that, at least on the surface, social rights protection remained as strong as before and appears to form a tangible proportion of the Constitution. Similarly, the 1993 Constitution continued to oblige the government to undertake positive steps to facilitate one's social and economic rights. However, there has been a change with regard to collective rights: while the provisions concerning overall equality are still in place (art. 19, parts 2 and 3), more "unusual" collective rights such as the right of nations to self-determination discussed above are not mentioned in the chapter. By itself, the Russian Constitution provided a strong mechanism for social rights protection. The Constitutional Court, obliged to examine all potential violations of the Constitution by the state bodies, has examined a considerable number of cases concerning social rights.[51] Russian citizens also recognize this role of state institutions, which is proven by the fact that, on average, human rights non-governmental organizations (NGOs) see the state as playing a key role in guaranteeing social rights.[52]

Additionally, the Constitution provides for using international law mechanisms, including for human rights protection. Part 4 of article 15 of the Russian Constitution reads:

49 Jordan Paust, 'Transnational Freedom of Speech: Legal Aspects of the Helsinki Final Act' [1982] 45 *Law and Contemporary Problems* 53, 59.

50 Giddon Gottlieb, 'Global Bargaining: The Legal and Diplomatic Framework' in Nicholas Onuf (ed.), *Law-Making in the Global Community* (Carolina Academic Press, 1982) 121.

51 Andrea Chandler, 'Citizenship, Social Rights and Judicial Review in Regime Transition: The Case of Russia' [2014] 21(4) *Democratization* 743.

52 Eleanor Bindman, 'The State, Civil Society and Social Rights in Contemporary Russia' [2015] 31(3) *European Politics* 342.

> [t]he universally recognized norms of international law and international treaties and agreements of the Russian Federation shall be a component part of its legal system. If an international treaty or agreement of the Russian Federation fixes other rules than those envisaged by law, the rules of international agreement shall be applied.

Therefore, the constitutional framework recognizes (1) direct effect of international treaties; and (2) the supremacy of said treaties in the national legal system. As noted by Tamara Morshchakova, ex-justice of the Russian Constitutional Court (RCC), this article reaffirms the supremacy of international sources in Russian law through their elevation to the status of norms of constitutional significance.[53] It can also show that the list of rights in chapter 2 might not be interpreted as complete and can include other rights recognized by international treaties, an interpretation supported by inclusion of "other generally recognized rights and freedoms" (art. 55).[54] Therefore, one can conclude that the "westernization" of rights in the 1993 Constitution occurred not only by virtue of embracing a more individualistic concept in its text, but also via legal acceptance of international mechanisms (such as, as explained below, the European Convention of Human Rights (ECHR)). This contradicts the previously outlined Soviet approach that did not allow for international law to be applied in the domestic setting as something which only exists for settling disputes between sovereign nations.

## *10 ECHR and Collisions*

The ECHR appears to be a comparatively powerful instrument in protecting social rights. The nature of the Convention is that it not only obliges the signatory states to comply with its requirements, but also that the breaches of rights in question can be adjudicated and compensated for directly to individuals or via a change in law, which makes it different from similar legal instruments of the past. Most rights listed in the Convention, however, are more traditional personal and political rights, such as the right to life (art. 2) and the freedom of expression (art. 10). The property rights and education rights are dealt with under the Protocol 1 of the Convention (arts. 1 and 2 respectively). Moreover, article 14 (anti-discrimination) was also used in conjunction with the social rights-based claims, therefore, on the one hand, challenging the arbitrary division between personal and social rights, but, on the other hand, seemingly prioritizing personal rights-based claims in their strength. However, despite the lack of explicit references to social rights, the jurisprudence of the European Court of Human Rights (ECtHR) increasingly recognizes "the interdependent and indivisible nature of civil and

53 Морщакова Т. Конституционная и судебная имплементация Европейской Конвенции по правам человека // Сравнительное конституционное обозрение. 2016. №2(111). С.182–189 (Constitutional and Judicial Implementation of the European Convention on Human Rights).

54 Gennady Danilenko, 'The New Russian Constitution and International Law' [1994] 88(3) *AJIL* 451.

political rights and socio-economic rights."[55] There have been cases where social rights-related matters were argued via article 2 (the right to life),[56] article 3 (protection from inhuman and degrading treatment),[57] and article 8 (right to private and family life).[58] This does not only demonstrate that the social rights/political rights distinction is not entirely suitable for hard cases, but also shows the willingness of Strasbourg to utilize the "living instrument" approach and expand the Convention to situations not covered by it before.

Part II will examine Russia's response to the ECHR, which was ratified by Russia in 1998, together with Protocols 1, 4, and 7. At first, it was positive: before the Convention was signed, the highest Russian courts cited Strasbourg jurisprudence in their decisions. Surprisingly, the Convention was even referred to as "binding" three times.[59] In 2001, President Putin stated that Russia "[did] not consider the [ECtHR] as a competitor of [its] judicial system and affirmed the need for dialogue ('constructive work') with the court."[60] Therefore, the cooperation in question seemed to be successful from the very start. However, as the political climate changed, the Convention started to be treated with suspicion. There were, later, calls for leaving the Strasbourg regime or abolishing the aforementioned part 4 article 15 of the Constitution overall in order to preserve Russia's sovereignty and the supremacy of Russian law to international arrangements. These calls were often supported not only by fringe groups like Narodno-Osvoboditel'noe Dvizhenie (NOD), but also by the political establishment: Alexander Bastrykin, the chief of the State Investigative Bureau (Sledstvennyi Komitet) has publicly endorsed this possible change, while the Parliament member Evgenii Fyodorov has raised this question in the Lower Chamber (state Duma).

There were several specific events that indicated the change in attitudes. One of them was the 2011 *Markin* [61] case, the first time the ECtHR overruled the RCC. Zorkin, the Chief Justice of the RCC, objected to it on both political and legal grounds, reasserting Russian national sovereignty and the supremacy of the Constitution in Russian law.[62] In Zorkin's opinion, the legitimacy of the "living instrument" approach was not as absolute and could be challenged, since the Constitution was still unclear on the hierarchy of norms, creating a never-ending dispute regarding which norms should prevail in case of a clash. Many ECtHR cases were described as "politicized" by Russian officials, including *Georgia* v.

55 Liam Thornton, 'The European Convention on Human Rights: A Socio-Economic Rights Charter?' in Suzanne Egan, Liam Thornton, and Judy Walsh (eds), *Ireland and the European Convention on Human Rights: 60 Years and Beyond* (Bloomsbury, 2014).
56 Ibid.
57 Ibid.
58 Ibid.
59 Alexei Trochev, *Judging Russia: Constitutional Court in Russian Politics, 1990–2006* (CUP, 2008) 175.
60 Ibid.
61 App. No. 30078/06, 48, ECtHR 2010.
62 William E. Pomeranz, 'Uneasy Partners: Russia and the European Court of Human Rights' Human Rights Brief 19, no. 3 (2012) 17.

*Russia* [63] and *Ukraine* v. *Russia* [64] – two decisions made in the course of ongoing international conflict, in which the ECtHR allegedly expressed bias by ruling against Russia. The *Yukos* [65] case, although not concerned with two state-level actors, also had political undertones since the claimants argued that Russian officials were not acting in good faith and used tax evasion proceedings to provoke the bankruptcy of Yukos for political reasons. In 2015, the Russian Parliament, following the RCC's advice, adopted a federal law legitimizing "constitutional brakes": allowing Russia not to comply with ECtHR rulings if they directly contradict the Constitution. This device was deployed first in *Anchugov and Gladkov* [66] and then in *Yukos.*[67] It was considered a major blow to Strasbourg, and further solidified the tension between national and supranational systems. It might be the case that the next step will be leaving the ECtHR regime full stop, following the previously indicated calls for doing so.

## II Russia and Socioeconomic Rights: Specific Cases

This section of the chapter will examine some of the social rights claims brought in the ECtHR against Russia. It will be divided into two parts: social security cases that had to deal with the state obligations to provide for the most vulnerable, and the *Yukos* case, which fit a more libertarian and less state-based model of property. These cases will be summarized, and the Russian response to them (i.e. whether the remedy was granted) will be analyzed. All in all, I will argue that the case law represents a practical problem caused by retaining the theoretical distinction between the Russian and the western models after the collapse of the Soviet Union.

### *1 Social Security and Pensions Cases*

Two cases, *Burdov* v. *Russia*[68] and *Makarova and others* v. *Russia*[69] (along with some other decisions such as *Plotnikovy* v. *Russia*[70] and *Pozhakhirina* v. *Russia*),[71] appeared to be the easiest in terms of facts and legal concepts involved. Both applicants were granted some kind of social relief by the decisions of the Russian courts, but the judgments were not enforced due to cited lack of funds. The appellants claimed their right to peaceful enjoyment of their possessions (art. 1 of Protocol 1) was infringed in conjunction with the right of access to a court (art. 6 para. 1). Strasbourg easily found a violation of the rights in question,

63 ECHR 211 (2016).
64 App. No. 20958/14, ECtHR 2014.
65 App. No. 14902/04. ECtHR 2014.
66 Decision (*Postanovlenie*) of the RCC, 19.04.2016.
67 Decision (*Postanovlenie*) of the RCC, 19.01.2017.
68 App. No. 33509/04, ECtHR 2009.
69 App. No. 7023/03, ECtHR 2005.
70 App. No. 43883/0, ECtHR 2005.
71 App. No. 25964/02, ECtHR 2005.

ordering respective compensations to be paid. These decisions appear to be relatively uncontroversial compared to other judgments against Russia, especially since they aimed to uphold the already existing Russian judgments as to the sum of one's benefits rather than adjusting them. The government's response to these decisions has been positive and accommodating and, in case of *Burdov*, involved executing more than 5,000 other domestic decisions on indexing of payments to other victims of the Chernobyl disaster. The Russian government allocated the social security authorities the necessary resources to meet their financial obligations arising from similar judgments. In addition, on April 2, 2004, the Russian Parliament amended the legislation on social insurance for Chernobyl victims. This, however, can also be explained by the special (informal) status of Chernobyl (and other disasters) victims in the state's hierarchy of claimants – the RCC and the other state bodies saw the responsibility to compensate them as "absolute."[72]

When confronted with supposed substantial and not procedural violations of one's social rights, the ECtHR appeared to be less willing to grant a compensation. In *Larioshina* v. *Russia*,[73] the applicant claimed that her old-age pension was not enough to live on, and the authorities' refusal to recalculate it amounted to a violation of her property rights. Moreover, the court has indicated that a severely insufficient amount of social benefits could be considered, in principle, in the light of inhuman and degrading treatment (art. 3). However, Strasbourg found no such violation, expressly highlighting that it cannot substitute itself for national authorities and impinge on their sovereignty to exercise pensions policy. Moreover, the applicant failed to apply for additional benefits, thus not utilizing an alternative course of action. In addition, the loss suffered by the appellant was not severe enough to trigger article 3.

On the other hand, a delay in pensions was found to be a sufficient violation of the applicant's property rights. In *Solodyuk* v. *Russia*[74] it caused the actual value of pensions to decrease because of inflation. Taking into account the amount of loss suffered and the length of delays, as well as the fact that old-age pensions were the major source of one's income, Strasbourg found a violation of rights. The consequences of the violation were made good by an award of just satisfaction, and no further individual measures were required. To prevent new violations, the Committee of Ministers asked the Russian authorities to notify it of measures taken or envisaged to prevent delays in pension payments and to ensure that pensions held their value.[75]

One can, however, say, that *Markin*,[76] being a social security-related case, has provoked a substantial backlash by the Russian government. The case concerned the provision that allowed women in the armed forces to take a leave of absence in order to look after their children until they were 3 years old. The male applicant,

72 Chandler (n. 50) 752.
73 App. No. 56869/00, ECtHR 2002.
74 App. No. 9384/81, ECtHR 2004.
75 'Social Security as a Human Right: the Protection Awarded by the European Court of Human Rights' *Human Rights Files* No. 23.
76 App. No. 30078/06, 48, ECtHR 2010.

also an army officer, wanted to use these provisions himself, and alleged that the gender discrepancy was discriminatory. Unsurprisingly, Strasbourg upheld his claim. While this outcome would not have been considered controversial in the West, Russia's Constitutional Court President, Valeriy Zorkin, spoke disapprovingly of the decision. He claimed that the European court failed to take into account the social underlining of this policy: the importance of both the family and the functioning of the defense structures for Russian society and culture.[77] Zorkin has also claimed that individual states should have been able to enjoy a wider margin of appreciation with regard to issues of this kind. However, one can say that this case was neither social nor political – it was a hybrid, and contained a strong (anti-discrimination) political element. Hence, the response to it has been less amicable than to other cases on related subject matters, especially since Zorkin's attitude was not an outlier – the RCC has tried to maintain traditional gender roles rather than strive for more progressive concepts of gender equality, as can be demonstrated by some of the domestic cases.[78]

Overall, it can be said that in cases of social security measures, Russia and the ECtHR's relations have not been that difficult. Overall, while infringements occurred, they were settled in a measured way consistent with international law principles, ECtHR jurisprudence, and good sense. The ECtHR has adopted a collaborative approach, devising ways to solve social problems in question together with Russian authorities. The only exception is *Markin*, which appears to really be a political case in disguise, touching on ideological and political differences between Russia and the West.

## *2* Yukos

The *Yukos*[79] case, on the other hand, was more controversial, and deserves more analysis. Yukos, a Russian company, was investigated in relation to its tax liabilities. The authorities alleged that Yukos had evaded tax, and sought an extremely large figure by way of compensation (over €1.3 billion in respect of tax in the year 2000, together with almost €1 billion in interest and €1 billion in penalties). The company was legally obliged to pay the compensation within five days, and was declared insolvent when it failed to do so. The company challenged the decision in the ECtHR, arguing that the manner in which the compensation was claimed, and the tax proceedings took place were "unlawful, arbitrary, and disproportionate" – therefore claiming violations under article 6(1) of the Convention (right to a fair hearing), as well as article 1 of Protocol 1 (right to property). The Court found in favor of the applicants, noting, in particular: (1) that article 6(1) was violated as Yukos had no time to prepare its case; (2) that the penalties were calculated in an unlawful manner; and (3) the rigid and inflexible enforcement of the court order was disproportionate in timing and substance. In a later decision concerning the

77 Valeriy Zorkin, 'Predel Ustupchivosti' *Rossiyskaya Gazeta* (October 29, 2010).
78 Chandler (n. 50) 756.
79 App. No. 14902/04. ECtHR 2014.

award of just satisfaction, Strasbourg made its largest ever award of compensation, ordering Russia to pay in the region of €1.9 billion to the shareholders of the company at the time of its liquidation. Russia did not take the decision well. In particular, it was identified as a catalyst to constitutional change in Russia's relationship with the ECtHR as indicated above.[80] This was confirmed in 2017, when the federal law provisions were applied to *Yukos*: the decision was found to be impossible to implement since it apparently contradicted the constitutional obligation to pay taxes. This, however, seems to be quite a stretch since the obligation to pay taxes was not disputed by the claimants, and can be attributed to the politics of Yukos rather than the need to preserve the Constitution.

The case differed from prior litigation involving Russia, as it did not focus on providing social benefits that the Russian government already intended to provide, but was about misuse of penalties Russia was legally entitled to impose. Therefore, the case was concerned with the limits of state power in relation to one's individual assets, which makes it follow a more libertarian model rather than a social security model. This, however, did not go down well in Russia – with the ECtHR decision being virtually overruled by the RCC.

## III The Apparent Paradox

Historical and contemporary evaluation of Russia's approach to human rights presents an interesting paradox. On the one hand, the Soviets, on both the national and then international planes, have developed a human rights approach distinct from the west: it focused on socioeconomic rights at least as much (if not more) as personal and political rights. Grounded in Marxist philosophy and socialist understanding of fairness, this was integrated into the western human rights canon with mixed success. However, after the collapse of the Soviet Union, Russia has seemingly changed its approach. While Russia is a different jurisdiction from that of the past, many legal constructs (such as emphasis on social rights in the Constitution) remained, as well as attitudes toward the role of the state, as evidenced by the vision of the state as the main protector of social rights expressed by the NGOs[81] and the use of Soviet rhetoric when talking about social rights by Russian citizens.[82] When social rights were finally integrated into international legal doctrine via instruments such as the ECtHR, Russia, however, did not manage to catch up with these developments. This, however, will be explained in this part of the chapter. Three explanations will be explored: Green's two theories of collective rights, differences between economic models, peculiarities of Russian legal system, and political factors.

80 Lauri Mälksoo, 'Russia's Constitutional Court Defies the European Court of Human Rights' [2016] *European Constitutional Law Review* 377.
81 Bindman (n. 52).
82 Laura Henry, 'Redefining Citizenship in Russia' [2009] 56(6) *Problems of Post-Communism* 51.

### *1 Rights to Collective Goods vs Rights of Collective Agents*

Green outlines two views of collective rights: rights to collective goods and rights of collective agents.[83] The latter view states that collective rights are the rights possessed by, say, governments and corporations (including corresponding duties), while the former focuses on collective interests of individuals with respect to public or shared goods. When this concept is applied to the current situation, one can deduce that the Soviet model focused on the former, while the modern international social rights framework is based on the latter. Specifically, the Soviet approach emphasized anti-individualism and the interests of community groups such as classes, national minority groups, and even states. Green argues that the latter approach (collective goods) would be a better device to be deployed by anti-individualists, however, it does not mean that it was adopted in fact: it is clear, judging by the elements of the Soviet doctrine (including, inter alia, emphasis on sovereignty and national self-determination as *human* rights), that the rights in question were usually framed collectively. On the other hand, the ECtHR emphasizes individual rights to collective goods (such as the social security fund). This difference in approaches also has a flip side: more collectivist doctrine includes *rights* of collective agents, such as governments, and thus is statist by nature. This can explain why Russia, used to a less curtailed state power, could not deal with the more individual rights-based approach adopted in *Yukos*. This analysis, however, has its faults. For instance, the Soviet model was not entirely focused on rights of collective agents: the clauses proposed by the Soviet delegation concerning nutrition and housing were aimed at individual agents. This can, however, be interpreted as imposing a collective obligation on a state as an agent; this view will be supported by the Soviets' insistence on the importance of human rights guarantees. Still, the explanation provided here remains only one of the variables potentially influencing the disconnect between a historical approach and the modern doctrine that Russia does not necessarily ascribe to.

### *2 Capitalism and Socialism*

Another possible explanation of the paradox is the disconnect between a more socialist and a more capitalist system. Some say that socialist states, possessing the means of production, have more capability of fulfilling its citizens' socio-economic needs than countries relying on free market mechanisms.[84] Howard and Donnelly, however, write that communist regimes, while being capable of producing social goods, are incompatible with social rights, since communist regimes do not respect personal and private property unconditionally on the

83 Green (n. 2).

84 Joop de Kort, 'How Right Are Economic and Social Rights? The Interaction Between Law and Economics in Human Rights' in Ferdinand Feldbrugge and William B. Simons (eds), *Human Rights in Russia and Eastern Europe: Essays in Honor of Ger P. van den Berg* (Martinus Nijhoff, 2002).

individual discharging their obligations to the state.[85] This, in my view, stands true as applied to the situation in question. The Soviets, ascribing to the socialist system and focusing on social security provided by the state, did not consider other possible economic rights such as property rights. On the other hand, more modern and westernized legal devices have pushed for a more balanced (even though still not entirely capitalist) model, combining both types of social rights. Modern Russia, being used to the former type of rights and not the latter, succeeded in complying with the ECtHR decisions on social welfare, unlike the differently motivated *Yukos* case. This can be doubted because of the formal change in regime and economic system in Russia, but the fact remains that there has been, among all innovations, a lot of continuity with the Soviet state in terms of both legal rules and practices employed and human resources utilized in the justice system. Moreover, de Kort says that the very process of shifting from socialism to capitalism, inevitably coupled with a major blow to Russian economy, could have negatively affected the state's ability to address socioeconomic rights violations incurring economic cost.[86] This, however, cannot explain the disconnect between responses to private property-type cases and social welfare-type cases as well as other possible theories. Overall, shift from communism to mixed economy has defined Russia's capability of protecting socioeconomic rights, both because of the Soviet legacy and the sudden shift.

### *3 Positive and Negative Rights*

The interplay between rights and obligations and the distinction between positive and negative rights might have also influenced Russia's approach. The Soviet Union focused on positive obligations of the state and the use of state power in order to achieve the common good rather than possible limits of such power in the form of negative rights. Therefore, modern Russia appeared to be more suited to complying with the requirements of the former rather than the latter type – this is why the *Yukos* case was not received well. This explanation, however, does not account for greater practicality of complying with negative rights requirements and lower amount of resources that are needed. Therefore, it can only be used in conjunction with other factors as indicated above. Moreover, one can argue that the distinction between positive and negative rights is a fallacious one, since they are interdependent:[87] therefore, in order to fully secure property security, the state should undertake specific steps – this is the rationale of the same article being used in ECtHR cases about property and about social security.

85 Rhoda Howard and Jack Donnelly, 'Human Dignity, Human Rights, and Political Regimes' [1986] 80(3) *American Political Science Review* 801, 810.

86 de Kort (n. 84).

87 Elizabeth Ashford, 'The Alleged Dichotomy Between Positive and Negative Rights and Duties' in Charles Beitz and Robert Goodin (eds), *Global Basic Rights* (OUP, 2011).

## *4 National System*

Another possibility of a slightly different approach to property rights in Russia stems from a substantive difference in legal setups between the Russian and western systems have in relation to property in general on the national plane. This occurs in two ways: in relation to right-holders and in relation to the rights themselves. As for the rights-holders, the Russian doctrine focuses, primarily, on individuals rather than companies. As Starzhenetsky notes, the concept of a "legal personality" meaning anything other than an individual can be criticized as it is perceived as somewhat artificial; companies cannot experience the same distress as individuals when their property rights are being violated.[88] Reaching only this, surface-level analysis, and failing to notice that cases including companies always include a series of individual claims, the Russian judiciary is less sympathetic to the plight of entities such as Yukos. This, on the one hand, is surprising considering the emphasis on possibly collectivist nature of human rights in the Soviet and Russian cultures. However, this collectivism, as one should note, has been influenced by socialist rather than capitalist ideas, and thus does not naturally include corporate entities. Another gap identified by Starzhenetsky is the narrower conception of property rights as used in the national Russian law and legal philosophy.[89] Property rights, at most, include tangible "things" rather than other types of property interests. Gadzhiev rightly noted that "the ECtHR sees property as a much broader entity than the Russian civil law doctrine."[90] This, in turn, could have also caused confusion with regard to the understanding of the Convention by the national courts. In practice, most individuals engaging in commerce are reported to distrust the Russian institutions as providing insufficient protection of one's property and often resorting to extralegal and even illegal means of doing so.[91] All in all, one can say that while the operation of the Convention is legally independent from national law, it still stays true that peculiarities of the national legal system and philosophy can hinder a country's receptiveness to decisions based on said Convention.

## *5 Merely Politics?*

Finally, one can argue that there has not been any paradox whatsoever, and the *Yukos* decision in question remains an outlier solely motivated by politics. In the light of the other social rights cases, the Russia's response was no worse than the reaction of its western counterparts. Therefore, Russia has inherited the Soviet approach to human rights, but like its predecessor, it is willing and able to depart from it in the event of a political threat or disagreement. This explanation, while

88 Vladislv Starzhenetskii, *Rossiia i Sovet Evropy: Pravo Sobstvennosti* (Gorodets, 2004).

89 Ibid.

90 Gadis Gadzhiev, *Kommentarii k Konventsii o Zachite Prav Cheloveka i Osnovnykh Svobod I Praktike Ee Primeneniia* (Norma, 2002).

91 Jordan Gans-Morse, 'Demand for Law and the Security of Property Rights: The Case of Post-Soviet Russia' [2017] 111(2) *American Political Science Review* 338.

plausible, appears to be very simplistic and close to the usual canons of analyzing Russian law – while politics might have played its part, one can argue that there have been other factors at play, such as the rights-of-collective-agents approach or more socialist approach as identified above. Still, ruling out political factors would mean ignoring the real-life context of the decisions in question.

## IV Concluding Observations

Therefore, the Soviet Union championed a human rights approach based on socioeconomic, positive, and collective (in the sense of rights of collective agents) rights. This view of human rights was not fully assimilated into the western canon, however, the latter has gradually become more sympathetic toward social rights. One would expect Russia to succeed in implementing social rights, but this success was partial – it only extended to some types of social rights and not the others. It can be explained by the fact that Russia was only used to social rights which were consistent with the Soviet model – personal property rights, for instance, were more individualistic and based on a capitalist system. Moreover, it can be argued that, possibly due to that, the present Russian legal and ideological property context was less expansive than the western (ECtHR) view, which led to confusion and rejection on Russia's part. Therefore, Russia, despite its unique human rights heritage, can only conform to the modern social rights canon to an extent. This is not all due to ideological factors – political differences could also affect the situation, but one should examine the historical foundations of Russian approaches to human rights in order to fully understand the challenges faced today.

# Part II

# Social Systems, Constitutionalism, and Legal Ideology

# 4 Living Constitutionalism in Russia

*Maria Smirnova and Chris Thornhill*

## 1 Introduction

In most polities, it is now acknowledged, formally, that constitutions are constructed by a range of processes, which widen the meaning of the constitution beyond the original scope of the constitution as text.[1] Different polities have developed distinct doctrines to account for the ongoing evolution of their systems of constitutional law. Such doctrines, often originating within judicial bodies and court rulings, are usually grouped together as theories of *living constitutionalism.*

This doctrine first assumed clear shape in Canada in the 1920s, in the living tree doctrine of the Constitution;[2] it was then exponentially expanded in Canadian jurisprudence through the 1980s, owing to the implementation of the Charter of Rights and Freedoms.[3] This doctrine also assumed great importance in the consolidation of constitutional theory and practice in the post-1949 Federal Republic of Germany (FRG). At a theoretical level, the doctrine of the *lebende Verfassung* played an important role in embedding the *Grundgesetz* (originally seen as a provisional document) in the society of the FRG in the 1950s. It then acquired great practical impact through decisions of the Constitutional Court, which between the 1950s and the 1970s articulated a pervasive hierarchy of constitutional norms, based in human rights, for all parts of society.[4] Aspects of this doctrine have been

1 Research for this chapter was funded by the European Research Council (Advanced Grant: 323656-STC). This chapter was presented in draft form at a roundtable discussion at the Institute of Legislation and Comparative Law under the Government of the Russian Federation (Moscow, March 3, 2017) and at a seminar at Kazan National Research Technological University (Kazan, March 2, 2017). We wish to record our thanks to the organizers of these events and to all participants, for their very stimulating comments and questions.

2 See *Henrietta Muir Edwards and others (Appeal No. 121 of 1928)* v. *The Attorney General of Canada* (Canada) [1929] UKPC 86 (October 18, 1929).

3 Note further arboreal symbolism in the opinion that a constitution is "drafted with an eye to the future" and must be "capable of growth" in *Hunter* v. *Southam Inc* [1984] 2 SCR 145. Likewise, note the view that "[n]arrow and technical interpretation" can "stunt the growth of the law and hence the community it serves" in *Law Society of Upper Canada* v. *Skapinker* [1984] 1 SCR 357.

4 See West German Constitutional Court 1 400/51 (Lüth) (15.1.1958) 42.

reflected in the superior courts in the USA.[5] Similar ideas have proven very influential in India, where courts have employed both the basic structure doctrine and social rights jurisprudence to enlarge the substance of the Constitution.[6] Such ideas have also been articulated in Spain and in some parts of Latin America in the concept of the *block of constitutionality*, which allows superior courts to determine the normative hierarchy of constitutional law and even to generate new constitutional rights.[7] Additionally, the reception of these ideas has become visible in parts of Africa, notably in South Africa and in Kenya.[8] In fact, this doctrine is now even established, with restrictions, in the UK.[9] A theory close to the doctrine of the living constitution is also reflected in some supranational judicial systems. This is visible, for example, in the European Union, where the constitution-making role of the European Court of Justice is widely recognized.[10] Under the European Convention on Human Rights (ECHR), the European Court of Human Rights (ECtHR) has clearly defined itself as an agent authorized to construct constitutional norms. Moreover, national courts within the European Convention system also espouse a living-tree construction of the ECHR, and they see themselves as participants in a constitutional conversation with the ECtHR and other courts.[11]

5 See the early formulation of this doctrine, by Wendell Holmes, in *Missouri* v. *Holland*, 252 US 416 (1920). An expanded variation on this doctrine is at the core of the most famous recent articulation of US–American constitutional philosophy: Bruce Ackerman, *We the People*, vol I: *Foundations* (Harvard UP, 1991). In some respects the doctrine of the living constitution was already anticipated by John Marshall who argued that a "provision is made in a Constitution intended to endure for ages to come, and consequently to be adapted to the various crises of human affairs": *McCulloch* v. *Maryland*, 17 US 316 (1819). It is persuasively argued that originalism is an ideologically generated doctrine, caused by the realist impulse of the Supreme Court in the 1950s and 1960s. See Johnathan O'Neill, *Originalism in American Law and Politics. A Constitutional History* (Johns Hopkins UP, 2005) 30.

6 See *I C Golak Nath & Ors* v. *State of Punjab & Anr* (1967), *Kesavananda Bharati* v. *State of Kerela* (1973).

7 The origins of this doctrine can be traced to a freedom-of-association case heard in 1971 by the French Conseil Constitutionnel (71-44 DC, 1971). For the Spanish elaboration of this doctrine, which widely informed Latin American constitutional law, see Spanish Constitutional Court 38/1983. This doctrine is most prominent in Colombia. In 1995, the Colombian Constitutional Court defined the block of constitutionality as the set of "norms and principles which, without appearing formally in the articulated text of the constitution, are used as parameters for controlling the constitutionality of laws" (C-225/95).

8 For South Africa, see the classic case *S* v. *Makwanyane and Another* (CCT3/94) [1995] 168. In Kenya, see *In Re Estate of Lerionka Ole Ntutu (Deceased)* [2008] eKLR.

9 By the late 1970s, the English judiciary had carved out the idea that Parliament was bound to recognition of a body of common law rights. See as primary exemplification the ruling in *Morris* v. *Beardmore* [1980] 2 *All ER* 753.

10 See classical analysis in Alec Stone Sweet, *Governing with Judges: Constitutional Politics in Europe* (OUP, 2000), Joseph H. H. Weiler, 'The Transformation of Europe' *Yale Law Journal* 100 (1991) 2404–83.

11 For one example in the UK, see *Brown* v. *Stott (Procurator Fiscal, Dunfermline) and another* [2001] 2 *All ER* 97 (Bingham LJ), for examples in Norway, see Mads

Broadly, the doctrine of living constitutionalism has a number of separate implications. Presented schematically, this doctrine can be identified in three separate theoretical variations.

First, this doctrine promotes a theory of judicial interpretation, which specifically empowers judges to develop and entrench new positions in constitutional law, and which assigns to judicial findings a key role in adapting the constitution to evolving societal conditions. In many recent cases, creative patterns of judicial constitutional construction are observable at the interface between domestic and international law. Indeed, living constitutionalism is typically connected to the solidification of international norms in domestic public law;[12] to the use of proportionality, aligning domestic standards to international law;[13] and to the creation of new rights, often linked to the imputation of immediate effect in national legal systems to rights that are defined in the international domain.[14] In each respect, living constitutionalism gives effect to international human rights as aspirational normative elements of a modern society.

Second, in some settings, this doctrine is construed, in part, as a framework for integrating new subjects in the process of constitutional implementation, and it serves to open the formation of constitutional law toward society as a whole. Although according high sociological importance to judges, this doctrine is consciously proposed as a theory of popular sovereignty, enabling a constant constructive alignment of the constitution to the popular will in society at large. In this respect, the doctrine of living constitutionalism is integrally connected with a theory of citizenship, which envisages ways in which constitutional law can be made sensitive to emerging citizenship practices in society. Such ideas have been applied in order to encourage increased access to law, to promote legal mobilization, and even to facilitate public law litigation, enabling multiple legal subjects to acquire influence on the formation of constitutional law.[15] For example, living constitutionalism has clearly embraced the role of social movements and strategic

Andenas and Eirik Bjorge, 'The Norwegian Court Applies the ECHR by Building upon Its Underlying Principles' *European Public Law* (2013) 19(2) 241–6, 242.

12 See for example cases (nn. 8 and 18).

13 For example, in Canada, proportionality is, arguably, a primary basis for the living tree approach. See Andrée Lajoie and Henry Quillinan, 'Emerging Constitutional Norms: Continuous Judicial Amendment of the Constitution: The Proportionality Test as a Moving Target' *Law and Contemporary Problems* 55(1) (1992) 285–302, 286. In the UK, judges have claimed that use of proportionality means that they have a duty to make a "sociological assessment" of the impact of administrative acts and to ensure accordance of such acts with higher rights norms. See *Wilson* v. *First County Trust Ltd* (No 2) [2003] UKHL 40 142 (Hobhouse LJ). On the more general constitutional implications of proportionality, see Anne Peters, 'Verhältnissmässigkeit als globales Verfassungsprinzip' in Björnstern Baade, Sebastian Ehricht, Matthäus Funk, Robert Frau, Mirka Möldner, Isabella Risini, and Torsten Stirner (eds), *Verhältnismäßigkeit im Völkerrecht* (Mohr Siebeck, 2015) 1–20; Alec Stone Sweet and Jud Mathews, 'Proportionality Balancing and Constitutionalism' (2008) 47 *Columbia Journal of Transnational Law* 73–165.

14 See discussion in Chris Thornhill, *The Sociology of Law and the Global Transformation of Democracy* (CUP, 2018).

15 See a classic example in the Indian case *S.P. Gupta* v. *President of India* (1981).

litigants as sources of constitutional impetus.[16] Moreover, it has embraced the role of public interest organizations as drivers of new patterns of constitutional construction.[17] Typically, again, such widening of constitutional formation through the promotion of new modes of legal subject formation is often supported by reliance on international human rights law.[18] Underlying this aspect of the contemporary theory of living constitutionalism we can find an expanded model of the citizen, in which acts of citizenship linked to litigation articulate national norms with global norms, and approximate national constitutions to the global legal order.[19]

Generally, the doctrine of the living constitution has a vital, multivalent place in much contemporary constitutional law. It is used to capture both the deep-lying processes of social transformation in national societies and the deep lines of refraction between national and international law. Moreover, such ideas tend to be associated with politically progressive patterns of constitutional legal formation, and their exponents tend to find support among more liberal sectors of the legal community.[20] In many cases, these ideas are seen to articulate a paradigmatic openness in the legal community, and they appear as attempts to commit the system of public law to ongoing modernization and strategic improvement. In particular, they appear as part of an endeavor to ensure that the people, in its contemporary form, remains an active source of legally binding norms: the living constitution is widely construed as an evolving expression of the primary sovereignty of the people, in which courts act in conjunction with other political institutions to capture moments of deep transformation in the popular will and the societal form of citizenship.[21] In each case, acts of litigation are observed as primary citizenship practices, forming constitutive links between government and society, and creating de facto constituent openings for constitutional revision.

## 2 The Living Constitution in Russia

Despite the wide diffusion of the doctrine of living constitutionalism, such concepts are rarely identified in Russia, and there is little research on constructive processes of constitutional actualization in the Russian setting.

16 See the Canadian case *Canada (Attorney General)* v. *Downtown Eastside Sex Workers United Against Violence Society* [2012] SCC 45.
17 In the USA, *Brown* v. *Board of Education* (1954) set the paradigm for this.
18 Many most important public interest cases reflected the deep impact of international law. A key example is the leading case heard by the Colombian Constitutional Court, T-024/05, concerning mass violation of the rights of displaced persons.
19 For this concept, see Thornhill (n. 14).
20 For discussion of this, see Aileen Kavanagh, 'The Idea of a Living Constitution' (2003) 16(1) *Canadian Journal of Law and Jurisprudence* 55–89, 79; Howard Gillman, 'The Collapse of Constitutional Originalism and the Rise of the Notion of the "Living Constitution" in the Course of American State-Building' (1997) 11 *Studies in American Political Development* 191–247, 192.
21 See most famously Bruce Ackerman, 'The Living Constitution' (2007) 120(7) *Harvard Law Review* 1737–1812, 1758, 1791; Bruce Ackerman, *We the People, III: The Civil Rights Revolution* (Harvard UP, 2014) 32, 34, 812, 127, 170, 329.

The absence of such inquiry can be attributed to a number of reasons. The lack of such research is partly the result of a general suspicion that the normative purchase of constitutional law in Russia is weak.[22] This is partly the result of a suspicion that constitutional law in Russia is subject to strong political control, and that constitutional jurisprudence is linked to clearly reactionary interests.[23] Moreover, it is partly caused by the fact that, especially outside Russia, Russian constitutional law is seen as detached from society, as existing in a purely formal legal domain, with minimal bearing on actual sociopolitical practices.[24] In fact, some Russian authors share the view that in Russia the Constitution exists mainly as a nominal, fictional document, such that constitutional norms are so remote from reality that they lose any practical meaning.[25] Lack of such research is also a result of the general fact that Russia is seen, at best, as a recalcitrant player in international legal orders, and the impact of international law in Russian legal system is not assessed favorably. Factually, moreover, legal openings for distinctive citizenship practices are not extensive in Russia. It is only in the very recent past that public interest litigation has become more accessible, without the assistance of public prosecutors, although it is still subject to restriction.[26] The basic function of public interest litigation as a line of exchange between state and society is thus not strongly consolidated in Russia. Generally, debates about

22 For an early example, see Richard Rose, 'Russia as an Hour-Glass Society: A Constitution without Citizens' (1995) 4 *East European Constitutional Review* 34–42.

23 Armen Mazmanyan, 'Judicialization of Politics: The Post-Soviet Way' *International Journal of Constitutional Law* (2015) 13(1) 200–18, 214; Carla L. Thorson, *Politics, Judicial Review and the Russian Constitutional Court* (Palgrave, 2012) 152.

24 Richard Sakwa, 'The Dual State in Russia' (2010) 26(3) *Post-Soviet Affairs* 185–206.

25 Медушевский А., 'Российская модель конституционных преобразований в сравнительной перспективе.' Конституционное право: восточноевропейское обозрение (Medushevsky A., 'Russian model of constitutional reforms in a comparative perspective' 2 (43) (2003) *Constitutional L: East European Rev*) 148–66, 155; Старилов Ю. Н. '"Корректировка" конституции как "развертывание" ее "потенциала." Правовые реформы в современной России: значение, результаты, перспективы: материалы научно-практической конференции, посвященной 50-летнему юбилею юридического факультета Воронежского государственого университета' (Воронеж, 20–21 ноября 2008 г.)' (Воронеж: Издательство Воронежского Государственного Университета, 2009) Выпуск 5, часть 1 (Starilov Yu. N., '"Adjustment" of the Constitution as a "Deployment" of Its "Potential" in Legal Reforms in Modern Russia: Significance, Results, Prospects: Materials of the Scientific–Practical Conference Dedicated to the 50th Anniversary of the Law Faculty of the Voronezh State University (Voronezh, November 20–21 2008) (Voronezh State University, 2009), vol. V, pt 1, 56–82, 79, 81); Шахрай С. М., О Конституции: Основной закон как инструмент правовых и социально-политических преобразований (Наука, 2013); Sergey Shakhrai, *About the Constitution: The Basic Law as the Instrument of Legal and Socio-Political Transformation* (Nauka, 2013) 26–7; Кабышев В. Т., 'Конституционные ожидания,' Конституционное и муниципальное право (Kabyshev V. T., 'Constitutional Expectations' (2013) 11 *Constitutional and Municipal Law*) 24–7, 25. All translations from Russian into English are by Maria Smirnova.

26 It has become possible for citizens to initiate certain cases in public interest through NGOs, as opposed to more traditional public prosecutors, with the adoption of the Federal Law No. 212-FZ of July 21, 2014 On the Basics of Citizens' Control; see art. 10(1)(7) (Федеральный закон от 21 июля 2014 г. № 212-ФЗ 'Об основах общественного контроля в Российской Федерации').

participatory citizenship are not fully elaborated in Russia. Citizenship is still most often understood as a synonym for patriotism.[27] Only very occasionally is citizenship interpreted as a participatory practice or as "social activity" of an individual person.[28] On these different grounds, sociopolitical conditions in Russia have not naturally favored debate about living constitutionalism.

This chapter seeks to alter and correct these perceptions. It argues that constitutional doctrine and practice in Russia need to be positioned within the wide context of debate on living constitutional adaption. In fact, it argues that a modified theory of living constitutionalism has particular relevance for explaining the role of constitutional law in Russian society more widely, so that elements of living constitutionalism can be understood in a broad sociological perspective. To set out these claims, the chapter focuses on four sets of legal data. First, it examines theories of living constitutionalism in relevant theoretical and doctrinal literature in Russia. Second, it assesses judicial rulings showing examples of constructive constitutional formation, including use of proportionality, assimilation of international law, and participation of Russian courts in discussion with the ECtHR. Third, it considers examples in which we can observe the formation of new constitutional subjects. Fourth, it sets out a theoretical analysis of emerging citizenship practices in Russia, illustrating how, as in other societies, theories and practices relating to living constitutionalism reflect new, evolving patterns of citizenship. In this respect, it argues that living constitutionalism in Russia institutionalizes citizenship practices of a very distinctive kind, adapted to the overarching nature of the Russian polity. In some respects, modes of citizenship enacted through living constitutionalism have greater effect on constitutional law than in other polities.

## *(a) Theoretical Foundations: Questions of Doctrine*

### *(i) Constitutional Axioms*

Despite localized skepticism about the social relevance of the constitution, the theory of the living constitutionalism is well established in Russian constitutional

27 Дебердеева Т. Х., 'Национальная идея в России: гражданственность в содружестве с патриотизмом,' Совет ректоров (Deberdeeva, T. Kh., 'National Idea in Russia: Citizenship in Conjunction with Patriotism' 1 (2010) *The Council of Rectors*) 60–5; Рожкова Л. В., Васильева Н. Д., 'Гражданственность и патриотизм как основания социальной консолидации российского общества,' Мониторинг общественного мнения: экономические и социальные перемены (Rozhkova, L. V. and Vasilyeva, N. D. 'Citizenship and Patriotism as the Basis of Social Consolidation of the Russian Society' 3 (121) (2014) *Monitoring of Public Opinion: Economic and Social Changes*) 123–9; Богданов А. П., Хутин А. Ф., 'Патриотизм и гражданственность как факторы укрепления государства,' Знание. Понимание. Умение (Bogdanov, A. P. and Hutin, A. F. 'Patriotism and Citizenship as Factors of State-Building' (2012) 4 *Knowledge: Understanding Skills*) 123–7.

28 Евгений Тарибо, Российское гражданство и вытекающие из него права и обязанности в практике судебного конституционного контроля (Taribo, Evgeny, *Russian Citizenship and the Ensuing Rights and Obligations in the Practice of Judicial Constitutional Review*) (NWAPA, 2011) 116.

discourse. In fact, it is almost axiomatic in Russian legal doctrine that the text of the 1993 Constitution does not form a definitive legal reality. Instead, the Constitution is seen as a declaration of national objectives, which need to be realized through subsequent interpretation and constitutional practice.[29] For different reasons, the idea of the constitution as a living document has particular significance for the Russian context.

On one hand, concretely, the claim that the Constitution is a "living instrument" is linked to the conditions in which the Constitution was drafted in the early 1990s.[30] During this process, original drafts for the Constitution had to be recurrently revised in order to meet the demands of different stakeholders in the constitution-making process, and to pacify opposing factions following the breakdown of the Soviet Union.[31] The authors of the Constitution were confronted with very pressing and immediate intergroup conflicts, and they were expected, as a matter of priority, to write a document that would both "restore the collapsed social agreement" and provide "an efficient instrument of transformation of the socioeconomic system."[32] Accordingly, the Constitution reflected the rivalries within the Constitutional Assembly, and it did not result from full consensus between different parties that contributed to its creation.[33] As a result, some provisions in the Constitution were formulated at a high level of abstraction,

29 Shakhrai (n. 25) 25.

30 The idea of the Constitution as a "living instrument" was mentioned by President Medvedev in his response to a suggestion to amend the text of the Constitution in order to include a new consultative body that consists of heads of regions. This body was created in 2000 to assist the president in decision-making after the method of formation of the upper chamber of Parliament – the Council of the Federation – was altered. Although the amendments were never introduced, the discussion was based on the concept of "living constitution." See Олеся Белобородова 'Конституция – живой инструмент: Дмитрий Медведев пообещал найти место Госсовету в основном Законе страны' (Olesya Beloborodova, 'Constitution is a living instrument: Dmitry Medvedev promised to find a place for the State Council in the main law of the country') *Vzglyad*, August 31, 2010, https://vz.ru/politics/2010/8/31/429092.html (accessed January 10, 2018). Two years later President Putin referred to the concept of "living constitution" again in his conversation with RCC judges. He insisted that despite the Constitution being "a living instrument," the role of the RCC judges is firmly to defend the foundations of the constitutional order and to be "very delicate" with its text to ensure its stability. See 'Конституция должна быть стабильной, уверен Путин' ('The Constitution should be stable, Putin is assured') *RIA Novosti*, December 12, 2012, https://ria.ru/politics/20121212/914506140.html (accessed January 10, 2018).

31 For example, as Shakhrai mentioned, initially there was no consensus among the drafters even in such technical issues as the length of the president's term. Shakhrai (n. 25) 146.

32 Гаджиев Г.А. Рецензия на книгу: Шахрай С. М., 'О Конституции: основной закон как инструмент правовых и социально-политических преобразований.' (Gadzhiyev GA, Book review: Shakhrai S. M., 'On The Constitution: The Basic Law as an Instrument of Legal and Socio-Political Transformations') (2013) 5 *Pravovedenie* 257–64, 259.

33 See Edward Morgan-Jones, *Constitutional Bargaining in Russia, 1990–93: Institutions and Uncertainty* (Routledge, 2010).

to avoid exacerbating existing conflicts between rival parties. For this reason, it was assumed by the drafters that some provisions would only take flesh incrementally, and that democratic institutions and processes would evolve more fully over time.[34]

The idea of the Russian Constitution as a document requiring incremental realization is also linked, not only to day-to-day problems during the drafting process, but to the longer-term political objectives of transitional elites in the early 1990s. Notably, leading figures in the transitional period possessed an elevated understanding of the purposes of constitutional law, and they created a highly programmatic Constitution, conceived as a "normative model of the future,"[35] and as a "normative programme for the modernisation of the Russian society."[36] The Constitution was imputed a core "organizing role" in the formation of a democratic political order,[37] and it expressed strategic goals for the development of society and state, to be realized in subsequent normative acts, decisions and actions.[38] Moreover, early judges on the Russian Constitutional Court (RCC), which pre-existed the drafting of the Constitution,[39] assumed for themselves a central role in the implementation of the Constitution. Many RCC judges were strongly committed to enhancing the role of the courts in the consolidation of democracy, and, in their own self-description, they were "great idealists," committed to the legal realization of a "happy democratic future."[40] Although these programmatic visions did not become a full reality, the idea that the Constitution forms a blueprint for social transformation and institutional construction is still imprinted in Russian constitutional law.[41] At a doctrinal level, this is reflected in the theory of "constitutional potential,"[42] which argues that there is an inevitable

34 Gadzhiyev (n. 32) 259; Tamara Morschakova, in 'Конституция России: менять, адаптировать или не трогать?' ('Russian Constitution: To Change, to Adapt or Not to Touch?') *Oblgazeta* (2015) 230.
35 Shakhrai (n. 25) 299.
36 Kabyshev (n. 25) 25.
37 Shakhrai (n. 25) 15
38 Ibid., 16.
39 The RCC was created on July 12, 1991. It actively participated in the settlement of the constitutional crisis of 1992–1993. Its judges, the leading experts on constitutional law, played a major role in the work of the Constitutional Conference drafting the text of the 1993 Constitution.
40 'Тайна совещательной комнаты. На вопросы Михаила Барщевского отвечает глава Конституционного суда РФ Валерий Зорькин.' (The secret of the advisory room. Mikhail Barshchevsky's questions are answered by the head of the Constitutional Court Valery Zorkin) *Rossiyskaya Gazeta* 5612 (236) (2011).
41 Kabyshev (n. 25) 24, Борисов Г. А. 'Освоение потенциала Конституции РФ: проблемы и перспективы' Научные труды РАЮН (Москва: Юрист, 2002), Выпуск 2, Том 2 (Borisov, G. A. 'Exploring the Potential of the Constitution: Problems and Prospects') (2002) 2(2) *RAYUN Proceedings* 195–200, 196.
42 See, for example, Добрынин Н. М., 'Конституционализм в новейшей истории России: потенциал и возможности' (Dobrynin, N. M. 'Constitutionalism in Russia's Recent History: Its Potential and Opportunities') *Gosudarstvo i Pravo* 2 (2009) 5–8, 5, Малый А. Ф., 'Модификация Конституции: ожидания и возможности' Научные труды РАЮН (Москва: Юрист, 2014) Выпуск 14, Том 1 (Maliy, A. F. 'Modification of

gap between the factual or real constitution and the constitutional text,[43] such that the "forward-looking programmatic nature of the Constitution requires a long process to realise its potential."[44] Indicatively, as late as 2008, the Report on the Current State of Legislation in Russia averred that Russian constitutionalism is a substantive strategy for creating a new quality of life.[45]

On the other hand, more conceptually, the idea that the Constitution has a living substance has deep origins in recent Russian constitutional history.[46] RCC Judge Bondar claims that the *roots* of the "living constitutionalism" doctrine lie in the Saratov school of legal thought – the main school of Russian constitutionalism since the 1960s. On this account, the main ideas of living constitutionalism were promoted by the school's founder, Isaac Farber.[47]

Such ideas remain palpable in contemporary debate. For example, Bondar imputes an axiological function to the Constitution. He argues that the Constitution reflects "the national cultural code" and the "sociocultural image of a multi-national society." Accordingly, it possesses "an inherent normative energy in its development, transformation and maturation as a unique political and legal phenomenon."[48] Owing to the "incompatibility of the Constitutional text with

the Constitution: Expectations and Opportunities') 14(1) *RAYUN Proceedings* (2014) 613–16, 616, Шахрай С. М. 'О творческом потенциале действующей Конституции Российской Федерации,' Современный конституционализм: вызовы и перспективы: материалы международной научно-практической конференции, посвященной 20-летию Конституции Российской Федерации (Санкт-Петербург, 14–15 ноября 2013 г.) (Москва: Норма, 2014) (Shakhrai, S. M. 'On the Creative Potential of the Current Constitution of the Russian Federation' in *Modern Constitutionalism: Challenges and Prospects: Proceedings of International Scientific–Practical Conference dedicated to the 20th anniversary of the Constitution of the Russian Federation* (St. Petersburg, November 14–15, 2013) (Norma, 2014) 83–108, 83.

43 Интервью с Виктором Шейнисом 'Это был не консенсусный документ, а Конституция победителя: Российская Конституция: Взгляд из 2008' (Interview with Viktor Sheinis, 'This was not a consensus document, but the Constitution of the winner: Russian Constitution: View from 2008') *Neprikosnovennyy zapas. Debaty o politike i culture* 5 (2008) 27–48, 43.

44 See Borisov (n. 41) 195.

45 Доклад Совета Федерации Федерального Собрания Российской Федерации 2007 года 'О состоянии законодательства в Российской Федерации' Под общей редакцией Г. Э. Бурбулиса и С. М. Миронова (Москва: Совет Федерации, 2008) (GE Burbulis and SM Mironov (eds), *Report on the Current State of Legislation in the Russian Federation in 2007*) (Council of the Federation, 2008) 512.

46 William B. Simons (ed.), *The Constitutions of the Communist World* (Sijthoff & Noordhoff, 1980) xv.

47 Бондарь Н. С. 'У истоков доктрины 'живого' (реального) отечественного конституционализма,' Вестник Саратовской государственной юридической академии (Bondar, N. S., 'At the origins of the doctrine of the "living" (real) domestic constitutionalism' (2013) 4(93) *Bulletin of the Saratov State Law Academy*) 42–7, 45.

48 Бондарь Н. С., 'По какой Конституции живет Россия: прошлого или нынешнего, XXI века?' Журнал зарубежного законодательства и сравнительного правоведения (N. S. Bondar, 'Under which Constitution Does Russia Live: The Past or the Present, the 21st Century?' (2013) 6(43) *Journal of Foreign Legislation and Comparative Law*) 976–85, 978.

reality," moreover, he argues that the Constitution "should contain immanently inherent points of growth and self-development."[49] In consequence, he concludes that the "Constitution is a living organism."[50] Similarly, RCC Chairman Zorkin has argued that "the Constitution must not be understood exclusively as a normative text." Instead, he claims, it should be viewed as "a historically formed (and still developing) axiological set of principles and norms, inherent in a specific society in a given phase of its development and shared by the majority of its members."[51] For this reason, the Constitution should be considered, not as "a recalcitrant text" or as a "dusty manuscript," but as a living organism, possessing an "independent existence" and the "potential to change."[52]

Naturally, this conceptual analysis of the Constitution does not enjoy a full consensus. The idea of living constitutionalism is contested by theorists of a more strictly positivist orientation, who deny that the Constitution in its given form possesses any transformative power.[53] Moreover, many observers claim that the current Constitution is simply discredited because of the manifest material gap between its normative content and social reality,[54] especially concerning the Constitution's provisions for a multi-party political system.[55] Such observers argue that the Constitution is redundant, and that a new Constitution should be adopted, following the "natural cycle" of constitutional development and reflecting the current demands of the Russian society.[56] Additionally, some

49 Ibid., 976.

50 Ibid., 980.

51 Valery Zorkin, 'Constitutional Justice in the Transitional Phase of the Historical Development of Russia' May 17, 2016, www.ksrf.ru/ru/News/Speech/Pages/ViewItem.aspx?ParamId=77 (accessed January 10, 2018).

52 Аничкин Е. С., '"Преобразование" Конституции Российской Федерации (к вопросу о дискуссии вокруг одной правовой категории)' *Конституционное и муниципальное право* (Anichkin, E. S. '"Transformation" of the Constitution of the Russian Federation (to the issue of discussion around one legal category)' *Constitutional and Municipal Law*) 22 (2008) 2–6, 2.

53 According to Starilov, "potential of the Constitution is an overused concept," Старилов Ю. Н., '"Корректировка" конституции как "развертывание" ее "потенциала," Правовые реформы в современной России: значение, результаты, перспективы: материалы *научно-практической конференции, посвященной 50-летнему юбилею юридического факультета Воронежского государственого университета* (Воронеж, 20–21 ноября 2008 г.) (Воронеж, 2009) Выпуск 5, часть 1 (Starilov, Yu. N., '"Adjustment" of the Constitution as a form of "deployment" of its "potential" in legal reforms in modern Russia: significance, results, prospects: materials of the scientific–practical conference dedicated to the 50th anniversary of the law faculty of the Voronezh State University (Voronezh, November 20–21, 2008) 5 (2009), Part 1) 56–82, 75.

54 Borisov (n. 41) 195.

55 Лебедев В. А., 'Конституционный идеал и политическая реальность: парадоксы российской многопартийности,' *Конституционное и муниципальное право* (Lebedev, V. A., 'Constitutional ideal and political reality: Paradoxes of the Russian multiparty system' *Constitutional and Municipal Law*) 8 (2013) 23–27, 25.

56 Such demand is expressed by some academics and politicians, see, for example, *Научный макет новой Конституции России. Для научной дискуссии и обсуждения* (Москва: Научный Эксперт, 2011) (*Scientific Blueprint for the New Constitution of the*

theorists who support the Constitution claim that it was "oversized," and "far ahead of the existing reality," creating expectations that could not realistically be fulfilled.[57]

Despite these criticisms, however, the view is predominant that the Constitution today leaves enough room for "political creativity,"[58] and it retains validity as a matrix that both stabilizes social reality and facilitates the representation of changing social interests.

### *(ii) Judicial Interpretation*

Contemporary scholarship has also shown recognition for the role of the RCC in transforming and expanding constitutional norms.[59]

For instance, Bondar argues that constitutional justice is "an important instrument of sociocultural transformation of the Constitution and the whole system of Russian constitutionalism."[60] He states that constitutional justice is an instrument of sociocultural modernization of the Constitution and a generator of "living constitutionalism,"[61] such that it is through the process of constitutional review that constitutionalism becomes "living."[62] When resolving particular constitutional disputes or providing interpretation of the Constitution, Bondar continues, the RCC has the duty to observe the transformative dynamics in society and to identify the normative form of society created by such processes. The normativity inhering in society then affects legal normativity, i.e. the material content of the relevant provision of the Constitution.[63] In this respect, Bondar moves close to a classical living-constitutionalist theory of the role of the courts in guaranteeing a

*Russian Federation* (Moscow: Nauchniy Expert, 2011), Алексей Навальный, 'Нужно ли менять Конституцию?' (Alexey Navalny, 'Does the Constitution Need Changing?') https://navalny.com/issues/нужно-ли-менять-конституцию-116/ (accessed January 10, 2018), 'Бастрыкин: нужно менять Конституцию РФ' ('Bastrykin: It is Necessary to Change the Russian Constitution'), February 26, 2015, https://regnum.ru/news/polit/1899609.html (accessed January 10, 2018), 'КПРФ предлагает изменить Конституцию России' ('The Russian Communist Party Proposes to Replace the Russian Constitution'), January 18, 2017, www.rline.tv/news/2017-01-18-kprf-predlagaet-izmenit-konstitutsiyu-rossii (accessed January 10, 2018).

57 Старилов Ю. Н., 'Будущее Конституции Российской Федерации: "реализация без изменений", "преобразование" или "неизбежность пересмотра""? (Часть 1) Право и политика (Starilov, Yu. N. 'The future of the Constitution of the Russian Federation: "implementation without changes," "transformation," or "the inevitability of revision"?' (pt 1) 1 (2005) *Law and Politics*) 4–24, 7, 23.

58 Shakhrai (n. 25) 94.

59 Kabyshev (n. 25) 26, Mitykov, 'The Key Role in "Soft Transformation" of the Constitution Belongs to Constitutional Judicial Review' Митюков М. А., 'О преобразовании Конституции Российской Федерации' *Право и власть* (Mityukov, M. A. 'On the transformation of the Constitution of the Russian Federation' 1 (2001) *Law and Power*) 105–12, 109.

60 Bondar (n. 48) 980.

61 Ibid.

62 Ibid., 981.

63 Ibid.

running articulation of the sovereign will of society. Similarly, Zorkin has argued that the Constitution should be interpreted as a living document, crafted in part by judges, to ensure that it reflects social reality at a given moment. He claimed that judges are entitled to make "piecemeal corrections [...] that do not change the main features of the Constitution."[64] Through these arguments, the RCC has assumed a tacit mandate to interpret the Constitution in a dynamic way, to coordinate the legislative fabric woven around its frame, and to adapt it to societal conditions.

There is no full agreement among Russian scholars on the role of the RCC in the transformation of the Constitution. Some judges, such as Zorkin, Bondar, and Mityukov, insist that judicial transformation is the most adequate way of elaborating the Constitution in contemporary conditions.[65] At the same time, judicial interventions in constitutional construction have been criticized. For example, Vitruk, one of the first RCC judges (1991–2003), argued that judicial transformation of the constitution "can be misused dramatically to transform the state into a 'managed democracy' with strong authoritarian tendencies."[66] He warned that the RCC often "uses political and social considerations as a justification for transformation." For this reason, he claimed, the term "living constitution" is sometimes misused,[67] and it is a mistake to "impose too much responsibility for the transformation of the Constitution on the nineteen judges of the RCC, and to disregard all the hard work of those people who wrote the text."[68] In a contrasting line of argument, Khabrieva claims that the jurisprudence of the RCC is always subject to informal institutional constraint.[69] In particular, given the status and reputational prestige attached to the RCC, judges on the Court are unlikely to risk their security by promoting radical or transformative doctrines, and they are unlikely to adopt counter-systemic or anti-government arguments.[70] On this account, the efficacy of living constitutionalism is always limited.

64 Anichkin (n. 52) 2.

65 Ibid., 4.

66 Витрук Н. В., 'К вопросу о "живом конституционализме" в контексте соотношения конституции и политики' *Конституционное право и политика: сборник материалов международной научной конференции* (Юридический факультет МГУ, 28–30 марта 2012 года) (Юрист, 2012) (Vitruk, N. V., 'On the question of "living constitutionalism" in the context of the correlation between the constitution and politics' in *Constitutional law and politics: a collection of materials of the international research conference* (Law Faculty of the Moscow State University, March 28–30, 2012) (Jurist 2012) 72–80, 76.

67 Ibid., 75.

68 Ibid.

69 Хабриева Т. Я., 'Развитие правового потенциала Конституции и деятельность Конституционного Суда РФ по ее толкованию,' *Российский конституционализм: проблемы и решения* (Москва: Издательство Института государства и права РАН, 1999) (Khabrieva T. Ya., 'Development of the Legal Potential of the Constitution and the Activity of the Constitutional Court of the Russian Federation towards Its Interpretation,' *Russian Constitutionalism: Problems and Solutions* (Institute of State and Law 1999)) 185–95, 194.

70 Бондарь Н. С. *Судебный конституционализм: доктрина и практика* (2-е издание, Москва: Норма, 2015) (Nikolay Bondar, *Judicial Constitutionalism: Doctrine and Practice* (2nd edn, Norma, 2015) 82, 89.

Despite these divergent views, by most standards, the RCC plays an important role in the actualization of the Constitution.

One example of dynamic interpretation of the Constitution is evident in the fact that the RCC modifies its own previous decisions when new social or political realities necessitate such changes. Indicatively, Zorkin explained in one of his annual meetings with the Russian President that some of the Court's earlier rulings on property rights, on protection of civil and political rights had been "slightly modified, as life commanded." He clarified that none of the positions had been completely reversed "from black to white," but small alterations had become necessary "in light of the new reality and new circumstances."[71] A further example of dynamic interpretation is visible in the fact that some judgements of the superior courts have impacted more broadly on the position of the Constitution in society. Notably, some leading rulings have corrected important gaps and imperfections in constitutional reality.[72] In fact, they have created new principles for construction of the constitution, often using international norms in so doing.

This is exemplified by the following processes.

First, over a long period of time, the superior courts in Russia have interpreted the provisions for the direct effect of international law in the Constitution to promote very constructive legal principles, using international norms to harden and to expand rights protected under domestic constitutional law. In 2003, by way of example, the Supreme Court issued the Plenary Ruling No. 5 On Application by the Courts of General Jurisdiction of the Universally Recognized Principles and Norms of International Law and International Treaties of the Russian Federation, which was intended to encourage the use of international law in all courts. Similarly, a 2009 ruling of the Supreme Court Plenum and a 2012 RCC ruling both used international law to expand the scope of responsibility for agents performing public functions, insisting that private organizations with a special public status could be subject to standard norms of public liability.[73] In 2013, this

71 'Встреча с судьями Конституционного Суда. В ходе рабочей поездки в Санкт-Петербург Владимир Путин встретился с судьями Конституционного Суда' ('Meeting with the Judges of the Constitutional Court. During his working trip to St. Petersburg, Vladimir Putin met with the judges of the Constitutional Court') December 14, 2015, http://kremlin.ru/events/president/news/50925 (accessed January 10, 2018).

72 See more, 'Потенциал развития конституции: Пути конституционной модернизации Российской Федерации': предварительные тезисы доклада и инициативные проекты трех новых глав Конституции Российской Федерации (Совместный экспертный доклад Фонда конституционных реформ и Журнала *Конституционный вестник*) (Москва, 2013) ('The potential of the development of the Constitution: The ways of constitutional modernization of the Russian Federation': preliminary abstracts of the report and the initiative drafts of three new chapters of the Constitution of the Russian Federation (Joint Expert Report of the Constitutional Reform Foundation and *Constitutional Herald*) (2013).

73 See item 5 of the Supreme Court of the Russian Federation Plenary Ruling No. 2 of February 10, 2009 (void since September 27, 2016 when a new Plenary Ruling No. 36

principle was solidified in a federal law.[74] In 2013, the Supreme Court set out guidelines for deportation cases, advising lower courts to take article 8 ECHR into consideration in all cases concerning administrative deportation of foreign citizens.[75] In cases of legal uncertainty, moreover, courts apply international law even if it places additional restrictions on public agencies. For example, in February 2017, a regional court in Voronezh reached an unpopular decision on the basis of the Constitution and international law. The court declared legal a protest against the war in Syria and against lack of direct elections in the appointment of the city's mayor. In this case, the court deemed the demonstration lawful, noting that the public meeting had been agreed with the local authorities, while the measures used to prevent the protest did not constitute a legitimate and proportionate limitation of the constitutional freedom of assembly. Importantly, in support of this conclusion, the regional court referred to article 11 ECHR and the ECtHR jurisprudence.[76] By any reasonable standard, such processes indicate that international law has considerable impact as a source of norms to expand the purchase of the Constitution.

In recent years, to be sure, actors in the political branches have sought to place limits on the impact of international law in Russian domestic law, and this has been partly replicated in the RCC. For example, the ECtHR ruling on the Yukos Oil Company,[77] led to a number of politically motivated decisions, designed to restrict the influence of European jurisprudence in Russia. First, the RCC issued the Ruling on Merits No. 21-P of 14 July 2015 on the supremacy of the Constitution in cases in which its rulings conflict with rulings issued by international courts and tribunals. Second, the Federal Constitutional Law On the Constitutional Court of the Russian Federation was amended to allow the Court to adopt

has clarified issues of application of similar provisions of the Administrative Litigation Code), and RCC Ruling on Merits No. 19-P of July 18, 2012.

74 Федеральный закон от 7 мая 2013 г. № 80-ФЗ 'О внесении изменений в статью 5.59 Кодекса Российской Федерации об административных правонарушениях и статьи 1 и 2 Федерального закона "О порядке рассмотрения обращений граждан Российской Федерации"' (Federal Law No. 80-FZ of 7 May 2013 On Amendments to Article 5.59 of the Code of Administrative Offences and arts 1 and 2 of the Federal Law On Regulations Concerning Consideration of Russian Citizens' Petitions).

75 Постановление Пленума Верховного Суда РФ от 24 марта 2005 г. № 5 (в редакции Постановления Пленума от 19 декабря 2013 г.) 'О некоторых вопросах, возникающих у судов при применении Кодекса Российской Федерации об административных правонарушениях' (Supreme Court Plenum Ruling No. 5 of 24 March 2005 'On Some Issues Arising from Application of the Code on Administrative Offenses by Courts' (amended on December 19, 2013)) para. 23.1.

76 'Суд в Воронеже прекратил административное производство за согласованные митинги' ('The Court in Voronezh Has Stopped the Administrative Proceedings of a Permitted Public Event') *OVD-info*, February 8, 2017 https://ovdinfo.org/express-news/2017/02/08/sud-v-voronezhe-prekratil-administrativnoe-proizvodstvo-za-soglasovannye (accessed January 10, 2018).

77 *OAO Neftyanaya Kompaniya Yukos* v. *Russia*, Application no. 14902/04, Judgment of 31 July 2014

decisions in exceptional cases when such contradiction occurs.[78] Third, the RCC considered whether it was possible to implement the ECtHR *Yukos* judgment, and it concluded that it was impossible as doing so would contravene the constitutional principles.[79] Finally, in March 2017 President Putin introduced a draft federal law on ratification of the ECHR Protocol No. 15 entrenching the subsidiary role of ECtHR in relation to national courts, which has been adopted by the Duma in just two months.[80] Although the ratification of the Protocol will not have an immediate effect,[81] it will, in conjunction with other measures aimed at weakening the effect of international law, certainly send a message to the Russian judges to apply the ECHR and the Court's jurisprudence more cautiously. In fact, this has already happened over the last two years. By 2013, the ECHR had acquired a very important position in Russian public law jurisprudence, with annual citation of the ECHR by regional courts reaching over 6,000 cases. In the period 2012–14, the number of rulings of regional courts referring to the ECHR almost doubled (from 3,800 to 7,800). The number of such citations peaked in 2015, with well over 8,300 rulings referring to the Convention. However, following the 2015 RCC Ruling No. 21-P on supremacy of the Constitution, the number of citations has started to decrease. In 2016 only 7,900 rulings of regional courts have referred to the Convention.[82] Similarly, the number of referrals to the ECtHR jurisprudence in Russian courts almost doubled in the years 2012–13, peaking at 5,200. Yet, by 2016 it had returned to its pre-2012 level of 3,400 citations per year.

Despite this, however, international law has not disappeared as a source of constructive jurisprudence in Russia. The courts themselves continue to refer to the ECHR with a positive attitude. Even the 2015 Supremacy of the Constitution Ruling itself (Ruling No. 21-P) is used to strengthen the domestic position of the Convention, not to undermine it. For example, the RCC ruled in 2016 that the Convention and the ECtHR judgments, to the extent that they interpret the conventional rights and freedoms in line with universal principles and norms of international law, constitute an inalienable part of the Russian legal system. Therefore, the Court opined, both federal legislator and law-applying bodies (a category that usually includes courts, police, prosecutors, and all other bodies bound by federal law) have an obligation to take into consideration the norms of the Convention in drafting and applying new legislation.[83]

78 Федеральный конституционный закон № 7-ФКЗ от 14 декабря 2015 г. (Federal Constitutional Law No. 7-FKZ of December 14, 2015).

79 Постановление Конституционного Суда РФ № 1-П от 19 января 2017 г. (RCC Ruling on Merits No. 1-P of January 19, 2017).

80 Федеральный закон от 1 мая 2017 г. № 79-ФЗ 'О ратификации Протокола N 15, вносящего изменения в Конвенцию о защите прав человека и основных свобод' (Federal Law No. 79-FZ of 1 May 2017 On ratification of Protocol No. 15 amending the Convention for the Protection of Human Rights and Fundamental Freedoms).

81 The Protocol will not enter into force until all 47 CoE countries ratify it, currently 12 more signatures are needed.

82 As reflected in the free legal database 'ConsultantPlus' available from: www.consultant.ru

83 Определение Конституционного Суда РФ № 117-О от 28 января 2016 г. (RCC Ruling on Admissibility No. 117-O of January 28, 2016).

Second, new lines of reasoning are emerging in Russia that directly reflect the influence of international law and the jurisprudence of the ECtHR. For example, the use of proportionality reasoning in RCC cases concerning freedom of assembly has changed the patterns of litigation for this right guaranteed in Article 31 of the Constitution. In 2007, the RCC rejected a claim challenging the constitutionality of a legislative norm prohibiting picketing in front of courts.[84] Without appealing to the proportionality argument or assessing the necessity of such limitation in a democratic society, the Court stated that a limitation is legitimate simply because it enforced the relevant statute and protected the constitutional order, morality, health, rights and interests of other persons, and it contributed to the defense and security of the state. This approach reflected a strict reading of the "limitation clause" in Article 55 of the Constitution. In this instance, the Court did not even attempt to establish the connection between independence of courts as a constitutional principle, the potentially detrimental effect that picketing can have on the courts' independence, and any of the legitimate interests protected by the limitation clause. The Constitutional Court, thus, did not question the legislator's discretion. Ten years later, in early 2017, the Court adopted a totally opposite position. According to recent amendments to the Criminal Code,[85] administrative offenses in violation of picketing rules can lead to criminal liability of up to five years' imprisonment. The first person convicted according to the new norm was an activist, Ildar Dadin. He challenged this legislation in the Constitutional Court. In the *Dadin* case the RCC appealed to "the constitutional principles of necessity and proportionality" to assess if such requalification of administrative offenses was necessary in a democratic society.[86] The Court suggested that the Duma should clarify the disputed norm as to take into account the actual public danger of the offense and other individual circumstances of the case.

These examples demonstrate how the Russian Constitution has experienced transformative interpretation by the RCC. As a result, the function of the RCC in controlling the organization of government and in contributing to the improvement and development of social practice has been significantly enhanced.[87] In fact, crucially, the RCC has played an important role in creating the basic vocabulary of public accountability. Concepts such as "public authority," constitutional liability,[88] constitutional

84 Определение Конституционного Суда № 428-О-О от 29 мая 2007 г. (RCC Ruling on Admissibility No. 428-O-O of May 29, 2007).

85 Art. 212.1 introduced by the Federal Law No. 258-FZ of 21 July 2014.

86 Постановление Конституционного Суда РФ № 2-П от 10 февраля 2017 г. (RCC Ruling on Merits No. 2-P of February 10, 2017).

87 Бондарь Н. С., 'Судебный конституционализм: постановка проблемы в контексте роли Конституционного Суда в утверждении "живого" российского конституционализма' (Bondar, N. S. 'Judicial constitutionalism: statement of the problem in the context of the role of the Constitutional Court in the affirmation of "living" Russian constitutionalism') *Lex Russica* 2 (2009) 322–43, 338.

88 Постановление Конституционного Суда РФ № 9-П от 30 ноября 1992 (RCC Ruling on Merits No. 9-P of November 30, 1992), Постановление Конституционного Суда РФ № 10-П от 7 июня 2000 (RCC Ruling on Merits No. 10-P of June 7, 2000),

order,[89] public interest in legality of norms, and other concepts that define the current constitutional order, first appeared in RCC judgments.[90] In this regard, the jurisprudence of the RCC has played an important role in guaranteeing that elements of constitutional doctrine are translated into practice, and that they frame the accountability structures of government.

One example of this is evident in the fact that the RCC's jurisprudence regarding the rule of law has shaped the institutional structure of civil society. Notably, the RCC ruled that public authorities have an obligation to protect the autonomy of civil society.[91] Further, the RCC established instruments to ensure that civil society organizations exercise control of the activities of the state, including the state's financial activities.[92] Likewise, an RCC ruling provided that the Public Prosecutor's functions should be amended to include the right to appeal to the RCC in public interest matters.[93] Additionally, the jurisprudence of the RCC has shaped the current balance of powers between the federal center and the regions. The status of the Republics was amended by RCC Ruling 10-P/2000. In Rulings 13-O/1997, 1-P 1998, the legislative model for the devolution of federal power to the subjects was modified to replace the previous treaty-based system of devolution.[94] The official language of the republics was established by the RCC Ruling 16-P/2004.[95] The procedure for changing the official names of the regions was also established by the RCC.[96] Importantly, the principles concerning the formation of the Council of Federation were set out by the RCC. Through this decision, the arrangement in which governors and heads of regional legislatures sat *ex officio* in the Council (1996–2002) was suspended, and the Council now comprises appointed professional representatives from the executive and legislative branches (2002–2012). Since 2012, it also comprises directly

Определение Конституционного Суда РФ № 534-О от 27 декабря 2000 г. (RCC Ruling on Admissibility No. 534-O of December 27, 2005).

89 Постановление Конституционного Суда РФ № 12-П от 14 июля 1997 г. (RCC Ruling on Merits No. 12-P of July 14, 1997), Определение Конституционного Суда РФ № 797-О-О от 4 декабря 2007 г. (RCC Ruling on Admissibility No. 797-O-O of December 4, 2007).

90 Bondar (n. 87) 238.

91 Постановление Конституционного Суда РФ № 12-П от 19 декабря 2005 (RCC Ruling on Merits No. 12-P of December 19, 2005).

92 Постановление Конституционного Суда РФ № 12-П от 17 июня 2004 (RCC Ruling on Merits No. 12-P of June 17, 2004).

93 Аничкин Е. С., 'Преобразование Конституции Российской Федерации: понятие, виды, пределы,' Российский юридический журнал (Anichkin E. S., 'Transformation of the Constitution of the Russian Federation: concept, types, limits' 6 (2008) *Russian Law Journal*) 26–32, 29.

94 Shakhrai calls this a change of paradigm (n. 25) 339.

95 Аничкин Е. С., 'Федеративное устройство России в решениях Конституционного суда РФ: от буквального толкования к "преобразованию" конституционных основ' Правоведение.(Anichkin, E. S., 'The federal structure of Russia in the rulings of the Constitutional Court of the Russian Federation: from a literal interpretation to the "transformation" of constitutional order' 6 (2008) *Jurisprudence*) 56–65, 59.

96 Anichkin (n. 95) 29.

elected members.[97] Indicatively, all these constitutional changes were introduced and implemented without alteration of the constitutional text.[98]

## 3 From Norms to Facts

Significant in the above analyses is the fact that, across the spectrum of political and doctrinal persuasion, opinion converges around the claim that Russian constitutional reality is marked by an at times acute discrepancy between constitutional norms and social facts. In particular, the claim is widespread that a living constitutionalist approach is required for *remedial purposes*, to rectify the failure of the 1993 Constitution, in its societal reality, to live up to its original promises, and to ensure that the Constitution gains at least some traction in societal life. In this context, living constitutionalism in Russia differs from its expression in other polities. In other settings, living constitutionalism is driven by the claim that it helps to translate new social demands into constitutional form. By contrast, in Russia, living constitutionalism is primarily focused on the endeavor to render the Constitution socially meaningful, and to acquire intensified recognition for constitutional law. As a result, living constitutionalism acquires a distinctively *curative* or *compensatory* character, in a reality in which constitutional order is perceived as precarious.

This compensatory aspect of living constitutionalism in Russia has been noted by opponents of the current government. For example, Svetlana Vasilieva interprets the "living constitution" doctrine as an instrument for compensating for the lack of general political participation. She claims that, as the Russian political system is marked by weak institutionalization of political opposition,[99] the constitutional commitment to the establishment of Parliament as a representative body for the entire country has been thwarted.[100] She sees this situation as characterized by the "lack of balance between the normative model of *narodovlastie* (Russian: sovereignty of the people) set out by the Constitution and constitutional practice itself."[101] She argues, however, that, through judicial engagement, the constitutional concept of *narodovlastie* has assumed a meaning that deviates from

97 Shakhrai (n. 42) 95.

98 For more examples of the transforming effect of RCC jurisprudence, see Безруков А. В., 'Проблемы реализации конституционных преобразований при сохранении стабильности Конституции Российской Федерации,' Конституционное и муниципальное право (Bezrukov A. V., 'Problems of implementation of constitutional reforms while maintaining the stability of the Constitution of the Russian Federation' 2 (2014) *Constitutional and Municipal Law*) 3–7, 5; Shakhrai (n. 25) 192–4 (on electoral system); Bondar (n. 70) 346.

99 Васильева С., 'Издержки демократии и потенциал Конституции Российской Федерации для развития технологий общественного участия,' Сравнительное конституционное обозрение (Svetlana Vasilyeva, 'Costs of Democracy and the Potential of the Constitution of the Russian Federation for the Development of Technologies for Public Participation' 6(67) (2008) *Comparative Constitutional Review*) 68–75, 73.

100 Ibid., 70.

101 Ibid., 69.

that established in the Constitution, and it *acts as an evolving expression of the primary sovereignty of the people*. For example, the practice of three readings of a draft law in the state Duma was not established by the Constitution, but by subsequent legislation. The same analysis is applied to other legislative practices invented by the Duma itself, including lobbyism, public consultations, etc.[102] Further, feedback mechanisms such as petitions, public meetings, reports of public bodies, etc. have been introduced into constitutional practice. These mechanisms "are used instead of the mechanisms of classic democratic participation."[103] Living constitutionalism is seen, thus, as a form of political practice that is used to assuage problems caused by weaknesses in the representative functions of the political system.

At a different level, the claim that living constitutionalism is a strategy for compensating for constitutional shortcomings is not only promoted by critics of the political regime. Leading actors in the political system expressly identify living constitutionalism as a vital constitutional doctrine, and they consciously extract compensatory functions from it. Putin himself has repeatedly supported the doctrine. For example, Putin noted in one of his annual conversations with the RCC judges that the "constitutional process is never finished forever." He concluded that the input of the RCC in the creation of the "so called living constitution" is impossible to overvalue.[104] Indeed, he referred to the Constitution as "a living contemporary law with a substantial potential for development."[105] More broadly, living constitutionalism – at least *sensu lato* – is strategically stimulated by the government under Putin, and many policies have been introduced to encourage individual citizens to enter situations in which the fabric of the Constitution is subject to expansive interpretation.

On this basis, we can see that living constitutionalism, defined as a practice of alignment between the constitutional text and societal reality, is observed in Russia, simultaneously, from two sides, and in two distinct paradigms – from the judicial side and from the governmental side. Both of these sides promote living constitutionalism, seeking to bring life to the Constitution, and to heighten its correlation with societal reality. However, both sides do this for distinct motives, one mainly for normative or doctrinal reasons, one, as discussed below, mainly for

102 Ibid., 70.
103 Ibid., 71.
104 'Встреча с судьями Конституционного Суда. В преддверии Дня Конституции Владимир Путин встретился с судьями Конституционного Суда Российской Федерации' (Meeting with judges of the Constitutional Court. On the eve of the Constitution Day, Vladimir Putin met with the judges of the Constitutional Court of the Russian Federation) December 8, 2014, http://kremlin.ru/events/president/news/47194 (accessed January 10, 2018).
105 'Встреча с судьями Конституционного Суда. Накануне вечером состоялась встреча Владимира Путина с судьями Конституционного Суда. Встреча приурочена к 20-летию Конституции России' (Meeting with judges of the Constitutional Court. Last night Vladimir Putin met with the judges of the Constitutional Court. The meeting is dedicated to the 20th anniversary of the Russian Constitution) December 13, 2013, http://kremlin.ru/events/president/news/19832 (accessed January 10, 2018).

functional or systemic reasons. We can see that, observed as a living text, the Constitution itself contains two different sets of valences and meanings, and the process of bringing life to the Constitution is tied to two sets of quite distinct prerogatives. From the judicial side, the Constitution appears, primarily, as a document possessing untapped normative potential. From the governmental side, the Constitution possesses a more functional meaning, and strategies for widening the scope of constitutional norms are expected to bring distinctive functional benefits. Whilst courts may comprehend their promotion of living constitutionalism as a normative exercise, the government promotes the exercise of such jurisprudence as part of a functional process, in which the Constitution acts, not solely as a normative order, but as a construction for stabilizing the foundations of government in society and for extending state capacity. Indeed, living constitutionalism acquires particular functional importance in the context of the transition initiated in 1991 and, above all, of the seismic institutional collapse that occurred in Russia before Putin came to power.

The extent to which living constitutionalism is an important public policy commitment for the Russian government is seen on the *supply side* of the law.[106] Notably, since 2000, the government has taken steps to encourage constructive engagement with the law and more expansive penetration of the constitution. In 2001–2, all of the major procedural codes were renewed in accordance with the Constitution and Russia's international obligations.[107] Moreover, these policies were flanked by an express injunction to use international law, as it was seen as an instrument for establishing legal uniformity across society, and for consolidating the "unity of legal space" across the Russian Federation.[108] In consequence, as discussed, the RCC often uses international law in order to explain the purpose or the scope of a constitutional norm.[109] Moreover, it has introduced measures to

106 Kathryn Hendley, 'Rewriting the Rules of the Game in Russia: The Neglected Issue of the Demand for Law' (1999) 8 *East European Constitutional Review* 89–95.

107 Уголовно-процессуальный кодекс Российской Федерации от 18 декабря 2001 г. № 174-ФЗ (Criminal Procedure Code of the Russian Federation No. 174-FZ of December 18, 2001), Кодекс Российской Федерации об административных правонарушениях от 30 декабря 2001 г. № 195-ФЗ (Code of the Russian Federation on Administrative Offenses No. 195-FZ of December 30, 2001), Арбитражный процессуальный кодекс Российской Федерации от 24 июля 2002 г. № 95-ФЗ (Arbitration Procedure Code No. 95-FZ of July 24, 2002), Гражданский процессуальный кодекс Российской Федерации от 14 ноября 2002 г. № 138-ФЗ (Civil Procedure Code of the Russian Federation No. 138-FZ of November 14, 2002).

108 Указ Президента РФ от 10 августа 2000 г. № 1486 'О дополнительных мерах по обеспечению единства правового пространства Российской Федерации' (Presidential Decree No. 1486 of August 10, 2000: On Additional Measures to Ensure the Unity of the Legal Space in the Russian Federation).

109 For example, in RCC Ruling on Merits No. 19-P of July 18, 2012 (Постановление Конституционного Суда РФ № 19-П от 18 июля 2012 г.) the court constructed an expansive interpretation of the right to petition public authorities (art. 33 of the Constitution) on the basis of international law. In particular, the Court referred to the Universal Declaration of Human Rights, the ICCPR, and the UN GA Declaration on the Right and Responsibility of Individuals, Groups and Organs of Society to Promote

ensure broadened application of the Constitution in select areas of legal practice, especially administrative law.[110]

The extent to which living constitutionalism is an important public policy commitment for the Russian government is also seen on the *demand side* of the law. Notably, since 2000, extensive judicial reform programs have been introduced to increase public access to law, and to simplify litigation procedures.[111] After 2000, Putin introduced a large package of judicial reforms, which were designed to increase access to courts, and to promote public confidence in legal institutions. Central to these reforms was legislation designed to clarify procedural rules for court hearings,[112] and to minimize litigation costs,[113] which clearly increased legal opportunities for Russian citizens.[114] In 2009, a special

and Protect Universally Recognized Human Rights and Fundamental Freedoms (53/144 of March 8, 1999). The latter reference is the most important in this instance. The Court concluded that the constitutional right to petition public authorities should, in view of the Declaration, be understood as including the right of legal entities to petition public authorities. Moreover, the Court concluded that the term "public authorities" should apply to some private entities performing public functions.

110 In RCC Ruling on Merits No. 1-P of January 15, 2002 (Постановление Конституционного Суда РФ № 1-П от 15 января 2002 г.) the Court referred to ICCPR to reveal the normative content of art. 32(2) of the Constitution establishing the electoral rights of all Russian citizens. On this basis the Court held unconstitutional a normative provision whereby it was impossible for a local court to nullify the results of general elections in the local district even if one of the candidates was illegally banned from participating in the elections. Respective provisions of the federal legislation were invalidated by the Court.

111 Постановление Правительства РФ от 20 ноября 2001 г. № 805 'О федеральной целевой программе "Развитие судебной системы России" на 2002–2006 годы' (Government of the Russian Federation Decree No. 805 of January 20, 2001 'On the Federal Target Program Development of the Russian Judicial System in 2002–6'), Постановление Правительства РФ от 21 сентября 2006 г. № 583 'О федеральной целевой программе "Развитие судебной системы России" на 2007–12 годы' (Government of the Russian Federation Decree No. 583 of September 21, 2006 On the Federal Target Program 'Development of the Russian Judicial System in 2007–12'), Постановление Правительства РФ от 27 декабря 2012 г. № 1406 'О федеральной целевой программе "Развитие судебной системы России на 2013–20 годы' (Government of the Russian Federation Decree No. 1406 of December 27, 2012 On the Federal Target Program Development of the Russian Judicial System in 2013–20).

112 All procedural codes were adopted during the early years of Putin's presidency see (n. 108).

113 Since 2004 all fees for all legal actions are consolidated in one document, the Tax Code (Налоговый Кодекс Российской Федерации, Часть 2), chapter 25.3 of the Second Part of the Code, as introduced by the Federal Law No. 127-FZ of November 2, 2004. The court fee is now established as a firm figure, 100 rubles ($2 in 2004) for judicial review claims initiated by individuals. In more than ten years this amount has only risen slightly, to 300 rubles.

114 On litigation and opportunity structures, see Amy Kapczynski, 'The Access to Knowledge Mobilization and the New Politics of Intellectual Property" 117 (2008) *Yale Law Journal* 805–85; Bruce M. Wilson and Juan Carlos Rodríguez Cordero, 'Legal Opportunity Structures and Social Movements: The Effects of Institutional Change on Costa Rican Politics' (2006) 39(3) *Comparative Political Studies* 325–51, 327; Lisa Vanhala, 'Legal Opportunity Structures and the Paradox of Legal Mobilization by the Environmental Movement in the UK" (2012) 46(3) *Law & Society Review* 523–56, 525.

federal law was passed to ensure open access to information about the functions of the judicial system.[115] In particular, central to these measures has been the endeavor to facilitate administrative litigation, and to impose stricter constitutional principles on administrative agencies. This is evident in the introduction of the Administrative Litigation Code (2015). This has also been reflected in policies and legislative acts to permit public interest litigation on constitutional questions (PIL), and to facilitate new modes of litigation, by new legal subjects, against public bodies.[116]

Overall, widened and transformative engagement with the Constitution has been a key strategic target for different governmental executives in Russia, and the government is clearly committed to strengthening the articulation between citizens and the normative order of the Constitution. As a result, the doctrine of living constitutionalism acquires a distinctive political–sociological significance in the Russian context. It moves beyond the simple level of doctrinal controversy or jurisprudential method to assume core significance in the basic dimensions of interaction between government and society. On this basis, in fact, living constitutionalism appears as a quite distinctive sociological phenomenon, and it is designed to perform certain very particular political–sociological functions. Consequently, living constitutionalism in Russia needs to be seen in terms of its sociological consequences, and promotion of this doctrine has a series of important systemic outcomes, as outlined below.

### *(a) Enhancement of Legitimacy*

Living constitutionalism appears, first, as a technique for solidifying the perceived legitimacy of the Russian Constitution itself. It is widely recorded that many Russian citizens are disappointed by the enforcement of the Constitution, and by

115 Федеральный закон от 22 декабря 2008 г. № 262-ФЗ 'Об обеспечении доступа к информации о деятельности судов в Российской Федерации' (Federal Law No. 262-FZ of December 22, 2008 On Ensuring Access to Information about Activities of Courts in the Russian Federation).

116 For example, a number of recent legislative amendments have served to widen access to PIL. This is reflected in the fact that new subjects have been established that can bring PIL cases to courts. These subjects now supplement the more traditional mode of representation by public prosecutors. These are: federal and regional ombudspersons (art. 40(1) Administrative Litigation Code (Кодекс административного судопроизводства), entered into force on 1 September 2015), The Federal Service for Supervision in Communications, Information Technology and Mass Media (*Roskomnadzor*) (art. 23(1) of the Federal Law No. 152-FZ of July 27, 2006 On Personal Data (Федеральный закон 'О защите персональных данных'), as amended by Federal Law No. 261-FZ of July 25, 2011), Federal Chamber of Lawyers (art. 35(2) of the Federal Law No. 63-FZ of May 31, 2002 On Advocacy and the Legal Profession in the Russian Federation (Федеральный закон 'Об адвокатской деятельности и адвокатуре в Российской Федерации'), as amended by the Federal Law No. 160-FZ of February 2, 2016), Associations of citizen's oversight (Federal Law No. 212-FZ of July 21, 2014 'On the Basics of Citizens' Control' (Федеральный закон 'Об основах общественного контроля')) and other new proxies.

its gaps and internal contradictions.[117] Moreover, it is widely noted, not lastly by architects of the Constitution, that the ideals of the Constitution have not taken root in Russian society.[118] For example, Viktor Sheinis argues that the brand of democratic constitutionalism promoted in the early 1990s did not reflect the given "self-consciousness" of the Russian people,[119] and that Russians have remained attached to personalistic ideals of government.[120] Nonetheless, the policies outlined above appear to have impacted beneficially on public attitudes to the Constitution, and the promotion of increasing use of law has been flanked by an increase in favorable perceptions of the Constitution. Indicatively, *Levada* polls show that, between 1997 and 2015, the number of respondents who thought that the Constitution protected their human rights increased from 12 percent to 48 percent, while the number of respondents denying that the Constitution possesses significant power has decreased from 46 percent to just 13 percent.[121] Similar results are demonstrated in surveys conducted by the Public Opinion Foundation (FOM) in 2001 and 2007. The number of respondents satisfied with the Constitution has increased in this period from 28 percent to 41 percent, while the number of dissatisfied has decreased from 38 percent to 20 percent.[122] Importantly, the number of those who believe that the Constitution is "just a formality" decreased in this period from 47 percent to 38 percent.[123]

On this basis, the promotion of constitutional engagement among citizens performs clear legitimational functions for the government, and it expands its basis of support in society.

### *(b) Creating Legal Consistency*

Very early in the post-1991 development of Russian constitutionalism, courts were accorded an important gap-filling function. That is, courts were instructed to apply

117 Баринов Э. Э., Белохонова А. О., 'Конституция 1993 года как символ постсоветской эпохи России,' Философия права (Emil Barinov and Alina Belohonova, 'The 1993 Constitution as a Symbol of the Post-Soviet Era in Russia' (2014) 1(62) *Legal Philosophy*) 66–8, 66; 'Россияне в 20-летие Конституции не возражают против ее изменения и уверены, что власти вообще ее не соблюдают' ('Russians on the 20th Anniversary of the Constitution do not Object to Amending it and are Convinced that the Authorities do not Observe it at all') *News.ru*, December 12, 2013, www.newsru.com/russia/12dec2013/const.html (accessed January 10, 2018).

118 Sheinis (n. 43) 42.

119 Ibid.

120 Пивоваров Ю. С., 'Между казачеством и кнутом (К столетию русской конституции и русского парламента)' Полис. Политические исследования (Yu. S. Pivovarov, 'Between the Cossacks and the Whip, to the Centenary of the Russian Constitution and of the Russian Parliament' (2006) 2 *Polis: Political Studies* 5–26, 10).

121 'Россияне о Конституции' (Russians about the Constitution). *Levada*, December 10, 2015, www.levada.ru/2015/12/10/rossiyane-o-konstitutsii-4 (accessed January 10, 2018).

122 'Отношение к Конституции' (Attitude to the Constitution) *FOM*, December 13, 2007, http://bd.fom.ru/report/cat/pow_con/d074926 (accessed January 10, 2018).

123 Ibid.

constitutional norms directly in all cases where such application did not depend upon the existence of a clarifying federal law, or where there exists a gap in regulation that inhibited the full realization of a particular human right.[124] This instruction was originally conceived as provisional emergency measure, intended to stabilize the legal order during the systemic restructuring after 1991. However, this measure created a framework in which courts assumed particular authority in constitutional enforcement, and they were able to apply constitutional norms as the immediate basis for all rulings and statutory interpretation. In consequence, notably, courts were invited, effectively, to promote jurisprudence close to living constitutionalism, and they were given a high degree of latitude in implementing constitutional norms. Before 2013, moreover, the courts were instructed to make independent decisions on the unconstitutionality of a legislative norm that entered into force either before or after the Constitution was adopted. The courts could independently decide not to apply a contradictory or outdated norm and instead directly to apply a norm of the Constitution.[125] Since 2013, the courts have been allowed to apply the Constitution directly in the intermediary period between the moment when a norm is declared unconstitutional by the RCC and the moment in which necessary action is taken by the legislature. Living constitutionalism thus became a doctrine with a core function for the state, as it served as a principle for establishing a more complete, gapless legal order, often acting as a proxy for legislation. By 2013, most of the gaps in the legal order had been filled, and in many cases the wording of legislation was slightly altered to ensure greater coherence within the unified legal system.[126]

In these respects, the courts acquired a function of distinctive importance for Russian society as a whole. Above all, they assumed a vital role in fleshing out a consistent legal order, often performing de facto legislative functions in so doing. For example, in one case, the regional court of Volgograd Oblast upheld the decision of a lower court, confirming a person's right to retire with benefits after a certain period of employment and military service in the area of the Far North. This decision was deemed correct despite an existing gap in the federal legislation as concerning the question whether the period of military service should count toward early retirement. In its ruling, the first instance court directly applied the constitutional principle that legal certainty should be guaranteed in pension regulations.[127]

124 Постановление Пленума Верховного Суда РФ от 31 октября 1995 г. № 8 'О некоторых вопросах применения судами Конституции Российской Федерации при осуществлении правосудия' (Supreme Court of the Russian Federation Plenary Resolution No. 8 of October 31, 1995 'On Some Issues of Application by the Courts of the Constitution of the Russian Federation in the Administration of Justice') para. 2.

125 Лебедев В. М., 'Прямое действие Конституции РФ и роль судов,' Государство и право (Lebedev, V. M., 'Direct Application of the Constitution and the Role of Courts' (1996) 4 *State and the Law*) 3–7, 4.

126 Постановление Пленума Верховного Суда РФ от 16 апреля 2013 г. № 9 (Supreme Court of the Russian Federation Plenary Resolution No. 9 of April 16, 2013).

127 Апелляционное Определение Волгоградского Областного Суда по делу № 33-4917/2013 от 16 мая 2013 г. (Appellate Ruling of Volgograd Oblast Court No. 33-4917/2013 of May 16, 2013).

### *(c) Promoting Societal Constitutionalization*

As we have discussed elsewhere, political elites in Russia have repeatedly observed low societal penetration of formal legal norms as a phenomenon that undermines government performance and weakens societal integrity generally.[128] This perception is shaped by the belief that Russian society has not been fully subject to principles of formal legality, and that, owing in part to historical experiences of institutional debilitation, public institutions lacked hard foundations. In particular, this view is shaped by the claim that institutional weakness was caused by the fact that societal actors had no trust in judicial institutions, preferring instead to seek justice by private means.

Against this background, policies designed to expand access to law have been designed to intensify the basic structural reach of the state and to heighten the authority of the distinctively public domain in society. Central to Putin's early judicial reforms, indicatively, was the attempt to use the law to build the capacity of state institutions, after the systemic crises of the Yeltsin era. Indeed, Putin's judicial reforms were originally meant to solidify the state's control of society, promoting a model of statehood based in a *dictatorship of law*: he expressly declared that a state not consistently governed by law is a *weak state.* [129] Notably, Zorkin stated that, for the first ten years after the 1993 Constitution came into force, "the biggest and the most real threat to the country was a collapse of the state," and he identified strict application of constitutional law in the superior courts as a precondition for prevention of state fragmentation.[130] Putin clearly viewed his policies as a remedy for this when he announced his plans for judicial reform in 2001; he claimed that common unwillingness to place trust in the state had led to the promotion of "shadow justice," which blocked the penetration of formal authority and diluted the power of the central state.[131] As a result, the judicial policies introduced by Putin were partly designed to encourage people to initiate litigation because litigation itself was seen as a practice that could help to widen the reach of formal constitutional norms and so to harden the societal position of formal institutions.

Although they were tied to a wider strategy of *verticalization*, intended to strengthen the governmental executive, Putin's judicial policies also had a

128 Maria Smirnova and Chris Thornhill, 'A Sociological Approach to the Russian Constitution' (2016) 15(6) *Comparative Sociology* 747–93.

129 'Открытое письмо Владимира Путина к российским избирателям' ('Open Letter from Vladimir Putin to the Russian Voters') *Kommersant* 32, February 25, 2000.

130 Валерий Зорькин, 'Апология Вестфальской системы,' (Valeriy Zorkin, 'Apologia of the Westphalian System') *Rossiyskaya Gazeta*, July 13, 2004.

131 Послание Федеральному Собранию Российской Федерации (Annual Address of the President of the Russian Federation to the Federal Assembly), delivered on April 2, 2001. As background to Putin's policies, see the account of shadow justice in Владимир Баранов, 'О теневом праве,' Новая правовая мысль (Vladimir Baranov, 'On the Shadow Law' 1 (2002) *New Legal Thought*) 13–20. By 2012, Putin claimed that great success had been achieved in ending shadow justice. See Speech of the President of the Russian Federation at the VIII National Congress of Judges, December 18, 2012.

normative, constitutional dimension. In fact, Putin expressly argued that the intensification of state structures presupposed the consolidation of constitutional rights in society, and that this could be best accomplished through more extensive use of law and increasing litigation. He justified his legal/judicial reforms by claiming that "the development and strengthening of the judiciary as an independent branch of government" was required to give full effect to the Constitution, including "the rights and freedoms" that it enshrined.[132] Moreover, policies promoting expanded access to law were closely linked to principles derived from international law. All the new procedural codes instruct the courts to resolve disputes by referring to international treaties, alongside relevant domestic legislation.[133] Some of the legislation promoting transparency of courts and litigation is a result of international cooperation with the Council of Europe.[134]

In such instances, living constitutionalism and systemic functions were inseparable. Indeed, constitutional engagement was expressly envisaged as part of a systemic-functional process, imprinting a deepening normative grammar on society as a whole, imposing a sharper constitutional grammar on society as a whole and stabilizing the basic integrational structure of the state itself.

### *(d) Reinforcing State Sovereignty*

The functional promotion of living constitutionalism is also manifest in the controversies about federalism in Russia. Importantly, the Constitution was created in a setting in which governmental system was threatened, among other factors, by the erosion of the federal system established in the Soviet Union. By 1993, the basic state structure of the Russian Federation was clearly imperiled by the ebbing of authority from the national government to the regions and to regional leadership groups. This weakening of the federal center then became acutely unsettling during Yeltsin's presidency. One strategy that sustained Yeltsin's presidency after 1993 was that he entered a series of bilateral treaties with different regions in the federation, and he devolved power, on a contractual basis, to regional rulers in order to secure political support. These treaties obviously led to a dispersal of power from the federal center, and they fragmented the basic structure of the political system. Many regional subjects

132 Постановление Правительства РФ от 20 ноября 2001 г. № 805 'О федеральной целевой программе 'Развитие судебной системы России' на 2002–6 годы' (Government of the Russian Federation Decree No. 805 of January 20, 2001 On the Federal Target Program Development of the Russian Judicial System in 2002–6).

133 Art. 11(1) of the Civil Procedure Code, art. 13(1) of the *Arbitrazh* Procedure Code, art. 15(1) of the Administrative Litigation Code.

134 See Federal Law No. 262-FZ of December 22, 2009 On Ensuring Access to Information about Activities of Courts in the Russian Federation. Internal regulations of the Supreme Court (in force 2009–11) mentioned that the Supreme Court "in cooperation with the Council of Europe develops and implements joint programs aimed at further promoting judicial and legal reform in the Russian Federation and increasing efficiency and transparency of justice in Russia" (para. 8.2).

of the federation were able to assume semi-autonomous positions within the federal polity as a whole.[135] Moreover, these treaties meant that center–periphery relations in the Russian Federation were highly asymmetrical, as different treaties were negotiated on very unequal terms. Overall, increasing centrifugality directly undermined the cohesion of the governmental system as a whole.

In addition to promoting engagement with constitutional law as a cure for the prevalence of shadow justice, therefore, Putin promoted judicial restructuring as a strategy for tying the regions more closely to Moscow and for creating a *unified legal space* across the whole of the Russian Federation.[136] Indeed, Putin first announced his legal/judicial reforms by explaining that many powers granted to federal subjects were exercised in breach of the Constitution, and by declaring his intention to combat some regional legislation on grounds of unconstitutionality.[137] This strategy was strongly backed by the RCC, which in leading rulings agreed that some republics had arrogated powers without constitutional authority.[138] As discussed, the promotion of a unified legal space was closely linked to the constructive incorporation of international law in domestic law, and principles of international law were expected to articulate the basic constitutional grammar for the Russian legal space.

Importantly, these aspects of Putin's policies were built on doctrines of living constitutionalism that were already endorsed in the high judiciary. In fact, the doctrine of direct application of the Constitution had acquired distinctive significance amidst centrifugal tendencies of the early 1990s in Russia. Proponents of this doctrine argued that "immediate application of the federal Constitution" acted as a means "of strengthening the unity of the state in Russia while preserving its federative nature."[139] In this context, it was also argued that direct application

135 Andrew Konitzer and Stephen K. Wergren, 'Federalism and Political Recentralization in the Russian Federation: United Russia as the Party of Power' (2006) 36(4) *Publius* 503–22, 503; Graeme B. Robertson, *The Politics of Protest in Hybrid Regimes: Managing Dissent in Post-Communist Russia* (CUP, 2011) 109–10.

136 One of Putin's most important early orders was Decree No. 1486 of August 10, 2000: On Additional Measures to Ensure the Unity of the Legal Space in the Russian Federation (Указ Президента РФ 'О дополнительных мерах по обеспечению единства правового пространства Российской Федерации'). See Robert Sharlet, 'Putin and the Politics of Law in Russia' (2001) 17(3) *Post-Soviet Affairs* 195–234, 203; J. Kahn, *Federalism, Democratization, and the Rule of Law* (OUP, 2002) 234–8.

137 Kahn (n. 136) 245. See details in EastWest Institute, Russian Regional Rep. 6(1) January 10, 2000.

138 See Определение Конституционного Суда РФ № 92-О от 27 июня 2000 (RCC Ruling on Admissibility No. 92-O of 27 June 2000), Постановление Конституционного Суда РФ № 10-П от 7 июня 2000 (RCC Ruling on Merits No. 10-P of June 7, 2000).

139 Эбзеев Б. С., 'Прямое действие Конституции Российской Федерации (некоторые методологические аспекты)' Известия высших учебных заведений. Правоведение (Boris Ebzeev, 'Direct Application of the Constitution of the Russian Federation (Some Methodological Aspects)' 1 (1996) *Higher Educational Institutions Rev: Jurisprudence*) 5–15, 9.

of the Constitution served to meet "popular demand" or a "social imperative" for deeper assimilation of constitutional law in the society.[140]

In this respect, Russia again displays a hybrid form of living constitutionalism, whose promotion is partly the result of political-systemic motives. Whereas more classical concepts of living constitutionalism envision an expansion of societal influence in government, in the Russian setting the widening of constitutional order was clearly expected to serve an intensification of systemic control in society.

### (e) Forming National Citizenship

It has often been observed that the collapse of the Soviet Union left a citizenship vacuum in the Russian Federation. That is, on one hand, the principles of citizenship and national membership of the dominant socioethnic group in the Soviet Union, the Russians, had only been weakly institutionalized before 1991, such that an all-Soviet model of citizenship was, at best, inchoate.[141] On the other hand, this meant that, after 1991, the Russian Federation did not possess a simple pattern of national citizenship, able to bring cohesion to the new polity – a problem which became especially acute amidst the institutional crises, which occurred in the 1990s. Indeed, it remains the case that, partly owing to the lack of single concept of citizenship, systemic integration in the Russian Federation is low, and the convergence of society around inclusionary institutions is limited.[142]

This fact has distinctive importance as background to legal reform policies in Russia. Manifestly, Putin's policies of verticalization and legal unification can be understood in this context, as they were intended to supply a unitary basis for constructions of citizenship in the Russian Federation. In this context, living constitutionalism acquires particular systemic importance.

On one hand, Putin has attempted recurrently to introduce legislation to compensate for the weak articulation of citizenship, and to obtain by other means the benefits of systemic cohesion usually brought about by shared experiences of citizenship. This has been partly pursued through the formation of United Russia as a national party. It has also been pursued through attempts to formulate a unifying "national idea" as the foundation for Russian citizenship.[143] In this sense, the

140 Пимонов В. А., 'Прямое действие Конституции: от правовой теории к практике,' Психология и право (V. A. Pimonov, 'Direct Application of the Constitution: From Legal Theory to Practice' 4 (2013) *Psychology and Law*).

141 See Yuri Sleznine, 'The USSR as a Communal Apartment, or How a Socialist State Promoted Ethnic Particularism' (1994) 53(2) *Slavic Review* 414–52.

142 Grigorii V. Golosov, 'The Idiosyncratic Dynamics of Party System Nationalization in Russia' (2015) 31(5) *Post-Soviet Affairs* 397–419, 401.

143 It was "competitiveness of the nation" in 2004, "sovereign democracy" in 2005, "preservation of the people" in 2011, and "patriotism" in 2016. See 'Путин назвал единственно возможную для России национальную идею' ('Putin Named the Only Possible National Idea for Russia') *RBC*, February 3, 2016, www.rbc.ru/politics/03/02/2016/56b1f8a79a7947060162a5a7 (accessed January 10, 2018). On patriotism as a national idea see also Лебедева Г. Н., 'Патриотизм как национальная идея,' Царскосельские чтения (G. N. Lebedeva, 'Patriotism as a National Idea.' *Tsarskoselskie*

national idea is understood as a shared set of values, directing the development of society as a whole, regardless of nationality, social status, religion and other factors.[144] As such, it is based in a shared perception of national identity and awareness of the purpose of the nation's existence.[145] The lack of a clear national idea is often perceived as a threat to national identity and territorial integrity of Russia.[146] Accordingly, the absence of a unifying ethic of citizenship is observed as an important source of systemic weakness.

On the other hand, the invigoration of constitutional norms in society can also be seen as a process designed to stimulate societal nationalization and intensified national citizenship. At a normative/symbolic level, as in other countries, collective engagement with the Constitution promotes national unity because the increasing recognition of constitutionally defined obligations links societal actors, as members of a national collective, more closely to the state. Indeed, it is easy to find a concentrated expression of the national idea in the Preamble of the Russian Constitution. It could be argued that Constitution itself, as a mechanism of consolidation of the society, is a national idea, while constitutionalism, as a belief of the supremacy of the Constitution, is the national ideology.[147] At a more functional level, however, the function of the Constitution as a focus of systemic unity is evident in the fact that litigation relating to constitutional norms has a factually unifying impact on society. Notably, such litigation is widely distributed across society, and it links actors in different regions of the Russian Federation

*readings)* (2016) 12–24, Банкерова Е. И., 'Феномен патриотизма как идеологическая основа гражданского правового государства,' Вестник Иркутского государственного технического университета (Elena Bankerova, 'Phenomenon of Patriotism as an Ideological Basis of a Civil Rule of Law State' (2012) 9(68) *Irkutsk State Technical University Bulletin*) 325–30. On the development of post-Soviet state ideology see Горева Н. А., 'Идеологический дискурс как механизм легитимации политического режима в современной России,' Вестник Воронежского государственного университета. Серия: Лингвистика и межкультурная коммуникация (N. A. Goreva, 'Ideological Discourse as a Mechanism of Legitimization of the Political Regime in Contemporary Russia' (2010) 1 *Bulletin of Voronezh State University*) 180–2.

144 For various interpretations of the term, see Чудомех В. Н., 'Российская национальная идея: проблема конкретизации и формализации в государственном статусе,' Известия Саратовского университета. Новая серия. Серия Социология. Политология (V. N. Chudomekh, 'Russian National Idea: The Problem of Concretization and Formalization in the State Status' (2017) 1 *Saratov University Bulletin*) 98–103, 101.

145 Радченко В. И., 'Национальная идея и идеология государства в Конституции Российской Федерации,' Вестник Саратовской государственной юридической академии (Vasiliy Radchenko, 'National Idea and State Ideology in the Constitution of the Russian Federation' (2015) 2(103) *Saratov State Law Academy Bulletin*) 110–15, 111.

146 Владимир Якунин, 'Государственная идеология и национальная идея: конституционно-ценностный подход,' Власть (Vladimir Yakunin, 'State Ideology and the National Idea: The Constitutional Value Approach' (2007) 3 *Power*) 3–12, 4.

147 On constitutionalism as state ideology, see Поярков С. Ю., 'Ценностные основания идеологии российского конституционализма,' Конституционное и муниципальное право (S. Yu. Poyarkov, 'Axiological Foundations of Russian Constitutionalism as an Ideology' (2013) 6 *Constitutional and Municipal Law*) 18–20.

immediately to normative constructs attached to the political center. Public opinion surveys have indicated that, at different points in society, Russian citizens are increasingly willing to resolve their problems in courts, and the penetration of law into society is rising.[148] Even in regions where formal litigation is less widespread, in fact, more informal dispute resolution methods are increasingly incorporated in the formal legal system.[149] As mentioned, procedures promoting litigation are closely tied to international legal imperatives. Indeed, access to litigation procedures in lower courts in remote regions is specifically protected through application of article 6 ECHR. Both the regular courts and the Supreme Court now systematically take into account relevant practice of the ECtHR, including in cases concerning access to courts.[150]

In this respect, once more, the attempt to bring life to the Constitution through widespread engagement with constitutional values acts, quite materially, to remedy core systemic problems in the Russian polity. Notably, functions of integration conventionally assigned to the exercise of citizenship rights through political organizations are translated into functions of the legal system, such that a model of citizenship through legal engagement becomes a core, compensatory pattern of societal integration.

## 4 Concluding Observations

A number of conclusions can be drawn from this analysis. First, a distinctive but pervasive variant on the doctrine of living constitutionalism is visible in Russia, and Russian constitutional lawyers are progressive participants in debates about the living constitution. Second, living constitutionalism in Russia exists in a bi-perspectival framework, and it is observed and promoted by different parties for different reasons. On one hand, it figures as part of the attempt to adapt the Constitution to changing social conditions. On the other hand, it is an important part of a functional process of systemic formation, in which leading political actors

148 Отчет ВЦИОМ об оценке деятельности судов в РФ (Report on the results of the Nationwide Mass Survey of Russian Citizens on the Topic: 'Assessment of the Activity of Courts in the Russian Federation') (WCIOM 2007), https://wciom.ru/database/open_projects/otsenka_deyatelnosti_sudov_v_rossii (accessed January 10, 2018).

149 'В Комитете гражданских инициатив представили доклад "Северный Кавказ и современная модель демократического развития"' ('The Committee of Civil Initiatives Presents their Report North Caucasus and the Contemporary Model of Democratic Development') April 1, 2016, https://komitetgi.ru/news/news/2775 (accessed January 10, 2018).

150 In 2007 the Supreme Court applied art. 6 ECHR to overturn decisions of lower courts as violating the principle of legal certainty in matters of substantive law (provision of pension). See Определение Верховного Суда РФ № 6-В07–28 от 2 ноября 2007 г. (Supreme Court Ruling No. 6-V07–28 of November 2, 2007). See in more detail on application of art. 6: Антон Бурков, Конвенция о защите прав человека в судах России (Anton Burkov, *Convention for Protection of Human Rights in Russian Courts*) (Kluwer, 2010).

perceive vital engagement with the Constitution as a means of cementing the societal foundation of the state.

Through this dual function of the Constitution, we are able to observe certain limits of political authoritarianism, both in Russia and generally. We can see that, in the Russian setting, the government relies on constitutional law as a medium of social integration, institutional construction, and normative stabilization. The use of international law to support the authority of constitutional norms has proven particularly important in the pursuit of such goals. In applying constitutional law to bring such benefits, however, legal institutions necessarily operate at a certain level of autonomy, and they create normative structures that are not entirely dictated by political actors. As discussed above, the promotion of living constitutionalism as a pattern of systemic formation has led, within the legal system, to the reinforcement and expansion of constitutional norms, to the extension of constitutional norms to new actors, and to the promotion of new lines of judicial reasoning. Moreover, it has led to the introduction of new laws on standing and the construction of new concepts of public interests. Outside the legal system, this has led to expansion of human rights provisions, to claims for new rights, to new judicial rulings, and even to new legislation to protect different rights.[151]

Through this dual function of the Constitution, further, we can, at least in outline, identify a further phenomenon that is sociologically distinctive for the Russian context. In this setting, classical political organs, such as parliamentary bodies, political parties, voluntary political organizations, have only been able to play a limited role in processes of national formation and national citizenship construction. As a result, the elaboration of citizenship patterns, central to the construction of a fully nationalized political system, has remained weak, and the level of systemic unity in society as a whole is reduced. Against this background, the legal system becomes a core repository of citizenship practices in the wider trajectory of systemic expansion, which underpins the construction of national society. Indeed, this may demonstrate a more general tendency in citizenship formation in partly authoritarian societies. In this respect, paradoxically, international law becomes a central element in the construction of national society, and the weak capacities of national political institutions for the construction of integrational models of citizenship are partly compensated by norms extracted from the international arena.

151 For instance, through litigation on the basis of international law it has become possible for a single father to claim "maternal capital," a certificate of monetary support granted to parents for birth of their second child and all subsequent children. Such certificate can be spent on housing, education, integration of disabled children, pension, and other social benefits. In 2014 a court in the Moscow Region, in spite of the lack of federal legislation, upheld the right of a single father of twins born through in-vitro insemination and registered as having no mother. The court referred to the CRC principle of best interests of the child to fill the gap of legal regulation and to create a new right. See Апелляционное определение Московского областного суда от 29 сентября 2014 г. по делу № 33–21541/2014 (Appellate Court of Moscow Region Ruling No. 33-21541/2014 of September 29, 2014).

# 5 "Sovereign Democracy" and International Law: Legitimation and Legal Ideology

*P. Sean Morris*

## 1 General Background on What Triggered Sovereign Democracy

The participation of Russia in international law has been, and remains, a matter of its vested interests only. Moreover, contemporary international law with its mission of globalization has been viewed in Russia as an attempt at removing the sovereignty of the Russian state. But, where Russia participates in the treaty system of international law, such participation is at best a result of a compromise, due to the failure of diplomacy or negotiations. Thus, on the one hand, Russia is cautious of Westsphalian international law that reduces the sovereignty of the nation state, and, on the other, Russia accepts the treaty system of international law based on the various *compromissory* clauses in those treaties that are "designed to address the concerns" of different states.[1] This acceptance of international law by Russia, wary of Westphalianism, but cautiously embracing the treaty system of international law, allows Russia to carve out a unique and fascinating approach to international law.[2] Often time, that approach can be caught up in an ideological maelstrom, and, one such maelstrom was *sovereign democracy* where debates on sovereignty, national identity, great power status, and *Russianness* captured the Russian intelligentsia during the second term (2004–2008) of Vladimir Putin's first presidency (2000–2008).

The *Georgia* v. *Russia* case at the International Court of Justice (ICJ) in 2011 was one of the few international cases where Russia's vision of sovereign democracy played out in a legal setting and confirmed Russia's resurgence to great power status. In the case, which was as a result of an armed conflict in 2008 between Russia and Georgia and the self-determination status of two breakaway regions in Georgia, the ICJ essentially ruled that modern treaty law in the international legal system is a series of compromises due to the failure of negotiations and diplomacy

1 *Application of the International Convention on the Elimination of all Forms of Racial Discrimination (Georgia* v. *Russian Federation)*, Preliminary Objections, Judgment, ICJ Reports 2011, p. 70, para. 143.

2 Lauri Malksoo, *Russian Approaches to International Law* (OUP, 2015); Bill Bowring, *Law, Rights and Ideology in Russia: Landmarks in the Destiny of a Great Power* (Routledge, 2013); Axel Kaehne, *Political and Social Thought in Post-Soviet Russia* (Routledge, 2007).

on the interests of states. Yet, what was crucial about that dispute, was how Russia perceived itself in international relations, especially on key issues of state sovereignty and the interests of Russia as a great power. This conception of renewed great power status had its origin in a domestic ideology that reawakened conservatism in Russia. This was even more evident in the fact that the *Georgia v. Russia* case as litigated before the ICJ was not actually about the armed conflict between the two former Soviet states in 2008, but, rather, whether Russia violated an international treaty on racial discrimination during the armed conflict. Eventually, the ICJ upheld Russia's objections to the case (with strong dissent among the Court's rank where dissenters accused the court of bias),[3] leaving Russia victorious on two fronts. The first victory for Russia was the ruling itself, and the second victory was the "acquisition" of territories that were *de jure* Georgia. These victories were, as this chapter posits, as a result of the ideology of sovereign democracy – a form of Russia exceptionalism.

At the end of the Cold War, the world was plunged into a new conflict. This was a silent conflict in which the victors of the Cold War represented by capitalist states had to choose to disband their huge military industrial complexes to fit the new era of integrating post-Soviet states in the world of pure capitalism, or continue to reassert capitalist hegemony through warfare and farcical conflicts. The latter was chosen and there was a sense of urgency to fight new enemies such as radical Islamic terrorism, and, at the same time, spread the deeds of democracy and human rights on an industrial scale around the world. In this mission to democratize the post-Soviet world and fight Islamic terrorism – the most important country that the western capitalist states wrestled with on the ideological front during the Cold War – Russia – was ignored, and/or its concerns were dismissed by the international community. Apart from being coerced into negotiations for capitalist instruments such as the World Trade Organization (WTO) charter, and human rights treaties such as the European Convention on Human Rights (ECHR) – the West, throughout the 1990s and the early 2000s no longer saw Russia as a credible player in international relations. The order of the day was unipolarity (*Pax Americana*). Russia was left on its own to sink into the dismal abyss of pre Peter the Great Russia – a backward country whose people were neither European nor necessarily Asians. Simply Russians.

Having lost its seat at the table of the superpowers in the chaotic years of the 1990s and early 2000s – Russia watched as the United States rolled into various nations through conflict interventions (presumably with the strategic aim of capturing natural resources), or as the United States built military bases on Russia's doorsteps in the so-called "near abroad" of the former Soviet commune. Further insults to Russia were the eastward expansion of the European Union (EU) as former satellite and constituent states of the ex-Soviet Union were painting their red

3 Dissenting opinion of Judge Abraham (n. 1) 158, para. 4; dissenting opinion of Judge Trinidade (n. 1) 239, who invariably made references to "great power" status (e.g. para. 39).

coats blue in the great 2004 accession.[4] Russia was not seen as a great power and its role was literally reduced to that of supplying the new *colonial* outlook of western capitalist states through hydrocarbons, minerals, grains, and other resources. Moreover, Russia did not meet the financial requisites to have a seat at the table where money matters – and was excluded from the most powerful financial club of capitalist states the Group of Seven (G7); although Russia occasionally dined as "G7 plus one." As the insults and humiliations mounted on Russia in the grand game of great power politics (and sometimes in the practice of international law), the once most powerful alternative to a nuclear-armed United States – Russia was in pain. It was during these dark moments that Russia underwent a period of soul-searching to restore its great power status led by Vladimir Putin – the enigmatic KGB-trained international lawyer, former provincial bureaucrat, former prime minister, and president (2000–2008), (2012–2018), (2018–2024) respectively. As president, Putin during his first term surrounded himself with loyalists and removed from influential positions business barons, state bureaucrats, and powerful political appointees. By the time Putin was getting ready to run for a second term as president in 2004, his sights were set on restoring Russia's rightful place in the world as a powerful country, an alternative to the West.

In order for Russia to regain great power status, Putin saw his tasks to include that of restoring Russia's pride in international relations and the international legal process; a reformed military with quick strike capabilities; a new military doctrine with nuclear deployment; economic and social reforms; and most importantly the Kremlin as the prime decision-maker through a system of vertical power with a single command structure to manage the Russian democratic process: the answer was sovereign democracy. The new ideological doctrine of sovereign democracy would grow as a phenomenon that was uniquely Russian combining elements of past ideologies such as communism, capitalism, and fascism. The ideology of sovereign democracy was both intellectually chaotic, and, at the same time, embodied Russian philosophical traditions that portrayed Russia as a collective entity where the people coalesce into an *obshina* – for the greater good of the fatherland. In that obshina, a strong *sovereign* as head of state and the shield of the Orthodox Church were all that mattered. Democracy as a western phenomenon, notion, and concept is alien to such obshina. But, in the modern Russia, where sovereign democracy as an idea once thrived, it was an opportunity for Russia to demonstrate a grand strategy at the international level covering economic independence, military might, and control over domestic political sovereignty.[5] It was

4 On May 1, 2004 ten countries acceded to the European Union, of which three were former Soviet countries, Estonia, Latvia, and Lithuania, and five were former soviet satellites: Hungary, Czech Republic, Slovakia, Slovenia, and Poland; see Francis Snyder (ed.), *Enlargement and the New Europe after 2004* (Bruylant, 2005).

5 Graeme Herd, 'Security Strategy: Sovereign Democracy and Great Power Aspirations' in Mark Galeotti (ed.), *Politics of Security in Modern Russia* (Ashgate, 2010) 9 (also noting that sovereign democracy identified with the wresting of the Russian economy and resources from the oligarchs and the chaotic 1990s, safeguards against western intervention in domestic politics such as Ukraine and Georgia, single administrative

only then, Russia would no longer be seen as at the periphery of great power status, but as a key player in global affairs. In this regard, Russia was no longer keen on creating a path that leads to the salvation of western democracy. What mattered was a strong Russia, a Russia capable of maintaining its pride and defending its people internally and externally. Russia was prepared to attack hegemony with hegemony and Vladimir Putin was keen on putting a stop to western "crusades"[6] especially those that affected the national interests of Russia. For Putin, the world was uncharacteristically about power relations, and any imbalance in such power relations shifts the gravity of force unfavorably to a single nation.

From 1993 through to 2003 the United States was mostly unchallenged in global affairs. This was because of what Putin called the overnight disappearance of the Soviet Union. Therefore, the United States was able to dilute the laws of wars through the invasion of Iraq in 2003 and the Kosovo conflict in 1999/2008. On all occasions international law and international relations were *scientific* fields that failed miserably: international relations failed to orient Russia westwards through constructive dialogue and international law failed when the US invaded Iraq in 2003. By 2004 when the Iraq war was in full swing – a number of other events were quietly taking shape in Russia's near abroad beginning with Ukraine and the Orange Revolution and other notable colored revolutions in Georgia and Kyrgyzstan. These former Soviet countries were shedding the final coat of enhanced ruling, a form of authoritarianism, and were embracing the gospel according to the American crusaders – liberal democracy. These were not only threats to the cohesive nature of the Russian Federation but were also a direct challenge to the Kremlin. Moreover, for Russia, the Cold War relic military organization, the North Atlantic Military Organization (NATO) adopted new military doctrines that were seen as counterproductive to the post-Soviet world order.

While these developments were taking place, a little-known Kremlin bureaucrat Vladislav Surkov, whose initial task as a *politologist* (the Kremlin's chief political ideologue) was to shape the intellectual discourse of the Kremlin's policies introduced the concept of "sovereign democracy" to the Moscow intelligentsia and the upper echelons of the Kremlin-controlled ruling political party – Edinnaya Rossia (United Russia). The aim was to explain how Russia's control over political and foreign relations would further mature. The new ideology of sovereign democracy was for a statist approach to policies that were compatible with Russia's history

bureaucratic chain of command, and a means of breaking patterns of revolutions endemic to Russia). But see Valentina Fedotova, 'Sovereign Democracy and a National Model of Modernism' in Abdusalam A. Guseinov (ed.), *Democracy for Russia, Russia for Democracy* (Russian Academy of Science 2008) 12–15 (original Russian, В.Г. Федотова, Суверенная Демократия и Национальная Модель Модернизма); Victoria Hudson, 'Sovereign Democracy as a Discourse of Russian Identity' in Philipp Casula and Jeronim Perovic (eds), *Identities and Politics During the Putin Presidency: The Discursive Foundations of Russia's Stability* (Columbia UP, 2009) 189–210.

6 Ronald Dannreuther, 'Russia and the Arab Spring: Supporting the Counter-Revolution' (2015) 37 *Journal of European Integration* 77, 83 quoting Putin as likening UN Resolution 1973 for intervention in Libya to a "medieval appeal for a crusade."

and was largely defined to include how political powers and authorities control the decision-making process of the Russian people. There is no precise definition of sovereign democracy, as it emanated from concepts such as vertical power, managed democracy, and *Russianness.* Surkov, however, contended that the core elements of sovereign democracy emanated from a unique political culture in Russia that requires "(a) political unity through centralization of governmental competence"; (b) "idealization of the means of political struggle"; and (c) "personification of political institutions."[7] In other words, sovereign democracy ought to be construed so that the sovereign (Kremlin ruler) centralizes authority in a top-down manner for the effective implementation of laws and policies. Although within and outside of Russia there have been various interpretations and analyses on the true meaning of sovereign democracy,[8] there is no consensus as to its relevance, but it certainly attracted (and still does) huge interest from scholars and in the general intellectual discourse in Russia. Furthermore, the intellectual and political pursuit of sovereign democracy as a new ideology would test the fields of international law and international relations. At the peak of the intellectual debate of sovereign democracy in Russia (2006–2008) its first external test was during Russia's engagement in the armed conflict in Georgia in the summer of 2008

7 Mikhail Antonov, 'Conservatism in Russia and Sovereignty in Human Rights' (2014) 39 *Review of Central and East European Law* 1, 29.

8 One of the finest treatments of the ideological notion of sovereign democracy by a Russian author for a western audience is Viatcheslav Morozov's, 'Sovereignty and Democracy in Contemporary Russia: A Modern Subject Faces the Post-modern World' (2008) 11 *Journal of International Relations and Development* 152 (noting that sovereign democracy was a symptomatic and ideology that suffered from genealogical greatness in Russia's Soviet past). See Vladislav Surkov, 'Nationalism of the Future: A Few Paragraphs in Favour Sovereign Democracy' in Abdusalam Guseinov (ed.), *Democracy for Russia, Russia for Democracy* (Russian Academy of Science, 2008) 71–86 (Владислав Сурков, Национализация Будущего. Параграфы pro Суверенную Демократию), an English translation can be found in Vladimir Surkov, 'Nationalisation of the Future: Paragraphs pro Sovereign Democracy' (2009) 47 *Russian Studies in Philosophy* 8. Note that the English title of Surkov's publication in this note is mine and may differ slightly from other translations. There is evidence that prior to and after Surkov's publication, sovereign democracy as an ideology was already creeping into Russian society based on Putin's ascent to the presidency in 2008, and both the popular press and the academic literature was inundated with discussions on sovereign democracy. See Михаил Рогожников, 'Что такое "суверенная демократия"' 14 ноя 2005, Эксперт №43 (489) [Mikhail Rogozhinikov, 'What Is Sovereign Democracy? 43 *Ekspert* 489, November 14, 2005]; Andrey Kokoshin, 'Real Sovereignty and Sovereign Democracy' (October 13, 2006) 4 *Russia in Global Affairs*; Филиппов А.В, История России. 1945–2008 гг. Книга для учителя, (2008), глава 6, Суверенная демократия; А. А. Казанцев, «Суверенная демократия» в современной России: структура концепта и идеологемы [AA Kazansev, 'Sovereign Democracy in Contemporary Russia: The Structure of the Concept and Ideologism']. Derek Averre, '"Sovereign Democracy" and Russia's Relations with the European Union' (2007) 15 *Demokratizatsiya* 173–90; Sergei Prozornov, 'The Paradox of Infra-liberalism: Towards a Genealogy of "Managed Democracy" in Putin's Russia' in Alexander Woll and Harald Wydra (eds), *Democracy and Myth in Russia and Eastern Europe*, (Routledge, 2008), 186–202; Herd (n. 5); but see Fedotova (n. 5).

where Russia challenged the international rules of armed conflict and state recognition by asserting Russian sovereignty over Georgian territory. Another crucial test for the ideology of sovereign democracy in Russia was how it influenced the domestic legislative process by rolling back what was considered liberal gains toward the rule of law and the western system of democracy. For all intent and purposes, 2008 was the year as a result of the armed conflict with Georgia (and cyberattacks on Georgia and Estonia) that Russia restored its place at the table of great powers. More importantly, the ideology of sovereign democracy that flourished in the mid 2000s in Russia played a crucial role in that restoration of great power status.

## 2 The Western Origins of Sovereign Democracy

Although the ideology of sovereign democracy that flourished in the mid 2000s in Russia first appeared as a homegrown ideology, its roots were actually more European – intellectual offshoots of Thomas Hobbes (1588–1679) and Carl Schmitt (1888–1985). Hobbes and Schmitt developed their most important works while conflicts (ideological and armed) were raging in their homelands. Hobbes wrote most of his works during the English Civil War, and some of Schmitt's works appeared before and after World War II. Therefore, decoding the legal, philosophical, and sociological impact of sovereign democracy as a political thought or ideology on Russia requires taking into consideration the influence of past western intellectual thoughts. This is a natural trajectory, given that Russia's homegrown ideologies are often complex or mostly rooted in its Orthodox and Slavophilic nationalism. The external impacts of non-Russian ideologies, such as Marxism, however are often more devastating. Nevertheless, the impact of foreign ideological thoughts has been supreme to Russia's search for a place in the world. Furthermore, Russia believes that a void has been left open due to hegemonic actions by a single state or the moral decline of shared traditional values. If western intellectual influence on Russia thrived for a while through Marxism and communism, Russia ironically reincarnated the chief Nazi legal ideologue Carl Schmitt as the intellectual grandfather of sovereign democracy, or its version of conservatism. But prior to Marx, there was also an English connection – a variant of conservatism that fits the Russian narrative.

### *(a) Hobbesian Natural Right to Sovereign Authority*

The works of Hobbes has had a profound impact beyond the shores of England, as his works, are largely seen, from a legal perspective, as the ideological bedrock of legal positivism. Furthermore, from a sociological point of view, Hobbes's works are undeniably *the* great pillar of social theory. Taken together, these two aspects of Hobbes's works create an ideological circle in which those who are at the helm of government (sovereign) can use to formulate an ideal governance of society. Given that Hobbes penned his works during the English Civil War, there is no doubt that some of his main concerns were governance and the rule of law. Two of Hobbes's main works captured these visions: *The Elements of Law, Natural and Politic* (1650) and *Leviathan, or the Matter, Form and Power of a*

*Commonwealth Ecclesiastical and Civil* (1651). If Hobbes was writing during a time of great uncertainty as the English Civil War ravaged the land, and departed from the legal and political thought of previous philosophers that shaped English democracy, then Russia in the mid 2000s had a similar awakening. Although Russia was immune from internal armed conflicts in the mid 2000s, the ideological[9] conflict that was ongoing, in terms of Russia as a "civil society," had at its core, conservatism.[10] If Hobbes was similarly concerned about conservatism, or rather, in a sociological interpretation of *Leviathan*, a conservative society flourishing within a social order, on the account that members of the society yield to a sovereign authority for their own wellbeing, then Russia during the First Putin Presidency (FPP) was charmed by these Hobbesian thoughts. The ideological conservatism that was brewing in Putin's Russia was that society should submit to a sovereign authority, and that central authority should be able to maintain stability and social cohesion through regulation. In Hobbesian terms, there was a *natural right* to sovereign authority especially if sovereign authority can also mean the central political seat of rulers in a nation state. What this means in modern times is the endorsement of a natural right to submit to a sovereign authority where enhanced ruling or a form of authoritarianism is acceptable in the political order of some societies. Although Hobbes's endorsement of a sovereign authority appeals to a form of conservatism that is based on the *natural order* of nature or a higher *omnipotent order* [11] as one of the best forms of social cohesion in a society he was appealing not only to England but to lands far and near with the same kindred spirit and traditions of the Christian world.

But a crucial Hobbesian element that seems to resonate with any comparison to modern Russia was the fact that Hobbes saw irresistible might as irresistible right[12] and the implication of this is that it has universal appeal and a "reason for action"[13] which, incidentally, sovereign democracy on some occasions had been

9 See also Samuel Huntington, 'Conservativism as an Ideology' (1957) 51 *American Political Science Review* 454; Thomas Parland, *The Extreme Nationalist Threat in Russia: The Growing Influence of Western Ideas* (Routledge, 2005).

10 See also Sergei Prozornov, 'Russian Conservatism in the Putin Presidency: The Dispersion of a Hegemonic Discourse' (2005) 10 *Journal of Political Ideologies* 121. I sometimes use "civil society" in two contexts. The first is a general reference to the engaged members that form part of a society – "we the people," to protect civil liberties and in a different context. I also refer to civil society as part of a broader civilizational discourse that has been ongoing in Russia where demarcations among the state, socioeconomic conditions, and the general populace are drawn and the engagement of the people in the society–state relationship discourse through various formal and informal entities. But see Sergej Ljubownikow, Jo Crotty, and Peter Rodgers, 'The State and Civil Society in Post-Soviet Russia: The Development of a Russian-style Civil Society' (2013) 13 *Progress in Development Studies* 153.

11 See Ross Harrison, *Hobbes, Locke, and Confusion's Masterpiece: An Examination of Seventeenth-Century Political Philosophy* (CUP, 2003) 22 (discussing political power as a form of divinity).

12 Ibid., 46, quoting Hobbes, *Leviathan* 31.5, p. 187: "to those therefore whose power is irresistible, the dominion of all men adhereth naturally by their excellence of power."

13 Ibid.

seen as a reason for action through Russia's irresistible military might. But, the main point is this: Hobbes and his emphasis on natural law and social order served as part of the intellectual foundational elements of sovereign democracy as an ideology due to its vision of conservatism in traditional societies. In light of this, the next question is then how to interpret Hobbes within the realm of international law and then make a direct linkage to Russian sovereign democracy.

For Hobbes, the law of nations, or its contemporary version, international law was deeply rooted in the laws of nature. By identifying natural law with the laws of nations emanated from how Hobbes viewed the state at constant war and thereby international in nature. Again, one must take into consideration that the English Civil War along with various claims to the English throne from continental sovereigns somehow influenced Hobbes's thinking. In any case, Hobbes believed that all sections of society, sovereign rulers, the sovereign subjects (the people) had a natural right, that, in the event of war, they have unlimited powers to defend the commonwealth (the nation). In order words, during conflicts, for Hobbes, the rulers of commonwealths have sovereign (authoritarian) rights and powers that determine how the commonwealth behave at the broader international level. As such, the sovereign rights and powers that the central authority of the commonwealth possesses "served to point to the presence of a basic framework of normative regulation for the relations among commonwealths."[14] This Hobbesian position could explain the nature of sovereign democracy during the early 2000s (2000–2004) in Russia. But there was a problem. Russia was not at war with any nations and Russia's position in international law was fairly "western" during that time, in that, it was in tune with the western conception of international law with no serious derogation.

It was during this relative period of calm that Russia turned inwards and began ideologically soul-searching that started with the Russian political leadership and intelligentsia. But the Hobbesian view of the world was not entirely satisfactory, and the ideas of a twentieth-century legal and political luminary that served as chief counsel to Nazi Germany – Carl Schmitt – began to take hold during Russia's inward turn. Hobbes and Schmitt shared a few personal traits. Both were born in the 88th year of their respective century; they both viewed man as a dangerous creature; and both were strong defenders of an *omnipotent politic* in their writings and reflected through a sovereign authority in the state against liberal dilutions. Like Hobbes who was writing during the English Civil War, Schmitt wrote most of his works during turmoil and conflict, whether it was upheavals during the Weimar Republic, or the rise of national socialism and its armed conflicts across Europe. Moreover, one of Schmitt's best-known works was an analysis of *Leviathan* [15] originally published in 1938, and was among other things on the

14 Charles Covell, *Hobbes, Realism and the Tradition of International Law* (Palgrave Macmillan, 2004) 61.

15 Carl Schmitt, *The Leviathan in the State Theory of Thomas Hobbes: Meaning and Failure of a Political Symbol* (trans. George Schwab and Erna Hilfstein) (Greenwood Press, 1996).

political philosophy of Hobbes. Russia's acceptance of Schmitt's political and legal conservative theory through the ideology of sovereign democracy was of course a bit of a paradox. However, let me try to extrapolate the intellectual theories of Schmitt and its eventual reception in Russia.

### *(b) Schmitt's Conservative Appeal to Russia*

As a leading intellectual during the Weimar period, one of Schmitt's targets was parliamentarianism, as evidenced by his 1923 work[16] and its entrenchment in the Weimar Constitution.[17] Schmitt's theory on authoritarianism was quite appealing, and conservative academics over the years have investigated and found his writings non-ideological. Needles, to say, there have also been a number of critics of Schmitt's writings.[18] For contemporary political conservatives and intellectuals in the academic world – the paradoxical world of Schmitt confronted legitimate questions pertaining to "liberalism and democracy," "politics and ethics," "enemies of state legitimation," and how this latter interacts with "domestic and international politics."[19] For conservatives in Russia during the mid 2000s Schmitt's take on liberalism and democracy represented their own views on the peculiarity of Russia as a state and how it should develop and interact with the rest of the world. Therefore, for a start, Russia, the conservatives believe, should continue on a *dictatorial* trajectory, in that Russia, for centuries has been accustomed to strong leadership (sovereign authority) and this must be reflected in the Russian rights and constitutional discourse. Mirroring the attempts to impose dictatorial powers under article 48 of the Weimar Constitution (on presidential powers and executive government by decree), Russia actually followed suit in 2008 and amended its Constitution and raised the presidential term from four to six years. The thinking behind Schmitt's view was that politics "cannot be made safe" and any such plans would "result in the abandonment of the state to private interests and to "society."[20] Whether or not this was the same reasoning behind the amendment of the Russian Constitution that raised the presidential term in 2008, is a different matter; what is certain is that by the end of 2024 Vladimir Putin's iron grip on the politics of Russia will be more than a quarter century.

The reception of Schmitt in the conservative and intellectual circles in Russia was similar to the rise of Schmitt in western academic literature, especially in the English-speaking world, that is, to look beyond the ideology of Schmitt, and concentrate on his scholarly treatment of his political philosophy. Therefore, similarly to how Hegel (and Hobbes) was influential on the Bolsheviks prior to

16 Carl Schmitt, *The Crisis of Parliamentary Democracy* (trans. Ellen Kennedy) (MIT Press, 1986).
17 Carl Schmitt, *The Concept of the Political* (expanded edn, trans. and introduction by George Schwab, with foreword by Tracy Strong, notes by Leo Strauss) (University of Chicago Press, 2007) ix.
18 e.g. Matilda Arvidsson, Leila Brannstrom, and Panu Minkkinen (eds), *The Contemporary Relevance of Carl Schmitt: Law, Politics and Theology* (Routledge, 2016).
19 Schmitt (n. 17), xiii.
20 Ibid., xv.

and during the Russian Revolution, Schmitt too, rose in prominence, during the ideological renewal of the Russian state in the 2000s. Schmitt, like Hobbes, offered contemporary Russian intellectual revolutionaries a *seventh alternative* away from the realms of capitalism, socialism, fascism, communism, liberalism, and Marxism, to that of sovereign democracy (Russian exceptionalism) – where *democracy* in Schmittian language – means direct representation of the people "by the political leadership."[21] In Russia, it was the political leadership (sovereign authority) that endorsed the need for a new ideological path that was compatible with Russia's own development. Schmitt's works advance the legitimacy of authority and conservatism, a more appealing allure to Russia[22] that has, according to Vladimir Putin, authoritarianism (super-centralized state) planted in its very genetic code.[23] As such, there was an urgent need for an ideological solution and alternative to the forms of state management such as liberal democracy, but with an intellectual base built on past experience. This was because all other forms of state management and their liberal undertones were not compatible with the challenges Russia faced in the contemporary world, including how to forge its own ideological pathway.

## 3 The Rise and Fall of Sovereign Democracy as Contemporary Ideology in Russia

As an ideological concept to portray Russian exceptionalism, sovereign democracy had various layers and served as an ideological counter-narrative to western hegemony in Vladimir's Putin Russia and how Russia is viewed in global affairs. The term itself is a bit of a paradox and even Russians were trying to come to grips with its literal pronunciation (Суверенная демократия/*Suverennaja Demokratija* or суверенитет демократии/*Suverenitet Demokratii*).[24] However, it was a term coined to reflect Russia as an autonomous political subject in the global arena. And, in the context of international legal relations, sovereign democracy was an identification of Russia's struggle for recognition within the modern system of international law and the classic doctrine of sovereignty.[25] There are a few ironies in the term

21 Benno Teschke, 'Fatal Attraction: A Critique of Carl Schmitt's International Political and Legal Theory' (2011) 3 *International Theory* 179, 192.

22 See also Vladimir Gligorov, 'Benjamin Constant and Carl Schmitt Go to Russia' (1997) 8. *Constitutional Political Economy* 271, 277 (noting that Schmitt's approach can be found in the 1993 Russian Constitution).

23 See Sean Cannady and Paul Kubicek, 'Nationalism and Legitimation for Authoritarianism: A Comparison of Nicholas I and Vladimir Putin' (2014) 5 *Journal of Eurasian Studies* 1, 6. Russian history in general has a tradition of blaming the Mongol invasion in medieval times for the introduction of autocracy in Russia, so it is likely that Putin was referring to this in general.

24 Valeria A. Lebedev and Valerii V. Kireev, 'Суверенная демократия или суверенитет демократии?' [Suverennaja Demokratija ili Suverenitet Demokratii?], (2008), Research Center for Constitutional–Legal Problems, Chelyabinsk University.

25 See David Held, 'The Changing Structure of International Law: Sovereignty Transformed?' in David Held and Anthony McGrew (eds), *The Global Transformations Reader: An Introduction to the Globalization Debate* (Polity 2003).

sovereign democracy itself. The first is that it literally conveys a form of democratic space, where parties' and pluralists' ideas thrive. However, because of changes to electoral laws in Russia a number of parties that once flourished in opposition disappeared, as they failed to gain the minimum threshold to sit in the lower chamber (Duma). Thus, United Russia, the Kremlin-controlled party dominated the political system under Putin, mirroring communist one-party rule. This was different from the number of political parties that emerged in the post-Soviet *democratic chaos* in Russia, where liberal, left-wing, communist, nationalist, right-wing, and other parties reflect a pluralistic[26] society competing for a voice among the nations of Russia.

Another irony in the term "sovereign democracy" is its conveyance of the sovereign: destined to be ruler over subjects, and this latter description also fits the messianic mission that Russia often assumes: a divine duty to uphold the laws of God, conservatism, and the natural order. Some of Russia's liberal neighbors such as Sweden have had instances where politics was dominated by a single political party. The same situation occurred in Japan for the first 50 years in its post-1945 make-up – a single party flourished in open democracy. Because Russia under Putin was not reviving the Communist Party, there were hopes that the country would go down the same route and democratically open up at its own pace. Russia, perhaps, was genuinely building a political center that was strong, so that democracy could flourish at a later stage. Therefore, if the political center were strong, the country's pride on the international stage would be fully restored. It can be argued that sovereign democracy from the political party perspective was good for Russia as compared to the haste and political humiliation after the collapse of the Soviet Union. But it was the ideological aspect of sovereign democracy that was more crucial and the impact of that ideological discourse on international law, in particular, when seen as an alternative approach to universal norms, human rights or democracy as understood in the West.

The chief intellectual architect of Russia's sovereign democracy ideology Vladislav Surkov saw sovereign democracy as a way of breaking away from the West and imposition of its values on Russia. Russia has a strong history as a unitary state that goes back hundreds of years, and has a special place in the evolution of centers of power that controls and influences weaker or internal subjects of larger states within its realm. In Surkov's vision, sovereign democracy was Russia's post-Soviet answer in "maintaining state sovereignty and the preservation of state control" to "insulate political power from international criticisms,"[27] by projecting Russia as an alternative to the West and/or the East. Russia was finally embracing its destiny – and sovereign democracy *was* the answer. Embracing its destiny under the rubric of sovereign democracy meant that Russia was finally able to act with impunity as a sovereign state under the rules that make up the international system and project its hegemony in both its near abroad and further afield. The Georgia

26 e.g. Vladimir Gelman, 'From "Feckless Pluralism" to "Dominant Power Politics": The Transformation of Russia's Party System' (2006) 13 *Democratization* 545.

27 Antonov (n. 7) 1, 28.

conflict of 2008 and the Crimean crisis of 2014 are examples of Russia's hegemony from a sovereign democracy point of view: international legal rules were only meant to supplement Russia's hegemony.

Because Russia was never a part of the traditional development of international law in the Westphalian context, or, at least has a rocky relationship with western development of international law from the Westphalian conception of sovereignty to the modern application of international legal rules, sovereign democracy presented an opportunity to chart's Russia's relationship with international law in the post-Soviet global hegemonic sense. If the concept of sovereign democracy began as a political public relations project in the halls of the Kremlin, intellectual scholars on all sides in Russia took on the concept from the discourse in the mass media and turned sovereign democracy into a "social science." Books and dissertations offering various interpretations and conceptions of sovereign democracy began to emerge.[28] However, there are two foundational elements on the emergence of sovereign democracy in Russia that accurately explain its rise and eventual fall from the intellectual and academic circles. The first was its Hobbesian/Schmittian intellectual foundation, as sketched out above. In the Hobbesian/Schmittian foundations the sovereign authority (ruler) was able to implement statist policies and seek legitimation of enhanced ruling. The second element was political nationalism. By political nationalism I mean how ideologues in the state political leadership extolled the virtues of nationalism as a way of justifying sovereign democracy to the point that sovereign democracy eventually failed to subdue civil society.[29]

However, most Russians embraced conservatism manifested through religion (including Orthodox and Muslims) and those espoused through isolationism. Therefore, the inward turn that Russia took in the mid 2000s toward homegrown conservatism through sovereign democracy was a rejection of the liberal western order that did not fit Russia. Russian leadership under Vladimir Putin concentrated on two main projects: (a) restoring Russia as a great power in international politics; and (b) putting an end to the economic and political turmoil that plagued Russia in its first decade as a post-Soviet state. In order to achieve those objectives the Russian people needed a (state) sanctioned ideology that conveys Russian exceptionalism. Furthermore, such (state) sanctioned ideology must emanate from strong political leadership (sovereign authority) that extolled the virtues

28 e.g. Дмитрий Орлов, Андраник Мигранян, Михаил Рогожников (eds), Суверенная демократия: от идеи к доктрине. Сборник статей, (Европа, 2005/10) (Dmitri Orlov, Andranik Migranyan and Mikhail Rogozhinikov (eds), *Sovereign Democracy: From Idea to Doctrine – Collected Essays*, Europa 2005/10); Матвиенко, Яна Юрьевна, Институционально-правовые модели легитимации суверенной демократии в современной России, (Jana Yurevna, *An Institutional–Legal Model of Legitimacy for Sovereign Democracy in Contemporary Russia*, Rostov on the Don, 2008) (a dissertation in Russian legal sciences on the concept of sovereign democracy), http://law.edu.ru/book/book.asp?bookID=1292726

29 e.g. David White, *The Russian Democratic Party Yabloko: Opposition in a Managed Democracy* (Ashgate 2006) (discussing the peak of the liberal political party Yabloko in the first decade of post-Soviet Russia).

of Hobbesian and Schmittian enhanced ruling be legitimized by the rule of law. As such, democracy as a notion and practice would need new meaning, and form part of a new ideology that had the tacit blessing of the state. That ideology should moreover, in Schmittian terms,[30] serve president and statist policies.

As an ideology, sovereign democracy initiated genuine debate within Russian society. Yet it became obvious that one of the hidden agendas for this ideology was the smooth transfer of power from the president to the prime minister in 2008, where they swapped position, until the effective amendment of the Russian Constitution was in place, that would allow Putin to run for a second presidency in 2012. The main political party United Russia had already vanquished all major political parties, and saw a return to the Russians mindset of a one-party system. Sovereign democracy as an ideology was part of this one-party reformation in which, as the ruling party, the *ideology* of sovereign democracy "was vital to solving the problem of succession, the most dangerous source of instability in autocratic regimes."[31] Although the then Prime Minister, Dmitri Medvedev, stood in as president from 2008 to 2012, the real succession was the return of the former president, Vladimir Putin to the Kremlin in 2012 with a new mandate and extended presidential term, as a result of the ideology of sovereign democracy from his first presidential term.

However, by Putin's second presidency in 2012, sovereign democracy was an idea that no longer had any value in pure debating terms. It was time to shift sovereign democracy from moot to practice. Moreover, the Kremlin had new priorities. For one, the notion of sovereign democracy as an ideology during the FPP confirmed that its main purpose was the smooth return of Putin to the presidency via a constitutional amendment that the ruling party successfully orchestrated in the lower legislature – the Duma. Second, a vast majority of the Russian "civil society" and even external Kremlinologists never bought the idea. Both Russians and the world were wary of ideologies and sovereign democracy as an ideology spectacularly failed from the onset, as it never inspired the *narod* (Russian people) beyond the walls of the Kremlin (and a clique of the Moscow intelligentsia). Yet, during its formative years, sovereign democracy successfully created a new legal landscape in Russia. The next section examines the fundamental legislative and constitutional shift that occurred during the formative years of the ideology of sovereign democracy in Russia – a period in which most western liberal democracies accused Russia of rebuilding authoritarianism by depriving civil liberties and other notions of western liberalism.

## 4 The Legal Foundations of Sovereign Democracy in Russia

There were two distinct legal developments in Russia that "entrenched" sovereign democracy as part of state ideology during its rise and the period of Russian

30 Weimar Constitution, art. 48.

31 Ivan Krastev, 'Paradoxes of the New Authoritarianism' (2011) 22 *Journal of Democracy* 5, 12.

renewal in the mid 2000s. The first was the amendment of the Russian Constitution raising the presidential term from four years to six years. Furthermore, new electoral laws were an offshoot of the constitutional amendment. Another legal development that aided and abetted the ideology of sovereign democracy was the series of legislation on civil liberties that were enacted during the same period as Russia underwent this new ideological revolution. The impact of these developments is long-lasting, in particular the constitutional amendment on presidential terms, given that they originated in the sovereign democracy movement. It is these two developments that are examined in the rest of this section of the chapter to extrapolate the legal impact of sovereign democracy and how its ideological development influenced the legislative and statist agenda during second term of Putin's first presidency.

### *(a) Sovereign Democracy on the Domestic Legislative Front*

One of the concerns of Carl Schmitt regarding political rule was that politics was never a safe vehicle for driving effective state policies as such; states fare better under enhanced ruling. The provisions of article 48 of the Weimar Constitution was one aspect of enhanced ruling where presidential powers were substantially expanded. The argument goes that, in some situations, the state should not be abandoned to private interests.[32] If there was ever a parallel that could be drawn with Russia, where, as a nation state, it was abandoned to private interests, it was the post-Soviet decade (1992–2002) in which capitalism ran wild and a new breed of private business barons effectively ruled Russia. This club of private concerns has been immortalized as oligarchs – super business barons of Russia. Upon Putin's election to the presidency in 2000, it was clear that the oligarchy presented a problem between political governance and business. By 2003 in the famous gathering of business barons with Putin in the Kremlin, the president issued them with an ultimatum – pursue business and stay out of politics. Some heeded, and others did not. Those who did not heed Putin's ultimatum saw their business empire gradually returned to the state and a sleuth of legislation that "renationalized" strategic industries began to take shape. These legislative efforts were further signals that sovereign democracy was coming to Russia, and, as per Carl Schmitt, the Russian state should not be abandoned to private interests. However, although, the legislative changes began with concerns of the Russian business barons, there were a number of legislative developments affecting every sphere of Russian society.

Between 2000 and 2008 President Putin signed into law dozens of laws and hundreds of decrees. Most of those with the greatest impact on society and that drew criticism from outside had to do with civil liberties in Russia. Furthermore, direct democracy in the regions and other federal subjects were discarded in favor of appointment by the Kremlin (sovereign ruler) of governors and heads of federal subjects. The laws that some believed crippled civil liberties included those that

32 (n. 20).

changed the rules for holding a referendum by amending legislation in 2004[33] to allow the direct appointment of governors as opposed to by popular vote. Furthermore, the law on the election of parliamentarians was also amended in 2004 raising the electoral threshold to 7 percent up from 5 percent.[34] Thus, in relation to the rules on federal governors, the *internal sovereignty* of regions and provinces would no longer be in competition with the sovereignty of the Federation.[35] In a sense, these were the core actions that legitimized sovereign democracy and enhanced ruling by the Kremlin during Putin's first presidency. But, by addressing those laws, we can get some sense of how the ideology of sovereign democracy matured in various legislative and other normative acts before making a public debut. The legal legitimation of sovereign democracy that began with the various legislative acts throughout Putin's first presidency were seen as a rejection of the democratic legal order consistent with western democracies. The various legislative developments concerning electoral matters and civil liberties were generally seen as part of the "sovereign/managed democracy" mantra, but given the rapid switch from "managed democracy" to "sovereign democracy" during the period, as both terms were being debated, it is best, in my opinion, to group those legislative actions as part of the broader sovereign democracy ideology.

### *(i) Freedom of Assembly/Civil Liberties and the Tide of Sovereign Democracy*

The (alleged) legal assault on freedom of assembly, free speech, religion, and other civil liberties during the period of sovereign democracy was a dual dance of conservatism and experimentation with western standards of human rights.[36] Three particular groups of legislation (on assembly, religious beliefs, and NGOs)[37] with

33 Federal Law No. 159-FZ, December 11, 2004.

34 Federal Law No. 175-FZ, December 20, 2002, as amended on December 28, 2004; Federal Law No. 51-FZ, May 18, 2005.

35 e.g. Federal Law No. 119-FZ, on the Division of Power Between Federation and Federal Subjects, with amendments May 20, 2002.

36 A number of laws were introduced or modified existing legislation that were seen as an assault on civil liberties, these include, but not limited to, public associations, Federal Law No. 82-FZ on Public Associations (1995, amended 2004); religious associations, Federal Law No. 125-FZ Law on Freedom of Conscience and on Religious Associations; charitable activities, Federal Law No. 135-FZ on Charitable Activities and Organizations (1995, amended 2004); use of the federal prosecutor, Federal Law on the Prosecutor's Office of the Russian Federation (1992, amended 2004). Also, art. 129 Russian Constitution; and freedom of assembly, Federal Law on Rallies, Meetings, Demonstrations, Marches and Picketing (2004, as amended 2010); art. 31 CON. See also Code of Administrative Offences (2001, as amended 2012). Federal Law No. 54-FZ on Assemblies, Meetings, Demonstrations, Processions and Picketing, June 19, 2004. The cases at the ECtHR are rather voluminous, but see e.g. *Barankevich* v. *Russia* (2007).

37 In 2006 the 1996 Russian legislation regulating NGOs was amended requiring them to report all forms of external assistance, Federal Law of the Russian Federation on Amendments to Certain Legislative Acts of the Russian Federation, January 10, 2006, Russian Gazette. See also *Makhmudov* v. *Russia*, Appl. No. 35082/04, July 26, 2007.

constitutional significance became the target of criticisms from the West, yet fully endorsed by some parts of Russian society and legislators. Naturally, the odd internal critiques were present in Russia regarding this legislation, but those internal critiques did not form opposition strong enough to roll back the legislative developments on civil liberties in the Russian Federation.

On the religious front, Jehovah's Witnesses, Scientologists,[38] and the odd evangelical,[39] were impacted from laws that were meant to curtail their activities in the Russian Federation, where Orthodoxy is all but a state-sanctioned religion. While discussions on the curtailing of religious freedom was not new, a broad discussion is not possible in this chapter;[40] suffice to say that given Russia's pluralistic and multiethnic society, the freedom of religion and belief is widely tolerated or an ongoing experiment in which the wider world could look up to as a form of social cohesion and harmony. Naturally, there are challenges. Given the role of the Orthodox Church in Russia's history, Russia must still navigate the many beliefs of its peoples. The *Rossiannis* (ethnic Russians) tend to subscribe to Orthodoxy as a unifying element, but not necessarily as believers in a strict sense, while *Russkiies* (the many peoples of Russia) comprise Judaism, Islam, and Buddhism among other religions. The law on freedom of religion or belief[41] recognized the multiethnic beliefs of Russians and guarantees their "legal relationships in the field of human rights and the rights of every citizen to the freedom of conscience and faith as well as the legal status of religious associations."[42] Yet the law on freedom of religion and belief had been a *victim* of sovereign democracy in Russia – at least for some *foreign* religious organizations such as Jehovah's Witnesses,[43] the Church of Scientology,[44] and the Unification Church.[45] For instance, the Church of Scientology Surgut City had been refused registration and complained to the ECtHR. The ECtHR is significant because it is the first transnational court to dispense *justice* based on western standards regarding civil liberties in the Russian Federation. Furthermore, the caseload from Russia grew gradually over the years, and the ECtHR found that Russia violated some form of civil

38 See *Church of Scientology Moscow* v. *Russia*, Appl. No. 18147/02, April 5, 2007, ECtHR.

39 *Barankevich* v. *Russia*, Appl. No. 10519/03, July 27, 2007.

40 But see Chapter 7, in this volume; Mikhail Antonov and Ekaterina Samokhina, 'The Realist and Rhetorical Dimensions of the Protection of Religious Feelings in Russia' (2015) 40 *Review of Central and East European Law* 229–84.

41 Federal Law No. 125-FZ of September 26, 1997 on the Freedom of Conscience and Religious Associations (1997, as amended 2008); also re arts 14, 19, and 28 of the Constitution. Noticeably, ECtHR case law include Application Nos 76836/01 and 32782/03) *Kimlya and Others* v. *Russia*, 3 December 2009; ECtHR (Application No. 2512/04) *Nolan and K.* v. *Russia*, February 12, 2009; ECtHR (Application No. 302/02) *Jehovah's Witnesses of Moscow and Others* v. *Russia*, June 10, 2010.

42 Ibid., art. 1.

43 *Jehovah's Witnesses* (n. 41).

44 *Kimlya* (Scientology) (n. 41).

45 *Nolan* (n. 41).

liberties from 2002 through to 2007. Thus, where the ECtHR was hearing around 2 percent of cases from Russia in 2002 that figure would change dramatically by 2007 to 22 percent. Not only was Russia found to be violating its international obligations in the ECHR (and by extension other international law instruments such as the ICCPR and the UCHR), Russia was also creating a *blockade* against future notion of rights that were not endemic in Russian society. Thus, for example, rights that could be claimed for personal reasons between same-sex couples, or rights that were seen within the framework of extremism could be deterred by law: "propaganda" of same-sex contact and extremism would have its limits.[46] Any promotion of extremist activities whether by individuals or organizations (even in the form of a right to assembly) were now subjected to the laws needed to construct Russia's new form of conservatism.

Naturally, there was genuine concern in Russia to curb criminal activities that posed a threat to law enforcement. Elements of extremism in that context was at the forefront given the vacuum created during the dark years of liberalism (1992–2002) in Russia. It was that same opportunity – the threat of criminalistics extremism that allowed for the enactment of rules that responded to those threats; and also to curtail organizations that expressed their views on *extremist* activities that threatened the Russian state. Such organizations fell into the domain of social, religious, nationalist, cultural, and many others. Yet, ironically, the law on extremism of 2002, for example, declared that its purpose was to protect "the rights and freedoms of persons and citizens, the principles of the constitutional system, and the integrity and security of the Russian Federation."[47] The latter clause of this part of the preamble alluded to the early beginnings of sovereign democracy because part of the argument advanced for sovereign democracy was to protect *Russianness*; that is, the integrity, moral fiber, and security of the Russian state. The enactment of the law on extremism in 2002, for example, was not so much about the genuine concern of criminalistics extremism: its enactment was part of the broader vision of enhanced ruling that the Kremlin began to quietly consolidate. This is because, had there been a commission for example to examine the legislative proposal for the 2002 law on extremism and the content of other laws including the Russian Constitution, then arguably, the 2002 law would have been unnecessary. But, having said that, one should not ignore the fact that the law defined extremism[48] that was lacking in other legislation. However, given that, as posited, that the 2002 law on extremism was the foundation for what was to come regarding a crackdown on civil liberties in other areas and expanding sovereign democracy, it was no surprise that laws banning religious organizations or laws *de-democratizing* the federal electoral process would follow in the ensuing years.

46 e.g. On Counteracting Extremist Activity, Federal Law No. 114-FZ (July 25, 2002); Code of Administrative Violations, art. 6.13, June 26, 2013.
47 Federal Law No. 114-FZ (n. 46) preamble.
48 Ibid., art. 1.

### *(ii) Constitutional Amendment and Electoral Laws*

In a series of unprecedented protests as a result of the 2011 parliamentary elections in Russia that caught the Kremlin off guard, the people rose up against what they saw were rigged election results and the dictatorship of Putin. However, the 2011 protests were already sewn in the sovereign democracy/*vertikalnaya vlast* paradigm from 2002 to 2008. For one, this paradigm had only one strategic aim in mind, which was not obvious at the time: the amendment of the Russian Constitution (and subsequent presidential election in 2012; and the second Putin presidency), especially in relation to the presidential term increasing from four to six years. Moreover, the various reforms in the electoral laws was a further aim of this paradigm, and, in 2011, the people's protest was a rejection of sovereign democracy/*vertikalnaya vlast*. In other words, the sovereign democracy/*vertikalnaya vlast* paradigm on the domestic legislative front in Russia was designed and executed with a particular result in mind through policies and legal changes that bolstered enhanced ruling. For an effective explanation of this, the narrative must turn to the sequence of events from 1991 through to 2008.

The Russian Constitution of 1993[49] emerged after a trial-by-error process in the 1991 Constitution when it became clear that the Soviet Union was on course to disband. That process began in 1990 when the Congress of People's Deputies of Soviet Russia[50] was elected and a constitutional commission was set up by Boris Yeltsin who forced Soviet leader Mikhail Gorbachev to sign the disbandment of the Soviet Union on live television. When the first draft of the Russian Constitution was produced in 1990 one of its core appeals was the system of popular vote to elect a president of Soviet Russia.[51] But as different forms of internal strife rocked Soviet Russia and the Soviet Union on a whole in 1991, Yeltsin comfortably won the presidency of Soviet Russia in the summer of 1991 – six months shy of the disbandment of the Soviet Union in December 1991. However, as Yeltsin turned his attention to more pressing economic matters, members of the Congress of Deputies in 1992 began to demand a more active role in economic reform. This led to tension between Yeltsin and the Congress of Deputies that culminated in Yeltsin shelling the Parliament building in Moscow, and shortly after new parliamentary elections alongside a constitutional plebiscite. A new Russian Constitution was adopted on December 12, 1993 and its only significant amendment was in 2008 to largely prolong the presidential term.[52] The 1993 Constitution in the rest of this chapter is referred to as the Yeltsin Constitution, so as to make distinctions later, when discussing the Putin amendments of 2008.

49 Constitution of the Russian Federation, December 12, 1993, Oxford Constitutions of the World, OCW CD 1023. In this chapter, I refer to this as the "Yeltsin Constitution."

50 By this I mean Russia as constituent republic of the USSR.

51 This paragraph and the next is based largely on Timothy Colton and Cindy Skach, 'The Russian Predicament' (2005) 16 *Journal of Democracy* 113, 115; see also Jane Henderson, *The Constitution of the Russian Federation: A Contextual Analysis* (Hart 2011) ch. 3.

52 Russian Constitution, amended 2008.

The Yeltsin Constitution in some ways opened with a Schmittian overtone as it proclaims in the preamble that the Russian people revived "the sovereign statehood of Russia and asserting the strength of its democratic foundations." And, from there, with two sections and 137 articles, the Yeltsin Constitution addressed civil liberties, the constituent parts that make up the Federation, legislative institutions, the governance structures, the judiciary, local government, procedure for amendments, and the presidency. The presidency is covered in chapter four (arts. 80–93) where article 81(1) sets the presidential term limit to four years; article 81 (3) states that the presidential term shall be no more than two consecutive terms, and covers other presidential powers. Another important article worth mentioning for the purposes of this chapter is article 13(2) which state that "no ideology shall be proclaimed as State or compulsory ideology." The attempts at fostering sovereign democracy as an ideology in Russia in the mid 2000s were not legally state sanctioned as that would have been unconstitutional. However, those attempts were widely supported by the executive (government and presidency) and were technically short of being state sanctioned.

But let me briefly return to chapter four of the Russian Constitution in this section to then compare it with article 48 of the Weimar Constitution. According to article 80(1) of the Yeltsin Constitution, the president is the "guardian of the constitution." What this means is not so clear-cut. Clearly, that provision appears to elevate the presidency into some form of "tsar emperor" or "sovereign" and therefore above domestic political entrapments.[53] In any event, article 80, in general, gives a summary on the role of the president. Furthermore, according to external Russian constitutionalist scholars such as Jane Henderson, "the provisions of Article 80 on the role of the President have been used to justify the extension of presidential powers by implication."[54] A noticeable thing about the Yeltsin Constitution was the absence of a vice president. The president exercises powers to nominate a prime minister and other key functionaries to institutions such as the central bank, but the Yeltsin Constitution excluded the position of a vice president. However, in the past, it was vice presidents' attempts to seize power that made the Yeltsin Constitution exclude the role of a vice president. But article 92 provides for the prime minster to be acting president in the event the president is unable to fulfil his duties. One of the key roles of the president under the Yeltsin Constitution was that the president was "to protect the sovereignty of the Russian Federation, its independence and State integrity, and shall ensure the coordinated functioning and interaction of the organs of State power."[55] Furthermore, article 87(1) provides that the president can implement martial law if there is a threat or aggression against the Russian Federation.

Upon reading these provisions of the Yeltsin Constitution, one begins to see the Schmittian call for enhanced ruling by the sovereign. Under article 87(3), the president's power to implement martial law should be in conjunction with a

53 See also Henderson (n. 51) 110.
54 Ibid., 129.
55 Russian Constitution (1993), art. 80(2).

federal constitutional law: "the regime of martial law shall be defined by federal constitutional law." However, prior to 2002, there was no federal constitutional law that helped to define or implement martial law. That law was only implemented in January 2002[56] heralding another legislative development in sovereign democracy (then branded as managed democracy or vertical power). According to Schmitt, via article 48 of the Weimar Constitution, the president can introduce a state of emergency as part of enhanced ruling. And in article 88 of the Yeltsin Constitution, the president in conjunction with federal constitutional law[57] can "introduce a state of emergency" in Russia provided the legislature is informed. Although these characteristic traits are not unique to Russia, and can be found in other constitutions, what is interesting is that the provision sets in motion a pathway in which sovereign democracy as an ideology aligns with the political concept of Schmitt.

In fact, a proper reading of the Yeltsin Constitution can reveal its Schmittian characteristics that provide for enhanced ruling by authoritative sovereign[58] prompting the observation that the Yeltsin Constitution was "at least one-third more powerful than was the president of the Weimar Republic."[59] Thus, in a similar way Schmitt viewed the sovereign as "he who decides on the state of exception," the presidential powers under the Yeltsin Constitution evoke a similar sentiment. It is against this backdrop that in 2008 President Dmitri Medvedev signed into law amendments to the Russian Constitution primarily extending the presidential term from four to six years and the lower legislature the Duma from four to five years.[60] The amendments saw changes to articles 81.1 and 96.1 of the Yeltsin Constitution respectively. Although the 2008 amendments to the Yeltsin Constitution was carried out rather quickly, those amendments were not carried out by Putin himself, but by his successor who had been in the job less than a year.

The electoral process itself was also a casualty of sovereign democracy in that electoral laws were fine-tuned to fit the narrative of political authority from the Kremlin.[61] The electoral laws that came into effect during the FPP broadly fall into three categories: (a) on political parties;[62] (b) on the election of the pre-

56 Federal Constitutional Law of January 30, 2002.

57 Federal Constitutional Law of May 30, 2001; see also art. 90(1) noting that the president can "issue edicts and regulations."

58 See also Henderson (n. 51) 130 expressing similar thoughts: "the President's powers are impressive, and when the 1993 Constitution was first examined by Western scholars there was serious disquiet that it set up the possibility of a presidential dictatorship." See similar views in Colton and Skach (n. 51).

59 Colton and Skach (n. 51) 119; see also Alexander Dormin, *The Limits of Russian Democratisation: Emergency Powers and States of Emergency* (Routledge, 2006); Peter Bernholz, 'The Constitution of Totalitarianism' (1991) 147 *Journal of Institutional and Theoretical Economics* 425.

60 Federal Constitutional Laws No. 6–7 of December 30, 2008, Constitution of the Russian Federation of December 25, 1993, with amendments to 30 December 2008.

61 See Cameron Ross, 'Regional Elections and Electoral Authoritarianism in Russia' (2011) 63 *Europe–Asia Studies* 641.

62 Federal Law No. 95-FZ on Political Parties, July 11, 2001, amended 2011.

sident,[63] governors[64] and parliamentarians[65] and other regional representatives;[66] and (c) on legislation on referendums.[67] Of these three categories, the most contentious has been the 2001 legislation on political parties[68] requiring them to be fully established in all regions of the Federation and setting a minimum membership threshold. These and other requirements in the original legislation were seen as "draconian" in comparison to western standards. However, in general these requirements were not novel as similar legislation in Europe has parallel provisions. Since 2001 the law on political parties has been amended several times; some amendments were in light of criticisms, while others were mostly on harmonizing procedural requirements.

But there have been numerous cases on Russia before the ECtHR that challenged the various legislative developments. One notable case *Artyomov* v. *Russia* [69] questioned the constitutionality of the laws on political parties. In *Artyomov* v. *Russia* the issue was whether a political party that sought registration could be associated only with a certain ethnic group. When the ECtHR was called upon to decide on the matter its ruling was not surprising. For the ECtHR, Russia violated the applicant's right to freedom of association. Yet, prior to the ECtHR's decision, the Constitutional Court of the Russian Federation was extolling the pluralistic and religious make-up of the Russian Federation when it decided similar cases in the 1990s. One of the interesting and often overlooked points of the decision in the Russian Constitutional Court was the fact that its ruling came out during the early public discourse on the meaning, concept, and context of "civil society" (a discourse that later ran parallel to sovereign democracy) in Russia that began in early 2003. Thus, for the Russian Constitutional Court: "contemporary Russian society, including political parties and religious associations, has not yet acquired substantial experience of democratic coexistence."[70] The Russian Constitutional Court engaged the language of civil society in the form of democratic coexistence

63 Federal Law on the Election of the President of the Russian Federation, January 10, 2003.

64 Federal Law on Modifications and Additions to the Federal Law on General Principles of the Organizations of Legislative (Representative) and Executive Bodies of State Power of the Subjects of the Russian Federation, July 29, 2000.

65 Federal Law No. 175-FZ (n. 34).

66 Federal Law No. 131-FZ on General Principles of Organization of Local-Self Government in the Russian Federation, October 6, 2003, transferring powers to federal organs.

67 Federal Law No. 67-FZ on Basic Guarantees of Electoral Rights and the Right of Citizens of the Russian Federation to Participate in a Referendum, June 12, 2002. The amendments to this legislation over the years covers among other things a severe restriction on the use of media (propaganda material) during election campaigns.

68 Federal Law No. 95-FZ (n. 62). For a non-legal discussion see generally Laura Petrone, 'Institutionalizing Pluralism in Russia: A New Authoritarianism?' (2011) 27 *Journal of Communist Studies and Transition Politics* 166 (discussing electoral competition and unique Russian peculiarities such as electoral authoritarianism and competitive authoritarianism).

69 *Artyomov* v. *Russia*, Appl. No. 17582/05, December 7, 2006.

70 Ibid., p. 3.

to justify the denial of a political party that was only promoting a certain ethnic group. This was a minor coup for liberalism, yet when the language and debate in Russia changed dramatically in 2004–5 to that of sovereign democracy, the Russian Constitutional Court also aligned itself with that language and debate to justify the denial of justice in several cases.

### *(b) The Failure of International Law and the Legitimation of Sovereign Democracy*

Global conflicts beyond the borders of Russia and President Putin's tacit support for conservatism in Russia coupled with a renewed pride in the Russian people encouraged the population to embrace the Kremlin's enhanced ruling. Moreover, Russia began to see international law as a diluted organism with various elements of decay that could no longer speak of universalism. The decay of international law from a Russian perspective began with the 2003 invasion of Iraq, and since then international law represents a hegemonic tool for western nations to use as disguise to justify their interventions in conflicts or to create conflicts. The Iraq War and the Kosovo conflicts made Russia wary of how international law was being abused to represent the unilateral actions of the United States. Thus, from the perspective of Putin's sovereign democracy, international law was finally a spaghetti bowl in which different strands of spaghetti could be removed from the bowl. In other words, international law was now a system to justify what suits the hegemon's political agenda. The participation of Russia in the diplomatic and international legal process to prevent a war in Iraq was a valuable lesson that strengthened the Kremlin's position to restore Russia as a great power. Moscow had realized that it can also use or circumnavigate international law to defend the territorial integrity of Russia and to defend Russians abroad. For Moscow, it had a sovereign right to contain external forces that threatens Russia and international law was a convenient tool to defend or legitimize its actions.

#### *(i) The Iraq War: Seen But Not Heard*

The most significant moment in the post-Cold War era that relegated Russia to the edges of international legal relations was the illusive war on terror in Iraq (2003–2011). Russia had quietly conceded that it was not in a position to deter the US bombings of Belgrade in 1999 and Russo-American relations were not severely damaged. However, the Iraq war changed the dynamics of how international law fit in to the post-Cold War world of Russo-American relationships and the plurality of the world order. Thus, while Russia was quietly nurturing sovereign democracy at home it was not in a position to demonstrate the fruits of this intellectual and (policy) revolution that affected all spheres of Russian society and on the international plane.

Thus, as the US and its partners of coalition of the willing embarked on a campaign in Iraq, and, in the process, severely dented the system of international law, and ushered in a new doctrine of preemptive strike,[71] Russia actively voiced

71 National Security Strategy of the United States (White House, 2002).

its opposition. Yet, for the first time, Russia felt that it no longer mattered on the world stage. For Russia was unable to contain the US via the supremacy of the UN Security Council which embraces the principles and virtues of international law and normative authority of the UN Charter necessary for world peace. Russia found allies in unlikely places such as France and Germany in its opposition to the war. Russia's alliance with France and Germany to oppose the Iraq War was part of an effort to rebuild brand Russia in international relations, where a multipolar world exercises and upholds international law and avoids destabilization.

But Russia also had a domestic situation that was a replica of the international scene. Russia, as a multi-ethnic country with various religious groups and counting over 20 million Muslims, fear the breakup of its own Federation, and other threats posed by *civil* groups, and regional political instability. To counter such a threat, required the concentration of power in Moscow and the containment of groups through various legislative efforts. Only the full containment of the domestic situation could then allow Russia to act on the international stage with confidence in its own interests. But, for Russia to be successful in defending or pursing strategic interests through the use of force, then, international law would need to be portrayed as irrelevant. The seeds on the irrelevancy of international law from the Kremlin's point of view were already sewn by the Iraq War.

A key line of opposition to the war that Russia constantly deployed was that the stability the UN Charter created in the post-World War II era was being eroded. For Russia, the UN Charter and the realm of international law were being turned into weak columns for the political rhetoric of a single hegemonic power and it was dangerous. For one, Russia, had already conceded, a number of strategic treaty law pillars to the US in the post-September, 11 world, such as the US withdrawal from the ABM treaty[72] and the enlargement of NATO. The UN Charter for its part outlaws the unilateral use of force except in self-defense,[73] unless authorized by the UN Security Council or the self-defense provisions of article 51. The proposed UN resolution on the use of force in Iraq in March 2003 was vehemently opposed by France, Russia, and Germany. Thus, on that basis, the US invasion of Iraq had been on shaky legal grounds from the beginning. The weak legal premise for the Iraq War helped to shape the domestic context of the legal and policy developments in Russia in earnest. First, entities that were suspected to be a threat to the Russian state through external influences were now the subject of various restrictive rules. Second, Russia as a sovereign nation (in the Westphalian context) should be able to project that sovereignty externally as a unified and strong nation, with little or no internal challenges.

As such, the Iraq War propelled Russia to examine its national sovereignty, and what were the factors that posed a threat to the nation state of Russia.

72 See e.g. Emily Penney, 'Is That Legal? The United States' Unilateral Withdrawal from the Anti-Ballistic Missile Treaty' (2002) 51 *Catholic University Law Review* 1287.

73 UN Charter, art. 2(4): "All members shall refrain in their international relations from the threat or use of force against the territorial integrity or political independence of any state."

Furthermore, by determining the *internal threats* to the sovereignty of the Russian state, it would, therefore, be in a position to align the changing nature of international law in the hegemonic world of the Iraq War. Because the new system of international law was also being shaped by how other international actors such as international organizations (e.g. the COE) or NGOs have on the domestic state,[74] diluting those positions was then a policy goal. In other words, for Russia to coexist with elements that threaten its civilization, such as external NGOs, unruly ethnic minorities, and the new norms of international law (preemptive strikes), there must be a degree of control. It was against this background that Russia made the *preemptive* strike shortly after the commencement of the Iraq War with referendums and legislative changes that embarked on the road to sovereign democracy. By the time the theater of war commend in Iraq in 2003, Putin, in an address to the nation, reiterated the relevance of international law. At the same time, he indicated that as a "political mistake" the war would open the door to global instability.[75] Putin saw the Anglo-American venture in Iraq as futile and warned that: "Perhaps for the first time since the end of the Cold War, the world community has encountered such a grave crisis. In essence, the danger of an undermining of the foundations of global stability and international law."[76] In that same address, Putin, for the first time, introduced a concept that went almost unrecognized: "immutable sovereignty."[77] This was Putin echoing the notion of sovereign democracy, a term, he purposefully avoided, but referred to in various forms as part of his vision of vertical power. Whether or not Putin had in mind a religious undertone to his 2003 proclamation, what was clear, in the ensuing years, as the notion of sovereign democracy occupied the intellectual and policy debates in Russia – Russia was to be seen as also having a *messianic* duty in the world.

The Iraq War presented Putin with an unexpected gift – that was orchestrated by the people. There was strong opposition to the Iraq War in Russia, and even though opposition to the war from official government sources was well known domestically and internationally, Russian *civil society* and people were angrier than the diplomatic side the government conveyed. Hospitable sentiments that were extended to the American people after September, 11 were suddenly rescinded by ordinary Russians. The powerful corpus of the mass media rallied the Russian people in their opposition to the Iraq War, and further actions by the US such as pulling out of the ABM treaty, the eastward expansion of NATO, and the

74 See also Bertjan Verbeek, 'Does Might Still Make Right? International Relations Theory and the Use of International Law Regarding the 2003 Iraq War' (2012) 42 *Netherlands Yearbook of International Law* 193–214; Símona Tutuianu, *Towards Global Justice: Sovereignty in an Interdependent World* (Springer, 2012) 43–94.

75 Kremlin, President Vladimir Putin, statement on Iraq at a Kremlin meeting, March 20, 2003.

76 Kremlin, March 28, 2003, also cited in Galia Golan, 'Russia and the Iraq War: Was Putin's Policy a Failure?' (2004) 37 *Communist and Post-Communist Studies* 429–59, 447.

77 Golan (n. 76) 447.

prolonging of the Jackson–Vanik amendment led the Russian people to adopt a chilly attitude to the "western agenda." It was this mini revolution by the people during the Iraq War that Putin tapped into for a number of legislative and policy goals under the rubric of sovereign democracy (Putin called it *immutable sovereignty*) that began life as various forms of *vertikalnaya vlast* or "managed democracy." It should be noted that Putin, in his first two and a half years as president was, in general, moving westward into the family of nations of civilized states, but was stopped in his tracks, not by the Russian people or angry army generals, but by the Iraq War. It was during vociferous opposition to the Iraq war in Russia that a pattern began to play out (democratically) that started to embolden Putin's sovereign democracy mantra and how those domestic situations would affect legal changes.

But even though Putin saw the dangers of the Iraq War, he also knew that domestic rules were also necessary to *defend* the Russian state from its own *extremist* elements, and, in 2004, as the debate turned to sovereign democracy, Russia adopted a law curtailing assembly and demonstrations.[78] The events for the 2004 law on extremism was a product of the Iraq War. During the second week of the Iraq war, a demonstration by the Central Islamic Board of Muslims broke out in the Southern Russian republic of Bashkortostan's capital city Ufa. The demands of the demonstrators were simple: jihad against the United States.[79] The regional prosecutor later intervened and cautioned the demonstration organizers that their declaration amounted to a criminal act and was subject to prosecution. Because the Iraq war galvanized all sections of Russian society, the very nature of the Russian state was also vulnerable to demonstrations by various ethnic and religious groups. But the most important lesson for Russia during the Iraq war was that its voice was ignored on the international stage as it pleaded for the principles of international law to be respected, and, having its voice ignored, it found itself in a position where it was seen but not heard. It was a lesson that Russia would later turn to its advantage, as it too, similar to how the United States justified the Iraq War as part of the elusive war on terror, and therefore, constituted self-defense; Russia's first use of force in an international conflict since Putin came to power began in Georgia in 2008, which was legally justified as self-defense.

### *(ii) Seen and Heard: Russia and the Use of Force in Armed Conflict with Georgia (2008)*

The Russo-Georgian conflict in 2008 – the first instance where Russia used force in an armed conflict beyond its territorial borders during Putin's control of the Kremlin – was the crowning moment of how sovereign democracy as a political ideology had permeated and solidified the leadership in Russia. Russia was confident that the Iraqi War was a prime example of how nations can take preemptive strike against external threats. The Iraq War has been a very dark spot in international law and created loopholes for other states to pursue their national interest without fear of legal accountability.

78 Federal Law, No. 54-FZ (n. 36).
79 Golan (n. 76) 447.

Because the Soviet Union was a complex pluralistic constellation held together by a communist ideology, the problem of identity and ethno-nationalism that plagued the Soviet republics and also the micro republics within the larger Soviet republics were not given full attention by the political powers in Moscow. Thus, when the Soviet Union disappeared in December 1991, not only were the larger republics such as Ukraine, Georgia, Kazakhstan, and minor ones such as Armenia and Moldova gained independence, but constituent micro *ethno-republic* within those republics were also seeking their independence. Thus, micro ethno-republics such as Abkhazia and South Ossetia in Georgia claimed their own independence. Other micro ethno-republics such as Transnistria in Moldova and Chechnya also attempted to separate from their larger siblings, but those attempts were put down largely based on military interventions from their larger siblings.

The quest for independence by these micro ethno-republics never disappeared and they enjoyed relative autonomy as "independent states" as their larger quest for self-determination remained frozen in international law. By 2008 as sovereign democracy was no longer an academic moot among the Russian elite and concerned members of the civil society the thaw of the early 1990s regarding the self-determination of micro ethnic-republics such as Abkhazia and South Ossetia flared up and pitted Russia against Georgia in a five-day conflict in the summer of 2008. Russia subsequently recognized the independence of South Ossetia and Abkhazia while the rest of the international community still views them as part of Georgia. For Russia, if Kosovo and East Timor, aided and abetted by the international community can unilaterally declare independence from sovereign states, then South Ossetia and Abkhazia, with the help of Russia (and the use of force)[80] can also become independent states.

For Russia, South Ossetians and Abkhazians were facing Georgian "oppression"[81] and that was good enough cause to support their quest for independence. However, Russia had armed forces stationed in South Ossetia (and other breakaway republics in the region) that were part of various agreements reached in the early 1990s during major conflicts in the region. But Russia claimed that in 2008 its forces in South Ossetia came under attack from Georgian forces. As a result its response amounted to self-defense and therefore was not violating article 51 of the UN Charter. The situation regarding Georgia was different, however, and could not be equated to self-defense, given that Abkhazia had Russian "peacekeeping" forces and Georgia sustained continued aerial bombardment from Russian forces.

80 In a strict legal sense, because Russia invaded the territory of Georgia, by all accounts, such use of force in international law was illegal, given that the UN Charter (art. 2(4)) prohibits the use of force. However, art. 51 of the UN Charter permits the use of force for self-defense and with the consent of the Security Council (chapter VII).

81 In fact, this argument was used a year later by Russia before the ICJ during submissions of the Kosovo case that self-determination is legal "only in extreme circumstances, when the people concerned is continuously subjected to most severe forms of oppression that endangers the very existence of the people." Russia's written statement (April 16, 2009) 39–40.

But, the thinking was that, when Russia took five days to oust Georgian troops from the break-away Georgian provinces of South Ossetia and Abkhazia in the summer of 2008, Russia was using the doctrine of preemptive strike as developed in the Iraq War to justify its self-defense in the region. The implication of that action saw a resurgent Russia where it reasserted itself in the international arena as a state that was exercising its sovereign statehood. For the first time since the collapse of the Soviet Union, Russia was directly taking part in an armed conflict with another sovereign state. This was in spite of and at the expense of a state in Russia's orbit of influence: the near abroad. Although Russia had supported the economic and cultural identity of the Abkhazia, South Ossetia, and other former Soviet regions that were part of a Soviet republic such as Nagorno-Karabakh in Armenia, Russia stayed away from any direct military intervention in those states, until 2008.

Russia's intervention in the conflict was, in part, because, as part of the discourse on sovereign democracy in Russia, the country should also be seen as militarily strong and to be able to reassert great power status. Although the buildup to the conflict was initially seen as insignificant in the hegemonic order of the day, the impact it had on international law would amount to a farce in the ICJ as Georgia would later complain that Russia violated an international agreement on racial discrimination during the armed conflict. Moreover, the Georgian conflict of 2008, again similar to how domestic opposition to the Iraq War in Russia, was a people's revolution that the Kremlin exploited to pursue sovereign democracy as an ideology, the Georgian conflict also was a gift to the Kremlin, without Russia making the first move. Russia, by 2008, was wary of American hegemonic ambitions in the South Caucasus, and also the fact that the United States was never receptive to Russia's proposal for an alliance to combat international terrorism.

One of the proclamations for the intervention in Georgia that Russia invoked was to protect "the lives and dignity" of Russians regardless of their place of abode.[82] That argument, and by also justifying Russia's intervention in the Georgian conflict as part of "privileged interest," Russia was able to project onto the world an international version of sovereign democracy. The debate on sovereign democracy during Putin's first presidency had also been largely cloaked in Russian ethno-nationalism. However, it would have been difficult to disturb the entity of the Russian Federation by singling out a particular ethnic group. Moreover, given that various colored revolutions had swept into places such as Ukraine and Georgia, sovereign democracy as a form of Russian ethno-nationalism was also meant to stop colored revolutions in their tracks in Russia. The chaos, from the Russians point of the view – in the new hegemonic world order, where the new Russia was helpless during the bombing of Belgrade in 1999 and various colored revolutions in the former Soviet republics – illustrated the need for Russia to reclaim its once great power status.

82 Vladimir Putin, speech, Valdai Club, September 12, 2008.

Thus, it was no surprise that at the Munich Security Conference in 2007, one of Putin's last acts during the second term of the first presidency, he told those in attendance that in light of the failure of the unipolar world, a world dominated by a single central authority can destroy itself from within.[83] Although Putin was speaking in the context of American hegemony, his comments were also closely tied to the general debate on sovereign democracy or vertical power that was taking place in Russia, leading up to his speech in Munich. Sovereign democracy in the domestic context had already gained the support of the Russian population due to the fact that the high price of oil was injecting foreign currency in the Russian economy and ordinary Russians saw a marked improvement in their lives during the first term of Putin's first presidency. But for sovereign democracy to make a mark externally it would require a strong sense of Russian ethno-nationalism and brute military force to correct mistakes in the international order. Thus, for Russia, an intervention in the frozen conflicts of the South Caucasus was to reestablish Russia's hegemony in the near abroad,[84] and to demonstrate the notion that sovereign democracy was ideologically driven as a geographic containment of western expansion.[85]

South Ossetia, *de jure*, part of Georgia, has proclaimed, de facto, independence since December 21, 1991 and a brief war (1991–1992) ended with the signing of the Sochi Agreement in 1992.[86] In a similar vein, after a brief war with Georgia, Abkhazia reached a similar truce with Georgia brokered by Russia.[87] Russia, for its part, supplied both self-proclaimed states with Russian passports, largely in part, as successor to the USSR, to fulfil pension and other social obligations. As, de facto independent states, arguably, they enjoy a right to self-defense in international law. Although not a part of the UN system, and hence, the UN Charter, both states relied on the argument that collective self-defense is exempted from the use-of-force principle in international law.[88] Russia, in part, relied on this argument, that according to article 51 of the UN Charter, members may engage in a form of collective self-defense to justify participation in the Georgian conflict. Although that argument never convinced the judges of the ICJ in the case of the US intervention in Panama,[89] a reliance on such an argument would also meet severe opposition at the ICJ in *Russia* v. *Georgia*. [90] At the ICJ, Judge Trinidade, in a

83 Vladimir Putin, prepared remarks at the 43rd Munich Conference on Security Policy (February 12, 2007).

84 See also Emmanuel Karagiannis, 'The 2008 Russian–Georgian War via the Lens of Offensive Realism' (2013) 22 *European Security* 74–93.

85 e.g. Thornike Gordadze, 'Georgian–Russia Relations in the 1990s' in Svante Cornell and Frederick Starr (eds), *The Guns of August 2008* (ME Sharpe, 2009) 46.

86 The Agreement on Principles of Settlement on the Georgian–Ossetian Conflict (Sochi Agreement, June 24, 1992).

87 Agreement on a Ceasefire and Separation of Forces, May 14, 1994.

88 Art. 51, UN Charter. The Charter also forms part of customary international law.

89 *Case Concerning Military and Paramilitary Activities in and Against Nicaragua (Nicaragua* v. *US) (Merits)*, Judgment, ICJ Reports 1986, 14.

90 But see, Natalia Lucak, 'Georgia v. Russian Federation: A Question of the Jurisdiction of the International Court of Justice' (2012) 27 *Maryland Journal of International Law* 323–54.

dissent, managed to make a connection of what really took place in Georgia: an armed conflict in international law.[91]

In the Georgian conflict, Russia reasserted itself into the international community of great powers, and effectively used two weapons for such accomplishments. The first was transforming the nature of sovereign democracy into the language of privileged interests and then deployed that language for part of its legal justification for the intervention in the South Caucasus. The second weapon was the nature and state of international law itself. Russia had seen how international law responds to the hegemony of military might in Iraq and would use the Georgian conflict as a laboratory for its own alignment of international law to hegemonic military might. In this context, international law provided Russia with a form of offensive realism that could not be achieved by diplomacy and also the opportunity to take advantage of the chaotic nature of international law during the bombing of Belgrade in 1999 and the Iraqi War of 2003. Yet, one unmistakable outcome of the Georgian conflict was that Russia, as a historic guarantor of the security of the nations and people in the South Caucasus, has actually brought peace to the region and remains only one of few countries that recognizes the states that were at the center of the conflict.[92]

## 5 Conclusion

The rise of sovereign democracy in Russia in the FPP was a natural inclination on the leadership of the Russian *narod* to portray Russia as the *other* – a beacon of conservatism, laboratory for ideologies, and great power status. Although a number of scholars have assessed the ideology of sovereign democracy in negative terms as part of the backwardness of Russia, those assessments lacked contextual rigidity based on normative developments in the nature of Russian civilizational discourse. Naturally, like most major ideological discourses there are certain loopholes that warrant fair criticism. But, having said that, my only problem with how the discourse on sovereign democracy developed in Russia was its lack of plurality. Russia is a diverse entity with various ethnicities and peoples, and, during the great debate on sovereign democracy, it was purely one sided – a discourse among *Russians for Russians*. That great divide in the discourse was perhaps one reason for sovereign democracy's failure to appeal beyond the European *metropols* of Russia. Thus sovereign democracy became the credo of *Russianness*, that is, the umbrella under which a single political, religious, and normative take on the external legal system is construed with a Russian identity for the purposes of a new dominion of legal norms beyond the worn-out Westphalian system. Yet, as this chapter demonstrated, the ideology of sovereign democracy did not enjoy continuity, at least in the general discourse; rather, it was abruptly abandoned.

91 *Georgia* v. *Russian Federation* (n. 1), Dissenting Opinion of Judge Trinidade, paras. 146, 147, 150, 158, 160.

92 See also, Susanna Badsasaryan and Svetlana Petrova, 'The Republic of Abkhazia as an Unrecognised State' (2017) 5 *Russian Law Journal* 98–118.

Sovereign democracy was abandoned in part due to the temporary changing of the guard in the Kremlin, where Dmitri Medvedev, stood as president from 2008 to 2012. During that time, there were purges of ideologues and other powerful forces took hold. However, upon Putin's resumption of the presidency in 2012 sovereign democracy returned in a guise. Because of the limited success in getting laws passed during Putin's second term in the first presidency, the situation changed in 2012, when laws were crafted under the protectorate of the ideology of sovereign democracy began to emerge including those on banning foreign NGOs. Nevertheless, Russia's experiment with the ideology of sovereign democracy was part of a carefully orchestrated effort to use the political process and legitimize constitutional amendment and secure the return of Putin to Kremlin with an extended presidential term in 2012. At the same time, the ideology of sovereign democracy was also in part to carve out Russia's own alternative to western liberal democracy and passage to a return of great power status with a unique identity[93] in the post-Soviet world. As an ideology, sovereign democracy was an elitist project without *narodniki* mobilization and was meant to be a cohesive consciousness to legitimize the legal structures of power that Putin created. The ultimate goal was to distinguish Russia from the West with a unique identity in modernism of the future. The advent of sovereign democracy in Russia was designed to ensure that enhanced ruling by the Kremlin achieved the desired legal changes in the domestic constitutional setting. Furthermore, sovereign democracy was effective in bolstering strategic changes in the Russian political system as a form of rhetoric for elusive aims of civil governance. The ultimate side effect of sovereign democracy through the centralization of power in Kremlin was the decimation of the very democratic process that began in the Yeltsin Constitution and the premise of Russian federalism.[94] Yet, it was through the rhetoric of "sovereign democracy" that Russia was able to restore itself as a great power in the world order.

93 On a similar point, see Andrey Makarychev, 'Russia's Search for International Identity Through the Sovereign Democracy Concept' (2008) 43 *International Spectator* 49; Andrei Medushevsky, 'Law and Justice in Post-Soviet Russia: Strategies of Constitutional Modernization' (2012) 3 *Journal of Eurasian Studies* 116–25; Alfred Evans, 'Putin's Legacy and Russia's Identity' (2008) 60 *Europe–Asia Studies* 899; and, generally, Iver Neumann, *Russia and the Idea of Europe: A Study of Identity and International Relations* (2nd edn, Routledge, 2017).

94 See also Ross (n. 61).

Part III

# Ethical Borders and Transplantation of Law and Morals

# 6 Russia and the Council of Europe

## An Incompatible Ideology, and a Transplanted Legal Regime?

*Bill Bowring*

## 1 Introduction

Russia's accession to the Council of Europe (CoE) in 1996 and ratification of the European Convention on Human Rights (ECHR) in 1998 saw the beginning not only of a wholly new Russian discourse on international law, but also of an unprecedented immersion in it. It is no exaggeration to say that in the almost 20 years since ratification of the ECHR, Russian law and practice have become saturated with the principles and case law emanating from Strasbourg. This remains the case whether or not Russia now "crashes out" of the COE as a result of sanctions suspending Russia's participation in the Parliamentary Assembly of the CoE following the annexation of Crimea in 2014;[1] and despite the Constitutional Court of the Russian Federation (CCRF) finding in two recent cases[2] that it was "impossible" for Russia to comply with judgments of the European Court of Human Rights (ECtHR).[3] Whereas the USSR had ratified and engaged with United Nations human rights instruments, notably the key UN human rights covenants and conventions,[4] these never impinged on the USSR's sovereignty or

1 'Russia May Crash Out of Council of Europe, Says Rights Chief' *Politico*, April 9, 2017. www.politico.eu/article/russia-may-crash-out-of-council-of-europe-says-rights-chief (accessed December 26, 2017).

2 No. 12-П/2016, April 19, 2016; No. 1-П/2017 January 19, 2017, and see https://rg.ru/2017/01/19/reg-szfo/konstitucionnyj-sud-rf-vynes-reshenie-po-delu-iukosa.html (accessed December 26, 2017).

3 *Anchugov and Gladkov* v. *Russia*, on prisoners' voting rights, Applications Nos 11157/04 and 15162/05, judgment of July 14, 2013; *OAO Neftyanaya Kompaniya Yukos* v. *Russia*, Application No. 14902/04, judgment (just satisfaction) of July 31, 2014.

4 Convention on the Prevention and Punishment of the Crime of Genocide, ratified by the USSR May 3, 1954; CERD – International Convention on the Elimination of All Forms of Racial Discrimination, ratified February 4, 1969; CCPR – International Covenant on Civil and Political Rights, ratified October 16, 1973; CESCR – International Covenant on Economic, Social and Cultural Rights, ratified October 16, 1973; CEDAW – Convention on the Elimination of All Forms of Discrimination against Women, ratified January 23, 1981; CAT – Convention against Torture and Other Cruel Inhuman or Degrading Treatment or Punishment, ratified March 3, 1987; CRC – Convention on the Rights of the Child, ratified August 16, 1990. See

the inviolable principle of non-interference in internal affairs, until, following a ruling of the USSR's Committee for Constitutional Supervision, on October 1, 1991, shortly before its demise just over a month later, the USSR accepted three individual complaints procedures.[5]

Relations between Russia and the CoE are now fraught as never before.[6] It is my contention that whatever happens – and Russia is as always entirely unpredictable – this intense 20-year experience will leave its indelible mark on Russia and its discourses on international law.

Furthermore, I seek to show that ratification of the ECHR was never a question of transplantation, but of restoration of the "great legal reforms" of the nineteenth century.[7]

In this chapter my strategy is that I start with the uncontestable empirical facts of the range of Russia's commitments to and engagement to the CoE.

Second, I present and comment on Russia's public statements as to its own perception of the significance of the CoE and its accession in 1996. These must of course be taken together with the deep engagement of the Russian judicial system with Strasbourg: the two resolutions of the Supreme Court of the Russian Federation giving guidance to the Courts of General Jurisdiction, first the Resolution of October 10, 2003 "On application by courts of general jurisdiction of the commonly recognized principles and norms of the international law and the international treaties of the Russian Federation,"[8] and second the Resolution of June 27, 2013 "On application of the European Convention on Human Rights by the courts of general jurisdiction."[9] Russia, according to a number of official pronouncements, has every intention of remaining in the CoE, for good reasons.

http://tbinternet.ohchr.org/_layouts/TreatyBodyExternal/Treaty.aspx?CountryID=144&Lang=EN (accessed December 26, 2017).

5 CAT, art. 22 – Individual complaints procedure under the Convention against Torture; CCPR-OP1 – Optional Protocol to the International Covenant on Civil and Political Rights; CERD, art. 14 – Individual complaints procedure under the International Convention on the Elimination of All Forms of Racial Discrimination. http://tbinternet.ohchr.org/_layouts/TreatyBodyExternal/Treaty.aspx?CountryID=144&Lang=EN (accessed December 26, 2017).

6 See Bill Bowring, 'Russian Cases in the ECtHR and the Question of Implementation' in Lauri Mälksoo and Wolfgang Benedek (eds), *Russia and the European Court of Human Rights: The Strasbourg Effect* (CUP, 2017) 188–221.

7 See Bill Bowring 'The Problem of "Legal Transplantation" and Human Rights' in *The Degradation of the International Legal Order? The Rehabilitation of Law and the Possibility of Politics* (Routledge, 2008) 183–206.

8 Ruling of the Plenary session of the Supreme Court of the Russian Federation No. 5 'On Application by Courts of General Jurisdiction of the Commonly Recognized Principles and Norms of the International Law and the International Treaties of the Russian Federation' October 10, 2003 at www.supcourt.ru/catalog.php?c1=English&c2=Documents&c3=&id=6801 (accessed December 30, 2017).

9 Ruling of the Plenary session of the Supreme Court of the Russian Federation No. 21 'On Application of the Convention for the Protection of Human Rights and Fundamental Freedoms of 4 November 1950 and Protocols thereto by the Courts of General Jurisdiction' June 27, 2013. Available in English at www.supcourt.ru/catalog.php?c1=English&c2=Documents&c3=&id=9155 (accessed December 30, 2017).

Third, I return to the CoE and its post-World War II history. What is its ideology? Does it have one? Is it based on a view of "morals"? I show that two leading contemporary scholars, a political scientist and a historian, have demonstrated, in a number of widely cited works, very different although convergent accounts of the origin and provenance of the CoE and ECtHR. My title has a question mark, for good reason. If there is doubt as to whether the CoE has a distinct and unmistakable ideology, is Russia any less ambiguous? It is perfectly proper to ask the question – what is Russia's ideology? Indeed, Russian journals and mass media are full of scholarly and journalistic articles asking just these questions. My fourth section engages with the vexed question of legal transplants.

I conclude by insisting that Russia from its origins in the expanding Moscow of the sixteenth century has been an integral part of the European political and legal orders, influencing and influenced by all the diverse currents of thought and action. And if Russia now seeks to see itself as essentially Eurasian, then the western European states, with, almost all of them, their histories of global colonial predation, have still to come to terms with their significance and legacy.[10]

## 2 Russia's Engagement with the CoE

Russia's most controversial and high-profile engagement with the CoE is, as indicated above, its ratification of the ECHR and frequent appearance as a defendant in the ECtHR. However, Russia is deeply embedded in a wide range of CoE activities. In a chapter concerning ideology, it is perhaps best to start with hard empirical facts.

At the ceremony held in Strasbourg on February 28, 1996, to mark Russia's entry into the CoE, the Russian Foreign Minister, Yevgeniy Primakov, handed over the documents affirming Russia's adherence to the Council's Charter.[11] He also signed the European Convention on Human Rights, the European Convention Against Torture, the European Charter on Local Self-Government, and the Framework Convention on Protection of National Minorities. I return to all of these below.

He did this pursuant to the obligations placed upon Russia in Parliamentary Assembly Opinion 193 (1996) of January 25, 1996,[12] confirmed in Committee of Ministers Resolution No. 96/2.[13] Paragraph 7 of the PACE Opinion set out 12

10 Bill Bowring 'Did the States Which Founded the UN Have Liberal or Illiberal Governments?' (2016) 15 *Baltic Yearbook of International Law* 31–44,

11 Bowring (n. 7) 175ff.

12 http://semantic-pace.net/tools/pdf.aspx?doc=aHR0cDovL2Fzc2VtYmx5LmNvZS5pbnQvbncveG1sL1hSZWYvWDJILURXLWV4dHIuYXNwP2ZpbGVpZD0xMzkzMiZsYW5nPUVO&xsl=aHR0cDovL3NlbWFudGljcGFjZS5uZXQvWHNsdC9QZGYvWFJlZi1XRC1BVC1YTUwyUERGLnhzbA==&xsltparams=ZmlsZWlkPTEzOTMy (accessed December 29, 2017).

13 https://search.coe.int/cm/Pages/result_details.aspx?ObjectId=090000168062c4fa (accessed December 29, 2017).

respects in which Russia was already seeking to conform with the fundamental principles of the CoE, more precisely, as set out in Article 3 of the CoE Charter:

> Every Member of the Council of Europe must accept the principles of the rule of law and the enjoyment by all persons within its jurisdiction of human rights and fundamental freedoms, and collaborate sincerely and effectively in the realisation of the aim of the Council.

Under paragraph 10 of its Opinion, the Parliamentary Assembly noted that "the Russian Federation shares fully its understanding and interpretation of the commitments entered into as spelt out in paragraph 7, and intends" followed by a detailed list of 25 commitments.[14]

14 10.1. to sign the European Convention on Human Rights at the moment of accession; to ratify the Convention and Protocols Nos 1, 2, 4, 7 and 11 within a year; to recognise, pending the entry into force; of Protocol No. 11, the right of individual application to the European Commission and the compulsory jurisdiction of the European Court (Articles 25 and 46 of the Convention); 10.2. to sign within one year and ratify within three years from the time of accession Protocol No. 6 to the European Convention on Human Rights on the abolition of the death penalty in time of peace, and to put into place a moratorium on executions with effect from the day of accession; 10.3. to sign and ratify within a year from the time of accession the European Convention for the Prevention of Torture and Inhuman or Degrading Treatment or Punishment; 10.4. to sign and ratify within a year from the time of accession the European Framework Convention for the Protection of National Minorities; to conduct its policy towards minorities on the principles set forth in Assembly Recommendation 1201 (1993), and to incorporate these principles into the legal and administrative system and practice of the country; Opinion 193 (1996): 10.5. to sign and ratify within a year from the time of accession the European Charter of Local Self-Government and the European Charter for Regional or Minority Languages; to study, with a view to ratification, the Council of Europe's Social Charter; and meanwhile to conduct its policy in accordance with the principles of these conventions; 10.6. to sign and ratify and meanwhile to apply the basic principles of other Council of Europe conventions – notably those on extradition; on mutual assistance in criminal matters; on the transfer of sentenced persons; and on the laundering, search, seizure and confiscation of the proceeds of crime; 10.7. to settle international as well as internal disputes by peaceful means (an obligation incumbent upon all member states of the Council of Europe), rejecting resolutely any forms of threats of force against its neighbours; 10.8. to settle outstanding international border disputes according to the principles of international law, abiding by the existing international treaties; 10.9. to ratify, within six months from the time of accession, the agreement of 21 October 1994 between the Russian and Moldovan Governments, and to continue the withdrawal of the 14th Army and its equipment from the territory of Moldova within a time-limit of three years from the date of signature of the agreement; 10.10. to fulfil its obligations under the Treaty on Conventional Armed Forces in Europe (CFE); 10.11. to denounce as wrong the concept of two different categories of foreign countries, whereby some are treated as a zone of special influence called the "near abroad;" 10.12. to negotiate claims for the return of cultural property to other European countries on an ad hoc basis that differentiates between types of property (archives, works of art, buildings, etc.) and of ownership (public, private or institutional); 10.13. to return without delay the property of religious institutions; 10.14. to

In paragraph 11, these are further described as "commitments and understandings" – certainly not as "recommendations."

In my view, the main reason the communist and nationalist majority in the State Duma voted in favor of accession to the CoE and ratification of the ECHR, was the fact that following the collapse of the USSR some 25 million ethnic Russians and Russian speakers were living outside the borders of the Russian Federation, and the CoE was seen as offering a comprehensive framework of opportunities for their protection.[15]

Of the more than 200 treaties promulgated by the CoE, Russia has, as of December 27, 2017, signed and ratified 63 treaties, has signed but not ratified 16, and has not signed 130. One of the treaties signed but not ratified is the European Charter for Regional or Minority Languages, the 'Languages Charter,' which it signed on May 10, 2001. I was an expert for the Council of Europe and European Union Joint Programme designed to assist ratification by Russia. The project failed – this was not my fault.

settle rapidly all issues related to the return of property claimed by Council of Europe member states, in particular the archives transferred to Moscow in 1945; 10.15. to cease to restrict – with immediate effect – international travel of persons aware of state secrets, with the exception of those restrictions which are generally accepted in Council of Europe member states, and to facilitate the consultation of archives kept in the Russian Federation; 10.16. to ensure that the application of the CIS Convention on Human Rights does not in any way interfere with the procedure and guarantees of the European Convention on Human Rights; 10.17. to revise the law on federal security services in order to bring it into line with Council of Europe principles and standards within one year from the time of accession: in particular, the right of the Federal Security Service (FSB) to possess and run pre-trial detention centres should be withdrawn; 10.18. to adopt a law on alternative military service, as foreseen in Article 59 of the constitution; 10.19. to reduce, if not eliminate, incidents of ill-treatment and deaths in the armed forces outside military conflicts; 10.20. to pursue legal reform with a view to bringing all legislation in line with Council of Europe principles and standards: in particular, Presidential Decree No. 1226 should be revised without delay; 10.21. to extend its international co-operation to prevent – and eliminate the ecological effects of - natural and technological disasters; 10.22. to sign and ratify within a year from the time of accession the General Agreement on Privileges and Immunities of the Council of Europe and its additional protocols; 10.23. to co-operate fully in the implementation of Assembly Order No. 508 (1995) on the honouring of obligations and commitments by member states of the Council of Europe, as well as in monitoring processes established by virtue of the Committee of Ministers' Declaration of 10 November 1994 (95th session); 10.24. to respect strictly the provisions of international humanitarian law, including in cases of armed conflict on its territory; 10.25. to co-operate in good faith with international humanitarian organisations and to enable them to carry on their activities on its territory in conformity with their mandates.

15 The author has represented ethnic Russian and Russian-speaking clients against Estonia and Latvia in several cases at the ECtHR, see for example the high-profile case concerning the 2007 "Bronze Soldier" disturbances in Tallin, *Korobov* v. *Estonia* (Application No. 10195/08, judgment of March 28, 2013). See https://news.postimees.ee/1184614/european-court-orders-estonia-to-pay-compensation-to-four-in-bronze-nights-case (accessed April 1, 2018). It can be said overall that Russia's accession to the CoE has indeed benefited Russians in the Baltics.

The CoE publishes a regularly updated overview of its action in Russia.[16] The highlights, which demonstrate the continuing intense relationship between Russia and the CoE, are considered in the following sections.

### (a) Prevention of Torture

The European Committee for the Prevention of Torture (CPT) visits places of detention (for juvenile or immigration detainees, police stations, psychiatric hospitals) in order to assess how persons deprived of their liberty are treated.[17] It gives no notice in advance, and CPT delegations, which include experienced prison managers, doctors, and psychiatrists, have the right to visit any place of detention, to be admitted, and to see anything they want to see and speak to any person they wish. The Russian member of the CPT, to 2019, is Olga Noyanova, Head of the International Relations Section, Office of the Human Rights Ombudsman of the Russian Federation.

Since ratification in 1998 the CPT has carried out 27 visits to Russia, 7 periodical and 20 ad hoc visits; 23 reports have been adopted, of which just three have been published (Russia has not accepted the automatic publication procedure). The CPT has made three public statements[18] on Russia, in 2001, 2003, and 2007. This is the CPT's "nuclear weapon." The CPT continues its regular visits. From November 30 to December 13, 2016 a CPT delegation carried out a periodic visit to Russia, to review the measures taken in response to recommendations made by the Committee after its previous visits. Particular attention was paid to the treatment and conditions of detention of persons in police custody and penitentiary establishments, including remand prisoners, juveniles, and prisoners serving life sentences. Further, the delegation examined the situation of patients held in civil and forensic psychiatric hospitals and of residents of social care homes. The delegation chose to visit a number of places of detention.[19]

16 www.coe.int/et/web/portal/russian-federation (accessed 27 December, 2017).

17 Although Russia has since 2013 – http://rm.coe.int/doc/0900001680697bd6 – not agreed to the publication of CPT reports, the CPT visits Russia regularly – www.coe.int/en/web/cpt/russian-federation

18 Under art. 10(2) of the European Convention for the Prevention of Torture and Inhuman or Degrading Treatment or Punishment, if a State Party:

> fails to co-operate or refuses to improve the situation in the light of the Committee's recommendations, the Committee may decide, after the Party has had an opportunity to make known its views, by a majority of two-thirds of its members to make a public statement on the matter.

19 Police establishments: Temporary detention facility (IVS) of the Internal Affairs Directorate of the South-Western Administrative District, Moscow; IVS at the Main Directorate of Internal Affairs of Krasnoyarsk region; IVS No. 5, Krasnoyarsk; IVS at the Main Directorate of Internal Affairs of Novosibirsk region; Penitentiary establishments: Pre-trial establishment (SIZO) No. 1 ("*Matrosskaya Tishina*"), Moscow; SIZO No. 2 ("*Butyrka*"), Moscow; SIZO No. 5, Moscow (unit for juveniles); SIZO No. 1, Krasnoyarsk (unit for juveniles); SIZO No. 1, Perm; Strict-Regime Colony No. 1, Solikamsk, Perm region; Colony No. 2

In addition, from November 28 to December 4, 2017 a CPT delegation carried out an ad hoc visit to the Chechen republic, its 12th, to review the treatment of persons deprived of their liberty by the police. Another objective of the visit was to examine the effectiveness of investigations into allegations of ill treatment of detained persons by law enforcement officials. The delegation visited a number of police establishments, a SIZO,[20] and the Republican Forensic Medical Bureau in Grozny.[21]

That is, the CPT organizes an intrusive and wide-ranging program of visits, putting the Russian penitentiary system under considerable pressure to comply and respond, which, by and large, it does.

### *(b) Fight against Racism*

The European Commission against Racism and Intolerance (ECRI) is an independent monitoring body which provides member states with concrete and practical advice on how to tackle problems of racism and intolerance in their country. Conclusions on the Russian Federation have been adopted on November 28, 1977, March 16, 2001, December 16, 2005, June 20, 2013, and March 17, 2016.[22] The last of these focused on issues in respect of which Russia had not implemented ECRI's recommendations. ECRI was especially concerned at the prohibition on grounds of "extremism" of the sacred texts of non-traditional religious groups such as those of Jehovah's Witnesses and certain Muslim groups. ECRI noted that the list of banned materials now exceeded 3,000 texts.

### *(c) Protection of Social Rights*

The European Social Charter guarantees social and economic human rights. It was adopted in 1961 and revised in 1996. The European Committee of Social Rights rules on the conformity of the situation in States with the European Social

(for life-sentenced prisoners), Solikamsk. In addition, the delegation went to SIZO No. 1 in Novosibirsk in order to interview persons who had recently been in police custody. Psychiatric hospitals: Krasnoyarsk regional psychoneurological dispensary No. 1; Federal specialized psychiatric hospital with intensive supervision, Novosibirsk; Psychiatric hospital No. 3, Novosibirsk; Social care homes: Shilinka psychoneurological boarding home, Krasnoyarsk region; Ob psychoneurological boarding home, Novosibirsk region. www.coe.int/en/web/cpt/-/council-of-europe-anti-torture-committee-visits-the-russian-federation (accessed December 28, 2017).

20 "Investigative isolator," the Russian name for pre-trial detention prisons.

21 Temporary Detention Facility (IVS) of Argun City Internal Affairs Division; IVS of Police Division No. 1 in Grozny (Leninskiy district); Police Division No. 2 in Grozny (Zavodskoy district); Shali District Internal Affairs Division and its IVS; Mesker-Yurt Police Station, Shali District; Headquarters and barracks of Special-Purpose Patrol-Sentry Police Regiment named after A. Kadyrov, Grozny. The delegation also went to SIZO No. 1 in Grozny in order to interview persons who had recently been in police custody. www.coe.int/en/web/cpt/-/council-of-europe-anti-torture-committee-visits-the-chechen-republic-of-the-russian-federation (accessed December 29, 2017).

22 www.coe.int/t/dghl/monitoring/ecri/country-by-country/russia/russianfederation_cbc_EN.asp? (accessed December 27, 2017).

Charter, the 1988 Additional Protocol and the Revised European Social Charter. The Russian Federation signed the Revised European Social Charter on September 14, 2000 and ratified it on October 16, 2009, accepting 67 of the Revised Charter's 98 paragraphs.[23] It has not yet accepted the Additional Protocol providing for a system of Collective Complaints – only 15 of the COE's 47 member states have done so. Since 2011 Russia has submitted six reports on the application of the Revised Charter. The sixth report, which was submitted on January 16, 2017, concerned the accepted provisions relating to Thematic Group 2 "Health, Social security and social protection," namely: Articles 3, 11, 12, 13, 14, 23, 30 of the Revised Charter. The Conclusions of the European Committee for Social Rights were published in January 2018. In some respects, Russia was found to be in compliance, but in respect of other articles, in the absence of necessary information the Committee was obliged to defer its conclusions.[24]

### *(d) Protection of Minorities*

The Framework Convention for the Protection of National Minorities (FCNM) provides for a monitoring system to evaluate how the treaty is implemented by State Parties. The Advisory Committee (AC) adopts recommendations to improve minority protection. In December 2016 Russia submitted its Fourth Periodical Report to the AC. A delegation of the AC visited Tyumen, Kazan, Krasnodar, and Moscow (group 1) and Murmansk and Moscow (group 2) from October 16 to 24, 2017 to evaluate progress.[25]

### *(e) Fight against Corruption*

The Group of States against Corruption (GRECO) monitors member states' compliance with the CoE anti-corruption standards with the objective to improve the capacity of its members to fight corruption. The Fourth Evaluation Round took place in 2016, but the report on Russia remains confidential. Materials of the Third Compliance Round for Russia, in 2011, have been published.[26] One of the five members elected to the GRECO Bureau for the fifth Evaluation Round starting in 2017 is Mr. Aslan Yusufov nominated by Russia,[27] with colleagues from Croatia, France, Czech Republic, Switzerland, Slovenia, and the UK.[28]

23 https://rm.coe.int/16805ac116 (accessed 27 December, 2017).
24 See www.coe.int/en/web/portal/-/european-committee-of-social-rights-annual-conclusions-for-2017 (accessed April 1, 2018).
25 www.coe.int/en/web/minorities/-/russian-federation-fourth-cycle-delegation-visit (accessed December 27, 2017).
26 www.coe.int/en/web/greco/evaluations/round-3 (accessed December 27, 2017).
27 Deputy Head of Department for Supervision over Compliance of the Anti-Corruption Legislation of the Prosecutor General's Office of the Russian Federation https://eng.genproc.gov.ru/smi/news/news-1146570/?print=1&ELEMENT_ID=1146570 (accessed December 27, 2017).
28 www.coe.int/en/web/greco/home (accessed December 27, 2017).

### *(f) Democracy through Law*

The European Commission for Democracy through Law – the Venice Commission – "plays a leading role in the adoption of constitutions that conform to the standards of Europe's constitutional heritage." The Venice Commission has adopted some 41 Opinions on proposed Russian legislation, the most recent of which was published on December 18, 2017.[29] The Russian members of the Commission are Ms. Taliya Khabrieva, Director, Institute for Legislation and Comparative Law, and the former Russian judge at the ECtHR, Anatoliy Kovler.[30]

There are several Russians in senior positions in the Secretariat of the CoE. Among them is Mikhail Borisovich Lobov, with whom I have been acquainted since 1996, who is now the Head of the Human Rights Policy and Cooperation Department in Directorate General I, Human Rights and Rule of Law. Another is Olga Sergeyevna Chernyshova, Head of Section in the Secretariat of the ECtHR. The continuing investment by the Russian government in reporting and representation at Strasbourg, involving a wide spectrum of government ministries and agencies cannot be underestimated. Nor can the focus this gives for civil society in Russia, which despite all obstacles put in its way continues a tireless monitoring of the activities of the authorities.

In an important article published in 2003,[31] the Canadian historian Pamela Jordan reviewed the experience of Russian membership for the previous seven years, including its willingness to pay compensation in respect of decisions of the ECtHR with which it profoundly disagreed, and to bring about certain required reforms, and concluded that:

> countries such as the Russian Federation appear to be motivated more to guard their existing interests in areas their governments have defined as national security concerns than to meet obligations and take part in social learning. Compliance tends to occur largely for instrumentalist reasons, and arguably the Council of Europe has been forced to adjust its expectations to justify keeping these members onboard.[32]

And in 2009 the political scientist and lawyer Alexei Trochev sought to assess the impact of ECtHR decisions on Russia.[33] He argued that the Russian judiciary may

29 www.venice.coe.int/webforms/documents/?country=26&year=all (accessed December 27, 2017).
30 www.venice.coe.int/WebForms/members/default.aspx?lang=EN (accessed December 27, 2017).
31 'Does Membership Have Its Privileges?: Entrance into the Council of Europe and Compliance with Human Rights Norms' (2003) 25(3) *Human Rights Quarterly* 660–88.
32 Ibid., 688.
33 Alexei Trochev, 'All Appeals Lead to Strasbourg? Unpacking the Impact of the European Court of Human Rights on Russia' (2009) 17(2) *Demokratizatsiya* 145–78; University of Wisconsin Legal Studies Research Paper No. 1082.

be the most Strasbourg-friendly branch of the Russian government.[34] His conclusion, based on detailed empirical research, was very much in line with my own impressions, but perhaps surprising for those who receive an unremittingly gloomy picture of Russia:

> the impact of the Strasbourg court's judgments on Russia is hard to exaggerate. Symbolically, it remains the most powerful court in the eyes of many Russians: week after week, the mass media informs them that the ECtHR routinely rules against the Russian government and that the government promptly pays out compensation awarded by this tribunal to all successful applicants. This remains true, although very few government officials are actually punished for committing the human rights violations, as identified by the Strasbourg tribunal. Moreover, the mere threat of litigation from the ECtHR forces government officials to take care of complainants, even if they do so half-heartedly, on a case-by-case basis, and only when following orders from the top. Responding to losses in Strasbourg, Russia has witnessed a flurry of legislative activity, as well as increased funding for the prison system and the judicial branch.[35]

I have shown in perhaps too much detail, but with references to a great deal more, that Russia is fully engaged in the structures and mechanisms of the CoE. That is, Russia is immersed in international law of a kind which does not permit mere window-dressing, but requires constant action and reaction. Russia's law and practice change significantly as a result, and in turn Russia participates in the development of international law.

## 3 Russia's View of the CoE; and the Impact on Russian Law and Practice of the Work of the ECtHR

The CoE rarely figures in President Putin's discourse except as an irritant, particularly with regard to Crimea and Donbas. And 2018 will see a number of controversial ECtHR judgments against Russia, particularly with regard to the 2008 war with Georgia – another CoE member, in the case of the NGOs designated as "foreign agents," and with respect to Russia's alleged complicity in the 2006 murder in London of Aleksandr Litvinenko, a case in which the author is a member of the team representing his widow.

On March 3, 2016 Sergei Lavrov, Russia's Foreign Minister published an article titled "Russia's Foreign Policy: Historical Background" in *Russia in Global Affairs.* [36] He started with an observation with which I entirely agree:

> History doesn't confirm the widespread belief that Russia has always camped in Europe's backyard and has been Europe's political outsider. I'd like to remind you that the adoption of Christianity in Russia in 988 – we marked

34 Ibid., 146.
35 Trochev (n. 33) 165
36 www.mid.ru/en/web/guest/foreign_policy/news/-/asset_publisher/cKNonkJE02Bw/content/id/2124391 (accessed 27 December, 2017).

> 1025 years of that event quite recently – boosted the development of state institutions, social relations and culture and eventually made Kievan Rus a full member of the European community. At that time, dynastic marriages were the best gauge of a country's role in the system of international relations. In the eleventh century, three daughters of Grand Prince Yaroslav the Wise became the queens of Norway and Denmark, Hungary and France. Yaroslav's sister married the Polish king and granddaughter the German emperor.

However, his account of subsequent history stresses the greatness of the Russian Empire and the disaster of the 1917 Revolution. For him the acme of Russian power was the reign of Catherine II, "when, as then Chancellor Alexander Bezborodko put it, 'Not a single cannon in Europe could be fired without our consent.'" Following 1991:

> Logically, we should have created a new foundation for European security by strengthening the military and political components of the Organisation for Security and Cooperation in Europe (OSCE) … Unfortunately, our Western partners chose differently. They opted to expand NATO eastward and to advance the geopolitical space they controlled closer to the Russian border. This is the essence of the systemic problems that have soured Russia's relations with the United States and the European Union.

He did not mention the CoE at all. Nor has he done so, except in passing, for several years.

In the context of the ongoing tension between Russia and the CoE, it is therefore instructive to consider the interview given by Russia's Permanent Representative (Ambassador) to the CoE, Ivan Soltanovsky, to the official daily *Rossiyskaya Gazeta*, published on September 14, 2017.[37] He started by emphasizing that:

> For over 20 years Russia, together with the UK, Germany, Italy, France and in recent years also Turkey, has been a member of the group of "principal contributors" to the budget of the Council of Europe which have shouldered the bulk of responsibility for the organisation's future … [we have] suspended the payment of the 2017 dues to the Council of Europe until the rights of the Russian Federal Assembly at PACE, which are stipulated by the Council of Europe's Charter, are fully restored.

He insisted that

> an information war with respect to Russia is underway in the West and our policy in the Council of Europe often becomes the subject of questionable

37 www.mid.ru/en/foreign_policy/news/-/asset_publisher/cKNonkJE02Bw/content/id/2864004

> political speculation … the West European members of the Council of Europe expected that after Russia's accession to the Council of Europe it would as if by magic fit into the Procrustean bed of Western political morality. As is only natural, this did not happen. Regrettably, the EU Expanding Europe concept has gained supporters in the West, which is about the European Union's domination and central role on the European continent. Against its will, the Strasbourg organisation has found itself on the sidelines.

He did not expand on his understanding of the "Procrustean bed," nor did he offer an opinion as to the nature of "Western political morality." I suspect that he had in mind the constant Russian assertion that the West is guilty of hypocrisy and "double standards" – a phrase which find its way into almost every official Russian statement concerning relations with the West. However, he insisted on Russia's continued commitment to the CoE, and I seek the reader's indulgence when I cite this passage from his long interview:

> I do not see any real alternative to the Council of Europe in Europe. Against the background of an emerging chronic crisis of other European institutions, the current political situation in Europe is giving the Council of Europe a chance to become a true centre of attraction for the entire continent. But for this, it should give up politicking, display the political will and, giving the Council of Europe a real "shake," set a course for cleansing the Strasbourg organisation of the backlog of double standards in all soft security areas.
>
> We have achieved the main goal of our joining the Council of Europe: we have benefited from the positive experience of other countries' development in many areas and also presented our vision of European development as well as our experience of ethnic relations to the community of nations that are represented in the Council of Europe. Over a period of the 20 years of our work at the council, Russia has joined over 60 legally binding conventions plus protocols of this organisation. We have amended our laws on corruption, for example, we have criminalised trading in influence and corrupt payment, as well as created mechanisms for interaction among the Council of Europe's counterterrorism agencies. There is no alternative to cooperation between Russia and Western countries, because we are geographic neighbours with a centuries-long shared history, even if some people refuse to remember this.

Here is another example of official Russian discourse concerning the CoE, also mixing regretful dissatisfaction with warm endorsement. The official web-site of the Embassy of the Russian Federation in London presents a fascinating overview of "Russia and the Council of Europe."[38] It starts:

> The Council of Europe has risen from the ashes of the World War II. Its activities in the humanitarian domain are aimed at ensuring security of every

38 https://rusemb.org.uk/rce (accessed December 28, 2017).

> European in its broader meaning. The better the guarantees of the social conditions of the human life are, the better the rights record is, the stronger the economy is, the more protected the individual is in society, the less reasons he or she has to resolve problems using force. In the conditions of the current crisis this is felt especially strongly ... the very concept of security has undergone qualitative transformation. The question is no longer about hostile States, against which old-style coalitions have to be created ... it is the unresolved problem of hard security, the relict agenda of the Cold War era, that hampers the effective development of such cooperation.

This is followed by fulsome praise for the CoE, followed by Russia's perception that the true objective of the suspension of the voting rights of Russia's delegation to PACE is the subordination of the CoE to the European Union and to NATO:

> The Council has proven its effectiveness not only in such critical areas as human rights, the rule of law, and the strengthening of democracy. It also contributes substantively to dealing with problems associated with new threats and challenges: terrorism, money laundering and corruption – these are all major issues to which the Council devotes heightened attention.
>
> The proposals to diminish the mandate and competence of our Organization are inadmissible, as well as the attempts to limit its independence, transform the Council of Europe into a subsidiary body of the other European structures. The Strasburg Organization must be the leading European lawmaker in the proper sense of the word.
>
> For this reason, Russia is especially keen on the accession of the EU to the ECHR and its representation on the ECtHR, as specified in Protocol 14 to the ECHR, and the Lisbon Treaty of the EU.
>
> We also favor the European Union's speedy accession to the European Convention on Human Rights, based on the recognition by the EU of the jurisdiction of the European Court of Human Rights on terms that are subject to ratification by all 47 member of the Council of Europe. We proceed from the fundamental importance of the fact that such an agreement would fully ensure the preservation of the supremacy of the European Convention on Human Rights for all of the Council of Europe area, and the central role of the European Court of Human Rights in relation to any breach of the Convention, no matter by whom: EU members or non members, the EU itself or its bodies and institutions.

Thus, a persistent and consistent message from Russia is that the CoE and ECtHR, of which Russia is a member, present the possibility of countering the inexorable expansion of the EU, of which it will never be a member.

Russia now has a new representative at the European Court of Human Rights, Mikhail Lvovich Galperin, relatively young to have been appointed, on May 19, 2017, to this position, and to the rank of Deputy Minister of Justice, closely following signing into law by President Putin, on May 5, 2017, of Russia's ratification of Protocol 15 to the ECHR.[39] Mr Galperin replaced Georgiy Matyushkin, who served for nine years. Mr Galperin was born in 1983, and graduated in law from St Petersburg State University, with an LLM in law from University of London (UCL and QMW) in 2010. His doctoral thesis was titled "Responsibility in contemporary civil procedure." He has acted as a judicial assistant in the USA, and worked for several years in the audit department of Ernst & Young.[40] He, like the Russian judge at Strasbourg, Dmitriy Dedov, is primarily a commercial lawyer.

In September 2017 Mr Galperin's boss, Alexandr Konovalov, the Minister of Justice of the Russian Federation, visited Strasbourg and met Guido Raimondi, President of the ECtHR, and Thorbjørn Jagland, Secretary General of the CoE. The press report of his visit referred to information he had given in February 2017: the ECtHR had become much more focused on paying attention to the problems of law enforcement in the Russian Federation. In 2016, the ECtHR received 5,500 complaints from Russia – 7 percent fewer than in 2015. However, the number of complaints communicated to Russia increased by 400 (up to 1,700), and the number of rulings in respect of Russia increased to 238 (in 2015–2016). As to the number of complaints submitted to the ECtHR per capita from the 47 countries of the CE, Russia is in 30th position. The annual number of complaints from Russia to the ECHR has reduced by more than half in five years (from 10–12,000 a year in 2011–2012), and the number of complaints pending against Russia in the ECtHR has dropped more than fourfold in four years – from 40,300 to 7,800 complaints.[41] Earlier, the Ministry of Justice sent to the Committee of Ministers of the CE reports on payments to applicants in the ECHR compensation for more than 424 million rubles.

Without doubt, the intended message is that Russia is no longer, if it ever was, an outlier in the CoE and ECHR system, but increasingly a normal European country.

It was in this vein that on December 20, 2017 Mr Galperin gave an exclusive interview to the legal web portal *legal.report*. [42] He started by insisting that

> Russia's participation in the ECtHR and the ECHR is a positive experience. Many important changes in our laws were the result of implementation of judgments of the ECtHR. For example, the well known case *Burdov v Russia* [the first "pilot judgment" against Russia] as to the execution of judicial decisions against the government. Also the protection of people in detention, and the improvement of their conditions of detention, and many other questions.

39 https://legal.report/article/02052017/putin-podpisal-zakon-o-novoj-roli-espch (accessed December 28, 2017).
40 www.hse.ru/staff/galper; and www.kommersant.ru/doc/3303129 (both accessed December 28, 2017).
41 http://tass.ru/obschestvo/4590814 (accessed December 28, 2017).
42 https://legal.report/article/20122017/syurprizy-espch-karmannye-arbitrazhi-i-novye-perspektivy-dlya-yuristov (accessed December 28, 2017).

> I repeat: our legal system for the last 20 years has developed largely under the influence of the ECtHR decisions. Without too much pathos I can say that participation in the ECtHR mechanism allows Russia not only to remain in the European legal field, but also to participate with some success in its formation and development.

This information has been substantiated by the CoE itself.[43] In 2016 PACE, assisted by the Human Rights Centre at the University of Essex, published a report on the impact of the ECHR in various countries.[44] The report identified a number of instances of positive impact.

- As a result of the pilot judgment in *Burdov* v. *Russia* in 2009 over non-enforcement of a domestic court judgment in favor of the applicant, Russia enacted a Federal Compensation Act, as well as a federal law to guarantee the effectiveness of the new remedy.
- In 2005 the Supreme Court of the Russian Federation followed up the CoM's 2004 Declaration and extended journalists' freedom of expression to criticism of public officials: public officials must accept that they will be subject to public scrutiny and criticism. In 2008 the Court closed a number of applications in view of this change.
- Following *Mikheyev* v. *Russia* (2006) and other similar judgments, on account of torture or inhuman and degrading treatment inflicted on persons held in police custody, and a lack of effective investigations into such acts, special investigation units were created within the Investigative Committee, tasked with investigating particularly complex crimes by police and other law enforcement bodies.
- There had been progress in the implementation of the Court's 2012 pilot judgment in *Ananyev and Others* v. *Russia* concerning inhuman and degrading conditions in Russian remand centers and the lack of an effective remedy. Russia presented and has been implementing an action plan as a result, monitored by the CoM.
- A number of measures have been taken to remedy numerous violations of the right to liberty, guaranteed by article 5 of the Convention, owing to unlawful and lengthy unreasoned (or poorly reasoned) detention on remand. Legislative changes were made between 2008 and 2011. Both the Constitutional Court and the Supreme Court have emphasized that a suspect or accused may

43 See Bill Bowring, 'Does Russia Have a Human Rights Future in the Council of Europe and OSCE?' in Doutje Lettinga and Lars van Troost (eds), *Shifting Power and Human Rights Diplomacy: Russia* (Amnesty International Netherlands, 2017), 53–63 at www.academia.edu/31979697/Shifting_Power_and_Human_Rights_Diplomacy_Russia?auto_accept_coauthor=true (accessed December 28, 2017).

44 PACE (Parliamentary Assembly of the Council of Europe) (2016) 'Impact of the European Convention on Human Rights in States Parties: Selected Examples' Council of Europe, January 8. Available at: www.assembly.coe.int/nw/xml/News/News-View-EN.asp?newsid=5968&lang=2&cat=5 (accessed December 28, 2017).

be detained only on the basis of a valid judicial decision. This was most recently monitored by the CoM in 2015.

## 4 Did the CoE Have Its Origins in "Western Morality"?

In this section I present and discuss the recent work of two leading scholars of the CoE and human rights, Andrew Moravcsik, a political scientist,[45] and Samuel Moyn, a historian.[46] It is curious that neither refers to the other – but their standpoints and analyses are markedly different if in the end convergent.

Starting in 1995, before Russia joined the CoE, Moravcsik asked the question "Under what conditions are effective international regimes for the promotion of human rights likely to emerge?"[47] He identified a mechanism of "shaming."[48] He noted the high level of compliance with judgments of the ECtHR,[49] and that only in the 1980s did the system begin to develop extensive constitutional case law. He put this delay down to the fact that ratification of the instrument and adherence to various of its specific provisions was voluntary.

Moravcsik returned to these questions in 1998.[50] Now the question was posed as follows: why would governments establish an arrangement that invades domestic sovereignty in this way? He distinguished between two main explanatory methods: the *realist* view which asserts that the most powerful democracies seek to externalize their values, coercing or enticing weaker and less democratic governments to accept human rights regimes, and the *ideational* view which argues that the most established democracies externalize their values, setting in motion a transnational process of diffusion and persuasion that socializes less democratic governments to accept such regimes. The ideational view was linked to liberalism and constructivism, and was characterized by a commitment to the transformative power of normative discourse and ideals.

45 Andrew Maitland Moravcsik (born 1957) is a professor of politics and director of the European Union Program at Princeton University. He is known for his research on European integration, international organizations, human rights,

46 Samuel Moyn (born 1972) is a professor of law and history at Yale University, which he joined in July 2017. Previously, he was a professor of history at Columbia University for 13 years and a professor of history and of law at Harvard University for three years. His research interests are in modern European intellectual history, with special interests in France and Germany, political and legal thought, historical and critical theory.

47 Andrew Moravcsik, 'Explaining International Human Rights Regimes: Liberal Theory and Western Europe' (1995) 1(2) *European Journal of International Relations* 157–89, 157.

48 Ibid., 168.

49 Ibid., 170–1.

50 Andrew Moravcsik, 'Explaining the Emergence of Human Rights Regimes: Liberal Democracy and Political Uncertainty in Postwar Europe' (1998) Working Paper Series 98-17, Weatherhead Center for International Affairs, Harvard University, at https://wcfia.harvard.edu/publications/explaining-emergence-human-rights-regimes-libera l-democracy-and-political (accessed December 28, 2017).

As against these, he proposed an *institutional liberal* view, and maintained that governments delegate for a self-interested reason, namely to combat future domestic political uncertainty. Therefore it was "not the most powerful or persuasive democracies, but weakly established democracies that favor enforceable (as opposed to merely rhetorical) human rights obligations, because such commitments help lock in democratic governance against non-democratic domestic opposition."[51] These theories were to be tested in respect of the ECHR. Looking closely at the diplomatic and other records, he concluded that "the strongest postwar advocates of binding human rights guarantees were recently re-established democracies, while more established democracies like Britain, Sweden, the Netherlands and Denmark uniformly sided with transitional regimes like Greece and Turkey in opposition to binding guarantees."

The timing of the negotiations in 1949 was, in his view, consistent with all three theories – realist, idealist, and liberal. "The first decade after World War II was one of emergent bipolar conflict, powerful democratic great powers, salient historical reminders of human rights violations, and the reestablishment of democratic governance."[52] He noted that:

> Austria, Belgium, France, Germany, Iceland, Ireland, and Italy supported creation of a Court of Human Rights and mandatory jurisdiction, while Denmark, Greece, Luxembourg, the Netherlands, Norway, Sweden, Turkey and the United Kingdom were opposed to anything except a court whose jurisdiction remained optional.[53]

Following analysis he argued that "There is almost no support for the realist or ideational view that the most democratic (or the most powerful) countries support human rights guarantees."[54] His conclusion was

> The most striking finding of this study – given the dominant role of altruistic motivations in nearly every scholarly treatment of human rights – is the near-total absence of evidence in favor of altruistic motivations or transnational socialization, once the analysis is properly controlled for sophisticated forms of self-interest.[55]

Moravcsik followed this analysis in an article published in 2000[56] (in which Russia was identified as a "transitional regime")[57] and in which he repeated that the origins of the ECHR lay in "self-interested efforts by newly established (or

51 Ibid., 1.
52 Ibid., 13.
53 Ibid.
54 Ibid., 15.
55 Ibid., 23.
56 Andrew Moravcsik, 'The Origins of Human Rights Regimes: Democratic Delegation in Postwar Europe' (2000) 55(2) *International Organization* 217–252.
57 Ibid., 229, n. 42.

reestablished) democracies to employ international commitments to consolidate democracy – 'locking in' the domestic political status quo against their non-democratic opponents."[58]

Moravcsik's articles on this topic have been widely cited, but perhaps best summed up by Mikael Rask Madsen in 2011:

> The original Convention had mainly sought to ensure liberal democracy in Europe. As argued by Andrew Moravcsik, the goal of the 1950 [ECHR] was predominantly to "lock in democratic governance against future opponents" and was by no means "a conversion to moral altruism" of the Member States.[59]

This was a "Cold war-inspired objective" – "the goal was hardly to alter substantially the protection of human rights in the Member States but collectively to guarantee against a return to totalitarianism in Western Europe."

Or as the late Ian Brownlie and Guy S. Goodwin-Gill put it in their introduction to the ECHR in their collection of human rights documents, referring to "the Council of Europe, an organisation created in 1949 as a sort of social and ideological counterpart to the military aspects of European cooperation represented in [NATO]. The Council of Europe was inspired partly by interest in the promotion of European unity and partly by the political desire for solidarity in the face of the ideology of Communism."[60]

Samuel Moyn caused a sensation in 2010 with his revisionist account of the history of human rights, as the "last utopia."[61] Perhaps his most provocative assertion was that "the drama of human rights is that they emerged in the 1970s, seemingly from nowhere."[62] He was able to give a more precise date: "The year of human rights, 1977, began with Carter's January 20 inauguration, which put 'human rights' in front of the viewing public for the first time in American history."[63] Furthermore, Moyn insisted that the 1789 Déclaration de Droits de l'Homme et du Citoyen was actually a political document about citizenship, and had nothing to do with the real human rights which emerged in the 1977. Turning to the CoE and the ECHR, Moyn referred to the "preeminent role Christianity could play in the postwar framing of human rights,"[64] and to the "sheer authenticity and passion with which Christian and conservative championship of 'human rights' took place."[65] He added that for many proponents of European

58 Ibid., 243–4.
59 Mikael Rask Madsen, 'The Protracted Institutionalisation of the Strasbourg Court: From Legal Diplomacy to Integrationist Jurisprudence' in Jonas Christoffersen and Mikael Rask Madsen (eds), *The European Court of Human Rights Between Law and Politics* (OUP, 2011), 43–60, 43–4.
60 *Brownlie's Documents on Human Rights* (6th edn, OUP, 2010) 679–80.
61 *The Last Utopia: Human Rights in History* (Harvard UP, 2010).
62 Ibid., 2.
63 Ibid., 155.
64 Ibid., 74.
65 Ibid., 75.

human rights "human rights, far from originating in 1789, were a Christian bequest to be defended against the legacy of the French Revolution – or even revolution as such – that still threatened."[66] He identified "political and civil rights, prioritized as the essence of Western European identity" and insisted that

> it would be a gross error to assume that the language of human rights, let alone the law of human rights mattered much in the beginning, The European Convention involved much more ideological signalling about the values on which Western European identity depended than it did legally enforceable guarantees.[67]

Moyn and Moravcsik, it seems to me, from their North American perspective, fail to note the striking fact that the ECHR follows the language of the 1789 Déclaration almost word for word, or the horror with which Edmund Burke, Jeremy Bentham, and A. V. Dicey in England identified the intellectual terrorism of the rights of man – a horror which persists to the present day in English reluctance to countenance the ECHR.[68] Dicey, writing at the end of the nineteenth century, reserved his sharpest criticism for the persistence of the 1789 Déclaration in the contemporary French and Belgian Constitutions.[69]

For sure, as Moyn asserts:

> From the beginning the energy in the movement to defend and define human rights as the essence of European civilisation in the European Convention came from conservatives – Churchill and his allies out or power, anxious about the spectre of socialism at home, and opposite numbers on the Continent worried about the impending triumph of materialism over spiritual values.[70]

This is to confirm the ideological, Cold War, content of the CoE and ECHR at their origin. But I contend that the revolutionary and scandalous – for common lawyers – content of the ECHR, with its roots in the 1789 Déclaration, has reemerged in the cases against the UK concerning Northern Ireland and Iraq, the Kurdish cases against Turkey, and the Chechen cases against Russia.[71]

Moyn has pursued his investigation of the Christian origins of human rights in the Mellon lectures he gave at the University of Pennsylvania, published in 2015 as *Christian Human Rights.* [72] His message is, as explained in his blog, that "my general thesis

66 Ibid., 76.

67 Ibid., 79.

68 See Bill Bowring, 'England's Terror of the French Revolution: The Historical Roots of Resistance to the Rights of Man and the Case Against the Human Rights Act' in Frederick Cowell (ed.), *Critically Examining the Case Against the 1998 Human Rights Act* (Routledge, 2017) 52–68.

69 See ibid. for full references.

70 Moyn (n. 61) 78–9.

71 I represented many Kurdish applicants against Turkey in the 1990s, and many Chechen applicants against Russia from 2000 onwards.

72 Samuel Moyn *Christian Human Rights* (University of Pennsylvania Press, 2015).

has been that through this lost and misremembered transwar era, it is best to see human rights as a project of the Christian right for the most part, not the secular left."[73]

In a long critical review article first published in the *Hedgehog Review* in 2016, Ronald Osborn referred to Moyn's thesis as "Conservatism by other means," and shows a number of Moyn's claims to be selective or even false.[74] In 2017 the *Kings Law Journal* published a symposium on Christian human rights. In his introduction,[75] Moyn made the claim that "The truth is that Europe and therefore the modern world drew nearly everything from Christianity in the long term."[76] This is, of course, as true of Russia, which took Orthodoxy from Byzantium, as it is of any European country. The problem is that throughout his recent interventions, when Moyn says "Christianity," he means Catholicism. His focus is Pope Pius XII, who was, very controversially, Pope from 1939 to 1958.

In his reply, Moyn states as follows:

> Something extraordinary has happened to the Christian faith of Western Europeans, for good or ill. Whether my commentators are coy, critical or celebratory about these developments, all agree that human rights have largely outlived their Christian phase – even if without the influence of Christianity at a specific juncture in its recent history, people might have had to find something else to believe in.[77]

My own conclusion is also that there is no monolithic western European morality or ideology against which some Russian discourse is to be counterposed. And most certainly not some western European "Christianity." Taking the broader view, and as, the evidence has shown, Russia has been and remain part of the discourse and ideology of "rights" and "laws," in continuing engagement with developments in Western European countries, whether based on "Christian values," or liberalism, or simply in terms of technical legal change.

## 5 Transplants?[78]

The theory of legal transplantation is a crucial domain within the theory of legal comparativism. The debate concerning "legal transplants" can be said to have begun in earnest in an exchange between Alan Watson and Otto Kahn-Freund in

73 https://tif.ssrc.org/2015/05/29/christian-human-rights-an-introduction (accessed December 29, 2017).

74 *Hedgehog Review* (2016) 18(1), at https://ronaldosborn.com/conservatism-by-other-means-samuel-moyns-christian-human-rights (accessed December 29, 2017).

75 Samuel Moyn, 'Introduction' (2017) 28(1) *King's Law Journal* 1–5. John Finnis, Lorenzo Zucca, and Thomas Pink provide trenchant critiques.

76 Ibid., 3.

77 Samuel Moyn, 'Tradition and Beyond: *Christian Human Rights* in Debate' 27–34, 34.

78 An extended exploration of these issues is to be found in Bowring (n. 7) 183–206.

the 1970s.[79] There is now an extensive and growing scholarly literature on legal transplants, especially as concerns the former Soviet Union and Eastern Europe. Most of it – with a few exceptions – concerns commercial law. Thus, Frédérique Dahan wrote:

> What is indisputable is that for the legal systems of Central and Eastern Europe, transplantation is a reality. Because transition economies cannot afford and do not wish to go through the same process of slow and tentative development as the developed economies did in the past in order to achieve their modern legal and regulatory structures, they must, to a large extent, import them.[80]

But importing a legal doctrine, mechanism, or even a statute is not the same as importing an automobile; and even the automobile may need adapting for left-hand driving. Scott Newton, commenting on Dahan's remark, points out that:

> the very term "transplantation," biased towards the technical, masks the political realities, for "legal transplantation" is always necessarily a species of the genus legislation. That is, even supposing a jurisdiction decides to import a foreign law lock, stock and barrel, it nonetheless must enact it, with all the sovereign political implications any enactment brings … in transplantation as in transition, the emphasis on product over process works to privilege legality over legitimacy.[81]

Most writers on transplantation, for the most part transplants in the commercial arena, do not share Newton's sensitivity to the issues.

No one can question the transformation of the Russian legal system since the mid 1980s – and especially since 1991, with accession to the CoE in 1996, and ratification of the ECHR in 1998. But it should be obvious that, especially in the spheres of constitutional and human rights, Russia has not been importing US models. Instead, it has, through its own choice, drawn closer once more to the western European mainstream.

The question is: what was there before? Was there a "legal culture" simply anathema to human rights? Was Russia simply the home of backwardness and despotism? Is it really the case that the Russians are condemned to catching up with the enlightened West from a position of legal barbarism? To answer these questions, the historical perspective is essential.

79 Otto Kahn-Freund, 'On Uses and Misuses of Comparative Law' (1974) 37 *Modern Law Review* 1; Alan Watson, 'Legal Transplants and Law Reform' (1976) 92 *Law Quarterly Review* 79–84; Alan Watson, *Legal Transplants: An Approach to Comparative Law* (2nd edn, University of Georgia Press, 1993).

80 'Law Reform in Central and Eastern Europe: The "Transplantation" of Secured Transactions Laws' (2000) 2(3) *European Journal of Law Reform* 369–84

81 'Transplantation and Transition: Legality and Legitimacy in the Kazakhstani Legislative Process' (2001) SOAS Working Paper 3.

I suggest just two examples.

Serfdom, *krepostnoye pravo*, was abolished in Russia in 1861. Slavery was finally abolished in the USA in 1866 – the American Anti-Slavery Society was founded in 1833.

Jury trial was introduced in a number of western European countries at about the same time as in Russia, 1864, though it had been strongly advocated by leading law reformers from the late eighteenth century. Jury trial was from 1993 available in nine of Russia's 85 regions, and since the enactment of the Criminal Procedural Code in 2000 has been extended to the rest of the country, including Chechnya.[82] This is not an innovation forced on Russia after defeat in the Cold War. It is the restoration of an effective system of jury trial for all serious criminal cases, presided over by independent judges, which existed in Russia from 1864 to 1917. Marina Nemytina, although pessimistic for the future of jury trial in today's Russia, insisted that in 1993:

> The first trials by jury were heralded as the reestablishment of the institution in Russia. Trial by jury was represented as not something borrowed from the West in the course of the democratic changes, but as a native legal tradition that was being revived.[83]

What is frequently neglected is any recognition of Russia's own prerevolutionary traditions, especially the reforms of Alexander II (1855–1881). Starting with the revolutionary Law on Emancipation of the Serfs in 1861, these reforms culminated in the laws of November 20, 1864.[84] The new laws introduced a truly adversarial criminal justice procedure, and made trial by jury obligatory in criminal proceedings. Judges were given the opportunity to establish real independence, in part by freeing them of the duty to gather evidence, and enabling them to act as a free umpire between the parties. The Prokuracy lost its powers of "general review of legality," and became a state prosecutor on the western model. The institution of Justices of the Peace was introduced. It is ironical that the Bolsheviks reinstated the pre-reform model of the Prokuracy.

Indeed, as Samuel Kucherov wrote in 1953: "Between 1864 and 1906, Russia offered the example of a state unique in political history, where the judicial power was based on democratic principles, whereas the legislature and executive powers remained completely autocratic."[85] A collection on jury trial in Russia contains an

82 See Gennady Esakov, 'The Russian Criminal Jury: Recent Developments, Practice, and Current Problems' (2012) 60(3) *American Journal of Comparative Law* 665–702; Stephen C. Thaman, 'Questions of Fact and Law in Russian Jury Trials: The Practice of the Cassational Courts under the Jury Laws of 1864 and 1993' (2001) 72 *Revue internationale de droit pénal* 415, 417–19.

83 'Trial by Jury: A Western or a Peculiarly Russian Model?' (2001) 72 *Revue internationale de droit pénal* 365 at www.cairn-int.info/article-E_RIDP_721_0365–trial-by-jury-a-western-or-a.htm (accessed December 29, 2017).

84 Chistyakov O. I. and Novitskaya T. E. (eds), *Reformi Aleksandr II* [Reforms of Aleksandr II] (Moscow, 1998).

85 Samuel Kucherov, *Courts, Lawyers and Trials under the Last Three Tsars* (Greenwood Press, 1975) 215.

extensive memoir by one of the most distinguished judges of the period, A. F. Koni.[86] Moreover, it also reproduces the advocates' speeches and judicial summings-up in some of the most famous trials, for example the trial in 1878 of Vera Zasulich, charged with the attempted murder of the governor of St Petersburg, Trepov, whom she had shot in broad daylight and before witnesses. Koni, who was presiding judge, refused to be pressured by the authorities, and Zasulich was acquitted, a verdict which was respected by the authorities.

It is noteworthy that in the major speeches made to legal audiences at the start of his presidency, Putin referred to just these issues. His speech of January 24, 2000[87] was delivered in his then capacity of Acting President to a colloquium of leaders of Republic, Krai, and Oblast courts. His main theme was the independence of the judiciary. He quoted Judge Koni, and referred to the necessity for correspondence with generally recognized norms of international law. Most important, he made explicit reference to the ratification by Russia of the European Convention on Human Rights and Fundamental Freedoms, which had therefore become a constituent part of the Russian legal system. Above all, he said, the jurisdiction of the ECtHR had been recognized. Therefore special attention must be given to those problems of the Russian judicial system that were likely to call forth a reaction from the European Court.

In order to understand these processes, we should look deeper still into Russian history and traditions. Gross errors by US and other western legal experts and commentators would be avoided by the realization that judicial independence, adversarial court proceedings, and trial by jury are not recent imports from the liberal West to the uncultured East, but the reinstatement of a rich and specifically Russian experience.

This history begins at a climactic time for the UK and for western Europe, and with a surprise for western scholars. A textbook on legal thought[88] points out that the first Russian professor of law, S. E. Desnitskiy (1740–1789), was a product not so much of the French Enlightenment, that is of Diderot and Rousseau, but of the Scottish Enlightenment.

Desnitskiy studied in Scotland, under Adam Smith and others, from 1761 to 1767, when he received a doctorate in civil and church law from the University of Glasgow. He was much influenced by the ideas of the Scottish Enlightenment, especially by the philosophy of David Hume, and especially by the Scottish emphasis on Roman law traditions and principles – the focus of Alan Watson's pathbreaking work on legal transplants.[89] On the basis of his lengthy researches in Scotland, in 1768 Desnitskiy sent the Empress Catherine II his "Remarks on the institutions of legislative, judicial and penitentiary powers in the Russian

86 S. Kazantsev, *Sud Prisyazhnikh* v. *Rossii: Gromkiye Ugolovniye Protsessi* [Trial by Jury in Russia: Great Criminal Trials] (Leniizdat, 1991).

87 http://kremlin.ru/events/president/transcripts/21536 (accessed December 29, 2017).

88 N. M. Azarkin, *Istoriya yuridicheskoi mysli Rossii: kurs lektsii* [History of Legal Thought in Russia: A Course of Lectures] (Moscow, 1999).

89 Watson, *Legal Transplants* (n. 80).

Empire" – however, his suggestions were entirely unacceptable, and the work was sent to the archives. Among other radical proposals, Desnitskii urged the abolition of serfdom. He survived Catherine's rejection of these ideas, and became a full professor of law in 1777, shortly after the Pugachev uprising. He published books introducing Russians to the ideas of Adam Smith and John Millar. At Catherine's own instruction, he translated into Russian volume I of *Blackstone's Commentaries*, and this was published in Moscow in 1780–83. His courses included the history of Russian law, Justinian's *Pandects*, and comparisons of Roman and Russian law.[90] He died in the year of the French Revolution, and the Declaration of the Rights of Man and of the Citizen.

It should be noted that Desnitskiy did not undertake a simple transmission of some already existing western liberalism to Russia. The period of his work was as much the period of the revolt of reason against autocracy in England as in Russia. Desnitskiy was born only a few years after Thomas Paine.[91]

V. S. Solovyev (1853–1900) was the next Russian to think deeply about issues of rights. He, like Radishchev, was not a lawyer, and his approach, while committed to enlightenment values, had a specifically religious focus to it. This spiritual, idealistic dimension to Russian rights discourse is characteristic and a specific and unique contribution. B. N. Chicherin (1828–1904) was the first lawyer to work through issues of liberalism in connection with law and rights. He argued for a constitutional monarchy and strong state, and strongly opposed Aleksandr Gertsen (Hertzen to us) – a writer who spent much of his life in exile in England. He did, however, draw on both Russian and European experience and traditions. Another lawyer, P. I. Novgorodtsev (1866–1924), was the chief exponent of a natural law, Kantian approach to questions of the relationship between the individual and law. He too was strongly influenced by the Russian spiritual heritage. One of the latest proponents of this trend was N. A. Berdyaev (1874–1948), a member of the *Vekhi* group, whose manifesto collection of articles appeared in 1909,[92] attracting the strongest criticism from Marxists and liberals alike.

For Berdyaev, inalienable human rights were the form of expression and existence on earth (Caesar's kingdom) of personal freedom, that is of the transcendental (and godlike) phenomena of the kingdom of Spirit. In his book *Gosudarstvo. Vlast i pravo. Iz istorii russkoi pravovoi mysli* ('The State. Power and Law. From the History of Russian Legal Thought'), Berdyaev wrote "The

90 William Butler, *Russian Law* (OUP, 1999) 24–5, 52–3; Archie Brown, 'The Father of Russian Jurisprudence: The Legal Thought of S. E. Desnitskii' in W. Butler (ed.), *Russian Law: Historical and Political Perspectives* (OUP, 1977) 117–42.

91 Paine left England for the American colonies in 1774, and began writing his extraordinarily influential *Common Sense* in 1775. Its publication in 1776 was a sensation, selling at least 100,000 copies in that year alone. Its content was entirely unacceptable to the English ruling elite. His *Rights of Man* appeared in 1791, and he was forced to leave England, remaining in France for ten years – he was imprisoned in 1793 after war broke out between England and France.

92 *Vekhi. Sbornik statei o russkoi intelligentsiya* [Landmarks: Articles on the Russian Intelligentsia] (paperback edn, St Petersburg 2011).

declaration of the rights of God and the declaration of human rights are one and the same declaration."

The point I wish to make by way of this brief survey is that there is a distinctively Russian approach to and thought about human rights which repays careful study by western scholars. These are thinkers of the first rank. Moreover, the account above is sufficient to show that while it is possible to speak of Russian culture, and even of Russian legal culture, it would be a grave mistake to ignore the complex and dynamic interplay of Russian and western European – especially Scottish! – histories and traditions.

## 6 Conclusion

I insist, as I have done in a number of publications,[93] that Russia's unexpected accession to the CoE, established as the CoE was as an ideological opponent of the USSR and its allies, and its ratification of the ECHR, did not at all represent the transplantation of alien concepts and mechanisms into hostile Russian soil, but rather a restoration of reforms adopted in the nineteenth century, as the result of the interaction between Russia and western Europe, especially Scotland, in the eighteenth century. It is in this context that the discourse of international law, more particularly human rights law, between Russia and the CoE since 1996 must be understood. Russia is as much a Christian, and increasingly a Muslim, country as any western European state, and has a rich history not only of legal and judicial reform but of intellectual contest concerning rights.

93 See in particular Bill Bowring, *Law, Rights and Ideology in Russia: Landmarks in the Destiny of a Great Power* (Routledge, 2013); Bill Bowring, 'Russian Cases in the ECtHR and the Question of Implementation' in Lauri Mälksoo and Wolfgang Benedek (eds), *Russia and the European Court of Human Rights: The Strasbourg Effect* (CUP, 2017) 188–221.

# 7 International Law and the Transnational Dimension of the Russian Orthodox Church

*Sebastian Rimestad*

## 1 Introduction: Culture, Religion, and International Law

In this contribution, I focus on the way the Russian Orthodox Church (ROC) posits itself as an actor of international law. This is particularly visible in relation to human rights law, but there are also other issues where the ROC attempts to or is called upon to become involved. The chapter is divided into four main parts. In this first part I discuss how religion and international law can and should interact. Then, a section provides the background, highlighting the transnational dimension of the ROC and its evolution. The third part focuses on human rights law, and the role the ROC envisages for itself within this discourse, before the final part covers other aspects of international law, and instances where the ROC is involved in legal disputes outside Russia.

Modern legal systems are generally conceived of as secular constructs, while religion should be confined to the private sphere of the individual. This is all the more applicable to international law, which is supposed to be universal and transcend religious or cultural differences. Religion is therefore often seen as incompatible with the concept of international law. Nevertheless, as Mashood Baderin explains, religion and international law do in fact interact, and they do so at four main levels. These levels are first, "in relation to the domestic laws of states where religion plays a formal role in national laws and policies."[1] This is not the case with Russia, since all religions are treated equally by the national laws of the officially secular Russian Federation, at least formally. Also the second level Baderin lists, pertaining to regional intergovernmental organizations, where religion may have a formal role to play, does not apply to the Russian case.

It is only at the third and fourth levels, which relate to individual religious beliefs and non-governmental religious organizations respectively, that the Russian case becomes interesting. International law not only operates on an interstate level, but impacts individuals and groups, who may act according to religious precepts and motivations. Therefore, international law cannot be considered a wholly secular domain, where religion does not figure. Important parts of

1 'Religion and International Law: Friends or Foes?' (2009) 5 *European Human Rights Law Review* 637–58, 652.

international law, especially the fields of human rights law, environmental law, or refugee law, touch upon spheres of societal life that for many people cannot be thought of without referring to religion.

That there is interaction between international law and religion does not yet say anything about the direction of this interaction. According to Baderin, "the relationship between religion and international law should be objectively perceived as double-edged – capable of being either amicable or adversarial, depending on what we, the human agents of the relationship, i.e. both religionists and secularists, want it to be."[2] Legal instruments in their own right are not *pro* or *contra* religion, just as much as religious arguments may both bolster and contest legal ones. It all depends on the strategic aim of the actors on both sides.

The most pertinent aspect of international law in relation to religion is the basic human right to freedom of conscience.[3] This right, which is enshrined in international human rights law,[4] guarantees the freedom of religion. These guarantees are not conceived of in terms of religious communities' rights, but rather the individual's right to profess his or her religious beliefs freely. Such a conception is the result of a long process of secularization, primarily in the areas of the world dominated by western Christian denominations. As a result, the societies outside the scope of western Christianity occasionally struggle to fully embrace the notion of individual human rights, seeing them as a form of western cultural colonialism. Such an approach is clearly visible in the case of the Arab world, which has adopted various alternative human rights charters since 1981.[5] A similar, yet less oppositionist stance is adopted by the ROC, which sees itself as a transnational actor with a moral compass of universal scope.

## 2 The ROC as a Transnational Actor

In order to assess the role of the ROC as a "transnational actor," we need to take two different aspects into account. One is the way the ROC can be construed as

2 Ibid., 657.

3 But see generally, Javaid Rehman and Susan Breau (eds), *Religion, Human Rights and International Law: A Critical Examination of Islamic State Practices* (Martinus Nijhoff, 2007); Malcolm Evans, *Religious Liberty and International Law in Europe* (CUP, 1997); Silvio Ferrari (ed.), *Routledge Handbook of Law and Religion* (Routledge, 2015); Martti Koskenniemi, Monica Garcia-Salmones Rovira, and Paolo Amorosa (eds), *International Law and Religion: Historical and Contemporary Perspectives* (OUP, 2017).

4 Such as art. 18 Universal Declaration of Human Rights, GA Res. 217A (III) UN Doc. A/810 (1948); art. 9 European Convention of Human Rights, 213 UNTS 221, entry into force September 3, 1953; 1981 UN Declaration on the Elimination of All Forms of Intolerance and of Discrimination Based on Religion or Belief, E/CN.4.RES/1981/15.

5 Ann Elizabeth Mayer, *Islam and Human Rights – Tradition and Politics* (3rd edn, Westview, 1999); Fuad Kandil, 'Verbreitete Haltungen und Einstellungen in arabisch-islamischen Gesellschaften zum aktuellen Menschenrechtsdiskurs' in Gerhard Höver (ed.), *Religion und Menschenrechte – Genese und Geltung* (Nomos, 2001).

an extension of the Russian government on issues of morality. Whereas church and state in western Europe are more or less fully independent from the political sphere, the relationship between the ROC and the Russian state is less clear-cut. This is the result of a very long historical process, culminating in the peculiar closeness between church and state in Russia that we can see today.

The second aspect is the emphasis of the ROC that, as a religious institution, it is per se transnational. God did not limit the proclamation of his gospel to a specific nation, and therefore, the ROC is responsible for all faithful, regardless of their place of residence. The close connection between the Russian nationality on the one hand and the Orthodox faith on the other has ensured that most of ROC faithful are ethnic Russians, living on the territory of the multi-ethnic Russian Federation. At the same time, there are millions of Russians living outside this territory all across the globe. The ROC sees it as it mission to cater morally and spiritually for these expat Russians and is even eager to institutionalize the transnational constituency.

Both of these aspects are highly complex and have a long historical background, which goes back to the eastern Roman (Byzantine) Empire. Christianity developed differently in the western Roman Empire than in the East. The western Empire had already crumbled by the fifth century AD, which facilitated the strict separation of the sacral/ecclesiastical and the secular/political spheres. The Augustinian theory of the two swords – differentiating strictly between papal and imperial authority – took hold in the West. The history of western Christianity can be viewed as a constant struggle over the boundary between the two types of authority. The high point of this struggle would be the Protestant Reformation, during which religious authority was clearly subordinated to worldly/political authority. The Roman Catholic Church tried to resist this subordination, but the Second Vatican Council in 1962–65 finally seemed to accomplish a similar transition also here.

In the Eastern Roman Empire, a unified political/imperial authority continued to exist until the Ottoman conquest of Constantinople (currently Istanbul) in 1453. As a result, religious and political authority never separated in the way it had done in the West. The head of the church (the Patriarch) and the Emperor both sat in the capital Constantinople and ruled the Empire together. Instead of the separation between their powers that developed in the West, the theory of a *symphonia of powers* developed. According to this theory, the Emperor and the Patriarch harmoniously exercised complementary authority.[6] This ideal was never fully achieved for any length of time, but the theory continued to inform the way most Eastern Christians conceived the relationship between worldly and religious authority. That is, the relationship was not seen as one of distinct but of complementary power.

Over the course of the centuries, and especially after the Ottoman conquest of Constantinople, the ideal of a *symphonia* stayed, but became unattainable among

6 John Meyendorff, *Rome, Constantinople, Moscow: Historical and Theological Studies* (St. Vladimir's Seminary Press, 1996) 131–9.

Greek Orthodox Christians. At the same time, the Russian Empire was rising further North. Since its Christianization at the end of the first millennium AD, the Empire had risen to claim the legitimate succession of the Eastern Roman Empire, which fell to the Muslim Ottomans in 1453. This was most clearly seen in the theory of the sixteenth-century monk Filofei of Pskov (1465–1542), who called Moscow the third Rome after the original Rome and Constantinople. Filofei tried to convince the Emperor of Muscovy that "both Romes fell, the third endures, and a fourth, there will not be."[7] This theory had been prepared by the marriage between Grand Prince Ivan III of Moscow (1440–1505) and the Byzantine Princess Zoë (1440/49–1503) in 1472, after which the Grand Prince took the title Emperor – or Tsar. Moreover, the theory of a *symphony of powers* was also applied to the relationship between the Tsar and the head of the Church in Russia, the Metropolitan of Moscow (from 1589 Patriarch).

The claim of Moscow as the third Rome was never explicitly used in official state doctrine, but has been a part of the geopolitical subtext ever since. The doctrine, which originally was conceived of as a warning to keep Russian Christianity pure, was transformed into a geopolitical claim to Russian superiority in the nineteenth century. The communist times in the twentieth century are seen by some as its continuation, proclaiming a special role for Russia on a global scale. In the post-Soviet era, the doctrine is mostly associated with rightwing ideologies, such as the Eurasianists, but it is also present in the subtext of many conventional Orthodox conceptions of Russian identity.[8]

Since the sixteenth century, influences from outside the Russian Empire have trickled in, challenging both the religious and political culture of the Empire. One of the most profound tests to the religious unity of the Russian Empire was the Great Schism (*Raskol*) in the mid-seventeenth century, when a significant portion of the Russian faithful accused the Patriarch of having fallen into heresy by adopting too many non-Orthodox traditions. The result was the emergence of the so-called Old Believers, who did not recognize Patriarch Nikon (1605–1681) as the legitimate head of the Church, and empire-wide religious unrest. Peace was restored only when the young Tsar Peter I the Great (1672–1725) in the year 1700 refused to let the Russian Church select a new Patriarch.

Two decades later, Peter restructured the Church completely after plans by Bishop Feofan Prokopovich (1681–1736). The latter had modelled the new structure on the German Lutheran churches, with a consistory (the Most Holy Synod) composed of clergymen but controlled by a lay functionary, the *Oberprokuror*.[9] Over the next two centuries, the Church of Russia was thus more or less subordinated to political authority without its own proactive leadership. Nevertheless, the ideal of a *symphonia of powers* survived in the collective consciousness

7 Ibid., 136; Tarja Langstrom, *Transformation in Russia and International Law* (Martinus Nijhoff, 2003) 21.

8 Dmitrii Sidorov, 'Post-Imperial Third Romes: Resurrections of a Russian Orthodox Geopolitical Metaphor' (2006) 11 *Geopolitics* 317–47.

9 Igor Schmolitsch, *Geschichte der Russischen Kirche 1700–1917* (Brill, 1964) 118–20.

of the Church. On the surface, a similar arrangement as in the (Protestant) West – political trumps religious authority – had been instituted also in the Russian case.

The twentieth century then saw new challenges and opportunities facing the Church. First, the general revolutionary mood in the Russian Empire also took hold of church officials, who organized a massive church council opening in August 1917. This council, called the Moscow *sobor*, reinstated the Patriarchate of Moscow and elected the first Patriarch for more than 200 years.[10] The Sobor continued to meet until September 1918, but the Bolshevik takeover in October 1917 hindered its work considerably, so that none of the other decisions taken were ever implemented in the Russian Church. Instead, the Church was subjected to persecution and attempted elimination by the Soviet authorities, who saw in it a surviving structure of the imperial state.

The Church of Russia survived the devastating early Soviet era and was rehabilitated as the ROC by Joseph Stalin during World War II, arguably in an attempt to boost the troops' morale during the war.[11] The incorporation of the territories of western Ukraine, Belarus, and the Baltic States into the Soviet Union during the war also contributed to the revival of the ROC.[12] However, contrary to the role it had envisaged in 1917, the revived ROC was not much more than an instrument in Soviet hands, unable to show initiative or public displays of religiosity. The Soviet regime used the Church to demonstrate its pacifism and adherence to basic principles of human rights law, for example. The Soviet Union, and thus the ROC, did not, however, fully embrace individual political and liberal rights, though, but mainly social and economic rights.

With the downfall of the Soviet Union, Russian society redefined itself. The communist ideology no longer defined public morality, and the ROC seemed able to fill the void. The political elite surrounding Boris Yeltsin saw the potential of the ROC, and the political and religious spheres were once again rather close allies. Patriarch Aleksii II of Moscow (1929–2008), who headed the ROC from 1990 until his death in December 2008, acted as an apolitical mediator, concerned mainly with the moral life of the Russian nation.[13] His successor, Kirill I (*1946), has a different approach. As a close friend and ally of Russian president Vladimir Putin, Kirill actively partakes in the political life, both within Russia and on the international scene.[14]

10 Dimitry Pospielovsky, *The Orthodox Church in the History of Russia* (St. Vladimir's Seminary Press, 1998) 191–204.

11 Daniela Kalkandjieva, *The Russian Orthodox Church, 1917–1948: From Decline to Resurrection* (Routledge, 2015) 179–83.

12 Wassilij Alexeev and Theofanis G. Stavrou, *The Great Revival: The Russian Church under German Occupation* (Burgess, 1976).

13 Łukasz Fajfer and Sebastian Rimestad, 'The Patriarchates of Constantinople and Moscow in a Global Age: A Comparison' (2010) 10 *International Journal for the Study of the Christian Church* 211, 219–20.

14 Gregory L. Freeze, 'Russian Orthodoxy in the Putin Era' (Task Force White Paper, Carnegie Endowment, February 9, 2017) http://carnegieendowment.org/2017/02/09/russian-orthodoxy-and-politics-in-putin-era-pub-67959 (accessed March 19, 2018).

Much of the history of the ROC can be constructed around its closeness to the Russian state apparatus. This closeness was not always chosen, nor was it always voluntary. However, there was only one short period (1917–1925) in which the ROC openly rejected being close to the state. At all other times, the church snuggled up to the political leadership, regardless of its political and ideological orientation.

## 3 The ROC as a Transnational Entity

The other aspect of the ROC is its transnational scope. The Orthodox Church is a potentially universal religious organization. However, its particular historical evolution has ensured that it caters primarily for ethnic Russians. Unlike the Roman Catholic Church, which developed independently from imperial power once the western Roman Empire had collapsed in the fourth century AD, the Orthodox Church remained tied to the Emperor of the Eastern Roman Empire. As such, it did not develop the same pretensions to universality as the Roman Church did. Instead, it developed an ecclesiology tying ecclesiastical jurisdiction with clearly delimited territory. Each bishop was to have jurisdiction in the specific territory of his diocese. Some bishops, called Metropolitans and Patriarchs, although jurisdictionally equal to the normal bishops, had prerogatives of honor. They decided in cases pertaining to more than one diocese and should guide the bishops of a region.

During the reign of the Muslim Ottomans over the lands of most Orthodox Christians (fifteenth to nineteenth centuries), the bishops retained much of their jurisdictional power, being responsible to the Sultan for tax collection and law and order among his Christian subjects. The main difference to the Byzantine Empire was that the territory was no longer the sole defining feature of the jurisdiction, but equally important was the identity of the subjects. Only Christians were subject to episcopal jurisdiction. When nationalism swept across the Ottoman Empire in the nineteenth century, a third layer was added to the question of ecclesiastical jurisdiction. The earlier idea of a strictly territorial diocese had transformed into the idea of a diocese, composed of Christians of a certain ethnicity. As a result, the Orthodox Church is currently divided into the Church of Serbia, the Church of Greece, and the ROC, among others.

In the age of digital technologies and globalization, the strict territorial limit of diocesan jurisdiction is further eroded and according to the current ROC statutes,

> the jurisdiction of the Russian Orthodox Church shall include persons of Orthodox confession living on the canonical territory of the Russian Orthodox Church in the [former Soviet Union and] Japan and also Orthodox Christians [wishing to belong to it] living in other countries.[15]

15 Statutes of the Russian Orthodox Church (2000, last amended 2013) s. I, para. 3. Cited from the English version, https://mospat.ru/en/documents/ustav (accessed March 19, 2018).

As well as those faithful living in the Russian Federation, the ROC also includes all Orthodox faithful in the "near abroad" (former Soviet Union) as well as all those who want to belong to the church beyond this geographic boundary. The ROC therefore considers itself a transnational entity.

The provisions in the statutes are primarily a concession to the large numbers of ethnic Russians living outside the Russian Federation. These fall into various groups, who have various reasons to wish to belong to the ROC. The oldest group is constituted by the Russian diaspora of the first wave of emigration – following the Russian Revolutions of 1917 – and its descendants. This group, originally numbering several millions, but rapidly dwindling due to age and assimilation, kept the ideal of the Russian Empire alive in exile and dreamt of a return to the pre-revolution status quo. They built up an imaginary "Russia Abroad" that flourished culturally and religiously.[16]

In terms of church organization, this first group was divided into four factions. First, there were those who remained loyal to the Patriarchate of Moscow, even after it had been forced to accept the Bolshevik authorities as legitimate. This group was the smallest one, and only grew after World War II as a result of a new influx of migrants. A second group of Orthodox exile Russians were the Russian Orthodox Church Outside Russia – a staunchly anti-Bolshevik organization that refused to recognize the Soviet-controlled ROC as legitimate and considered itself the last genuine remnant of the Orthodox Church of Russia. The third faction existed mainly in the USA, where it argued for the need to have an independent American Orthodox Church. This wish eventually came to fruition in 1970 with the establishment of the Orthodox Church in America, although this church is not recognized by all other orthodox churches. The final group was headed by Metropolitan Evlogii Georgievskii (1868–1946) of western Europe, based in Paris. In 1931, once he could no longer reconcile his pastoral mission with the Soviet demands to show loyalty, he switched from the jurisdiction of the Patriarchate of Moscow to that of Constantinople.

These four factions of the first Russian emigration were to become important for the later waves, when the Russian newcomers had to decide which of the four to join for their religious needs in the diaspora. The faction of those who remained loyal to Moscow, while the smallest between the world wars, became much more important after World War II, and especially during the third wave of emigration since the collapse of the Soviet Union. The other structures, except the Orthodox Church in America, are seen by the Moscow Patriarchates as remnants of a bygone era, which should disappear now that the Soviet regime is gone. The Russian Orthodox Church Outside Russia in 2007, with mediation help from Vladimir Putin, entered into a union with the ROC again. The Paris Exarchate under Constantinople jurisdiction has a rather hard time between the Patriarchates.

Next to the three waves of emigration that happened throughout the twentieth century, there is a very significant number of Russians who moved within the

16 Marc Raeff, *Russia Abroad: A Cultural History of the Russian Emigration 1919–1939* (OUP, 1990).

Soviet Union to find labor and livelihood, but now find themselves outside of the Russian Federation. These internal emigrants, in Estonia, Latvia, Central Asia, or Ukraine, often identify as Russian Orthodox, but happen to live in a different country. The ROC is sometimes for them the main way of expressing their Russianness.

The ROC has always been interested in keeping its members outside the boundaries of the Russian Federation. The decisiveness with which the ROC attempted to retain the control over the Orthodox Church in Estonia, Ukraine, and also Moldova is a case in point.[17] Another important avenue through which the ROC retains its control over the exile Russians is the concept of the "Russian world" (Русский Мир). This concept in principle exists on the level of secular politics. Mikhail Suslov, although an expert on current developments within the ROC, has no problem analyzing the concept of the Russian world without mentioning religious actors at all.[18] Next to its secular dimension, there is an important religious aspect to the Russian world however, especially since Patriarch Kirill I took office in 2009.

Since 1993, Kirill, then Metropolitan of Smolensk and Kaliningrad and head of the Moscow Patriarchate's Department of External Church Relations, has been the patron of an organization called the World Russian People's Council (WRPC, Всемирный Русский Народный Совет). This transnational organization, uniting Russian nationals from all over the world, perceives itself as the safeguard of Russian national identity and values. It gathers Russian cultural, political, and religious influencers yearly for about a week to discuss issues of Russian national cultural interest. The topics range from the role of the Russian idea in the modern world to how to combat alcoholism or drug abuse. The 2006 WRPC meeting met under the heading "Truth. Man. Land. Russia's Mission for the 21st Century." One of the documents it adopted was a "Declaration of Human Rights and Dignity." This two-page document proclaimed a specifically Russian version of the human rights discourse, which openly called to resist the universal institutionalization of human rights in their western guise.

## 4 The ROC and Human Rights

While the WRPC and the "Russian World" it champions are not openly religious phenomena, the ROC is definitely seen as the moral driving force behind many of their ideas and statements. Two years after the declaration, the ROC adopted a much more comprehensive document on human rights and dignity, which outlines the ROC's view. Looking at this document, Orthodox Christians "intended to propose their own, alternative vision of human rights, with a different

17 Katja Richters, *The Post-Soviet Russian Orthodox Church. Politics, Culture and Greater Russia* (Routledge, 2013) 75–127.

18 Mikhail Suslov, '"Russian World": Russia's Policy towards Its Diaspora' (2017) 103 *Russia.Nei.Visions*www.ifri.org/sites/default/files/atoms/files/suslov_russian_world_2017.pdf (accessed March 19, 2018).

foundational approach and with different orientations and emphases."[19] The ROC tends to portray human rights as partly incompatible with basic Christian teachings, which posit that man, as created by God, has a dignity based on moral values. The norms derived from human rights discourse "cannot be accepted if they contradict the divine truth and Christian morality."[20] This pertains particularly to such issues as the rights of sexual minorities, offensive acts (that which the Orthodox Church deems to be immoral behavior), and challenges to what ROC spokesmen perceive as national values.

Alexander Agadjanian, a Russian sociologist of religion, maintains that there is an ambivalent intent in these documents. They are both outward- and inward-oriented. On the one hand, they are meant to create an international platform for a discussion about human rights where the cornerstones are set by the ROC. On the other, they serve as guidance manuals for Orthodox believers who face a discourse which they perceive as impenetrable.[21] The ROC is not necessarily propagating an alternative human rights discourse, such as has been the case with the attempts to create Islamic discourses of human rights. Rather, it attempts to negotiate with the dominant western discourse for a relevant place for itself and its members. The ROC thereby purports not only to speak on behalf of its active members but, also, to express the opinion of the masses of Russian non-believers who are deemed to be implicit members of the Church.[22]

According to Hegumen Philaret Bulekov, the ROC's representative to the European institutions in Strasbourg at the time, writing in 2008, the ROC does not condemn human rights but, rather, seeks to enrich them:

> Offering her own interpretation of human rights and freedoms based on religious ideas, the Church enters as a rightful participant in the lively discussion which is underway on national and international levels and thus becomes a cause for continued evolution of the human rights concept. This involvement of the Church, just as other religious communities, reflects the present stage in this evolution. Because today any discussion on human rights cannot take place only in the "secular irreligious space," considering especially the fact that most of the people on our planet are still religious people.[23]

At the end of May 2012, Patriarch Kirill of Moscow also criticized the way human rights discourse is being propagated by the western world:

19 Alexander Agadjanian, *Russian Orthodox Vision of Human Rights* (Universität Erfurt, 2008) 6.
20 Ibid., 9.
21 Ibid., 15–16.
22 Ibid., 16.
23 Philaret Bulekov, 'Russian Orthodox Church formulates her basic teaching on human dignity, freedom and rights' (statement on the publication of the 2008 ROC paper on human rights, August 18, 2008) www.strasbourg-reor.org/?topicid=308 (accessed March 19, 2018).

> If the human rights industry loses its spiritual and moral dimension and becomes a tool of political propaganda used for promoting specific philosophies to the detriment of others, its fruit will bring mankind a lot of injustice and make people slaves of sin, excessive consumption, and pride. Now we, religious leaders, are expected to speak clearly about the harm of attempts to build a world without God.[24]

The ROC, thus, perceives human rights as a useful tool for countering injustice, but claims that the concept cannot work without reference to its theological foundations.[25] That does not preclude the ROC from taking part in the institutions of human rights to try to use the instruments available for their own benefit. The ROC has been directly and indirectly involved in about a dozen cases filed before the European Court of Human Rights (ECtHR). These cases have pertained to registration of parishes, opposition to "harmful sects," and LGBTQ demonstrations.[26] The ROC also aggressively comments on court decisions and on the work of the European institutions. For that purpose, the ROC opened a representation in Strasbourg in 2004, headed first by Philaret Bulekov and since 2011 by Philip Riabykh.

Two hallmark cases, where the ROC representation in Strasbourg commented were the 2013 case of a Romanian clergy trade union[27] and a case from the same year about the right to wear a baptismal cross at the workplace in the United Kingdom.[28] In the former case, the ROC had even been invited to present a third-party opinion, which was published in revised form.[29] The trade union had been founded without consulting the local bishop, who, according to the statutes of the Romanian Orthodox Church, has to agree to such an association. The third-party intervention, written by Riabykh and two Russian lawyers, clearly sides with the church, claiming that:

24 'Patriarch Kirill Criticizes Attempts to Promote Liberal System of Law in World' *Interfax*, May 30, 2012, at www.interfax-religion.com/?act=news&div=9406 (accessed March 19, 2018).

25 Alfons Bruening, '"Freedom" vs. "Morality": On Orthodox Anti-Westernism and Human Rights' in Alfons Bruening and Evert van der Zweerde (eds), *Orthodox Christianity and Human Rights* (Peeters, 2012) 125.

26 Sebastian Rimestad, 'The Interaction between the Moscow Patriarchate and the European Court of Human Rights' (2015) 40 *Review of Central and East European Law* 31, 40–4.

27 *Sindicatul "Păstorul Cel Bun"* v. *Romania* Appl. No. 2330/09 (ECtHR, 9 July 2013).

28 *Eweida and Others* v. *The United Kingdom* Appl. Nos 48420/10, 59842/10, 51671/10, and 36516/10 (ECtHR, May 27, 2013).

29 Philip Riabykh, Igor' Ponkin, and Alena Ponkina, 'Sur la reconnaissance de la compétence exclusive des groupements religieux afin d'instaurer leur structure intrinsèque et les normes intérieures des relations en tant qu'une des garanties de la liberté de la conscience dans l'État démocratique' (2012) 34 *Stato, Chiese e pluralismo confessionale* 1–22, at www.statoechiese.it/images/uploads/articoli_pdf/ryabykhponpan_sur_la.pdf (accessed March 26, 2018).

> if canon law of a religious organization does not admit the interference of non-canonical institutions in its internal affairs … then the secular state has no right to interfere or even presume the ability to interpret and judge on these canonical regulations.[30]

If religious stipulations should not influence secular courts, so the argument goes, then the secular courts should not be able to influence religious stipulations. The case ended with a judgment (by a majority of 11 judges to six) in favor of the Romanian state, which was allowed to prohibit the trade union on the basis of autonomy of religious institutions.

The other case involved four British citizens, complaining of discrimination for their Christian faith. Two of them were not allowed to wear their baptismal crosses at work, whereas the other two had lost their jobs for refusing to provide services for same-sex couples on religious grounds. The controversy, which had significant resonance in Russian media, ended with only the first complaint, that of a British Airways flight attendant, upheld, whereas the other three were dismissed.[31] Russian commentators, including Philip Riabykh, criticized the verdict, which would amount to a "a new era of persecution for European Christians."[32] Riabykh's wish that the case would be referred to the ECtHR Grand Chamber did not come true.

In a programmatic speech in mid 2012, Riabykh argued that there were three areas in which religious communities should have a voice vis-à-vis international human rights institutions.[33] First and foremost, Riabykh claimed, they should insist on the right to organize themselves according to their norms and traditions. According to Riabykh, there was a tendency in the recent rulings of the ECtHR to encourage individuals to complain about the hierarchical order of a religious organization or the criteria for the selection of clergy. A second area pertains to "believers' right to free participation in religious life and the support of the religious spirit through speech and practice."[34] This includes the support of religious instruction in state schools and religious symbols on public display. Finally, Riabykh says, religious communities should be accepted as equal partners in the discussion about socially relevant moral questions, including euthanasia, abortion, surrogate motherhood, same-sex partnerships, and adoption. A legalistic approach

30 Ibid., 10.

31 *Eweida and Others* v. *The United Kingdom* Appl. Nos 48420/10, 59842/10, 51671/10, and 36516/10 (ECtHR, 27 May 2013).

32 'Русская Православная церковь призвала ЕСПЧ пересмотреть дела о дискриминации христиан' (Russian Orthodox Church calls on the ECtHR to reconsider the case of discrimination of Christians) *ria Novosti* (January 17, 2013) http://strasbourg-reor.org/?topicid=1022 (accessed March 26, 2018). See also Milena Faustova, 'ЕСПЧ: за христианку, но против христиан' (ECtHR: for one Christian, but against the Christians) *Radio "Golos Rossii"* (January 17, 2013), at http://strasbourg-reor.org/?topicid=1023 (accessed March 26, 2018).

33 Philip Riabykh, 'Религия и права человека' (Religion and Human Rights) (speech from June 28, 2012), www.strasbourg-reor.org/?topicid=923 (accessed March 19, 2018).

34 Ibid.

to such questions would often "run counter to any religious view, teaching the integrity of human life."[35]

In all these discussions, one can clearly see how the ROC uses its leverage as a transnational actor to try and influence the way human rights law is institutionalized by the Council of Europe (CoE). The Russian Orthodox Representation to the CoE institutions in Strasbourg is simultaneously one of the most affluent and distinguished parishes of the ROC in France. An ambitious new church building for this parish in central Strasbourg was completed in 2018. This building, together with the outspoken parish priest, Philip Riabykh, are carefully chosen by the ROC leadership in order to provide a prestigious and visible presence vis-à-vis the CoE.

The ROC pursues a specific agenda in relation to human rights law. The main criticism of the dominant discourse is its emphasis on individual rights over and above collective rights. For the ROC, human rights require a theological foundation and cannot be based on the liberal conception of maximized freedom for each individual. God created humankind in his image, and the highest goal of an Orthodox Christian is *theosis* – becoming God-like. This goal is fundamentally different from the posited aim of western human rights, total freedom for the individual will.

The ROC pursues this agenda on the one hand as a transnational actor, purporting to represent all Russians all over the globe, and on the other hand, it looks out for allies in western societies. Its main strategic partners are often rightwing populist conservative movements, such as Front National in France, the UK Independence Party in the UK, or Alternative für Deutschland (AfD) in Germany. These movements are seen as allies in the fight against the rampant liberal individualism of mainstream political discourse. The discrepancy between transnationalism and exclusivist nationalism is not perceived as a problem, but the divide is actively bridged by focusing on common conservative ideals. A case in point was a Russian language AfD-poster for the 2017 German parliamentary elections, which read "Together for a strong German home."

Another strategic partner for the ROC in its struggle for a conservative mainstream are the heterodox religious community. Metropolitan Hilarion Alfeyev, currently head of the ROC Department of External Church Relations, has since 2008 argued that the ROC should join together with the Roman Catholic Church in a "strategic alliance" to counter secularism and protect Christian values. Since the advent of Pope Francis in 2013, these calls have become less vehement, though. Hilarion does not argue for an administrative or theological union, but simply a strategic partnership to influence the values of the political mainstream.

It is difficult to assess the effectiveness of these Russian Orthodox attempts to influence global opinions, but, within Russia, the ROC clearly has an influential voice on moral issues, which is communicated all across the world. However, this voice clearly does not have as much power in the western world as for example the

35 Ibid.

Roman Pope. The latter might not be followed, but his interventions are at least mostly taken seriously and reported on by a variety of media. When the Moscow Patriarch expresses his opinion on an issue, this is much less widely covered in western media.

## 5 The ROC in Other Aspects of International Law

The ROC is not only involved in human rights and moral issues, but occasionally also in at least two other aspects of international law. First, the ROC plays a role in some territorial conflicts in the former Soviet Union. In Estonia and in Moldova, for example, the ROC has been involved in lawsuits concerning the local Orthodox Church in the early 1990s. In the Estonian case, the Church of the Moscow Patriarchate could not register as it wanted to, and the ROC attempted to convince the international community that this amounted to a discrimination of the Russian minority in Estonia, but without avail.[36] The Estonian domestic lawsuit of the 1990s could not be referred to the ECtHR, since Estonia had not yet signed the European Convention on Human Rights at the time. In the Republic of Moldova, the ROC was the only legitimately registered Orthodox Church, and a split-off church structure, reporting to the Orthodox Church of Romania, complained to the ECtHR and won.[37] The Moldovan state had to register the Romanian Church in addition to the Russian one.[38]

In Ukraine, there are several Orthodox Church structures competing for the title of the legitimate Orthodox Church of Ukraine. However, only one of them is internationally recognized as a legitimate Orthodox Church, namely the Ukrainian Orthodox Church in the jurisdiction of the Patriarchate of Moscow (UOCMP). This church is an autonomous part of the ROC, and it vehemently refuses to acknowledge the legitimacy of any of the other churches in Ukraine, which thus have no official recognition from the rest of the Orthodox world. The Ukrainian part of the ROC contains more than one-third of all its parishes and it is therefore a very important part. Without Ukraine, the ROC would be much smaller and much less prestigious.[39]

After the controversial Russian annexation of Crimea in 2014, the ecclesiastical status of the peninsula remained unchanged. It is still administered by the UOCMP based in Kiev. At the same time, other religious organizations in Crimea, including other Orthodox churches, claim to be exposed to persecution under Russian administration. The situation of the Orthodox Church in Crimea is used aggressively in the propaganda war. The pro-Ukrainian news station TSN reported in March 2015 that the UOCMP had officially recognized the Russian

36 Richters (n. 17) 75–95; Sebastian Rimestad, 'Orthodox Churches in Estonia' in Lucian N. Leustean (ed.), *Eastern Christianity and Politics in the Twenty-First Century* (Routledge, 2014) 295.

37 *Metropolitan Church of Bessarabia and Others* v. *Moldova* App. No. 45701/99 (March 27, 2002).

38 Andrei Avram, 'Orthodox Churches in Moldova' in Leustean (ed.) (n. 36) 402.

39 Richters (n. 17) 111.

annexation of the peninsula and handed all its property over to the ROC.[40] The pro-Russian news outlet Komsomolskaya Pravda replied that this was not the case, since the UOCMP continued to administer the Crimea dioceses, which had just been reregistered under Russian laws.[41] This balancing act has enabled the UOCMP to refrain from legally acknowledging the Crimea annexation while de facto handing the ecclesiastical administration of the peninsula to the ROC.

With regard to the situation in the unrecognized people's republics of Donetsk and Luhansk (in eastern Ukraine), the ROC is caught in a dilemma. On the one hand, as a Christian church, it wants to condemn violence and promote peace, but, on the other, the pro-Russian separatists in eastern Ukraine clearly look to the ROC as their patron. One of the paramilitary units in the conflict was called the "Russian Orthodox Army," and the ROC (Moscow Patriarchate) is clearly the preferred religious actor in these new states. There are numerous reports of persecution of religious organizations that do not align themselves with the Moscow Patriarchate, while there are also attempts to bridge the political divides.[42]

In relation to international law, the ROC officially argues that it is up to the political leadership to take a stance on the issue of recognition. This does not stop the separatists and local actors from trying to use the ROC as leverage to achieve some official recognition. That is especially visible in break-away regions of other former Soviet republics. In the Georgian secessionist regions South Ossetia and Abkhazia as well as in Transnistria in the Republic of Moldova,[43] the local Orthodox Church is situated between the ROC and another independent Orthodox Church. In the former two regions, this is the Church of Georgia, whereas Transnistria is claimed also by the Church of Romania. In all three regions, the local Orthodox Church tries to use the ROC as a means to gain more recognition also in the secular sphere.[44] The three highly complex cases show that the Orthodox Church has its own complicated procedures and hierarchies, whereby the ROC acts just as strategically as the break-away jurisdictions and international law is just a tiny aspect of this action.

An entirely different point of contact between the ROC and international law is when the ROC attempts to take over properties situated outside the Russian Federation. In most cases, this does not pertain to international law as such, but to

40 'Церковный скандал или госизмена: УПЦ МП юридически признала Крым частью России и передала ей две епархии' (A Church scandal or state switch: the Ukrainian Orthodox Church (Moscow Patriarchate) juridically recognized Crimea as part of Russia and gave away two dioceses) (March 8, 2015), https://ru.tsn.ua/politika/cerkovnyy-skandal-ili-gosizmena-upc-mp-yuridicheski-priznala-krym-chastyu-rossii-i-peredala-ey-dve-eparhii-414611.html (accessed March 26, 2018).

41 Elena Chinkova, 'Крым для церкви наш или ваш?' (Is the Crimea for the Church Ours or Yours?) (June 15, 2015), www.kp.ru/daily/26391.5/3270493 (accessed March 26, 2018).

42 Brian Milakovsky, 'The Church: Caught between Russia and Ukraine' *Fair Observer* (December 14, 2016), www.fairobserver.com/region/europe/orthodox-church-ukraine-conflict-russian-separatists-latest-news-00164 (accessed March 19, 2018).

43 See also Chapter 9 in this volume.

44 Kimitaka Matsuzato, 'Orthodox Churches in Abkhazia, South Ossetia and Transnistria' in Leustean (ed.) (n. 36) 387.

the ROC using the national laws of different countries to its benefit. The most spectacular such lawsuits were carried out in France and Great Britain. The Russian Orthodox Cathedral at Ennismore Gardens in London had been purchased by the local Orthodox parish under the leadership of Metropolitan Anthony (Bloom, 1914–2003) in 1978. When the British diocese of the ROC split in 2006 between one faction remaining loyal to Moscow and the other switching to the Patriarchate of Constantinople, the question of the ownership of the cathedral surfaced. The London parish council was dominated by the faithful of the Constantinople faction, so the Moscow Patriarchate started a lawsuit to gain control of the Cathedral.[45] Despite the arguments of legal continuity between the group around Metropolitan Anthony that had collected the money to purchase the Cathedral and the current day parish council, the Moscow faction won the lawsuits and all appeals.[46]

In France, it started with the magnificent Orthodox Cathedral in Nice, which was built with imperial money in the nineteenth century. The ROC had no claims to the ownership of this cathedral, but the Russian state initiated a lawsuit against the Association Culturelle Orthodoxe Russe (ACOR-Nice), which had managed the Cathedral throughout the twentieth century.[47] After more than a decade of litigation, the Russian state won and passed all the rights to use the Cathedral to the ROC, in spite of loud protests from the members of ACOR-Nice. A similar lawsuit happened in Biarritz on the French Atlantic coast, again won by the Russian state.[48] In all of these lawsuits, the ROC seemed more interested in gaining prestige and access to property in foreign lands than understanding any local concerns.

The way the ROC has gone about securing representative properties in Madrid, Strasbourg, and Paris, to name just a few, also testifies to this. Using the Russian Federation as a broker and financier, the ROC has executed more or less questionable deals without consulting the local Orthodox faithful, who often have a rather negative view of the Moscow Patriarchate. The ROC seems more interested in pursuing the grand idea of influential centers of the "Russian world" across Europe than in integrating existing communities of exile Russians and other Orthodox faithful. In terms of international law, the ROC wants to establish embassies, representing the might and prestige of the Moscow Patriarchate, not cultural or religious associations to serve the spiritual needs of the local Orthodox.

45 *Dean* v. *Burn and others* [2009] EWHC 1250 (Ch).

46 Irina Shumovitch 'BBC Russian Service: farewell to old friends' *openDemocracy: Russia and beyond* January 31, 2011, www.opendemocracy.net/od-russia/irina-shumovitch/bbc-russian-service-farewell-to-old-friends (accessed March 19, 2018).

47 *ACOR Nice* v. *Fédération de Russie* CA Aix-en-Provence, 1re ch. b, 19 mai 2011, n° 10/01453.

48 *ACOR Biarritz* v. *Eglise Orthodoxe Russe* CA Pau, ch. civ. 1, 12 févr. 2008, n° 06/00060.

## 6 Conclusion

The ROC has become an important transnational actor at least since the collapse of the Soviet Union in the early 1990s. The ROC tries to take a specific position in the global civil society, which is consistent with its historical development. The implicit idea that Russia has a special role to play in the history of global salvation resonates strongly within most ROC discourses. As was mentioned in the beginning, there have long been explicit Russian messianic discourses around, such as the Slavophiles in the nineteenth century, the Soviet Socialists in the twentieth century, and the Eurasianists in present Russia.[49] The ROC acts as a breeding ground for these ideas, actively laboring for the spread of Russian values throughout the world.

There are several avenues through which the ROC is able to act as the champion of the Russian idea. On the one hand, it can use the international instruments available, such as the ECtHR to try to propagate its worldview. More efficiently, however, it can act as an official critic of these instruments, proposing alternative ways to achieve a harmonious society. The official ROC representation to the European institutions in Strasbourg is an effective actor of criticism, endorsed both by the Church and the Russian state to balance what is perceived as a too liberal and individualistic discourse of human rights at the European level.

At the same time, the ROC is eager to build up a presence in western Europe, akin to that of a state actor, a presence which provides it with prestige and representation. This eagerness is less obvious in the lands of the former Soviet Union, where the ROC also has a strong presence, but not as prestigious. In the disputed regions, the ROC has to act very pragmatically, in order to not jeopardize its arguments elsewhere and keep the appearance of being a neutral religious actor. Although it is mostly aligned with the Russian state, there are instances where pragmatic reasons force it to pursue a different path. The transnational dimension of the Orthodox Church certainly makes it an interesting actor on the international scene.

49 Sidorov (n. 8).

# Part IV

# The High Politics of Contemporary Russia in International Law

# 8 Foreign Policy Discourses as Part of Understanding Russia and International Law

*W. E. Butler*

## 1 Introduction

On December 18, 2017, the government of the United States issued a 67-page document titled the "National Security Strategy of the United States of America" which set out an image of the world as seen by the executive branch. This will have de facto replaced the "National Security Strategy" issued on February 6, 2015, which in turn replaced that of May 27, 2010, both issued by President Obama. The Obama administration strategies supplanted in succession 14 earlier iterations dating back to 1987.[1] None had or has legally binding force. These documents are political statements of objectives which may or may not actually influence policies pursued in practice.[2] They are general in nature, ranging widely across foreign, military, legal, and other policies, and supplemented by other documents, among them the National Military Strategy.

Shortly after the 2016 elections in the United States, on November 30, 2016, the Russian Federation issued its own Conception of Foreign Policy of the Russian Federation. This document superseded an earlier Conception confirmed by Edict of the President of the Russian Federation on February 2, 2013, and in reverse chronological order, the 2013 Conception replaced earlier versions of July 12, 2008, June 28, 2000, and April 23, 1993.

The determination that the Russian Federation, upon the dissolution of the former Soviet Union, was the "legal-continuer" (and not the legal successor) of the Union of Soviet Socialist Republics meant that all rights and obligations of the USSR instantaneously became those of the Russia without the process of succession occurring. The request of Russia, made in various forums and in various

1 The legal foundation for the issuance of national security strategies – the titles can vary slightly from one to another – is the so-called Goldwater–Nichols Act of October 4, 1986, Pub. L. 99-433, which introduced sweeping reforms in the structure of the United States military. Through 2017 there have been 17 in all. Each is prepared by the executive branch for submission to the Congress of the United States.

2 See M. Landler and D. E. Sanger, 'Mixed Signals as Trump Sets Security Policy' *New York Times*, December 19, 2017 (Washington edn) A1, A6: "The national security strategies of past administrations were sometimes strong predictors of future action" (A6, col. 2). Others experienced in foreign policy said: "national security strategies have a fairly short shelf life" (A6, col. 4).

communications, to be deemed the legal-continuer rather than the legal successor was accepted by the international community as a whole and by each state individually. Russia continued membership of the United Nations and other organizations, including as one of the five permanent members of the Security Council. Legal continuer it may have been, but not necessarily in matters of foreign policy. The internal quest began for new conceptions of foreign policy, while drawing upon advanced Soviet thinking insofar as it had progressed. At a minimum, this meant continuing an exercise already in progress during the late years of the Gorbachev perestroika: employing the "old thinking" and the "new thinking" to advantage, substituting words and phrases, as appropriate, to recognize and characterize Russia's new position in the world and/or new positions on old issues. The old Leninist/Stalinist ideas of "socialism in one country" might now be reshaped to encourage factors and trends furthering the development of international circumstances well disposed to building democracy in Russia; that is, creating an international environment that would nurture and facilitate desirable domestic outcomes. The second element – which has reappeared with greater prominence in the 2016 Conception of Foreign Policy – was to pursue the logic of "new political thinking" introduced by M. S. Gorbachev.

Initially, under Gorbachev the "new political thinking" was related to arms control and saving humankind from the horrors of a nuclear conflict – although international law figured strongly in the dialogue.[3] With the disappearance of the USSR and under the leadership of Boris Yeltsin (1931–2007), the initial impulse of Russian foreign policy in its "continuer" aspect was to emphasize the democratization of the world. It was believed that democratization might be achieved on the basis of the joint and several efforts of all democratic countries, among which Russia considered itself to be after 1991. To some, this was a massaging from the Soviet version of "socialist internationalism," this version based on the belief that democratic solidarity would flow from all democratic countries conducting themselves similarly because they shared common interests.

Early addresses on foreign policy by the Russian leadership in international forums and at home indicated that Russia faced continual choices – sometimes competing, sometimes complementary – between encouraging better relations with the "near abroad" (former Soviet republics which had become independent states and the countries of Central and Eastern Europe) or pursuing better relations with the United States, western Europe, not to mention the Near and Far East, Southeast Asia, Africa, Latin America, and elsewhere. No doubt much is to be made of the initial expectations of those who were pro-American or pro-western; they proved to be disappointed, an aspect much in evidence in the 2016 Conception of Foreign Policy.

The first post-Soviet conception of foreign policy was confirmed by a Regulation No. 284-рп, of the President of Russia dated April 23, 1993[4] under the title

3 See W. E. Butler (ed.), *Perestroika and International Law* (Dordrecht: Nijhoff, 1990).

4 The confirmation by a "regulation" did not in and of itself deprive the Conception of normative value, but this type of normative-legal act is routinely used for administrative material; often regulations are non-normative.

"Basic Provisions of the Conception of Foreign Policy of the Russian Federation." It had been prepared by a group of experts from the Ministry of Foreign Affairs, Ministry of Foreign Economic Relations, Ministry of Defense, Foreign Intelligence Service, apparatus of the Security Council, and two committees of the Supreme Soviet of the Russian Federation: the committee for international affairs and foreign policy links, and for defense and security. Iu. V. Skokov (1938–2013) acted as Chairman of the Inter-Departmental Foreign Policy Commission. Prior to being submitted to the President, the document was agreed with the relevant institutions and submitted for prior confirmation to the Security Council.[5]

The 1993 Conception was modified or supplemented – some would say supplanted – by the adoption of the 1993 Constitution of the Russian Federation and annual addresses or messages on foreign policy by the President of Russia and/or by the Minister of Foreign Affairs to the Federal Assembly of the Russian Federation. These in various ways emphasized that Russian interests might be best pursued not by confrontation with other powers, but by strengthening cooperation; moreover, the world, these materials stressed, was no longer bipolar, but multipolar. The implication was that military force would play a lesser role and law would become more important.

The Putin administration actively encouraged, or continued, the preparation of doctrinal and conceptual documents of various aspects of Russian domestic and foreign policies. Vladimir Putin took office as acting President of Russia on December 31, 1999. Within ten days he had confirmed an updated version of the Concept of National Security of Russia (January 10, 2000), followed by the Military Doctrine of Russia on April 21, 2000, and about two months later, on June 28, 2000, the Conception of Foreign Policy of Russia. In general, the 2000 Conception of Foreign Policy noted that the general situation around Russia had changed and required rethinking. Certain negative trends were in evidence, and matters that seemed promising in 1993 had proved in some cases to be otherwise.

The election of President Medvedev in 2008 was accompanied by the confirmation of the 2008 Conception of Foreign Policy. In addition to some adjustments made to accommodate changed circumstances, the 2008 Conception emphasized the modernization of Russia and the development of innovation policies in a world in which geopolitical competition was greatly aggravated. Most changes in the 2008 version were stylistic, sharpening the text and deleting extraneous verbiage. Since President Putin had become the Prime Minister, it is worthy of note that the 2008 Conception added to the list of structures effectuating measures for the realization of Russian foreign policy the "Government of the Russian Federation."

On February 12, 2013 President Putin confirmed a new version of the Conception of Foreign Policy. This version was prepared by the Ministry of Foreign Affairs working group pursuant to the Edict of the President of the Russian

5 See 'Концепция внешней политики Российской Федерации: сравнительный анализ' [Conception of Foreign Policy of the Russian Federation: Comparative Analysis], available at mgimo.ru, where no author is given.

Federation of May 7, 2012, "On Measures for the Realization of the Foreign Policy Course of the Russian Federation."[6] The document was ready by the assigned deadline (December 2012), but the adoption of the so-called "Magnitsky Law" in the United States resulted in some rethinking in Moscow, and the Conception was held back in order to introduce these. The final variant was submitted by President Putin to the Security Council of Russia on February 15, 2013. The basic principles of Russian foreign policy were said to be unchanged. Nonetheless, there were changes of emphasis and innovations.

The 2013 Conception stressed the importance of what was called "soft power" – resolving foreign policy tasks by using the potential of a civil society, informational, communications, humanitarian, and other alternative classical diplomatic methods and technologies while being aware of the damage that may be done by the destructive and unlawful uses of soft power for the purposes of exerting political pressure on sovereign states, interference in internal affairs, and manipulating public opinion and public consciousness. Information security, in other words, in this version of the Conception was moved to the forefront.

Globalization is accelerating, moving the world from unipolarity under the domination of the United States (2000) to multipolarity, with no estimate given as to how many "polarities" may be in the process of formation. The concept of "network diplomacy" was expanded in the 2013 version from its original appearance in 2000. This approach to diplomacy constitutes a transition from block approaches to resolving international problems to forming ad hoc temporary alliances with Russian participation for the resolution of particular issues; depending on the issue, membership may vary from one alliance to another.

The texts of the 2013 and earlier conceptions available on commercial databases omitted the text of the Presidential Edict. The text of the 2013 Conception was taken from the Kremlin website.[7] This treatment of the Conceptions raises issues: did either the confirming edict or the conceptions, or both, contain clauses or provisions that engaged state secrecy legislation? Was the failure to publish officially an effort to reduce the importance of the Conception or to eliminate questions of its normative force?

The preparation of the Conception of Foreign Policy of the Russian Federation is undertaken by the Ministry of Foreign Affairs pursuant to an explicit mandate set out in the Statute on the Ministry of July 11, 2004:[8]

> 2. The principal tasks of the Ministry of Foreign Affairs of the Russian Federation shall be:
>
> ...

6 СЗ РФ (2012), no. 19, item 2342.
7 The texts of the Conceptions of 2013, 2008, 2000, and 1993 are available on Consultant Plus.
8 СЗ РФ (2004), no. 28, item 2880, as amended; transl. in W. E. Butler (ed.), *Russian Public Law* (3rd edn, Wildy, Simmonds and Hill, 2013) 232.

(2) realization of the foreign policy course of the Russian Federation in accordance with the Conception of Foreign Policy of the Russian Federation confirmed by the President of the Russian Federation.

The 2016 Conception appeared with a greater measure of self-assurance. Both the confirming Edict and the Conception itself were gazetted, and the 2013 Conception was formally repealed. In the Soviet era, a document of this nature would have been treated as an exercise in propaganda. Not so in the post-Soviet era, which suggests that the document is to be taken seriously and plays a direct role in Russian foreign policy formulation – indeed, is itself an exercise in foreign policy formulation.

What, then, is the status – if any – of a "Conception" in the Russian legal system?

## 2 Legal Status of a Conception and Similar Documents

In a country with a history of economic planning, it is hardly surprising to see vestiges or elements of "soft" planning or orientation documentation in post-Soviet legal systems. This is a legacy of the planned economy which has been adapted and survived. Documents of this nature appear under various designations: strategy (including national strategy, state strategy); conception; doctrine; or fundamental principles. These, as a rule, undergo the same process as ordinary legislation; indeed, they are confirmed – depending at what level they are adopted – by laws, edicts, or decrees and sometimes by lower-level subordinate acts. They have been characterized as "sources of law of a political–ideological character";[9] if acted upon, they are capable of influencing virtually all other elements of the Russian legal system.

Although in substance these enactments may be "policy" documents, they are couched in legal form and language and undergo the same legislative process as normative legal documents, irrespective of from what level they may emerge. They may themselves generate or call for legislation or serve as justification for a "line on the budget." They enter into force, are often but not always gazetted, and are repealed as legislative acts. Both Russian and Belarus jurists have singled out state conceptions, programs, strategies, basic orientations, and similar documents as an "autonomous source of law which may be called a policy-program document"; these documents are believed by some to be of a doctrinal nature.[10]

9 See M. A. Mushinskii, 'Стратегии, концепции, доктрины в правовой системе Российской Федерации: проблемы статуса, юридической техники и соотношения друг с другом' [Strategies, Conceptions, and Doctrines in the Legal System of the Russian Federation: Problems of Status, Legal Technique, and Correlation with One Another], Юридическая техника [Legal Technique], no. 9 (2015) 488–99.

10 Ibid., 488, also citing N. V. Sil'chenko, 'Концепция совершенствования законодательства: понятие, структура, содержание' [Conception of Improving Legislation: Concept, Structure, Content], Веснік Канстытуцыйнага Суда Рэспублікі Беларусь [Herald of the Constitutional Court of the Republic Belarus], no. 3 (2001) 68–73.

Leaving aside the Soviet era, the presidents and governments of Russia seem to have introduced, returned to, or accelerated recourse to policy-program documents from 1996 onwards. There are three main types: strategies (or national strategies, state strategies); conceptions; and doctrines. Related miscellaneous documents include: national plan; fundamental principles of state policy. Unlike general legislation, it is common for policy-program documents to be adopted for designated periods, after which they will either lapse or be replaced for another period. More than 50 have been adopted since 1996.[11] The foreign policy Conceptions, however, have been an exception: they are not adopted for designated periods of time. Of the five enacted since 1993, all but one originate under the leadership of President Putin; the earliest dates from the presidency of Boris Yeltsin. The conceptions seem to be replaced when senior foreign policy officials believe a new version is desirable, although the years correspond roughly to election cycles in Russia.

Policy dialogue as a category suggests discourse about policy alternatives and choices, a discussion about why and how certain paths should be pursued over others – influenced by perceptions of what is important in the subject matter being considered, what trends are at work, and what desirable state policies may be to prevent or encourage certain outcomes. While these are not absent in Russia, the fact that strategies, conceptions, doctrines, and the like are embodied in normative legal acts puts a significantly different spin on their relevance and importance. In the quarter-century since foreign policy conceptions began to be produced in Russia, they have moved from being, it would seem, rapidly, even hastily, compiled statements of objectives and preferences to increasingly formal products of legislatively mandated working groups clothed in normative-type documents (presidential edicts) and embodying formulations increasingly noteworthy for legislative technique.

In this chapter, however, we concentrate upon one aspect of Russian foreign policy: the role of international law, especially in the 2016 Conception of Foreign Policy. Several general observations are appropriate. First, the predecessor 2013 Conception took between seven and eight months from authorization to proceed until final submission, and then in order to incorporate the considerations dictated by the so-called Magnitsky Act in the United States, was held up by another two months. But the very foundation of the 2013 version – the Edict of May 7, 2012 – did more than simply authorize the preparation of the Conception.[12] The title of the Edict in this case indicated the substance: "On Measures for the Realization of the Foreign Policy Course of the Russian Federation": five pages of

11 The figure comes from Mushinskii, but it is a low figure. He lists only those in force at the time he wrote and therefore omitted, for example, the Conceptions of Foreign Policy of 1993, 2000, and 2008. Had he attempted a list of all adopted after 1992, the list would have been considerable longer.

12 Point 3:

> The Ministry of Foreign Affairs of the Russian Federation shall: (a) submit in the established procedure before December 2012 the draft Conception of Foreign Policy of the Russian Federation in a new version; (b) ensure the coordination of work connected with the realization of the present Edict.

detail which doubtless served as the outline of the 2013 Conception. The point here is that the Edict remains in force and there was, so far as can be determined, no equivalent preparatory material or mandate for the 2016 Conception. It is unclear whether Russia decided that the formulations of 2013 had been overtaken by events fewer than four years later and required rethinking the conception, or whether tweaks were in order to introduce minor readjustments in policy in light of the outcome of the 2016 elections in the United States.

Second, although from 1993 onward international law with each generation of foreign policy conception acquired a more prominent and substantial role, the 2016 Conception of Foreign Policy accorded to international law an importance exceeding all previous versions – to which we shall return below.

Third, the 2016 Conception of Foreign Policy strongly reinforced the "multi-polarity" perception of Russian foreign policy, a perception that will, should it persist, reduce the significance of the United States in Russian foreign policy calculations and behavior:

> 4. The contemporary world is living through a period of profound changes, the essence of which consists in the forming of a polycentric international system. The structure of international relations continues to be complicated. As a result of the globalization process, new centers of economic and political influence are forming. A dispersion is occurring of world potential of power and development and the displacement thereof to the Asian-Pacific region. The possibilities are reducing for the historical West to dominate the world economy and politics. The diversity of cultures and civilizations in the world is sharply manifest, and the multiplicity of models for the development of States.[13]

Fourth, although in this chapter we shall concentrate upon the special section in the Conception of Foreign Policy dedicated to international law, in the larger sense most of the document is devoted to international law directly or indirectly. There are repeated reference to international law, but even where there are not, the subject matter being addressed relates either to individual aspects of international law (human rights, international organizations, law of the sea, Arctic, arms control, environment, and others) or to matters that have an international–legal dimension.

## 3 Supremacy of Law in International Relations

Thus reads the heading of the segment of the Conception of Foreign Policy dedicated exclusively to public international law. It appears with section III (although the word "Section" is not used in the Conception) titled: "Priorities of the Russian Federation in Resolving Global Problems" following a "subsection" (a word also not used in the Conception) titled: "Forming of a Just and Stable

13 This and all other references to the 2016 Conception of Foreign Policy are to my translation in W. E. Butler (ed. and trans.), *Russia & The Republics: Legal Materials* (loose-leaf service, Juris, 2006–).

World Structure." The rationale for the arrangement is set out in point 23 of the Conception:

> 23. The Russian Federation is conducting a foreign policy directed towards the creation of a stable and firm system of international relations on the basis of generally-recognized norms of international law and the principles of equality, mutual respect, noninterference in internal affairs of States for the purpose of ensuring the reliable and equal security of every member of the world community.

The allocation of a special subsection to the supremacy of law in international relations in the 2016 Conception of Foreign Policy was not an innovation. There was a subsection similarly positioned and titled in the 2008 and 2013 General Conceptions. What changed in 2016 was the formulation of the first subsection from "The Forming of a New World Structure" (2013) to "The Forming of a Just and Stable World Structure" – that is, the substitution of the words "just and stable" for "new." International law is the considerable beneficiary of this change.

The phrase "supremacy of law" is close to the 1993 Russian constitutional formulation of Russia being a "rule-of-law State."[14] But to those with a longer memory, the term "supremacy of law" in international relations sounds synonymous with the perestroika formulation "primacy of law in international relations" – a thread of continuity, perhaps, between late-Soviet and post-Soviet Russian foreign policy analysis.[15]

There continues to be a preference for the fundamental legal and organizational structures that came out of World War II, above all the United Nations and its sister agencies. For Russia, as indeed for much of postwar Soviet foreign policy, a stable and firm system of international relations is desirable whose justness originates in a system of relations based on "generally-recognized norms of international law" and the principles of equality, mutual respect, noninterference in internal affairs of states – central tenets, it should be recalled, of peaceful coexistence, although that term is no longer in fashion. The United Nations is the center of this system of international relations. That organization has "international legitimacy" and, in any event, as the Conception of Foreign Policy observed, there is a demonstrated lack of an alternative.

Russia would welcome steps to strengthen the role of the United Nations, but without changing key provisions and principles of the United Nations Charter. Russia is plainly apprehensive that any weakening or dilution of the role of the

14 Art. 1(1), 1993 Constitution of the Russian Federation. See Butler (n. 8) 4.

15 See G. I. Tunkin:

> The primacy of international law in politics or, to put it another way, the supremacy of international law in inter-State relations, is not a new issue. What is new is the situation in which the Soviet Union has raised this virtually forgotten question ... The most important question for the normal functioning of the inter-State system is the primacy of international law in politics. It is from this that the question is posed anew.
>
> ('On the Primacy of International Law in Politics' in Butler (ed.) (n. 3) 5)

United Nations may lead to Russia playing a less significant role in the international system. From the Russian perspective, the place of Russia on the United Nations Security Council is preserved to this day, even surviving the dissolution of the Soviet Union itself. Multipolarity there may be on the planet, but the end of the Cold War has seen nothing emerge that would justify fundamentally altering the postwar arrangements for organizing international society. The Conception of Foreign Policy counsels against any changes relating to "the outcome of the Second World War and actions undertaken or sanctioned as a result of the Second World War by governments bearing responsibility for such actions." Any measures to strengthen the potential of the United Nations with a view to adapting to new world realities should preserve the interstate nature of that Organization.

While Russia welcomes measures to enhance the effectiveness of the United Nations Security Council, including possible greater representation, any decision to create additional seats on the Security Council should be adopted on the basis of the most extensive consent of members of the United Nations while preserving the status of the five permanent members of the Security Council.

Development issues are viewed separately and have, in addition to the United Nations, an increasing number of other organizations concerned with regional aspects of "world development." For Russia, such bodies included the G-12, BRICS, and the Shanghai Organization of Cooperation (SOC) – the Eurasian organizations being created under Russian leadership are treated separately elsewhere in the Conception of Foreign Policy.

These general propositions with respect to the priorities for resolving world problems bring the Conception of Foreign Policy to the role of international law, set out in one lengthy, virtually full-page point 26 as follows with commentary on following each paragraph:

> 26. Russia consistently favors the strengthening of the legal foundations of international relations and complies in good faith with international–legal obligations. The maintenance and strengthening of international legality is one of the priority orientations of its activity in the international arena. The supremacy of law in international relations is called upon to ensure peaceful and fruitful cooperation of States when complying with the balance of their interests, and also to guarantee the stability of the world community as a whole. The Russian Federation intends to …

This provision is an endorsement of the role of international law in international relations and most especially of the principles of *pacta sunt servanda* and *bona fide*. Compliance with international obligations is views as a *sine qua non* of strengthening the legal foundations of international relations. The supremacy of law, implying international law but a definition open-ended enough to encompass national legal systems, here is to ensure peaceful and fruitful cooperation, the stability of the world community as a whole, and the balanced interests of states.

(a) maintain collective efforts for the strengthening of the legal foundations of inter-State relations;

"Collective efforts" here is a broad, almost limitless term that can refer to any international organization, including NGOs, the codification of international law, indeed, anything that contributes to or promotes the role of international law constructively.

(b) counteract attempts of individual States or groups of States to subject to revision generally-recognized principles of international law consolidated in the United Nations Charter, Declaration on the Principles of International Law Concerning Friendly Relations and Cooperation between States in Accordance with the Charter of the United Nations of 24 October 1970, the Final Act of the Conference on Security and Cooperation in Europe of 1 August 1975; attempts to arbitrarily interpret major international–legal norms and principles to the advantage of political competition and interests of individual States such as the non-use or threat of force, peaceful settlement of international disputes, respect for the sovereignty of States and their territorial integrity, right of peoples to self-determination, attempts to interfere in the internal affairs of States for the purposes of effectuating an unconstitutional change of power, including by means of support for non-State subjects, including terrorist and extremist organizations;

This formulation represents a strong commitment to the postwar United Nations arrangements, the 1970 Declaration on Principles of International Law, and the Helsinki Final Act as the legal foundations of the existing international order and resistance to efforts to alter those by re-interpretation or other emendation. The elements of continuity here between Soviet and post-Soviet diplomacy are extensive and strong, including a preference for anti-regime change policies.

(c) not allow the effectuation, under the pretext of the realization of the conception of "defense responsibility," of military interventions and other forms of outside interference violating norms of international law, in particular the principle of sovereign equality of States.

Here a modern formulation expressing a long-standing Soviet and post-Soviet preference for acceptance of the principle of sovereign equality of states, violated in the example given by various doctrines, of which the old "Brezhnev Doctrine" would have been one.

(d) further the progressive development of international law and the codification thereof, above all under the aegis of the United Nations, and also universal participation in international treaties of the United Nations and their uniform interpretation and application.

Likewise another long-standing principle of Soviet and post-Soviet international legal doctrine and foreign policy.

> (e) continue efforts for improvement of the mechanism of the application by the United Nations of sanctions, to proceed especially from the fact that a decision concerning the introduction of such sanctions should be adopted by the United Nations Security Council on a collegial basis after comprehensive consideration, above all by taking into account their effectiveness when fulfilling the tasks of the maintenance of international peace and security and averting a worsening of the humanitarian situation; further the exclusion from the practice of international interaction of illegal unilateral enforcement measures adopted in violation of the United Nations Charter and other norms of international law.

Sanctions are now part of international life to a much greater degree than previously. Russia imposed sanctions under United Nations and other auspices, is the victim of sanctions, and routinely debates the effectiveness of sanctions, including with respect to Iran, North Korea, Syria, and other venues. The general position expressed here has long been held in Soviet and post-Soviet Russian foreign policy.

> (f) activate the process of international–legal formalization of the State boundary of the Russian Federation, and also the boundaries of sea expanses within whose limits Russia exercises sovereign rights and jurisdiction, with the unconditional ensuring of her national interests, especially in the sphere of security and the economy, proceeding from the importance of strengthening trust and cooperation with neighboring States.

This formulation is post-Crimean in several respects and can be read at several levels. Russian land boundaries, and those of the other independent states, were supposedly fixed by the Almaty Agreements of December 21/22, 1991. To suggest they are not, as may this provision, reopens doors long believed to have been closed. The Almaty Agreements, it should be observed, reiterated the position on boundaries of the 1975 Helsinki Final Act.

Insofar as maritime boundaries are concerned, lateral boundaries between Russia and some neighbors remain to be determined, including territorial sea, exclusive economic zone, and continental shelf. The Conception of Foreign Policy provides for an expectation that these are on the Agenda and reasonably imminent.

In sum, international law is seen as a positive, reinforcing, stabilizing, pillar of the international system whose roots in the outcome of World War II should be retained and strengthened. In the Russian view, these roots may be consolidated and preserved, but not fundamentally altered.

## 4 Subsidiary Roles of International Law

The Conception of Foreign Policy does use the term "subsidiary role." We introduce the term to demonstrate how central international law is in fact to the

Russian conception of foreign policy. First, the Conception of Foreign Policy is based on law:

> 2. The legal foundation of the present Conception shall comprise the Constitution of the Russian Federation, generally-recognized principles and norms of international law, international treaties of the Russian Federation, federal laws, the Edict of the President of the Russian Federation of 7 May 2012, No. 605, 'On Measures for the Realization of the Foreign Policy Course of the Russian Federation,' the National Security Strategy of the Russian Federation, the Military Doctrine of the Russian Federation, normative legal acts of the Russian Federation regulating the activity of federal agencies of State power in the sphere of foreign policy, and also other normative legal acts of the Russian Federation in this sphere.

Second, the foreign policy activity of Russia aspires to achieve objectives or perform tasks which are legal in character, among them: ensuring the sovereignty and territorial integrity of the country, strengthening the rule-of-law state and democratic institutions; not permitting discrimination against Russian goods, services, or investments, using the possibilities of international and regional economic and financial organizations, strengthening international peace, forming good-neighborly relations with adjacent states, preventing tension and conflicts, developing bilateral and multilateral relations with foreign states, interstate associations, international organizations on the basis of principles of independence and sovereignty, expansion of international cooperation on a non-discriminatory basis, promoting the creation of network alliances, defense of rights and legal interests of Russia citizens and compatriots residing abroad, among others.

Third, international law is elevated to a major factor of influence on the behavior of states in international politics, together with economic, technological, informational, geopolitical, and military aspects (point 8). This role for international law affects responses to threats from global terrorism Russia favors at this conjuncture of history the creation of an extensive international anti-terrorist coalition "on a stable legal base" (point 15).

Fourth, Russia sees its autonomous and independent foreign policy course as one dictated by its national interests and is based on absolute "respect for international law" (point 21). In the world of international security policy, Russia endorses article 51 of the United Nations Charter as an "adequate legal foundation, not subject to revision, for the use of force by way of self-defense, including conditions of the existence of such threats to peace and security as international terrorism and dissemination of weapons of mass destruction" (point 32). International terrorism, in the Conception of Foreign Policy, is perceived as a major state task and a key priority. Measures to prevent the same are to be taken in accordance with international law and Russian legislation (point 33(c)) and the international community is to combine efforts to combat terrorism without politicization and in accordance with the "United Nations Charter and norms and principles of international law."

Fifth, international law is invoked when addressing international economic and ecological cooperation, including the taking of measures, in accordance with international norms and principles, in the domain of trade policy, the defense of rights and legal interests abroad of Russian citizens and compatriots.

Russia's relations with its immediate neighbors are characterized as "regional priorities." The Conception of Foreign Policy, no longer using the terminology of "great power," nonetheless sees Russia as a world power. Within the Commonwealth of Independent States the Russian Federation maintains "friendly relations" on the basis of equality, mutual advantage, respect, and taking into account one another's interests. International–legal instruments are important for the defense of their rights and legal interests in the educational, language, social, labor, humanitarian, and other spheres. The expansion of economic cooperation is seen within the framework of the 2011 Treaty on the Free Trade Zone.

The Euro-Atlantic region is viewed as being among Russia's regional priorities – a considerable downgrading in comparison with previous conceptions. The role of international law here is to encourage a transition to a "legally binding form of political declaration" concerning the indivisibility of security irrespective of the membership of states in military and political alliances. So far as NATO is concerned, Russia will take into account the degree of the readiness of that alliance for equal partnership, undeviating "compliance with the principles and norms of international law" (point 72), and real steps toward ensuring a common space of peace, security, and stability in the region.

It follows that Russia is opposed to the extraterritorial effectuation by the United States of its jurisdiction outside the framework of international law. Russia anticipates that the United States "will in its actions in the world arena strictly comply with norms of international law, especially those consolidated in the Charter of the United Nations" (point 74).

The law of the sea and the Arctic are singled out twice in the Conception of Foreign Policy. Marine expanses are important for economic development and strengthening security:

> [the] significance of marine expanses and sea lanes is striving for compliance with the requirements for safety of marine navigation that meet national interests in accordance with norms of the international law of the sea, including with respect to combatting international terrorism and counteracting piracy at sea and is developing responsible fishing and effectuating scientific-research activity on the World Ocean, taking measures in so doing for the defense of the marine environment. Russia intends to establish in accordance with international law external boundaries of its continental shelf, thereby expanding the opportunities for the exploration and extraction of the mineral resources thereof (point 44).

Russia is pursuing a line directed toward the preservation of peace, stability, and constructive international cooperation in the Arctic. The Russian Federation is proceeding from the sufficiency of the existing international–legal treaty-law base

> for the successful regulation by means of negotiations of all questions arising in the region, including the establishment of external boundaries of the continental shelf in the Northern Arctic Ocean. Russia believes that the Arctic states bear special responsibility for the stable development of the region and in this connection favors the strengthening of interaction in the format of the Arctic Council, the coastal Arctic "Five," and also the Council of the Barents/Euro-Arctic region. Russia will firmly counteract any attempts to bring into the Arctic elements of a policy of confrontation and military opposition, to politicize international interaction in the region as a whole. The use of the Northern Sea Route has a national transportation communication of Russia in the Arctic has material significance for the development of the region, and also the use thereof for the effectuation of transit carriages between Europe and Asia (point 76).

The above are virtually an exhaustive account of when and how international law is mentioned in the Conception of Foreign Policy, although many, perhaps most, policies mentioned in the Conception have an international legal aspect or depend upon international law in meaningful ways if they are to be actually achieved.

## 5 Formulation and Implementation of Foreign Policy in Russia

The final section of the Conception of Foreign Policy is devoted to an account of the agencies and officials in Russia who are responsible for the formulation and execution of foreign policy; that is, sets out the legal framework in general terms for foreign policy articulation. The President of the Russian Federation in accordance with the Constitution of the Russian Federation and federal laws determines the basic orientations of foreign policy of the state, effectuates the direction of foreign policy of the country, and as the head of state represents the Russian Federation in international relations (point 100).

The role of the Russian Parliament is next described. The Soviet of the Federation of the Federal Assembly of the Russian Federation and the state Duma of the Federal Assembly of the Russian Federation within the limits of their powers shall carry on work for legislative provision of the foreign policy course of the country and the fulfillment of international obligations of the Russian Federation, and also promote the enhancement of the effectiveness of parliamentary diplomacy (point 101).

The role of the Government of the Russian Federation is described as an executing rather than a formulating role. This observation refers to the government as a whole rather than to constituent parts thereof (for example, the Ministry of Foreign Affairs). With respect to foreign policy formulation, a key role is allocated to the Security Council of the Russian Federation:

> The Security Council of the Russian Federation shall effectuate the forming of the basic orientations of State foreign and military policy, forecasting, identification, analysis, and assessment of threats to the national security of Russia, preparation of proposals for the President of the Russian Federation

> concerning the application of special economic measures for the purposes of ensuring national security, consideration of questions of international cooperation in the domain of ensuring security, coordination of the activity of federal agencies of executive power and agencies of executive power of subjects of the Russian Federation for the realization of decisions adopted by the President of the Russian Federation in the domain of ensuring national security (point 103).

The Ministry of Foreign Affairs of the Russian Federation is assigned to work out a general foreign policy strategy of the Russian Federation and submit respective proposals to the President of the Russian Federation, effectuate the realization of a foreign policy course of the Russian Federation in accordance with the Conception of Foreign Policy and with the Edict of the President of the Russian Federation of May 7, 2012, No. 605, and also the coordination of activity of federal agencies of executive power in the domain of international relations and international cooperation in accordance with the Edict of the President of the Russian Federation of November 8, 2011, No. 1478, "On the Coordinating Role of the Ministry of Foreign Affairs of the Russian Federation in Conducting a Single Foreign Policy Line of the Russian Federation."

Russia pays considerable attention not only to Russian citizens outside the country, but also ethnic Russians who have emigrated abroad and may or may not have acquired a foreign citizenship. The support extended to these populations may be legal, humanitarian, economic, or cultural; whatever the type of assistance extended, Russians are reminded where their Motherland is located and that they are welcome to return as and when they wish. The Federal Agency for Affairs of the Commonwealth of Independent States, Compatriots Residing Abroad, and International Humanitarian Cooperation renders assistance to the Ministry of Foreign Affairs of the Russian Federation in conducting a single foreign policy line of the Russian Federation in the part concerning the coordination in the established procedure of programs in the sphere of international humanitarian cooperation.

Foreign policy is not an exclusive monopoly of the central federal authorities in Russia. The subjects of the Russian Federation (of which presently there are 85, if Crimea and Sevastopol are included in their number) effectuate international and foreign economic links in accordance with the Constitution of the Russian Federation, Federal Law of January 4, 1999, No. 4-FZ, "On the Coordination of International and Foreign Economic Links of Subjects of the Russian Federation," and other legislative acts. The Ministry of Foreign Affairs of the Russian Federation and other federal agencies of executive power renders to agencies of state power of subjects of the Russian Federation necessary legal and expert-consultative assistance in the development of international and foreign economic links, in the organization and conducting of negotiations, in working out texts of agreements of the effectuation of international and foreign economic links to be concluded by agencies of state power of subjects of the Russian Federation, in the fulfillment of the said agreements, and also ensure the defense of the rights and legal interests of subjects of the Russian Federation in foreign states, using for these purposes the possibilities of the Council of Heads of Subjects of the Russian Federation attached to the Ministry of Foreign Affairs of the Russian Federation. The development of interregional and frontier cooperation is an important reserve for bilateral links with respective regions and states in trade, economic, humanitarian, and other domains.

## 6 Russian Compliance with International Law

The extent to which any state complies with its obligations under international law is a legitimate issue which international lawyers have considered at various times. Violations of international law are considered to be inherent in the international legal system. As Onuma expressed the proposition: "Where there is law, there is always violation of the law."[16] How frequent and material are violations of international law? Henkin (1917–2010) suggested the probability that "almost all nations observe almost all principles of international law and almost all of their obligations almost all of the time."[17] The question is whether this is true of the Russian Federation in its Soviet and post-Soviet guise.

Why, in principle, should the response to this question with respect to the Russian Federation differ from that of any other state. Whether the response should differ we consider below, but the context in which the question is put has differed in the twentieth century onward with respect to Russia for several reasons. First, Soviet political authorities and international lawyers approached the system of international law with suspicion and hostility from the October 1917 Revolution onwards. Treaties concluded by imperial Russia were in many (but not all) instances treated as predatory or unequal; these were terminated unilaterally, among them treaties establishing or recognizing the regime of capitulations and consular jurisdiction in the Near and Far East. Certain treaties were left in abeyance (for example, Red Cross treaties), and their validity from the Russian point of view was left in doubt.

Second, Soviet jurists questioned the legitimacy of the international legal order of which their country was a part. At a maximum, they devised theories and explanations over time that either rendered the international legal system ideologically impossible as between bourgeois and socialist countries, or posited the development of a "socialist international law," or devised other theories that would enable Soviet Russia to pick and choose among international legal norms considered to be useful or acceptable and therefore universal in application and those which were fundamentally bourgeois in origin and therefore antithetical in principle to Soviet Russian interests.

Third, especially after World War II, Soviet Russia favored the emergence of a new international legal order which would embody an appropriate mixture of

16 Yasuaki Onuma, *International Law in a Transcivilizational World* (CUP, 2017) 244.
17 L. Henkin, *How Nations Behave: Law and Foreign Policy* (2nd edn, Columbia UP, 1979) 47.

bourgeois and socialist legal rules or norms and be of more or less universal application.

During the Stalinist era of the Cold War, it was fashionable to juxtapose the presumed law-abiding behavior of the West and the constant violations of international law on the part of Soviet Russia, including treaty violations. Lengthy lists of alleged violations emanated from the legislative and executive branches of the United States.[18] Characterizing state behavior as law-abiding or law-violative is no simple matter, however:

> Even the most legal-minded Western nations have at time admittedly violated international law. It would be extremely difficult, if not impossible, for any impartial scholar or group of scholars to determine and compare the frequency with which various states have, in different periods of history, violated international law. The most basic difficulty arises from the very nature of legal norms. Legal scholars increasingly recognize that no legal norm, whether expressed in writing in a treaty or not, is "plain" and admits of only one interpretation. In varying degrees, all norms have a rubber-like quality which permits them to be reinterpreted to fit new needs and conditions and renders almost hopeless the task of an "objective" interpreter.[19]

For Soviet Russia, international law was as much a defensive mechanism as it was an opportunity to reshape the international community along lines deemed more favorable to Soviet interests. Whatever the views of Soviet jurists on ideological matters – and they frequently advocated positions far in advance of Soviet state practice – the international legal practice of Soviet Russia was often, perhaps mostly, in line with positions considered to be consistent with international legal norms.[20]

In post-Soviet Russia there are elements of continuity and divergence in approaches to international law. Among the elements of continuity are the fact that Russia is accepted as the legal-continuer of the former Soviet Union, and not the legal successor. The theory of the late Academician G. I. Tunkin (1906–1993) regarding the concordant wills of states as the principal explanation for the formation of rules of international law continues to be widely accepted by Russian international lawyers and has no widely accepted successor or replacement. Contemporary Russian international lawyers are as at home with citing their Soviet

18 The length of the lists varied with the overall state of political relations at the time. Compare: 'Soviet Violations of Treaties and Agreement' *Department of State Bulletin*, XXIII, no. 574 (July 3, 1950) 8, with another list published in the *Congressional Record*, CIX (September 24, 1963) pt 13, 17827.

19 O. J. Lissitzyn, *International Law Today and Tomorrow* (Oceana, 1965) 58.

20 On the distinction between compliance with international legal rules and policy advocacy seeking a change of those rules, see W. E. Butler, *The Soviet Union and the Law of the Sea* (Johns Hopkins Press, 1971); E. Bykhovskaya, *State Immunity in Russian Perspective* (Wildy, Simmonds and Hill, 2008).

predecessors as they are with quoting their pre-1917 predecessors. On many matters there is a continuity of opinion because there is a continuity of interest.

The transition to a market economy has required adjustments in Soviet and post-Soviet legal doctrines in the domain of private international law. Some areas of concern continue to prove to be difficult, if not intractable: state immunity, for example, not least because state ownership of the instruments and means of production continues to survive in the post-Soviet economy. Although international commercial arbitration is extensively accepted in post-Soviet Russian practice, the same cannot be said of interstate arbitral or judicial settlement of disputes. The ideological rhetoric has softened, but the reluctance to submit Russian disputes to independent third-party settlement runs deep. The submission of minor maritime disputes to the International Tribunal on the Law of the Sea (arrest of vessels) generated severe criticism in the Russian international legal community even though the outcome was favorable to Russia.

The state monopoly of foreign trade is long abolished, but the interest of the state in the regulation of foreign economic relations continues to be strongly in evidence. Russia was among the last major countries to achieve admission to the World Trade Organization; membership is regarded by the majority of Russian economists to have been of marginal benefit to the Russian Federation.

In one domain, however, post-Soviet Russia departed from most countries of the world in a positive way. When drafting the 1993 Constitution of the Russian Federation, a provision was included which made international law an integral part of the Russian legal system:

> Generally-recognized principles and norms of international law and international treaties of the Russian Federation shall be an integral part of its legal system. If other rules have been established by an international treaty of the Russian Federation than provided for by a law, the rules of the international treaty shall apply.[21]

The second sentence of article 15(4) reiterated a position long-established in Soviet law, although narrowly interpreted by some Soviet jurists to apply only to branches of Soviet law in which this priority accorded to treaties was expressly stipulated and by some post-Soviet Russian international lawyers to apply only to treaties subject to ratification and duly ratified.[22] The first sentence, however, was a considerable innovation. To paraphrase what was sometimes said of the Monroe Doctrine, the architects of the Russian Constitution brought in international law to reduce the possibilities of a return to arbitrary policies of the former Soviet Union. Dissatisfaction, however, with certain positions taken by the European Court of Human Rights (ECtHR) which found that provisions of the 1993 Russian Constitution were not consistent with Russian obligations under the 1950 European Convention for Human Rights and Fundamental Freedoms led the

21 Art. 15(4), 1993 Constitution of the Russian Federation, transl. in Butler (n. 7) 7.
22 See W. E. Butler, *Russian Law* (3rd edn, OUP, 2009) 4.74.

Constitutional Court of the Russian Federation to deny enforcement to such judgments of the ECtHR.[23] For the moment, the outcome is to place the Russian Constitution higher in the hierarchy of sources of Russian law than international treaty engagements which may violate provisions of the Constitution. To be sure, in one sense this was a foreseeable conflict,[24] for the treaty provisions themselves existed at the moment when the Russian Federation acceded to the 1950 European Convention and passed without remark at the time of the accession; their application in a subsequent case by the ECtHR can hardly have been unexpected. Russia thus joined those parties to the 1950 European Convention who have expressed disquiet at some of the judgments rendered by the ECtHR. The extent to which this judicial policy may detract from a unified European approach to human rights remains to be seen.

It nonetheless remains the case that Russian domestic courts during the past two decades have been performing a remarkably different, a veritably revolutionary, role in comparison with preceding years. Individuals and juridical persons may and do invoke treaty rights directly in Russian courts pursuant to article 15(4) of the Russian Constitution. Judges are encouraged as part of their training to draw upon international acts when appropriate and are not necessarily dependent on counsel directing their attention to them. The fact that a large number of cases have been in Strasbourg against Russia, Ukraine, Turkey, Bulgaria, and other Central European states is no reflection on the courts, but rather an indication that these countries continue to share a different attitude toward the relationship between state and citizen and a different perception of human rights with respect to some Convention provisions.

## 7 Conclusions

From an international lawyer's point of view, the 2016 Conception of Foreign Policy of the Russian Federation would deserve high marks for its explicit acknowledgment of the role that international law does or should play in the formulation and execution of foreign policy. For the moment at least, international legal structures formulated in the aftermath of World War II continue to serve Russian interests and are zealously defended against material changes. They secure the stature of the Russian Federation in the world community; the Soviet Union had a material hand in shaping them; and on the whole they are regarded as serving Russian national interests.

23 See on this sequence of events and possible implications for enforcement of Yukos judgments in Russia, Lauri Mälksoo, 'Russia's Constitutional Court Defies the European Court of Human Rights' (2016) 12 *European Constitutional Law Review* 377–95; Mälksoo, 'Case Law in Russian Approaches to International Law' in A. Roberts et al. (eds), *Comparative International Law* (OUP, 2018) 337–52.

24 In the case of *Anchugov and Gladkov* v. *Russia*, the ECtHR held that art. 32 of the 1993 Russian Constitution, which prohibited convicted prisoners from voting in state elections or holding elected office, was not in accordance with Protocol 1, art. 3, of the 1950 Convention.

Moreover, the key legal instruments that emanated after the United Nations Charter – the 1970 Declaration on the Principles of International Law Concerning Friendly Relations and Cooperation between States in Accordance with the Charter of the United Nations, and the Helsinki Final Act – continue to be viewed as pillars of order in the world community. Even with the dissolution of the former Soviet Union and discarding of Marxist-Leninist ideology, there remain remarkable continuities in Soviet and post-Soviet perceptions of the moving forces in international law and relations. Russia continues to feel fundamentally comfortable in the twenty-first century with mid-twentieth-century international legal structures.

That is not to gainsay the forces of globalization and the emergence of what Russia sees as a multipolar international system. The 2016 Conception of Foreign Policy marks a decided Russian shift of preoccupation from the Euro/Atlantic to all parts of Asia and a vigorous Arctic policy. But these for the moment merely alter certain vectors of Russian development and are not perceived as necessitating fundamental new institutions or readjustments to the existing postwar structures.

International law is a major factor, in the Russian view, for the resolution of world problems and the maintenance of international peace and security.

# 9 The Changing Nature of the Contemporary Russian Interpretation of the Right to Self-Determination under International Law

*Tero Lundstedt*

## 1 Introduction

This chapter introduces the Russian interpretation of the right to self-determination by first analyzing the significant contribution of the Union of Soviet Socialist Republics (hereafter, USSR) to its evolution. Following, after accounting for the continuum in the Russian legal stance toward self-determination, the focus will be on the significant changes that have occurred since the unilateral declaration of independence by Kosovo in February 2008. The chapter concludes that Russian domestic concerns and its historic interpretations on statehood and self-determination are reflected in its international law positions.[1]

During the Cold War, the USSR saw itself having fulfilled the self-determination aspirations of its numerous peoples with autonomic units in a federal structure, and conceived self-determination only applicable to other states. Therewith, it was seen as a useful instrument to further policy goals,[2] and the USSR enthusiastically promoted people's right to self-determination, becoming the original prime mover of decolonization. Nevertheless, because of its territorial gains following World War II, in the context of Europe the USSR demonstrated staunch support for the territorial integrity of states, culminating in the signing of the Helsinki Final Act in 1975.[3]

With the dissolution of the USSR in 1991, the Russian Federation chose to retain the Soviet federal formula and, with it, the Soviet understanding of self-determination. The former Soviet border regime was transplanted, as the Russian 1993 Constitution legalized the continuation of all the former autonomous units. Alongside came the perception that the issue of self-determination was again solved within the federation and thus only applies to other states of the international community. Russia continued to respect the borders of the Helsinki Final Act consistently until

1 According to Mälksoo, this is a recurring theme in the Russian international law concept in general. L. Mälksoo, *Russian Approaches to International Law* (OUP, 2015) 189–91.

2 Numerous examples of territorial acquisitions are well summarized in M. Beissinger, 'Self-Determination as a Technology of Imperialism: The Soviet and Russian Experiences' (2015) 14(5) *Ethnopolitics* 479–87, 481–2.

3 The Helsinki Final Act was the final document of the Conference on Security and Cooperation in Europe. It reaffirmed all European borders to be inviolable and was signed by virtually all European states, the USSR, the USA, and Canada.

2008, after which some major changes have taken place. The changes are visible in, for example, the Russian Written Statement in the Kosovo hearings at the International Court of Justice (ICJ) in 2009,[4] in several statements of leading officials, and in the two latest Foreign Policy Concepts of the Russian Federation.[5]

To summarize briefly, before 2008 Russia maintained that the right to territorial integrity of states is stronger than the right to self-determination and there was no right to secession under international law.[6] This did not stop Russia from aiding separatism and helping to create several "frozen conflicts"[7] in the post-Soviet area in the early 1990s: in Moldova (Transnistria), in Georgia (Abkhazia and South Ossetia), and in Azerbaijan (Nagorno-Karabakh).[8] Yet, significantly, no secession was recognized. After Kosovo's independence a new, controversial element appeared; the so-called "remedial secession" doctrine,[9] according to which a legal secession breaching territorial integrity is seen possible under certain special circumstances. Russian official statements regarding remedial secession have always been careful to refer to it in relation to the alleged Kosovo "precedent,"[10] for

4 Accordance with International Law of the Unilateral Declaration of Independence by the Provisional Institutions of Self-Government of Kosovo, Written Statement by Russia Federation, April 16, 2009.

5 Concept of the Foreign Policy of the Russian Federation, February 12, 2013; and Foreign Policy Concept of the Russian Federation, December 1, 2016.

6 See section 3.

7 A "frozen conflict" is a legal situation in international relations where active fighting between the parties has ceased but only by a ceasefire agreement, not by formal peace treaty or power-sharing agreement. In the post-Soviet context, this has usually resulted from an armed uprising of separatists in a formerly autonomous unit which had lost this status after the independence of the host state. While the separatists were able to secure retreat of the host state's army from their territory – usually via Russian military aid – they have been unable to get international recognition for their independence, or to reach an agreement on any meaningful autonomy with the host state.

8 In addition, there was limited lobbying in the 1990s in the state Duma for the return of Crimea from Ukraine, and more extensive lobbying took place for the return of the city of Sevastopol. However, these issues seemed to have been settled when, in 1994, Russia and Ukraine were able to agree on the continuing presence of the Russian Black Sea Fleet in Crimea via a long-term lease agreement.

9 The alleged right to remedial secession is usually derived from the "safeguard clause" of the Declaration on Principles of International Law Concerning Friendly Relations and Cooperation Among States in Accordance with the Charter of the United Nations, UNGA Res. 2625 (XXV), October 24, 1970 (Friendly Relations Declaration):

> Nothing in the foregoing paragraphs shall be construed as authorizing or encouraging any action which would dismember or impair, totally or in part, the territorial integrity or political unity of sovereign and independent States conducting themselves in compliance with the principle of equal rights and self-determination ... and thus possessed of a government representing the whole people belonging to the territory without distinction.

10 In a common law legal system, a precedent is a principle or a rule established by a prior legal case, which is either binding or otherwise persuasive for a court when deciding subsequent similar cases. In the international law sphere, a precedent has an

instance by the March 2014 Presidential Address,[11] as well as the open letter written on behalf of the Executive Board of the Russian Association of International Law (RAIL).[12] The Soviet linkage is that the target groups for remedial secession are the former Soviet autonomous subunits, to which Kosovo has an obvious legal parallel status. Additionally, remedial secession is linked in the Russian doctrine of self-determination to a reliance on referendums[13] to define both the "will of the people" and, in Crimea, even who the "people" are.[14]

This chapter concludes that these changes have thus far affected Russian legal position only in the post-Soviet area, just as Russian official sources had been warning prior to Kosovo's independence.[15] However, despite its calls for consistency, Russia has been utilizing its new view of self-determination inconsistently. This is well demonstrated in its approaches to different frozen conflicts, displayed in both the official policy documents as well as its actions: in the dispute over Transnistria, Russia has supported the territorial integrity of Moldova (as long as it remains neutral); in Georgia, it has supported the independence of Abkhazia and South Ossetia; in Nagorno-Karabakh, it has pursued a neutral mediator role between Armenia and Azerbaijan;[16] whereas in Ukraine it has resorted to "remedial annexation,"[17] justified by the Kosovo precedent and a referendum. Russia has failed to establish a legal criterion that would justify these inconsistencies, and the different treatment appears to be solely due to the state of relations between Russia and the target country.

This chapter will proceed in chronological order. After analyzing the Soviet view on the right of self-determination, it will proceed to the contemporary stance of the Russian Federation, focusing on the major changes in 2008 and in 2014.

added political tone. For a precedent case to produce binding legal customary law, it needs to have both state practice and *opinio juris* (a belief that such practice is legally allowed).

11 Address by the President of the Russian Federation, March 18, 2014.

12 Letter to the Executive Council of the International Law Association, June 6, 2014.

13 Yet, under international law, "holding a free and fair referendum is only a necessary, but not a sufficient condition for a territorial realignment to be accepted as lawful by international law" (A. Peters, 'Sense and Nonsense of Territorial Referendums in Ukraine, and Why the 16 March Referendum in Crimea Does Not Justify Crimea's Alteration of Territorial Status under International Law' *EJIL: Talk!*, April 16, 2014. Additionally, in 1920, the International Commission of Jurists of the League of Nations noted that there was no right of national groups to secede by a simple expression of will.

14 In its Written Statement (n. 4), Russia insisted that former autonomous status was not determinative of whether one could be considered a "people." This is due to its fragile position, being composed of altogether 83 federal subjects (85 if one counts Crimea and Sevastopol).

15 Inter alia, referring to Kosovo, Abkhazia, and South Ossetia, Putin has called for "generally accepted, universal principles for resolving these problems" (press conference for the Russian and foreign media, January 31, 2006); and "any resolution on Kosovo will set a precedent in international practice" (*BBC*, January 17, 2008).

16 (n. 5) (2013) art. 49.

17 T. Lundstedt, '"Peaceful" and "Remedial" Annexations of Crimea' *Völkerrechtsblog*, January 19, 2018, doi:10.17176/20180113-184204.

## 2 The Complex History of the Soviet Interpretation of the Right to Self-Determination

The history of the right to self-determination – an international legal norm according to which people have the right to freely choose their political status without outside interference[18] – has its political origins in 1917–18. The USSR and later Russia have contributed significantly to the development of the right to self-determination on four separate occasions, all stemming from the Soviet ethnofederal legacy. This took place in the establishment of the USSR in 1917–24; in the USSR's promotion of the international codification of the right in the United Nations (UN) era; with the dissolution of the USSR and the application of the *uti possidetis* principle in 1991; and with the schisms over the relationship with the international law principles of territorial integrity of states and self-determination of peoples since 2008. In order to inspect the changes in the Russian interpretation, the chapter will account briefly the history of self-determination and the Soviet role in its development.

The original self-determination appeared as a political principle in the late stages of World War I with two mostly politically opposite ideologues: Woodrow Wilson and Vladimir Lenin.[19] At this time, the principle did not secure an affirmative international legal position, since the United States and the USSR both stayed outside the newly established League of Nations. Without a major political figure to promote self-determination, the League did not codify it in its Covenant.[20]

In the USSR setting, Lenin proclaimed the right to self-determination of the peoples of Russia as a propaganda tool to win support of the non-Russians for the Bolshevik Civil War effort. However, after the failed experiment of "War Communism" (1918–1924) the Bolsheviks decided to reorganize the state applying the right to self-determination, as a union of sovereign states.[21] Lenin insisted that the Bolshevik

18 Self-determination is one of the core principles of contemporary international law, arising from customary law, protected in the UN Charter, granted in the 1966 International Covenants on Civil and Political Rights and on Economic, Social and Cultural Rights to "all peoples," and enshrined in a number of other international treaties. The principle is, at the same time, vague in its substance, which has enabled states to take varying views with its application in relation to the principle of territorial integrity. According to art. 1 (2), the purpose of the UN is to "develop friendly relations among nations based on respect for the principle of equal rights and self-determination of peoples."

19 See J. Duursma, *Fragmentation and the International Relations of Micro-States: Self-Determination and Statehood* (CUP, 1996) 7–27.

20 The League of Nations-appointed Commission of Rapporteurs represented a thorough and multidimensional treatment of self-determination in 1920. According to the rapporteurs' categorization:

> The principle is not, properly speaking, a rule of international law and the League of Nations has not entered it in its Covenant … It is a principle of justice and of liberty, expressed by a vague and general formula which has given rise to most varied interpretations and differences of opinion.
>
> (Report of the Commission of Rapporteurs, League of Nations Docs. B7.21/68/106/VII (1921) 22–3)

21 The subject of federalism caused a major ideological split within the Bolshevik Party over the constitutional structure. The opposing sides were the "assimilationists," led

commitment to self-determination had to be demonstrated, first by a voluntary treaty of union and then by legalizing a right of secession in the union's constitution.[22]

Thus, in December 1922, the Treaty on the Creation of the USSR was adopted by the First Congress of Soviets of the USSR. It became the framework and the *Grundnorm* of the federation all throughout the Soviet era, to be included in all subsequent constitutions as an annex. In January 1924, the first Constitution of the USSR was adopted. It created a unique asymmetrical federal structure, based on the Marxist-Leninist national ideology, called ethnofederalism.[23] Under ethnofederalism, the USSR consisted of three levels of self-determining units for the national groups of the former Russian Empire, based on their size and "progression level" toward socialism. The demarcation of these units was based on what was conceived as preexisting national communities, defined by their ethnicity, religion, or language. Under Soviet constitutional theory, the first two levels were usually referred to as "states" and the lowest as "ethnoterritorial self-administrative units."[24] The highest units were the Soviet Socialist Republics (SSRs), such as Georgia and Ukraine. The second highest were the Autonomous Soviet Socialist Republics (ASSRs), such as Abkhazia (in Georgian SSR) and Crimea (in Ukrainian SSR). The lowest were the Autonomous Oblasts (AOs), such as South Ossetia (in Georgian SSR) and Nagorno-Karabakh (in Azerbaijani SSR).[25] The higher status was reserved for the most economically and culturally progressive ethnicities.[26] Promotion and demotion were possible within the system.[27]

The aim of the system was to retain the large, multinational state inherited from imperial Russia in an era of nation-states without seeming to reestablish imperialism.[28]

by Stalin, and the "autonomists," led by Lenin. T. Rakowska-Harmstone, 'The Dialectics of Nationalism in the USSR' *Problems of Communism*, May 1974, 1–22, 1.

22 "We want a voluntary union of nations … a union founded on … absolutely voluntary consent." Letter to the Workers and Peasants of Ukraine, December 28, 1919, in V. Lenin, *Collected Works, Vol. 30, September 1919–April 1920* (Progress, 1965) 293.

23 The term "ethnofederalism" was first used by Philip Roeder to describe the Soviet system of designing ethnic homelands to titular nationalities ('Soviet Federalism and Ethnic Mobilization' (1991) 43(2) *World Politics*). The *Great Soviet Encyclopedia* and the 1977 USSR Constitution art. 70 used the term "socialist federation" which – according to the former – is "based on the national-territorial principle" (Vol. 27, 1977) 255.

24 G. Ubiria, *Soviet Nation-Building in Central Asia: The Making of the Kazakh and Uzbek Nations* (Routledge, 2016) 96–7.

25 1936 USSR Constitution, arts 22–9.

26 See, inter alia, J. Larrain, 'Classical Political Economists and Marx on Colonialism and "Backward" Nations' in B. Jessop and R. Wheatley (eds), *Karl Marx's Social and Political Thought: Critical Assessments of Leading Political Philosophers, Second Series* (Routledge, 1999) 164–95, 174–5.

27 Later downgraded SSRs included the Karelo-Finnish SSR and the Abkhazian SSR (demoted to ASSRs), and the Bukharan People's SR (disbanded).

28 The Bolsheviks were strongly affected by the simultaneous collapses of the Austro-Hungarian, Ottoman, and Tsarist empires. As put by Martin, "Lenin and Stalin understood very well the danger of being labelled an empire in the age of nationalism" (T. Martin, *The Affirmative Action Empire: Nations and Nationalism in the Soviet Union, 1923–1939* (Cornell UP, 2001) 19).

As nationalism was conceived as a capitalist distortion, the ethnofederal model was to be transitory and the USSR itself a "negation" of all the previous states that had existed.[29] Thus, within the USSR framework, at least in theory, the right to self-determination was awarded to the peoples of Russia in a form of territorial autonomies, with the highest level of the SSRs being referred to as sovereign and possessing a constitutional right to free secession from the Union. However, the official ideology presented the system with two major restrictions. First, only the toilers of a nation, not the bourgeoisie, could enjoy self-determination.[30] Thus, the secession right of the SSRs became obsolete, as only the bourgeoisie would want to secede, and they did not have a right to self-determination. Second, the only party allowed was the Communist Party, which was unified throughout the country without ethnic divisions.

Based on its own nationality policy, the USSR then promoted the establishment of self-determination as a legal right in the international setting and was consistently involved in drafting international treaties and conventions referring to it.[31] Self-determination was first institutionalized as a *principle* in 1945 when it was enshrined in article 1(2) of the Charter of the UN by a supplement proposed by the Soviet delegation.[32] It gained a major status upgrade with the 1960 UN General Assembly's Declaration on the Granting of Independence to Colonial Countries and Peoples that equated the *right* to self-determination to a complete independence in a colonial context.[33] The Soviet role was decisive, as its delegation submitted the draft that became the 1960 Declaration.[34] The USSR found natural allies in its quest for codifying the right to self-determination from the newly independent African and South Asian states. The momentum continued, as self-determination was made a qualified legal right beyond decolonization context by the 1966 Covenants on Civil and Political Rights and on Economic, Social and Cultural Rights, both containing identical article 1(1): "All peoples have the right of self-determination. By virtue of that right they freely determine their political status and freely pursue their economic,

29 R. Suny, 'The Empire Strikes Out: Imperial Russia, "National" Identity, and Theories of Empire' in R. Suny and T. Martin (eds), *A State of Nations: Empire and Nation-Making in the Age of Lenin and Stalin* (OUP, 2001) 53.

30 V. Vujačić, *Nationalism, Myth, and the State in Russia and Serbia: Antecedents of the Dissolution of the Soviet Union and Yugoslavia* (CUP, 2015) 10.

31 According to the highly distinguished Soviet scholar G. L. Tunkin: "Having placed the right of nations to self-determination at the base of its policy on the nationality question, the Soviet government pressed for the recognition of the principle of self-determination of nations as a principle of international law" (*Theory of International Law* (trans. W. Butler) (Harvard UP, 1974) 61).

32 Ibid., 62.

33 UNGA Res. 1541 (XV), December 14, 1960, arts 2, 4, and 6. It went much further in its legal implications than a normal declaration, establishing a special committee devoted exclusively to decolonization and monitoring the implementation of the declaration.

34 This is well documented by Bowring, who calls this instance a "truly climatic moment in the development of contemporary international law" (B. Bowring, 'Positivism versus Self-Determination: The Contradictions of Soviet International Law' in S. Marks (ed.), *International Law on the Left: Revisiting Marxist Legacies* (CUP, 2008) 133–68, 160).

social and cultural development." The principle also appeared in paragraph 1 of the 1970 Friendly Relations Declaration, and the ICJ has, on several occasions, referred to it as an operative legal right.[35] Nevertheless, self-determination has always been a problematic international law norm for its vagueness,[36] and the 1970 Declaration seems to equate it, outside decolonization, to self-government rather than independent statehood.[37] Finally, the 1975 Helsinki Final Act identified most fully the content of self-determination at a regional level,[38] by extending its normative content to all nations and peoples.[39]

In the early 1990s, the previous restrictions on self-determination within the USSR were abolished with Mikhail Gorbachev's glasnost reforms. Most importantly, article 6 of the 1977 Constitution was repealed, thereby abolishing the Communist Party's monopoly on political power. New nationalist parties started immediately demanding their right to self-determination, made possible by reforms of free speech, and the USSR started to dissolve.[40] The final dissolution process started on December 8, 1991, as the heads of states of the SSRs of Russia, Ukraine, and Belarus met in Minsk and signed a treaty establishing the Commonwealth of Independent States (CIS). The treaty proclaimed that "the USSR as a subject of international law and a geopolitical reality no longer exists."[41] Two

35 See, e.g., *Western Sahara, Advisory Opinion*, ICJ Reports (1975) 12, 120–1; *Legal Consequences for States of the Continued Presence of South Africa in Namibia (South West Africa) notwithstanding Security Council Resolution 276* (1970), Advisory Opinion, ICJ Reports (1971) 16, 73–75.

36 See A. Cassese, *Self-Determination of Peoples: A Legal Reappraisal* (CUP, 1995); Mälksoo (n. 1) 159–62; H. Hannum, *Autonomy, Sovereignty, and Self-Determination: The Accommodation of Conflicting Rights* (University of Pennsylvania Press, 1990) 27; H. Hannum, 'Rethinking Self-Determination' (1993) 34(1) *Virginia Journal of International Law* 1–69, 2.

37 M. Nikouei and M. Zamani, 'The Secession of Crimea: Where Does International Law Stand?' (2016) 85(1) *Nordic Journal of International Law* 37–64, 49.

38 As described by Kuznetsov:

> After the decline of colonial empires, the issue of self-determination of peoples in the sense of the formation of autonomous States was basically resolved … Now the provisions of this principle are basically applicable to the peoples of existing sovereign States.
> (V. I Kuznetsov and G. V. Ivanenko, 'Principles of International Law' in V. I. Kuznetsov and B. R. Tuzmukhamedov, *International Law: A Russian Introduction* (ed. and trans. W. Butler) (Eleven Publishing, 2009) 129–62, 149)

39 The Act proclaims:

> By virtue of the principle of equal rights and self-determination of peoples, all peoples always have the right, in full freedom, to determine, when and as they wish, their internal and external political status, without external interference, and to pursue as they wish their political, economic, social and cultural development.
> (Conference on Security and Co-operation in Europe, Final Act, Helsinki 1975, 1. (a) VIII)

40 D. Barry et al., *Perestroika at the Crossroads* (Sharpe, 1991) 235.

41 Agreement on the Establishment of the Commonwealth of Independent States (Belavezha Accords), December 8, 1991, 31 ILM 138.

weeks later, eight more SSRs joined the CIS,[42] declaring that the USSR had now ceased to exist.[43] The SSRs agreed that Russia would continue the legal existence of the USSR,[44] and formally declared that all their border adjustments would be settled by the *uti possidetis juris* principle, if not agreed otherwise by the parties in question.[45]

*Uti possidetis (juris)*[46] is an international legal principle according to which the former administrative borders of a unit become international borders at the moment of independence.[47] It had been utilized previously in decolonization contexts in Spanish America in the early 1800s, and in Africa and Southeast Asia in the 1960s. In both cases, the successor states of the colonial empires agreed between themselves to apply *uti possidetis* and honor the former administrative borders.[48] In the 1990s, *uti possidetis* was applied outside the decolonization context in two ethnofederal dissolutions: by the common agreement in the USSR and by an outside insistence in the case of the Socialist Federal Republic of Yugoslavia (SFRY).[49] The SFRY situation was comparable to that of the USSR, as it had transplanted the Soviet ethnofederal model to its Constitution in 1946.

Yet, in the dissolutions of the USSR and the SFRY, only the highest level of self-determination units, the SSRs, were able to secure international recognition. Therewith, all the former SSRs, e.g. Estonia, Georgia, and Ukraine in the USSR, Serbia and Croatia in the SFRY, became independent states that inherited sovereignty over their former SSR area, including, in many cases, former ASSRs and AOs. This was highly problematic, since the ASSRs had gained considerable autonomy, close to equivalent to those of the SSRs, in the early

42 The Baltic States refused to participate and for a time Georgia experienced severe internal unrest.

43 Alma-Ata Declaration, December 21, 1991, 31 ILM 148.

44 *Decision by the Council of Heads of State of the Commonwealth of Independent States*, ILM 31 (1992), para. 1. In December 24, 1991, Russia announced its wish to continue membership of the USSR in the UN. Letter of the President of the Russian Federation to the UN Secretary-General, ILM 31 (1992) 138.

45 Belavezha Accords (n. 41) art. 5.

46 In its original form *uti possidetis juris* is based on a Roman civil law principle, according to which, when there was a completing claim on a property, an official edict would grant provisional possession over it during litigation to the person who already was physically possessing it.

47 For a good overview, see, inter alia, M. Shaw, 'Peoples, Territorialism and Boundaries' (1997) 8(3) *EJIL* 478–507; M. Shaw, 'The Heritage of States: The Principle of *uti possidetis juris* Today' (1997) 67(1) *British Yearbook of International Law* 75–154; J. Crawford (ed.), *Brownlie's Principles of Public International Law* (8th edn, OUP, 2012) 238–9.

48 Most Latin American states agreed to apply *uti possidetis* in the Treaty of Confederation (February 8, 1848), the African states in the 1963 *Charter of the Organization of African Unity*, art. III.3, and reaffirmed a year later in Resolution on Border Disputes ("Cairo Declaration"), September 10, 1964, AGH/RES.16(I).

49 The role of the Arbitration Committee on Yugoslavia, established by the European Community in 1991, has received a lot of scholarly attention. See, for example, P. Radan, *The Break-up of Yugoslavia and International Law* (Routledge, 2002); M. Craven, 'The European Community Arbitration Commission on Yugoslavia' (1995) 66(1) *British Yearbook of International Law* 333–413.

1990s.[50] The dissolution of the USSR resulted in the SSRs being recognized territorially fully sovereign, terminating all guarantees for the ASSRs of any meaningful autonomic status. The former SSRs confronted their ASSRs in different ways, but many chose a revocation or a substantial diminishing (e.g. Georgia in relation to the Abkhazian ASSR and the AO of South Ossetia, Azerbaijan in relation to the AO of Nagorno-Karabakh, Serbia in relation to Kosovo ASSR) of their autonomies. Usually, this destroyed the peacefulness of the dissolution, igniting ethnic violence. Moreover, this made many of the former SSRs highly vulnerable to claims of self-determination.

Next, I will account for the changes in the Russian doctrine of the right to self-determination since 1991. I will divide the changes in three sections: pre-Kosovo 1992–2008; pre-Crimea 2008–14, and the contemporary view since the annexation of Crimea.

## 3 Russian Policy toward the Former ASSRs and the Russian Diaspora, 1992–2008

Four distinct, yet interdependent, aspects of the Soviet legacy have shaped the contemporary Russian view of self-determination in the CIS area since 1991: ethnofederalism, Russian diaspora, a self-proclaimed "Sphere of Influence" and a policy of "passportization."

The legacy of ethnofederalism has haunted many of the former SSRs, since the USSR had altogether 20 ASSRs and eight AOs in 1991.[51] The ASSRs were the most susceptible to separatist demands, based on their previous high self-governing status. The Russian Federation was most affected, with 17 ASSRs and five AOs being located within its borders. Despite the proposal of the Rumiantsev Constitutional Commission of the Russian parliament calling for its abolition,[52] and unlike the other SSRs, Russia

50 The USSR passed a series of constitutional changes in the spring of 1990 in preparation for a renewed federal structure, promoting the ASSRs as close-to-equals with the SSRs. The changes included: Law on the Procedure for Resolving Questions Connected with a Union Republic's Secession from the USSR, April 3, 1990; Law on the Principles of Economic Relations between the USSR, the Union and Autonomous Republics, April 10, 1990; Law on the Free National Development of Citizens of the USSR Who Reside Outside Their Own National-Territorial Formations or Who Do Not Possess Such Formations on the Territory of the USSR, April 26, 1990; finally, Law on the Division of Powers between the USSR and the Subjects of the Federation, April 26, 1990. In the SFRY, the ASSRs had already secured a strong autonomy in the 1974 SFRY Constitution. Under the SFRY constitutional system, the SSRs were called Socialist Republics and the ASSRs were called Socialist Autonomous Provinces, but their self-governing rights – including the secession right for the Socialist Republics – were copied from and corresponded to the Soviet ethnofederal arrangements. Thus, for clarity's sake, I will use the terms SSRs and ASSRs to refer to the SFRY ethnofederal units as well.

51 USSR 1977 Constitution, arts 71, 85, 87, and 88.

52 The Commission proposed abolishing the ASSRs and AOs, and replacing them with about 50 provinces without ethnic labels and with equal status. J. Hughes, 'Managing Secession Potential in the Russian Federation' in J. Hughes and G. Sasse (eds), *Ethnicity and Territory in the Former Soviet Union: Regions in Conflict* (Routledge, 2002) 36–68, 46–7.

chose to retain the Soviet federal system by the 1992 Federal Treaty, followed by the 1993 Constitution. Some scholars have argued that this saved Russia from further fragmentation in the 1990s.[53] Nevertheless, like other former SSRs with ASSRs, Russia was faced with secessionist attempts. While it was able to negotiate a peaceful settlement via Treaty with the Tatarstan ASSR,[54] the conflict with Chechnya led to the establishment of the unrecognized Chechen Republic of Ichkeria (1991–2000) and to two bloody wars, until Russian control was reestablished. In 2000, the then President Putin said that the Chechnyan conflict was due to the "continuation of the collapse of the USSR," which had to be stopped or the Russian state might cease to exist.[55]

On top of numerous former autonomous units, the 14 other SSRs inherited a huge diaspora of 25.2 million Russians, who were transformed from a majority to a minority in their new homeland, ranging from 2 to 38 percent of the population.[56] While they lacked their own autonomous units, Russians usually resided in greater numbers within the ASSRs and AOs, which, already, had typically a more pro-Russian political elite than the successor states as a whole.

The Russian "Sphere of Influence" was first formulated in 1992 by Foreign Minister Kozyrev, when he insisted that Russia would not leave those regions that for centuries it had considered its spheres of interest.[57] In the spring of 1993, he asked the UN to recognize Russia's special responsibility for peacekeeping in the CIS area.[58] The Foreign Policy Concept of 1993 demanded that the relations with the CIS states have to be built on premises that they take Russian interests properly into account, especially by guaranteeing the rights of Russian diaspora.[59] Yet, as Trenin has pointed out, domestic problems in the 1990s deprived Moscow of resources to back up its ritual claims on its prime interests in the CIS area.[60] These insistencies came back in the mid 2000s, when the rhetoric of sphere of *influence* was replaced with the rhetoric of sphere of *interest*. For example, in 2003 Putin called the CIS area "the sphere of our strategic interests."[61]

53 e.g., see H. Hale, 'The Makeup and Breakup of Ethnofederal States: Why Russia Survives Where the USSR Fell' (2005) 3(1) *Perspectives on Politics* 55–70. Hale concludes that since none of the Russian provinces have over 50 percent of the population, the central government has capacity to thwart the kind of centrifugal forces that dissolved the USSR.

54 *On Delimitation of Jurisdictional Subjects and Mutual Delegation of Powers between the State Bodies of the Russian Federation and the State Bodies of the Republic of Tatarstan*, Moscow, February 15, 1994.

55 Quoted in F. Hill, 'The Real Reason Putin Supports Assad' *Foreign Affairs*, March 25, 2013.

56 T. Heleniak, 'Migration of the Russian Diaspora after the Breakup of the Soviet Union' (2004) 57(2) *Journal of International Affairs* 99–117, 99.

57 J. Sherr, *Hard Diplomacy and Soft Coercion: Russia's Influence Abroad* (Chatham House, 2013) 50.

58 D. Trenin, 'Russia's Sphere of Interest, not Influence' (2009) 32(4) *Washington Quarterly* 3–22, 8.

59 Conception of the Foreign Policy of the Russian Federation, April 23, 1993, s. IV.

60 Sherr (n. 57) 9.

61 Annual Address to the Federal Assembly, May 16, 2003. Additionally, in his annual address on April 25, 2005, Putin said that "Russia should continue its civilizing mission on the Eurasian continent … We consider international support for the respect of

Interest should be understood in this context as a lighter form of influence, without any straightforward political control.[62]

Finally, on top of the Russian diaspora, the Russian liberal Law on Nationality from the late 1990s gave the former citizens of the USSR wide opportunities to apply for Russian citizenship, and many minorities of the ASSRs and AOs have been eager to do so.[63] As a result, there has been fierce opposition in many of the former SSRs to the passportization policy of Moscow, and only Tajikistan has a formal agreement with Russia on dual citizenship,[64] whereas e.g. the laws of Ukraine, Georgia, and Moldova reject it.[65] While international law on nationality poses few restrictions on states to confer citizenship, Russia's policy of conferring its citizenship en masse on the citizens of another country seems arbitrary and abusive,[66] and the Independent International Fact-Finding Mission has condemned Russian passportization policy in South Ossetia and Abkhazia.[67]

For these four reasons, Russia already had a complex relationship with many of the former SSRs prior to 2008. Although Russia had agreed to honor their territorial integrity,[68] it contributed to the establishment of the frozen conflicts in their territories. The former ASSRs and AOs that had declared independence in the early 1990s included: the ASSRs of Chechnya and Tatarstan from Russia; the Crimean ASSR from Ukraine;[69] the Abkhazian ASSR and the South Ossetian AO from Georgia; the Transnistrian ASSR from Moldova;[70] and the AO of Nagorno-Karabakh from Azerbaijan. However, the "hot" period of these conflicts involving use of force was mostly finished by 1992, and the conflicts remained, apart from

the rights of Russians abroad an issue of major importance, one that cannot be the subject of political and diplomatic bargaining."

62 Trenin (n. 58) 12–13.

63 President Putin clarified who are Russian "compatriots" abroad thus: "those people who consider themselves part of the broad Russian community, they may not necessarily be ethnic Russians, but they consider themselves Russian people" (speech at Conference of Russian Ambassadors and Permanent Representatives, July 1, 2014).

64 A. Grigas, *Beyond Crimea: The New Russian Empire* (Yale UP, 2016) 41.

65 Ukrainian Law on Citizenship, art. 2 rejects it outright, and in Georgia and Moldova dual citizenship is only possible by presidential decree.

66 Well elaborated in K. Natoli, 'Weaponizing Nationality: An Analysis of Russia's Passport Policy in Georgia' (2010) 28 *Boston International Law Journal* 389–417, 416–17.

67 Independent International Fact-Finding Mission on the Conflict in Georgia (IIFFMCG), Report (II), September 2009, 183.

68 Under the auspices of the CIS, the inviolability of their former internal borders has been affirmed in several treaties: Belavezha Accords (n. 41) art. 5; Alma-Ata Declaration (n. 43) preamble and art. 1; Charter Establishing the Commonwealth of Independent States (January 22, 1993), 34 ILM 128, art. 3; Declaration on Respect of Sovereignty, Territorial Integrity and Inviolability of Boundaries of Member States, Bulletin of International Agreements No. 7, Moscow 1994, 9–10.

69 Crimea declared independence, dependent on a later referendum, in May 1992, but was incorporated back to Ukraine via an agreement later that year.

70 Transnistria had been ASSR until 1940, but was without ethnofederal status in 1991.

Chechnya, relatively peaceful until 2008.[71] Russia was often able to dominate the mediation formats in the conflicts between the former SSRs and ASSRs by using the auspices of the CIS and the ASSRs' elites' historical tendency to seek support from Moscow. Additionally, in Transnistria, Abkhazia and South Ossetia, the Kremlin was able to secure continued presence in the form of Russian peace-keepers,[72] and in Ukraine it received extraterritorial rights over the Sevastopol Naval Base.[73] The main ingredient of the Russian view on the realization of the right to self-determination of this time was its vehement support for the inherited *uti possidetis* borders. Even though several former ASSRs had voted in favor of the continuation of the USSR,[74] and had voiced their willingness to become part of the Russian Federation after the dissolution,[75] Russia remained committed to inherited borders and refused to recognize any territorial changes in the CIS area. Russia was keen to demonstrate that it was supporting separatism. Likewise, the Russian Constitutional Court denied any right to secession in the Tatarstan (1993) and Chechnya (1995) cases.[76] The main Russia scholars writing on self-determination prior to 2007–8 held a consistent view that self-determination does not justify breaching the territorial integrity of an existing state.[77] At this time, any reference to the "will of the people" meant the will of the population as a whole, not of the separatist unit.

Notwithstanding, the legal landscape and political position of the former ASSRs was altered with developments in the former SFRY. In 1999, after a controversial

71 Apart from the war between Abkhazia and Georgia, which lasted until the December 1993 ceasefire agreement.

72 In South Ossetia (jointly with Georgians) since the Sochi Agreement June 24, 1992; in Abkhazia since the Moscow Agreement May 14, 1994; in Transnistria since the establishment of the Joint Commission Control in July 21, 1992.

73 In three separate agreements, all signed on 28 May 1997.

74 Referendum on the Preservation of the Union of Soviet Socialist Republics. The posed question was "Do you consider necessary the preservation of the USSR as a renewed federation of equal sovereign republics in which the rights and freedom of an individual of any nationality will be fully guaranteed?" For example, in Abkhazia, the vote to preserve the USSR was 98.5 percent in favor, and in the Russian SSR the results in all its ASSRs were higher in favor (76.0–91.4 percent) than in the Russia proper (73 percent) (Direct Democracy, www.sudd.ch/event.php?lang=en&id=su011991).

75 e.g., a referendum in South Ossetia on January 19, 1992 registered 99. 9 percent vote for reunion with Russia with 96. 9 percent turnout (Direct Democracy, www.sudd.ch/event.php?lang=en&id=ge011992). In Transnistria, a referendum in 2006 was 98 percent support in favor of "free association with the Russian Federation" with 78.6 percent turnout (Direct Democracy, www.sudd.ch/event.php?lang=en&id=md012006).

76 J. Summers, 'Russia and Competing Spheres of Influence: The Case of Georgia, Abkhazia and South Ossetia' in M. Happold (ed.), *International Law in a Multipolar World* (Routledge, 2011) 91–113, 109.

77 These scholars included O. I. Tiunov (right to self-determination is limited by the principle of territorial integrity); S. V. Chernichenko (the legality of secession depends on the consent of the parent state). Quoted in O. Merezhko, 'Crimea's Annexation by Russia – Contradictions of the New Russian Doctrine of International Law' (2015) 75 (1) *Zeitschrift für ausländisches öffentliches Recht und Völkerrecht* 167–94, 178.

NATO intervention, UN Security Council Resolution 1244 had established a UN administration over the former ASSR of Kosovo, and obligated Serbs and Albanians to negotiate over the province's future status. The series of negotiations hit a final impasse in early 2007.[78] As Kosovo's declaration of independence started to seem imminent, the rhetoric of Russia and of the separatists in the CIS area started to change. Most of the western states planning to recognize Kosovo tried very hard to justify their decision by the fact that this case was so unique, *sui generis*, that it did not create a dangerous precedent on secession. Russia had been opposing Kosovo's independence consistently, and, rejecting the *sui generis* formula,[79] warned on several occasions that it would have major implications for the post-Soviet area.[80] Just a month prior to the Georgian War, President Medvedev stated that "We consider the Kosovo precedent as extremely dangerous and unsuccessful. We don't consider the decision made on this issue as a *causus sui generis*, but as an absolute precedent."[81] Also in 2007, an influential Russian international law textbook was published by the Diplomatic Academy of the Ministry of Foreign Affairs of Russia, under the aegis of the Russian Association of International Law. It concurred with the findings of the Canadian Supreme Court in its 1998 case,[82] which had affirmed that self-determination, even if confirmed by a clear free vote in favor of secession, was expected to be exercised within the framework of existing states. However, it could be exercised unilaterally under certain, limited circumstances. The textbook concluded that the question of secession may be resolved only by referendum of the people in question, and that remedial secession may be possible if the principle of equality and self-determination is not observed.[83]

78 Most plainly, Comprehensive Proposal for the Kosovo Status Settlement by the UN Special Envoy Ahtisaari, February 2, 2007, concluded that further negotiations were futile and recommended a supervised independence for Kosovo.

79 In the scholarly circles, the *sui generis* role of Kosovo is often called into question. In reality, in the international law setting *sui generis* circumstances are more common than unique. C. Rossi, 'Impaled on Morton's Fork: Kosovo, Crimea, and the *sui generis* Circumstance' (2016) 30(3) *Emory International Law Review* 353–90.

80 Already in 2006, Putin called for uniform solutions to territorial conflicts, adding that "Russia has never raised the issue of annexing any territories outside its current borders" ('Putin Urges Uniform Regional-Conflict Approaches' *Sputnik*, June 2, 2006). In November 2007, he insisted that "The principle of self-determination should apply not just to the peoples living in former Yugoslavia, but also to peoples, including the peoples of the Caucasus, in the post-Soviet area" (V. Pacer, *Russian Foreign Policy under Dmitry Medvedev, 2008–2012* (Routledge, 2016) 30–1). After Kosovo independence, the rhetoric hardened as the chairman of the Committee of the Post-Soviet Affairs, Alexei Ostrovsky, commented that "The world community should understand that from now on the resolution of conflicts in the ex-Soviet area cannot be seen in any other context from that of Kosovo" (*Javno* (Zagreb), March 13, 2008); and "We must review our foreign policy in response to new challenges" (*Financial Times*, March 16, 2008).

81 Interview, *Tanjug*, July 3, 2008.

82 *Reference re Secession of Quebec* [1998] 2 SCR 217, 1998 CanLII 793.

83 Kuznetsov and Ivanenko (n. 38) 149–50. The book was originally released in Russian in 2007. After Kosovo's independence, the right to remedial secession continued to be

One of the warnings that speaks volumes about the faltering Russian commitment to the territorial integrity of the former SSRs came from the Russian Envoy to NATO, Dmitry Rogozin, in early 2008. He described the Georgian decision to have a referendum on NATO membership excluding Abkhazian and South Ossetian provinces a:

> historic mistake, because in this way he personally excluded Abkhazia and South Ossetia from Georgia. As soon as Georgia gets some kind of prospect from Washington of NATO membership, the next day the process of real secession of these territories from Georgia will begin.[84]

Even more ominously, he said later that "it is unlikely that Ukraine would be able to maintain its current borders if it joined NATO."[85] Russia was warning that, in addition to its vehement opposition of NATO aspirations of the former SSRs, it would consider independence of the ASSR of Kosovo legitimizing territorial changes in the CIS area under some circumstances.

Thus, as Kosovo was quickly recognized by most western states and, ultimately, by 113 (59 percent) UN member states,[86] the Russian doctrine of the right to self-determination was altered accordingly.[87] This development has been reflected in Russian actions, official rhetoric, foreign policy, military, and national security documents. In sum, the previous consistency of Russia's dual stance on self-determination – officially supporting territorial integrity of states, despite its significant political, military, and economic support of separatism in the CIS area since 1992 – gave away to a more politically motivated interpretation. Fewer than six months later, Russia used this new interpretation to justify the dismantling of the former SSR of Georgia.

## 4 The Russian View of Self-determination in 2008–14

After the western recognition of Kosovo and subsequent Russian rhetoric, the relations between Georgia and Russia became very tense. The UN Security Council tried to intervene in April by reaffirming the territorial integrity of Georgia within its recognized borders and calling for peaceful settlement to the Georgian–Abkhazian conflict.[88] After a controversial Georgian attack against South

promoted, e.g., in a 2009 book by Ostoukhov (secession can only be legal when authorities of a state make internal self-determination impossible) Merezhko (n. 77) 180.

84 'Russia Warns Against Georgia NATO Membership' *Reuters*, March 11, 2008.

85 *Russian Newsweek*, February 25–March 2, 2008, 23.

86 Situation as at December 22, 2017.

87 The "traumatic" nature of Kosovo independence for Russia is well summarized in C. Borgen, 'Law, Rhetoric, Strategy: Russia and Self-Determination Before and After Crimea' (2015) 91 *International Law Studies* 216–80, 234–6.

88 UNSC Res. 1808 (2008), para. 1.

Ossetia on August 7, 2008,[89] a brief war between Georgia and Russia followed, after which Russia, for the first time, broke the taboo of territorial changes to the *uti possidetis* borders that it had promised to honor in several international agreements. When President Medvedev recognized the independencies of Abkhazia (former ASSR) and South Ossetia (former AO), he based this on three factors: the Georgian decision to opt for a "genocide" which dashed all hopes for peaceful coexistence (remedial secession); the freely expressed will of Abkhazians and Ossetians; and the right to self-determination.[90] He accused the West of ignoring Russian warnings over Kosovo and that it would now be impossible to deny the same right to Abkhazians and Ossetians.[91]

Thus, three new contentious aspects of Russia's interpretation of self-determination emerged: the will of the people can be determined by the people of the province, irrespective of the will of the population as a whole; human rights violations of the host state may justify territorial changes via remedial secession; and Kosovo is a legal precedent for these new interpretations. The situation was somewhat different on the academic side: at this point, the scholarly view in Russia still held that territorial integrity takes priority over the right to self-determination, and remedial secession should be seen as a rarity.[92]

As the official Russian rhetoric was questioning territorial integrity of some of the former SSRs,[93] even the legitimacy of the application of *uti possidetis* back in 1991 was being questioned. As a group of leading Russian defense analysts remarked at the 2012 Valdai Club:

> The entire Belavezha Accords system[94] of State and territorial structure, which took shape as a result of the 1991 national disaster, is illegitimate, random, unstable and therefore fraught with conflict.[95]

89 According to IIFFMCG, while Georgian attack was the beginning of large-scale hostilities, it was only the culminating point of a long period of increasing tensions (Report (I) (2009) 11).

90 Statement by President of Russia, August 26, 2008.

91 Interview, *Reuters*, August 26, 2008.

92 According to Moiseev, Russian international legal doctrine does not allow self-determination undermining territorial integrity (Happold (n. 76) 180).

93 President Putin said in a speech at the NATO summit April 2, 2008: "this policy puts us into a very complicated position at the post-Soviet space, because we have there enough situations similar to that with Kosovo – it is Transnistria, Southern Ossetia, Abkhazia, Karabakh"; and "Ukraine is not even a State. What is Ukraine? Part of its territories is Eastern Europe, but the greater part is a gift from us" ('Putin to the West: Hands off Ukraine" *Time*, May 25, 2009).

94 Belavezha Accords (n. 41). The reference is to the decisions to dissolve the Union and to apply *uti possidetis*.

95 M. Barabanov, K. Makienko, and R. Pukhov, 'Military Reform: Toward the New Look of the Russian Army' (2012) *Valdai Discussion Club Analytical Report* 9–10. The Valdai Discussion Club an influential annual forum where Russian officials meet with experts.

Russian officials had also repeatedly condemned the transfer of Crimea to Ukraine back in 1954, and called for its return to Russia.[96] Notwithstanding, Russia displays inconsistencies in this position, as it has never repudiated or questioned the numerous territorial transfers in its favor during the Soviet era.[97]

Russia's rhetoric was also hardening in relation to its diaspora and sphere of interest. First, Russia has seen itself entitled to protect the rights of Russians abroad if it feels that their rights are being violated, and this was used as an official justification for its military action in Georgia (protecting Russian peacekeepers and Russian passport holders).[98] In 2009, this new doctrine was codified in the Russian Federal Law amendment "On Defence," to legitimize military intervention if there is "discrimination and the suppression of rights, freedoms and legitimate interests of Russian Federation citizens in foreign countries." The Council of Europe has called the law "problematic" under international law.[99] When it is combined with the passportization policy in the former ASSRs, one could argue that Russia is unilaterally making itself a direct party in these separatist conflicts.

Second, sphere of interest came back to official rhetoric in late summer 2008. In his foreign policy principles,[100] President Medvedev listed regions of special interest as one of the main foreign policy areas, where Russia will have "special, cordial, long-term relations,"[101] and Foreign Minister Lavrov urged the West to acknowledge this "new reality."[102] Finally, Medvedev hinted that it was foolish to deny the existence of Russian special interests, because it would end up like the Georgian War.[103]

One could conclude that Russia seems convinced of its right to have a sphere of interest in the post-Soviet area, and it has modified its internal legislation and foreign policy to suit its needs. Further, it seems to be willing to make significant political sacrifices and risks to retain this sphere, calculating that at least NATO membership will exclude the post-Soviet states from it. Thus, not only did Georgian aspirations for western alignments lead to a brief war, but there was even a warning by the president that it would happen again if the existence of Russian special interests in the region were denied.

96 For example, the state Duma and Ministry of Foreign Affairs had, on January 23, 1992, condemned the transfer of Crimea to Ukraine (T. Kuzio, *Ukraine – Crimea – Russia: Triangle of Conflict* (Ibidem-Vertag, 2014) 15). Likewise, Prime Minister Chernomyrdin demanded in December 1996 that Ukraine recognize the "illegality" of its sovereignty over Sevastopol (ibid., 77).

97 Merezhko (n. 77) 175–6.

98 Official Russian justifications are listed in IIFFMCG, Report (III), September 2009, 429–40.

99 Council of Europe, 'Opinion on the Federal Law on the Amendments to the Federal Law on Defence of the Russian Federation' adopted by Venice Commission at its 85th Plenary Session (December, 2010).

100 Interview, *Rossiya-1, NTV*, August 31, 2008.

101 Interview, *Euronews*, September 3, 2008.

102 *Gazeta Wyborcza*, September 10, 2008.

103 Transcript of the Meeting with the Participants in the International Club Valdai, September 12, 2008.

In October 2008, Russia supported a Serbian draft for a resolution in the UN General Assembly that took the case of Kosovo independence to the ICJ. In its Written Statement, Russia gave a comprehensive overview on its stance of the right to self-determination, insisting that the Kosovo case can be solved through relevant principles and rules of international law, enshrined in the UN Charter, the 1966 Covenants, the 1970 Friendly Relations Declaration, and the Helsinki Final Act 1975. Based on these, Kosovo had, at most, the right to *internal* self-determination within Serbia, in similar manner "The peoples of the Russian Federation have chosen to exercise their right to self-determination through constituent entities."[104] This is a reference to the Russian position that is has solved any questions relating to self-determination in Russia with its Soviet-inspired federal structure, which is also the framework it tried to introduce in Moldova[105] in 2003 and, later, in Ukraine[106] in 2014. Additionally, Russia was simultaneously promoting the right to remedial secession, while denying its applicability to Kosovo. The bar for remedial secession was set high: "However, those conditions should be limited to truly extreme circumstances, such as an outright armed attack by the parent State, threatening the very existence of the people in question."[107] Outside this threshold, any disputes should be settled within the framework of the existing state. In September 2009, Russian UN Ambassador, Vitaly Churkin, clarified that the difference between Kosovo and Abkhazia and South Ossetia was that in 2008 nobody was threatening the population of Kosovo.[108]

The ICJ gave its Opinion in 2010, where the main finding was that a unilateral declaration of independence is not prohibited under international law. However, if a peremptory norm, such as use of force, is breached to achieve it, then the independence is illegal.[109] The ICJ did not address the legality of remedial secession or outside recognition of Kosovo's independence.[110]

A long stillness in the Russian official documentation and political initiatives came to an end with the introduction of a new Foreign Policy Concept (2008), National Security Strategy and a series of policy initiatives launched by the Medvedev

104 Written Statement (n. 4) para. 5.

105 Russian Draft Memorandum on the Basic Principles of the State Structure of a United State in Moldova (Kozak Memorandum), November 17, 2003.

106 Protocol on the Results of Consultations of the Trilateral Contact Group, signed in Minsk, September 5, 2014.

107 Ibid., para. 88. References are made to the Quebec case (n. 82), and to international law scholars favoring the right, such as C. Tomuchat ('Secession and Self-Determination' in M. Kohen (ed.), *Secession: International Law Perspectives* (CUP, 2006) 23–45, 41); Cassese (n. 36) 119).

108 B. Balayev, *The Right to Self-Determination in the South Caucasus: Nagorno Karabakh in Context* (Lexington, 2013) 58.

109 *Accordance with International Law of the Unilateral Declaration of Independence in Respect of Kosovo*, Advisory Opinion, ICJ, July 22, 2010, para. 81.

110 For scholarly views, see R. Falk, 'The Kosovo Advisory Opinion: Conflict Resolution and Precedent' (2011) 105(1) *AJIL* 50–60, 54; P. Hilpold, 'The International Court of Justice´s Advisory Opinion on Kosovo: Perspectives of a Delicate Question' (2009) (14) *Austrian Review of International and European Law* 259–310; Separate Opinion of Judge Keith, para. 1; and Separate Opinion of Judge Cançado Trindade, para. 26.

administration (2009),[111] Military Strategy (2010), and an updated Foreign Policy Concept (2013).[112] All the documents highlighted the importance of upholding general principles of international law, but, often, contained contradictory articles.

Particularly interesting is the 2013 Concept, which contains several questionable references to the Russian stance toward the former SSRs, added due to the key changes that had happened in 2008. First, there was a new statement that Russia "will maintain its active role in the political and diplomatic conflict settlement in the CIS space." However, the Concept proceeded to address the conflict settlement under special conditions for each of the disputes: according to article 49, Russia will participate in the settlement of the Transnistria problem on the "basis of respect for the sovereignty, territorial integrity and neutral status of the Republic of Moldova" with a special status for Transnistria; and in the settlement of the Nagorno-Karabakh conflict on the basis of territorial integrity and self-determination of peoples, with "future determination of the final legal status of Nagorno-Karabakh through a legally binding expression of will." Second, article 50 states:

> While respecting its Commonwealth partners' right to build relations with other international actors, Russia stands for the full implementation by the CIS Member States of their commitments within regional integration structures with Russian participation, ensuring further development of integration processes and mutually beneficial cooperation in the CIS space.

This ambiguous statement is an example of the pressure Russia is putting on the CIS states to choose Russian-led integration projects instead of the western ones.[113] The latest Foreign Policy Concept (2016) retains the same formulations of articles 49–50 of the 2013 Concept.

Thus, even before the Ukraine crisis, the inconsistencies in the Russian view on self-determination in the CIS area are observable: the former ASSRs are treated differently based on political goals, as the settlement in Transnistria is conditional on Moldova's remaining neutral, whereas Nagorno-Karabakh's political future would be settled by a referendum. Article 51 then promises assistance to Abkhazia and South Ossetia for their state formation, which are no longer mentioned as diplomatic conflicts in the CIS space. Still, the general tone of the Concept was reconciliatory toward the West and the former SSRs. Sadly, this became

111 These proposals included: confirming the basic principles of relations between states; emphasizing the role of the UN; a development of conflict settlement mechanisms; arms control; and cooperation in countering new threats, such as terrorism. All these should be codified in a legally binding document, a European security treaty. Address by Russian Minister of Foreign Affairs Sergey Lavrov at the opening of the OSCE Annual Security Review Conference, Vienna, June 23, 2009. Likely because of the Georgian War (2008), the proposals were met with suspicion by western states.

112 Russian Foreign Policy Doctrine (n. 5).

113 e.g. J. Headley, 'Russia's Complex Engagement with European Union Norms: Sovereign Democracy versus Post-Westphalianism?' in A. Björkdahl et al. (eds), *Importing EU Norms: Conceptual Framework and Empirical Findings* (Springer, 2015) 211–29, 223.

meaningless by Russian actions in 2014, using yet another former ASSR, Crimea, to achieve territorial dismemberment of another former SSR, Ukraine. After this, the events in Georgia in 2008 should no longer be seen as a one-off instance of escalating relationship with a neighboring state but, rather, as a continuum derived from the combination of Russian doctrine on the right to self-determination and its political attitude toward the sovereignty of the former SSRs.

## 5 The Russian Inconsistencies on Self-Determination after the Annexation of Crimea

Russia's aim in helping create and maintain frozen conflicts has been to use the leverage given by siding with the separatists to block the membership bids of the former SSRs in the western institutions, mainly, NATO and the European Union (EU).[114] Thus, not surprisingly, the crisis in Ukraine was ignited by the overthrow of a pro-Russian President and subsequent expressions of the willingness of the new leadership to join the EU. This gave Moscow the opportunity to use separatist tendencies in a former ASSR, where it had issued passports and had military presence, to further its policy goals. However, two new aspects have emerged, making the contemporary Russian stance on self-determination seem inconsistent: the legal justifications given for the annexation of Crimea are significantly weaker; and, unlike the former ASSRs, the separatists that Russia is actively supporting in Eastern Ukraine lack any previous autonomous status.[115]

In brief, after an uprising in the streets of Kiev, the fleeing of President Yanukovych, and his dismissal by the Ukrainian Parliament in February 2014, the Russian special forces took over the Crimean peninsula on February 27–28.[116] A hastily organized and internationally condemned referendum was held on March 16,[117] and Crimea was incorporated into Russia two days later. At first, Russian scholars remained silent, while officials were giving their international law interpretations "to the point of redesigning it."[118]

114 NATO's Supreme Allied Commander in Europe, Philip Breedlove, has argued that frozen conflicts are a tool that Russia uses as a veto to the target countries' EU and NATO memberships (*Reuters*, March 23, 2014).

115 The Russian international law doctrine has been unable to justify military involvement in the Donbass, and any active participation in the fighting is denied, and there has been no recognition rebel territories as independent.

116 This was first denied by Russian officials, but was admitted by Putin in a documentary *Crimea: The Road to Motherland* (Крым. Путь на Родину), *Rossiya-1*, March 15, 2015.

117 In addition to almost unanimous condemnation of the referendum by scholars, the Council of Europe described it as a violation of both Ukrainian law and general democratic rules on referendums. 'Opinion on Whether the Decision Taken by the Supreme Council of the Autonomous Republic of Crimea in Ukraine to Organise a Referendum on Becoming a Constituent Territory of the Russian Federation or Restoring Crimea's 1992 Constitution Is Compatible with Constitutional Principles' adopted by the Venice Commission at Its 98th Plenary Session (March, 2014).

118 A. Moiseienko, 'Guest Post: What Do Russian Lawyers Say about Crimea' *Opinio Juris*, September 24, 2014.

As in 2008, Russian legal argumentation over the secession right of Crimea was connected to the will of the people. As suggested by Chris Borgen, "The process of the referendum becomes a substitute for the substantive law of self-determination."[119] However, since the supporting remedial secession argument was so weak in this case,[120] Russia resorted to several other justifications, including the Kosovo precedent. The officials started instantly making references to the western views in the Kosovo hearings in the ICJ,[121] as well as to the controversial *sui generis* formulation.[122] The impact of Kosovo cannot be over-emphasized – before Kosovo's independence Russia supported separatism of the former Soviet subunits, but did not recognize even one as independent. Since Kosovo's independence, Russia has recognized three: Abkhazian and Crimean ASSRs and South Ossetian AO.

Other official Russian justifications for its action included correcting historical wrongs;[123] a view that the state of Ukraine had ceased to exist;[124] the requests by President Yanukovych and the Crimean Parliament to restore order;[125] and a partial quotation of the ICJ 2010 Advisory Opinion stating that there is no prohibition of declarations of independence under international law.[126] These arguments are not legally convincing.[127] There is no "correcting historical wrongs" under international law, and, in any case, Russia had recognized Ukraine's borders in several multilateral and reciprocal international treaties. The "disappearance" of the state of Ukraine because of a coup confuses recognition of states and

119 Borgen (n. 87) 248.

120 Four different international delegations visited Crimea in the spring of 2014 and all concluded that the Russian population was not in any kind of danger. *The Advisory Committee's Ad hoc Report on the Situation of National Minorities in Ukraine*, adopted on April 1, 2014, Council of Europe Doc. ACFC(2014)001, para. 15; Office of the United Nations High Commissioner for Human Rights, *Report on the Human Rights Situation in Ukraine*, June 15, 2014; Council of Europe Commissioner for Human Rights, 'Human Rights Abuses in Crimea Need to Be Addressed' September 12, 2014; Statement by the OSCE High Commissioner on National Minorities on Her Recent Visit to Ukraine, April 4, 2014.

121 (n. 11), quoting the US Written Statement.

122 Lavrov described Crimea as a "very special case, a unique case from all point of view." Interview, *ITAR-TASS*, September 20, 2014.

123 (n. 11).

124 Ibid.; P. Hilpold, 'Ukraine, Crimea and New International Law: Balancing International Law with Arguments Drawn from History' (2015) 14 *Chinese Journal of International Law* 237–70, 256–8; Merezhko (n. 77) 186–9.

125 The Russian Ambassador to the UN quoted Yanukovych's request at the UN Security Council meeting on March 3, 2014, S/PV.7125; Paul Lewis, Ian Traynor, and Luke Harding, 'Crimea Crisis: Pro-Russian Leader Appeals to Putin for Help' *Guardian*, February 28, 2014.

126 Quoted by Putin in his March 18, 2014 address.

127 Summarized (in Finnish) in T. Lundstedt and L. Hannikainen, 'Ajavatko Venäjän perustelut Krimin valtaukselle sen kansainvälisoikeudellisen doktriinin umpikujaan?' ['Do Russian Justifications for Annexation of Crimea Lead Its International Law Doctrine into a Dead End?'] (2016) 45(4) *Oikeus* 445–65, 457–61.

recognition of governments, and, again, would not affect multilateral treaties.[128] According to the Ukrainian Constitution, article 85(23), only the Parliament can ask for foreign intervention, not the president who, at any rate, did not have effective control over the country when making this request. Likewise, the Crimean Parliament did not have a right to ask for foreign intervention. Finally, the ICJ 2010 Opinion stated that while there is no general prohibition, a declaration of independence is deemed illegal if it's a result of an illegal act, such as use of force, by an outside state.[129]

Russian arguments failed to convince the international community, as the UN General Assembly voted 100 for and 11 against (with 58 abstentions) not to recognize changes in the status of Crimea.[130]

In June 2014, Russian scholars concurred with their government's views, as the most prominent members of the Russian International Law Association published an open letter to the International Law Association. In the letter they were surprised by the:

> disrespect to the will of the population of Crimea to exercise the right to self-determination provided for by the UN Charter ... It is impossible to ignore international legal precedents of realization of the principle of self-determination of peoples. The leadership of the USA and EU member States supported separation of Kosovo though there was no referendum and [no such will expressed by] the people in Kosovo ... but opposed in rigid tones the expressed will of [the Crimean] people by means of a referendum and against realization by Crimea people of the principles of self-determination of peoples.[131]

Many Russian scholars have chosen to follow the government's reinterpretations of the right to self-determination, although often this means completely disregarding what they have written on the subject for the past 20 years.[132] One reason for this is the federal law against secession.[133] Nevertheless, there are few noteworthy exceptions.[134]

128 These include the Helsinki Final Act (1975), Agreement on the Establishment of the CIS (n. 41), and the Memorandum on Security Assurances (Budapest Memorandum), December 5, 1994. Moreover, the Vienna Convention on the Law of Treaties, art. 62 excludes a possibility to unilaterally abolish a border treaty.

129 (n. 109).

130 UNGA Res. 68/262, March 27, 2014.

131 (n. 12).

132 Mälksoo has argued that if Russian scholars apply the earlier legal criteria they have supported for years, they must characterize annexation of Crimea as illegal (L. Mälksoo, 'Crimea and (the Lack of) Continuity in Russian Approaches to International Law' *EJIL: Talk!*, March 28, 2014.

133 In May 2014, a controversial art. 280.1 (on public calls to action for the violation of the territorial integrity of the Russian Federation) was added to the Criminal Code, making arguments against Russian annexation of Crimea illegal.

134 E. Lukyanova, 'On the Rule of Law in the Context of Russian Foreign Policy' (2015) 3(2) *Russian Law Journal* 10–36; M. Issaeva, 'Quarter of a Century on from the

The Russian government is, likewise, contradicting itself in many ways. It has explicitly demanded that its borders with Estonia follow the *uti possidetis* principle,[135] displaying obvious inconsistency when trying to re-draw its *uti possidetis* border with Ukraine. Furthermore, Russia is designating Crimeans as a "people" entitled to secession, whereas according to the Russian Constitutional Court case law and the Russian stance in the case of Kosovo, "people" was not simply the inhabitants of a province – who had a right at most to internal self-determination – but the whole people of the state, who alone had the full right to self-determination.[136] Even as the 2013 Foreign Policy Concept was displaying an equivocal attitude toward different ASSRs, it failed to even mention Crimea.[137] Finally, Russia used to consistently equate the right to remedial secession with the ASSR status, but is now providing the Eastern Ukraine rebels lacking any previous autonomous status with substantial political and military support, creating yet another frozen conflict.[138]

It is difficult to find any rationalization for the inconsistencies in the Russian stance on the right to self-determination in the post-Soviet area other than plain political calculations. When *uti possidetis* or Soviet territorial transfers work in favor of Russia, they are respected, but the transfer of Crimea is displayed as a "historical wrong." Additionally, the Foreign Policy Concepts have placed some SSRs in decisively different legal positions, for instance making Moldovan territorial integrity contingent upon its neutral status. Russia has been unable to justify these inconsistencies in legal terms.

## 6 Conclusions

Russia has utilized the vagueness of the right to self-determination to further its foreign policy goals, especially since 2008. It has had a good position for such an action: it has "solved" its own ASSR problem with giving them a constitutional right to internal self-determination within the Russian Federation, while other former SSRs with ASSRs had often mistreated their minorities, helping to create several frozen conflicts in the post-Soviet space. In addition, the former SSRs contain significant number of Russians, and this number has been appropriately expanded in the strategic ASSR areas with the passportization policy. Kosovo independence gave Russia at least an arguable legal and political precedent to utilize in its relations with the former SSRs.

Soviet Era: Reflections on Russian Doctrinal Responses to the Annexation of Crimea' (2017) 5(3) *Russian Law Journal* 86–112.

135 J. Vidmar, *Democratic Statehood in International Law: The Emergence of New States in Post-Cold War Practice* (Hart, 2013) 215.

136 See Written Statement (nn. 4 and 14).

137 In retrospect rather ominously, the 2013 Concept promises to contribute to Ukraine's participation in extended integration processes (n. 5) art. 48(e).

138 The local populace has not been enthusiastic for secession. In May 2014, only 27 percent of the Russian-speaking inhabitants of Eastern Ukraine supported secession. 'Despite Concerns about Governance, Ukrainians Want to Remain One Country' *Pew Research Center*, May 8, 2014.

Nevertheless, Russian actions do not seem to be based on its international law doctrine, as several inconsistencies can be detected. First, just like Georgia in 2008, in the late 1990s Russia had used extensive force to prevent the former ASSR of Chechnya achieving independence, claiming it was entirely an internal matter for Russia.[139] Second, Russia keeps on referring to the Kosovo precedent without recognizing Kosovo. This is problematic, since Russia thereby lacks *opinio juris*[140] to justify other secessions based on this precedent. However, Russia could claim that Kosovo has created a legal precedent for remedial secession, while maintaining that the conditions for it were not quite met there. This might work then in relation to the Georgian provinces, as there was verified violence and Russia could – if not convince – at least *argue* for remedial secession and linkage to Kosovo. Notwithstanding, this argument disregards Russia's own actions in Chechnya, and the fact that even a threat of violence was absent in Crimea. Third, previously Russia supported mistreated minorities in the former ASSRs, but the rebel territories in Eastern Ukraine lack both mistreatment and any former autonomous status. Last, Russia's arguing for "will of the Crimean people" is weak due to the flawed and condemned nature of the referendum, and its other legal justifications are even weaker and go against its own previous positions.

Therewith, I conclude that the Russian policy goals have started to override its otherwise consistent international law doctrine on self-determination, and this has become ever more pronounced since the annexation of Crimea. This is an unwelcome evolution, for Russia has been the most vocal UN Security Council permanent member state to call for consistent application of the most fundamental international law principles,[141] and has highlighted this point in all its official doctrine papers since 2008. The situation with Transnistria (former ASSR) and Nagorno-Karabakh (former AO) remain to be solved, and the former has applied to join Russia.[142] Finally, Russian support of the rebels in Eastern Ukraine without any prior history as a political unit produces new threat scenarios over the Russian diaspora and passportization policy in the post-Soviet area.

To conclude, the Russian international law doctrine seems to be in disarray, as many of its policy frameworks in the CIS area, such as the proclaimed sphere of interest, passportization, and promises to protect Russians abroad, are irreconcilable with international law. In relation to self-determination, the situation is not quite as drastic, as self-determination is a notoriously vague international legal norm. This is shown, for instance, in the conflicting views of states over the legality of Kosovo independence, or remedial secession in their Written Statements presented to the ICJ in 2009. That said, Russia has undisputedly overstretched its claim for remedial secession and Kosovo precedent – somewhat arguably with Abkhazia and South Ossetia, but implausible in relation to Crimea.

139 e.g. according to the then Prime Minister Putin, "everything that concerns the North Caucasus is Russia's internal matter" (*Ria Novosti*, October 27, 1999).

140 (n. 10).

141 Mälksoo (n. 1) 150–2.

142 'Moldova's Trans-Dniester Region Pleads to Join Russia' *BBC*, March 18, 2014.

# 10 The Principle of Territorial Integrity in Russian International Law Doctrine

## The Case of Crimea

*Christer Pursiainen and Tuomas Forsberg*[*]

## 1 Introduction

While Russia firmly defends its own sovereignty and territorial integrity and acts as a champion of international law in general, under President Vladimir Putin it has started to penetrate other post-Soviet sovereign countries by gradually seizing some of their separatism-minded regions. This is achieved, for instance, by granting Russian citizenship to their residents and placing Russian troops on their territory under the guise of peacekeeping or anti-terrorism operations, and de facto making them parts of Russia or at least Russia's military protectorates; or by proxy wars and outright military operations. This development concerns countries such as Georgia, Moldova, and Ukraine in particular, which have been reluctant to participate in the Russia-led reintegration of the post-Soviet space under the labels of Commonwealth of Independent States, Collective Security Treaty Organization, and the Eurasian Economic Union.

Russia's annexation of Crimea in March 2014 is ostensibly the clearest example of such behavior. This case is shortly discussed also in Chapter 9, but here it is considered in some more detail, both from the perspective of diplomatic struggles and Russian domestic international law debates. The western international law community is quite united in underlining that the annexation was not a legal act.[1] Politicians and other representatives of the West immediately expressed their disapproval, accusing Russia of violating international law, and the ensuing sanctions regime was established on this premise. The Russian leadership, by contrast, has vehemently denied that any violation of international law has taken place, that it was not an annexation but the "reunification" of Crimea with Russia, and that the western states themselves were effectively violating international law when they supported the "illegal" Ukrainian government and invoked the sanctions against Russia.

* We are very grateful to Prof. Roy Allison and Prof. Klaus Törnudd for their most valuable comments.

1 e.g. Thomas Grant, *Aggression against Ukraine: Territory, Responsibility and International Law* (Palgrave Macmillan, 2015); Ferdinand Feldbrugge, 'Ukraine, Russia and International Law' (2014) 39 *Review of Central and East European Law* 95.; Christian Marxsen, 'The Crimea Crisis - An International Law Perspective' (2014) 74 *Zeitschrift für ausländisches öffentliches Recht und Völkerrecht* [*Heidelberg Journal of International Law*] 367.

This chapter addresses the question of how this apparent discrepancy between deeds and letter has emerged in Russian international law doctrine and its domestic legal discourses.[2] Although the Russian foreign policy doctrine has put considerable emphasis on the primacy of the fundamental principles of international law, Russia has been depicted as a "non-native speaker" of it.[3] There has often been seen a need for distinct international norms and order for the post-Soviet space[4] owing to the tradition of applying a doctrine of "limited sovereignty"[5] in that area. Perhaps the most profound question in this context is whether Russia wants to revise the international legal order in general,[6] or whether it is transitioning to a post-factual world where discrepancies between the rhetoric concerning international norms and legal order and the country's behavior do not matter.

The Russian discourse(s) of international law before and after the annexation of Crimea has not been examined in great detail in English-language literature to date As Mälkoo has noted, "more needs to be said on this topic" of how the Russian international law community can switch from condemning violations such as the war against Iraq, or Kosovo's independence, to defending the annexation of Crimea under international law.[7]

The chapter starts with a brief look at the chain of events that led to Russia's annexation of Crimea, focusing in particular on the crucial decision points in terms of the legal formalization of the annexation. The chapter then reviews the immediate legal justifications provided by Russia for the annexation, followed by a brief overview of the international responses. Against this background, a major part of the chapter is dedicated to discussing not only official Russian documents but also legal expert debates in Russian academic journals, as well as those in the international law textbooks used in Russian universities. The Russian legal experts' interpretations and textbooks are interesting from the point of view of the broader discourse since the views may reflect deeper belief systems, worldviews, and identities compared to the tactical opinions expressed in Russia's diplomatic practice. Moreover, on that basis, we can also gain insights into the nature of the Russian international law community

2 Oleksandr Zadorozhnii, *Russian Doctrine of International Law after the Annexation of Crimea* (KIS Publishing, 2017); Lauri Mälksoo, *Russian Approaches to International Law* (OUP, 2015).
3 Anna Dolidze, 'The Non-Native Speakers of International Law: The Case of Russia' (2016) 15 *Baltic Yearbook of International Law* 77.
4 Michael Slobodchikoff, *Building Hegemonic Order Russia's Way: Order, Stability, and Predictability in the Post-Soviet Space* (Lexington Books, 2014).
5 Robert Jones, *The Soviet Concept of 'Limited Sovereignty' from Lenin to Gorbachev: The Brezhnev Doctrine* (Palgrave Macmillan, 1990); Ruth Deyermond, 'The Uses of Sovereignty in Twenty-first Century Russian Foreign Policy' (2016) 68 *Europe–Asia Studies* 957.; Katarzyna Kaczmarska, 'Russia's *droit de regard*: Pluralist Norms and the Sphere of Influence' (2015) 5 *Global Discourses* 434.
6 Roy Allison, 'Russian "Deniable" Intervention in Ukraine: How and Why Russia Broke the Rules' (2014) 90 *International Affairs* 1255; Roy Allison, 'Russia and the Post-2014 International Legal Order: Revisionism and Realpolitik' (2017) 93 *International Affairs* 519.
7 Mälksoo (n. 2) 192.

and assess the legal experts' freedom of thought and expression and overall positioning within the country's increasingly authoritarian political system.

We conclude that Russia is not intent upon dismantling international law – and rhetorically it indeed acts as a firm proponent of it – but it feels that it has the prerogative to interpret and enforce international law in the area of the former Soviet Union, often mirroring what it considers to be the western state practice elsewhere. Hence, Russia still wants to preserve the universal spirit of international law, but it is increasingly using it as an instrument for its own power political justifications, thus often paying only lip service to the basic principles of international law. In other words, Russia is trying to take control of interpretations of international law, and sees it as an arena for power struggles between the western-dominant system and the emerging multipolar system of the world where spheres of interests come into play and international law is doomed to yield in front of reality.

## 2 The Decision Points

There is no undisputed factual basis for the events leading up to the annexation of Crimea. Yet the basic narrative of the key decisions is generally shared by Russian as well as western analysts. Although the annexation of Crimea may have been planned and prepared beforehand, it was not until February 2014 that the issue became acute. After an all-night meeting, probably on February 22–23, 2014, in the presence of President Putin and four of his *siloviki* colleagues, Putin – by his own televised admission – decided to "start working on returning Crimea to Russia."[8] As a consequence, on February 26–28, 2014, Russian troops – armed uniformed individuals wearing no identifying insignia, namely the "little green men" – seized control of Crimea's public administration buildings, major transport routes, and airports, as stated in a 2016 International Criminal Court report.[9] Russian flags were duly raised in these locations. Under the control of these troops, the Crimean parliament held an emergency session and voted to dissolve the Crimean government, and replace the incumbent prime minister with a more Russia-friendly person, whose party had received 4 percent of the vote in the previous election.

For a considerable period of time, Russia denied its involvement in Crimea. True, on March 1, President Putin asked Russia's Federation Council to accept the decree "On the use of the Armed Forces of the Russian Federation on the territory of Ukraine."[10] This obvious post-factum domestic legal framework was however presented as if it were to be applied only if needed in the future. For

8 Tuomas Forsberg and Christer Pursiainen, 'The Psychological Dimension of Russian Foreign Policy: Putin and the Annexation of Crimea' (2017) 31(2) *Global Society* 226.

9 Report on Preliminary Examination Activities. International Criminal Court, November 14, 2016.

10 Постановление Совета Федератсии Федерального Собрания Российской Федерации от 1 марта 2014 г. Но. 48-СФ 'Об изпользовании Вооруженных Сил Российской Федерации на территории Украины' (Decree of the Federation Council of the

some time, Russia's leaders claimed that this decree was never used. It was not until mid-April that President Putin admitted for the first time that Russian troops had played a decisive role in these developments: "We had to take unavoidable steps so that events did not develop as they are currently developing in southeast Ukraine," he said in a televised program. "Of course our troops stood behind Crimea's self-defence forces."[11]

The formal incorporation of Crimea into the Russian Federation proceeded in three stages: declaration of independence, referendum, and "reunification." The Declaration of Independence of the Republic of Crimea by the Supreme Council of Crimea and the Sevastopol City Council was adopted on March 11, and the subsequent positive political statement by the Russian Ministry of Foreign Affairs. The second stage, a referendum, was organized on March 16 in Crimea with two alternatives, choosing between being reunited with Russia as a federal subject, or for Crimea to remain in Ukraine but under an earlier 1992 version of the Republic's Constitution. The Crimean authorities declared the official result as being 96.77 percent in favor of integrating the region into the Russian Federation with an 83.1 percent voter turnout. The third stage on March 18 was the signing of the treaty between the Russian Federation and the Republic of Crimea on the Acceptance of the Republic of Crimea into the Russian Federation and on the Creation of New Federative Entities within the Russian Federation. The treaty (see English translation)[12] is larded with legal jargon, referring to the UN and OSCE conventions. With unprecedented speed, the Russian parliamentarian bodies approved the related legislation.

## 3 Russia's Justification

Russia defended its behavior in the UN Security Council meeting as early as March 1, 2014, claiming that all the developments had been in accordance with international law. On March 3, before Russian troops were even supposed to be in Crimea by Russia's own account, Russia's representative issued the country's more detailed position,[13] which mainly consisted of five different legal justifications for the annexation that were all rejected by Ukraine and the western powers.

First, Russia noted that the current Ukrainian power was itself illegal. It supported this argument with reference to the agreement of February 21, 2014 between the then President Viktor Yanukovich and the Ukrainian opposition; the agreement concerned power-sharing between Yanukovich and the opposition during an agreed-upon transitional period, and was also signed by the foreign

Russian Federation on March 1, 2014 'On the use of the Armed Forces of the Russian Federation on the territory of Ukraine').

11 'Putin admits Russian forces were deployed to Crimea' (April 14, 2014), https://uk.reuters.com/article/russia-putin-crimea/putin-admits-russian-forces-were-deployed-to-crimea-idUKL6N0N921H20140417 (last accessed April 3, 2018).

12 Anatoly Pronin, 'Republic of Crimea: A Two-Day State' (2015) 3 *Russian Law Journal* 133.

13 UNSC, S/PV7125, March 3, 2014.

ministers of Germany, France, and Poland. Yet Russia's justification was discounted by the western powers and Ukraine. It was pointed out that Russia itself originally declined the power-sharing agreement and, furthermore, that Yanukovich himself had fled Kiev and had therefore renounced his position. Under these conditions, the Ukrainian parliament declared that Yanukovich had withdrawn from his duties in an unconstitutional manner, and they duly elected an acting president and prime minister until new elections could be organized.

Second, Russia claimed that it was a question of defending Russian citizens and compatriots and ensuring human rights in Crimea. This was necessary because the new illegal government was exploiting the fruits of their victory to trample over the rights and basic freedoms of the Russian-speaking people, not only in Crimea but in Ukraine at large. Crimea in particular was home to millions of Russian-speaking people, and the ultra-nationalists threatened their lives and legitimate interests. Russia's adversaries in the Security Council commented that no such reports had proceeded from any independent or neutral media to the effect that Russian speakers would have been repressed. This counterargument is plausible to a degree as it was indeed post factum confirmed in the report issued by the UN High Commissioner for Human Rights,[14] covering the period from November 2013 to September 2014: while no major human rights violations had been directed against any Russian-speaking contingent of the population before the annexation, afterwards, by contrast, the human rights of the pro-Ukrainian population, especially Crimean Tatars, had been severely repressed. The International Criminal Court confirmed this interpretation in the above-mentioned 2016 report.

Third, Russia argued that Russian troops had intervened in the situation only after the legitimately elected authorities of the Republic of Crimea had asked Russia to help them restore calm in Crimea. Western countries in the Security Council noted that international law does not allow subordinated authorities of any country to request military assistance from a neighboring country, especially when that neighboring country already exercises military power there.

Fourth, Russia referred to an invitation by President Yanukovich. While news reports just a few days earlier had stated that, in his first press conference in Moscow after his escape, Yanukovich bluntly rejected the right and possibility of Russian military interference, Russia's UN ambassador was suddenly and rather dramatically in possession of a photocopy of an invitation letter from his suitcase, dated 1 March. In it, Yanukovich – the incumbent legal president, as Russia claimed – was worried about overt acts of terror and violence that were committed under the influence of western countries, and asked the Russian president to use armed force to establish legitimacy, law and order, and stability in defense of the Crimean people. Other countries did not pay much attention to this justification because it lacked credibility from the start. To all intents and purposes, the Russians also understood that the invitation seemed fabricated, or signed under

14 Report of the United Nations High Commissioner for Human Rights on the situation of human rights in Ukraine. UNGA A/HRC/27/75, September 19, 2014.

pressure, as had been the case on numerous occasions in the Soviet invasion history, and they soon dropped it.

Fifth, Russia argued that its Black Sea fleet in Ukraine (Sevastopol) was threatened; thus it was a question of self-defense. Ukraine, followed by the western countries, noted that there was no evidence to that effect. By contrast, after Yanukovich's escape, Kiev had already stated that they were firmly committed to the bilateral agreement between Ukraine and Russia, scheduled to last until 2042. No threat or preparation thereof existed toward the Russian fleet stationed in Sevastopol. In this sense, the base was considerably more secure than it had been in 2005 at the time of the Orange Revolution, or during the 2008 tensions when NATO accepted that Ukraine would enter NATO. In those years the base extension agreement had not been signed and so its legal position was clearly more vulnerable.

About two weeks after this Security Council meeting, a sixth argument, the slogan "Crimea is Ours," based on historical and nostalgic but also legal reasoning, came more to the fore, showing that Russia's troops were there to stay. On March 18, the date when the annexation treaty was signed, President Putin addressed[15] state Duma deputies, Federation Council members, and heads of Russian regions as well as selected civil society representatives in the Kremlin. He started by saying that a referendum had been held in Crimea in full compliance with democratic procedures and international norms, whereby an overwhelming majority had voted for reunification with Russia. Added to this, everything in Crimea spoke of the history and pride it shared with Russia. The graves of Russian soldiers, whose bravery brought Crimea into the Russian Empire (under Catharina II), were also in Crimea. Thus, in people's hearts and minds, Crimea had always been an inseparable part of Russia. Putin literally condemned Nikita Khrushchev's 1954 decision to give Crimea to Ukraine, then part of the USSR. According to him, this decision had been made in clear violation of the constitutional norms that were in place even then. After the collapse of the USSR, Putin claimed, it was only when Crimea ended up as part of a different country that Russia realized it had not simply been robbed, but plundered. From the international law perspective, Putin also referred to the Kosovo precedent, and although Russia had always claimed the illegality of Kosovo's independence, now Putin said that the case mirrored the situation in Crimea. In other words, he claimed, the West was applying double standards by criticizing the Crimean case.

## 4 International Condemnation

The other countries in the post-Soviet space were alarmed about the developments. In April 2014, Russian Foreign Minister Sergey Lavrov was asked whether Russia might adopt the Crimean approach in other neighboring countries as well, as some nationalist Russian politicians had already suggested with great euphoria. The specific points of reference were Kazakhstan as well as Abkhazia, the southern

15 Address by President of the Russian Federation (March 18, 2014).

separatist region in Georgia. Lavrov firmly stated that it was "senseless to talk about such things appealing to the Crimean precedent. Crimea is an absolutely special case, this is Russian land, where a lot of Russian blood was spilt."[16]

The broader international community did not remain mere bystanders in the face of this development. A draft resolution was quickly put forward in the Security Council[17] on the day preceding the Crimean referendum, urging countries not to recognize the results. It referred to the UN Charter, the 1975 Helsinki Final Act of the CSCE, and the 1994 Budapest Memorandum, where Russia had opposed any use or threat of force that would affect the sovereignty, independence, unity, and territorial integrity of Ukraine within its internationally recognized borders. The resolution failed as a result of only 13 out of 15 votes in favor, coupled with Russia's obvious veto, and China's abstention.[18]

While the UN Security Council did not therefore collectively condemn Russia's action, the General Assembly agreed on a clear-cut resolution on March 27.[19] It stated that the Crimean referendum was not authorized by the Ukrainian government and, lacking validity, could not form the basis for any alteration in the status of the region. Consequently, the resolution called on all states, international organizations, and specialized agencies not to recognize any alteration to the status of Crimea, and to refrain from any action or interactions that might be interpreted as recognizing any such altered status.

Nor did the international community, as the UN General Assembly manifested, accept the argument that Kosovo could be used as justification for Crimea. Whereas Kosovo's declaration of independence had previously been held as not being in violation of international law by the International Court of Justice in 2010,[20] which was subsequently confirmed by the UN General Assembly, the Crimean independence declaration and referendum were deemed illegal and as being organized in the presence of foreign troops under threat of violence.[21]

The above-mentioned March 2014 UN General Assembly resolution, introduced by Canada, Costa Rica, Germany, Lithuania, Poland, and Ukraine, was approved by 100 countries. Among them was one CIS country, namely Azerbaijan. Eleven countries voted against, among them Armenia and Belarus from the CIS countries, and naturally Russia. The other CIS countries either abstained from

16 Speech by the Russian Foreign Minister, Sergey Lavrov, and his answers to questions during the First Forum of Young Diplomats of the CIS Countries, Moscow, April 25, 2014.

17 UNSC Security Council Draft Resolution/2014/189 14-26657 (E) 170314, March 15, 2014.

18 UNSC. Meetings coverage (March 15, 2014). Security Council Fails to Adopt Text Urging Member States Not to Recognize Planned 16 March Referendum in Ukraine's Crimea Region.

19 Resolution adopted by UNGA 68/262, 'Territorial integrity of Ukraine' March 27, 2014.

20 International Court of Justice. Advisory Opinion, July 22, 2010.

21 See the discussion in Enrico Milano, 'The Non-Recognition of Russia's Annexation of Crimea: Three Different Legal Approaches and One Unanswered Question' (2014) 1 *Questions of International Law* 35.

voting (58 countries altogether) or were absent, probably purposefully (24 countries). China was among those who abstained, stating that such a resolution would not be constructive in resolving the situation. Those who voted alongside Russia and could therefore be regarded as its most loyal allies in this type of issues – apart from the above-mentioned two CIS states – were Bolivia, Cuba, Nicaragua, North Korea, Sudan, Syria, Venezuela, and Zimbabwe.[22]

After two years, the International Criminal Court confirmed the UN General Assembly's interpretation by stating in its report that the situation within the territory of Crimea and Sevastopol amounted to an international armed conflict between Ukraine and Russia. The report labelled Russia's presence in Crimea as an occupation:

> This international armed conflict began at the latest on 26 February when the Russian Federation deployed members of its armed forces to gain control over parts of the Ukrainian territory without the consent of the Ukrainian Government. The law of international armed conflict would continue to apply after 18 March 2014 to the extent that the situation within the territory of Crimea and Sevastopol factually amounts to an on-going state of occupation. A determination of whether or not the initial intervention which led to the occupation is considered lawful or not is not required.[23]

## 5 The Russian International Law Community: Four Coping Strategies

A British academic authority on Russian affairs, Sakwa, calls Russia "neo-revisionist," meaning that the essence of Russia's approach is not an attempt to create new rules or to advance an alternative model of international order but to ensure the universal and consistent application of existing norms. Russia is thus not condemning the principles of international law and governance but the practices that accompany their implementation.[24]

The current chapter defends a more affirmative answer to the question. Revising the international order has been the main theme in almost all of Putin's main foreign policy speeches, like his (in)famous Munich speech in 2007, it is also proclaimed in official doctrines. Such major revision is necessitated by the move from a unipolar to a multipolar world, as the "Russian Federation's pursuit of an independent foreign and domestic policy provokes opposition from the United States and its allies, who are trying to maintain their dominance in world affairs."[25]

22 UN Res. Symbol A/RES/68/262. Meeting symbol A/68/PV.80 (March 27, 2014). Available at: United Nations Bibliographic Information System.

23 International Criminal Court 'Report on Preliminary Examination Activities' (The Hague, November 14, 2016), www.icc-cpi.int/iccdocs/otp/161114-otp-rep-pe_eng.pdf, para. 158 (last accessed April 4, 2018).

24 Richard Sakwa, *Russia Against the Rest: The Post-Cold War Crisis of World Order* (CUP, 2017)

25 Указ Президента Российской Федерации от 31 декабря 2015 года Н 683 'О Стратегии национальной безопасности Российской Федерации' (Decree of President of the

The Russian demand is that new rules of the game should be negotiated in the frame of the UN Security Council that would take into account the interests of all key players, i.e. great powers. All of the current Russian political elite seems to be socialized into the same way of thinking.

But what does this mean in terms of international law? And, more specifically, how does the above-described Crimean case comply with the Russian international law doctrine? How is international law, especially the parts concerning sovereignty, territorial integrity, and non-interference in internal affairs, understood in Russian international law textbooks and legal experts' debates? In order to address these questions, we begin by briefly reviewing the discursive developments before Crimea, and then take a closer look at the post-Crimean legal argumentation to ascertain whether there is any difference.

### *(a) Pre-Crimean International Law Debates*

During the Soviet era, one could distinguish between several periods of Soviet international law doctrine, sequentially reflecting different periods of Soviet foreign policy, sometimes in a very zigzag fashion. At a deeper level, on several occasions, the doctrine expounded two distinct and rivalling, yet partially overlapping systems of international law, reflecting the antagonistic rivalry of the two political world orders, socialist and capitalist. However, by the end of the Soviet Union, or even a couple of decades before that, the idea of universal international law had clearly gained the upper hand among both the Soviet political leadership as well as authoritative figures in the legal field.[26]

At the end of the 1990s, it seemed that a legally based international community that included Russia had gradually developed in the Russian international law community and political elite. The principle of compliance with international norms and rules had emerged at least at the level of discourse, and the overall tendency was evidently for ascribing increasing significance to international law, although the "illiteracy" vis-à-vis international law at the lower echelons remained widespread.[27] Nevertheless, those in power during President Boris Yeltsin's era seemed committed to integrating Russia into the international legislative and normative order.[28] This was also confirmed in the Russian Constitution of 1993, which states that the universally recognized norms of international law and international treaties and agreements of the Russian Federation shall be a component

Russian federation from December 31, 2015 Nr 683 'About the National Security of the Russian Federation'). Part 2, arts 12, 13.

26 Christer Pursiainen, '*Pacta sunt servanta*? The Development of the Sense of Community and the Principle of Obligation in Soviet and Russian Doctrines of International Law' (1998) 14(3) *Journal of Communist Studies and Transition Politics*.

27 George Ginsburgs, *From Soviet to Russian International Law: Studies in Continuity and Change* (Martinus Nijhoff, 1998) 122–3.

28 Pursiainen (n. 26); Tarja Långström, 'Russia in Transition: Reflections on International Law Doctrines' (1997) 66 *Nordic Journal of International Law* 475.

part of its legal system, and if a conflict between international law and domestic legislation were to arise, the former would prevail.[29]

In parallel, however, from the early 1990s onwards, a pluralistic competition over Russia's foreign policy line emerged. It allowed, contrary to what had mainly prevailed in the Soviet Union, that several "schools of thought" appeared simultaneously.[30] This competition extended from pro-western international liberalism or more national-interest-based realpolitik to Eurasianist or Slavophile ideas; the two latter saw Russia as representing a different civilization from the West and therefore it could not follow the rules of the West.

This ideological antagonism was also reflected in the debates on international law, which had begun to polarize. The rivalry between ideas and interpretations started to demarcate the field. The range of these sometimes fierce debates can perhaps be illustrated by two 1996 articles, one by Tikhomirov[31] and the other by Il'in.[32]

Following the official line, the former takes as its starting point the rapprochement between international and domestic laws, namely the transfer of international norms into the sphere of the domestic legal system and practice. Tikhomirov presents the view that a clear hierarchy of international law over domestic laws prevails and that the basic principles and norms are universal. These, in turn, are the generally recognized articles of the UN Charter, which deal with international peace and security, and which penetrate the whole legal system at other levels, such as CIS documents. While Tikhomirov admits that the international system still involved conflicts and collisions, he put forward a kind of normative list of those instruments that should be used in regulating such crises. The most important of these is the procedure concerning the peaceful resolution of disputes through negotiations, included in the OSCE norms, for instance. This is followed by the use of norms in conflict situations, sanctions by the UN and the OSCE, international courts of arbitration, other courts, and, finally, effective domestic processes for realizing the primacy of international law. Tikhomirov's approach accorded well with mainstream legal writing in Russia at that time, and with Russian textbooks on international law, e.g. Kolosov and Kuznetsov's 1995 textbook.[33]

29 Constitution of the Russian Federation 1993, ch. 1, art. 15, nr. 4.

30 Alexei Arbatov, 'Russia's Foreign Policy Alternatives' (1993) 18 *International Security* 5; Olga Alexandrova, 'Divergent Russian Foreign Policy Concepts' (1993) 4 *Aussenpolitik* 24; О. В. Лазебникова, *Запад и борба политических и научных кругах России по вопросам ее внешней политике в Европе* (Москва, Институт Европы, 1995) (O. V. Lazebnikova, *The West and the struggle within Russian political and scientific circles about the country's foreign policy in Europe*).

31 Ю. А. Тихомиров, 'Согласованность и коллизии норм' (1996) *Московский журнал международного права*, Но. 2 (Yu. A. Tikhomirov, 'Consistency and collision of norms').

32 Ю. Д. Ильин, 'Международное право и война в наши дни' (1996) Московскии журнал международного права, Но.1 (Yu. D. Il'in, 'International Law and the war in our times').

33 Ю. М. Колосов и В. И. Кузнецов (ред.) *Международное право* (Москва, Международные отношения, 1995) (Yu. M. Kolosov and V. I. Kuznetsov (eds) *International Law*).

An utterly different kind of picture was drawn by Il'in, for one, whose polemic and declarative article was published – as was Tikhomirov's – in the leading Russian periodical in the field (Eng. *Moscow Journal of International Law*). Il'in looked back to the 1970s and asked what had happened to international law in the subsequent period. He concluded that, in practice, legal norms had become worthless, and their real content had evaporated. Il'in criticized western practice and those Russian lawyers who follow the western example – those who spoke in defense of the self-limitation of state sovereignty and an increasing role for supranational institutions. One should not be deceived, Il'in said, since it was clear that the OSCE, the EU, NATO, the IMF, the G-7, and even the UN, were in their present-day form only instruments for the promotion of the international interests of western countries; the world had become an American hegemony. However, Il'in contended, forces also existed that stood against this trend. The Islamic world, the Slavonic peoples, India, Africa, Latin America – all of these were potential allies of Russia. And because international law is an instrument, it is of decisive importance who is in possession of this instrument.

Indeed, Il'in's instrumental (rather than normative) idea about the nature of international law is deeply rooted in Soviet/Russian lawmaking process. It was already present in the 1954 edition of the authoritative *Bol'shaya Sovetskaya Entsiklopediya* article on international law.[34] While there were striking contradictions in the two world systems, the one socialist and the other capitalist, the article noted, certain international law norms existed which were universally recognized and accepted, that is, they are binding from the point of view of both the socialist and the bourgeois sense of justice and the legal system. These included, above all, the institution of sovereignty, territorial integrity, the basic principles of the international law of contract, the legal status of international organizations, such as the UN Charter, and the so-called laws and conventions of war. However, these common principles and norms were to some degree contested, reflecting power relations between the two systems at their contemporary stage of development. Thus, both the conflict and the cooperation between these two systems was expressed in the application and interpretation of these norms.

In the mid 1990s, Il'in's anti-western approach seemed old-fashioned, a Soviet-time exception in the otherwise optimistic belief that Russia would be "westernized." And indeed, while Russia's foreign policy and domestic orientation gradually started to change after Putin came to power, this was not very visible at first in Russian international law debates. Marochkin in his 2012 article analyzed the development of Russian legal debate from the early 1990s to the early 2010s in 'Contemporary Approaches of the Russian Doctrine to International Law: Identical to Western Ones?' He concluded that while the current Russian doctrine was mostly free of the former Soviet ideological heritage, some scholars adhered to the once-held positions and did not notice changes. In

34 *Большая Советская Энциклопедия*, 'Международное право' Том 27 (Москва, Советская Энциклопедия, 1954) (*The Great Soviet Encyclopedia*, vol. 27, 'International Law') 21–4 [authors anonymized].

general, however, the Russian legal theory principles did not differ from the western ones in key aspects, and were based on the understanding of a universal legal community.[35]

There is, however, one issue over which the new Russia had consistently criticized, and continues to do so, western international law interpretation and state practices, namely humanitarian intervention. Bismillah in his 2013 article,[36] for instance, referred to western misuse of this concept in the cases of Iraq and Libya, that is, intervention without the proper authorization of the UN Security Council. Yasnokarskiy, in turn, discussed the same issue in his 2013 article[37] through the concept of Responsibility to Protect (R2P), which Russia had always disliked, seeing it as a smokescreen for western interference in other countries' internal affairs. Stopping short at directly accusing the West, the author argued that there was a potential conflict between the R2P and the non-interference principle, the latter being a more profound and traditional international law principle. However, as to Russia's position on the concept, the author emphasized that it remains well balanced and unchanged: Russia is against any interference in the sovereign affairs of an independent state. In this context, the point of reference was Russia's representative at the UN Security Council, the very same representative that had defended the legality of the annexation of Crimea a short spell later, who had always adamantly stressed that the idea of R2P should not lead to interference in internal affairs of states and should take place only when mandated by a Security Council resolution. Yasnokarskiy underlined his point further with a quotation by Foreign Minister Sergey Lavrov – another subsequent hardliner in defending his country's stance on Crimea – who had said that interference in the internal affairs of other countries would lead to complete chaos. The author finally refers to a Russian foreign policy principle whereby intranational conflicts should not be used to carry out regime change operations by providing external support to one of the opposing sides.

As we know, in practice Russia has regularly interfered in other post-Soviet countries' internal affairs by non-military and military means. It is therefore easy to conclude that Russia's actions and international law doctrine were in conflict over this issue even before Crimea. Indeed, the Russian–Georgian War in 2008 can be seen as relatively similar to the later Crimean annexation from the perspective of Russia's legal justification. Russian leaders and legal experts alike defended the country's behavior as not being in violation of any international law norms as the operation was pure self-defense to save the Russian peacekeepers that had been placed in South Ossetia against Georgian aggression, as

35 Sergei Marochkin, 'Contemporary Approaches of the Russian Doctrine to International Law: Identical to Western Ones?' (2012) 12 *Baltic Yearbook of International Law* 29.

36 M. Бисмиллах, 'Концепция "гуманитарной интервенции" и суверенитет государства' (2013) *Московский журнал международного права*, Но. 4 (92) (M. Bismillah, 'The concepts of "humanitarian intervention" and the state sovereignty').

37 Yu. A. Yasnosokirskii, 'The Principle of Non-Intervention and Responsibility to Protect (R2P' (2013) 3 *Matters of Russia and International Law* 9.

well as a humanitarian intervention to protect the Russian "compatriots" in South Ossetia.[38] It has nevertheless been noted that while Russia used humanitarian intervention or R2R as a political "trump card" in the 2008 war against Georgia to justify its action both internationally and for raising domestic support, it was still reluctant to more generally accept unilateral humanitarian intervention or R2P practice in international relations. This was originally related most clearly to the fear that humanitarian intervention might be applied against Russia over its campaign in Chechnya, or that the humanitarian intervention argument could be used as a means of pressure against Russia over Chechnya, and later that it could be used in justification of western support for "coloured revolutions" in CIS states.[39]

### *(b) Post-Crimean International Law Debates*

At first glance, Marochkin's 2012 view[40] that Russian international law doctrine did not differ markedly from western interpretation(s) still is accurate in spite of Russia's actions in 2014. This seems to be the case especially on the basis of official documents. Most Russian international law textbooks also convey the same picture: international law is understood as a universal order that Russia faithfully complies with. This, of course, creates an uncomfortable gap between the letter and the deeds. Upon closer inspection, however, there are some divergent discursive strategies on how to deal with this gap.

#### *(i) Official Doctrine*

As to Russia's official international law doctrine, the Foreign Policy Concept of the Russian Federation 2016,[41] which replaced the 2013 version,[42] is a case in point. There is no major visible difference between these pre- and post-Crimea documents. True, in the new version there is an article (61) that strongly condemns "the geopolitical expansion pursued" by the EU and NATO, whereas the previous document emphasized cooperation. In any case, the 2016 document pays homage to international law and its universal spirit. In its opening words it is said to be based on the generally recognized

38 Nikolai V. Ostrouhov, 'Territorial Integrity of the State in Contemporary International Law, and its Protection in the Russian Federation and in the Post-Soviet Space' (Moscow: Russian Peoples Friendship University, 2010) (unpublished doctoral dissertation).

39 Roy Allison, 'The Russian Case for Military Intervention in Georgia: International Law, Norms and Political Calculation' (2009) 18 *European Security* 173, 182.

40 Marochkin (n. 35).

41 Foreign Policy Concept of the Russian Federation (approved by the President of the Russian Federation Vladimir Putin on November 30, 2016, official English translation).

42 Foreign Policy Concept of the Russian Federation (approved by the President of the Russian Federation on February 12, 2013, unofficial translation on the site of Ministry of Foreign Affairs of the Russian Federation).

principles and rules of international law as well as international treaties of Russia. Later in the document, we find that Russia conducts an assertive and independent foreign policy guided by its national interests and at the same time based on unconditional respect for international law. Moreover, Russia's foreign policy is aimed at creating a stable and sustainable system of international relations based on the generally accepted norms of international law and principles of equal rights, mutual respect, and non-interference in domestic affairs of states. It also states that the UN should maintain its central role in regulating international relations and coordinating world politics, ensuring strict observance of the key provisions and principles of the UN Charter.

The foreign policy concept also includes a specific section entitled "Rule of Law in International Relations," which asserts that Russia consistently advocates strengthening the legal foundation of international relations and complies with its international legal obligations in good faith. In that spirit, Russia, it is formulated, opposes attempts by some states or groups of states to revise the generally accepted principles of international law and counters politically motivated and self-interested attempts by some states to arbitrarily interpret the fundamental international legal norms and principles such as non-use of force or threat of force, peaceful settlement of international disputes, respect for sovereignty and territorial integrity of states, right of peoples to self-determination. There should be no attempts to violate international law with "creative applications" of its norms. In particular, one should not interfere in the domestic affairs of other states with the aim of an unconstitutional change of regime, including by supporting non-state actors.

In other doctrines, for instance in the national security doctrine,[43] the spirit is the same and the US is usually named as the leader of this group of states that regularly violate international law. Thus, the official doctrine presents Russia as a firm supporter of universal international law, whereas it implicitly condemns western countries' use of international law as revisionist and opportunist, contravening the prevailing legal order.

### *(ii) Legal Experts' Discursive Strategies*

While it is rather obvious that in the Crimean case (as in many other cases) Russia was not following its own international law doctrine, it is interesting to look at the way in which more unofficial Russian international law debates explain or represent Russia's annexation of Crimea. Even if one were not dealing with the Crimean case as such, it is clear that this recent case must be in the mind of authors when they write about sovereignty, territorial integrity, non-use of violence or the threat thereof, prohibition to interfere in the internal affairs of other states, the R2P principle, and similar related issues.

43 Указ Президента Российской Федерации (n. 25) Part 2, art. 15ff.

The Russian Association of International Law gathered in April 2014 to form its collective opinion of the Crimean case.[44] Since that meeting, legal experts have also discussed the case and the principles in various articles and, more sparsely, in textbooks. When it comes to printed material, the time span from 2014 to the time of writing the current analysis in early 2018 is too short to start speaking about post-Crimean schools of thought. Nevertheless, one can still differentiate between at least four discursive strategies. Roughly speaking, these could be called "anti-West," "neutral," "balancing," and "dissident" variations.

The *anti-westerners* put most of their efforts into accusing the West. Russia is presented as a standard-bearer of international law, whereas the West by its deeds is intent upon dismantling the current legal order. One could understand this strategy as identifying closely with Russia's foreign policy language: indeed, it strongly resembles the blame games engaged in by Russian foreign policy leaders as well as their representatives in the UN Security Council in practical diplomatic disputes.

The circular letter signed by a certain Professor Kapustin on behalf of the Russian International Law Association[45] that was sent to the International Law Association in June 2014 quite clearly belongs to this category, albeit the tone of the argumentation in the letter is much more political than legal. In that, the Russian International Law Association accuses "the leaders of the USA and most of the EU Member States" of supporting the military coup d'état in Kiev. The rights of local inhabitants in southern and eastern Ukraine were not respected and "millions of Crimean residents will never forget this offence" insomuch as their referendum was deemed illegal by the West. The West is, in other words, hysterical when it comes to its views on Crimea and ignores its own actions and precedents elsewhere such as Kosovo.

This is also the approach adopted in a 2014 article by Moiseev, who is head of the Department of International Law at the Diplomatic Academy of the Ministry of Foreign Affairs. In his view, it is "still astonishing that [the western powers] assumed the position of non-recognition of the self-evident results of the Crimea referendum, which they allege was illegal and unconstitutional." Furthermore, he argues that "those who have seized power in Ukraine by armed force have committed a criminal offense and their actions cannot have legal force for the Russian Federation."[46]

Another typical example of this line of argumentation is by Likhachev, in his 2015 article[47] published by the Ministry for Foreign Affairs. The issue concerns

44 Anton Moiseienko, 'What Do Russian Lawyers Say about Crimea?' (September 24, 2014) *Opinio Juris* guest post, http://opiniojuris.org/2014/09/24/guest-post-russian-lawyers-say-crimea (last accessed April 4, 2018).

45 Russian International Law Association, 'Circular Letter to the Executive Council of the International Law Association' June 6, 2014, unofficial translation available at https://mgimo.ru/about/news/departments/252984 (last accessed April 4, 2018).

46 A. Moiseev, 'Some International Legal Positions on the Ukrainian Question' (2014) 60(4) *International Affairs: A Russian Journal of World Politics and International Relations* 84.

47 В. Н. Лихачев, 'Современное международное право: поиск идентичность' *Современное международное право. Теория и практика* (Дипломатическая Академия МИД России, Институт государства и права Россиыской Академий Наук, Москва,

the western violation of international humanitarian law and interference in the internal affairs of other countries. Referring to the post-Soviet space in particular, the biggest violator of international law is the US which, with its material and political support, contributed in 2008 to Georgia's aggressive behavior against the people of South Ossetia. Ukraine then followed the same pattern, as the US used the country to promote its geopolitical interest against Russia. This involved supporting the Ukrainian leaders' policy of extremism, ultra-nationalism, and cooperation with neo-Nazis, which violated the basic principles of international law. In so doing, both Ukraine and the US have undermined the UN Charter and several other conventions and legal principles. The EU, on the other hand, has undermined international humanitarian law by consistently violating international rules when it comes to allowing xenophobia, racism, aggressive nationalism, offensive treatment of minorities and refugees, as well as the rights of its own citizens and especially those of children. In the international arena, this is visible in the EU's ignorance of international humanitarian law conventions.

In a similar spirit, Ignatenko and Tiunov in their massive 2017 international law textbook[48] (which perhaps reflects the growing anti-western trend in Russian international law textbooks), present the principle of non-interference in the internal affairs of another country. The points of reference are again UN and OSCE documents, and they posit that interference in other countries' affairs poses a serious threat to international security and peace. The authors then mention that unfortunately one can find examples where countries do not follow international law in this question, namely certain countries of the EU, as well as naturally the US. Another norm – non-violation of state borders – is also discussed; in this context it is stated that Russia strictly adheres to this norm in its policy. Ukraine is not mentioned at all.

Voronin, Kulebjakin, and Nikolaev in their 2015 article,[49] published in the most prominent Russian journal on international law, belong to the same group, offering a forceful defense of Russia's official policy line. The authors start by claiming that the West actively supported the illegal coup d'état in Kiev. As for the Russian troops in Crimea, they had actually been in their military base in keeping with the agreement with Ukraine. The article claims that there is no evidence of the impact of the Russian military on the referendum arranged by the self-organized Crimean citizens, and that any alleged unmarked soldiers in Crimea cannot by any means be attributed to Russia. Obviously, this statement seems to

Оригинал-макет, 2015) (V. N. Likhachev, 'The contemporary international law: Looking for identity' *Contemporary International Law: Theory and Practice*).

48 Г. В. Игнатенко и О. И. Тиунов (ред.) *Международное право* (Москва, Норма ИНФРА-М., 2017) (G. V. Ignatenko and O. I. Tiunov (eds), *International Law*), esp. 158, 164, 165.

49 E. R. Voronin, V. N. Kulebjakin, and A. V. Nikolaev 'The State coup d'état in Kiev in February 2014. Evaluations and consequences from the perspective of International Law' (2015) 1 *Moscow Journal of International Law* 11–28).

contradict Putin's April 2014 recognition of Russia's presence in Crimea before annexation.

The *neutral* discursive strategy is instead most clearly visible in mainstream Russian university textbooks on international law. It is possible to read this strategy as an internal, even psychological defensive strategy from the perspective of the legal experts in question, where the aim is to keep one's own understanding of international law intact, thus avoiding evidence that contradicts it in Russia's foreign policy. It is also possible to read this approach as merely an academic insurance policy; it follows the official Russian doctrine on international law, but does not engage in discussion of the Crimean (or any other difficult) case. Indeed, in most textbooks published before and after 2014, the general picture is fairly similar to the official foreign policy concept of Russia referred to above, without any reference to Russia's actions, which sometimes appear to depart from, or be in violence of, the country's own official international law doctrine. In other words, Russian students of international law are routinely taught norms that are the complete opposite of Russia's foreign policy conduct in the cases of Crimea, eastern Ukraine, and many others.

It is a mystery, perhaps inherited from the Soviet era, as to why theory and practice are accepted as being so far apart in academic circles. For instance, a 2015 authoritative university textbook by Tuzmuhamedov,[50] published by the Russian Association of International Law, presents two relevant concepts in detail, namely that of the inviolability of borders and that of territorial integrity, in such a way that only with a great stretch of the imagination could one regard the annexation of Crimea as legal. The former concept, in this Russian account, denies any kind of complete or partial occupation of another state's territory, including transit of any kind of goods or troops, as well as interfering in information-technological measures, without the permission of the respective country. The latter concept reveals that no one is allowed to completely or partially break up the unity of another state. The reference points are both the UN Charter and OSCE rules and norms, and it is also stated that these principles form the foundation of international security and stability. It means that no direct or indirect threat against another country's territory is allowed. While the textbook admits that there are territorial changes in international politics, it notes that from the international law perspective this requires both the respective states' and their people's acceptance, and is to be carried out by peaceful means. Furthermore, the existence of internal domestic opposition welcoming territorial transformations does not make any difference. The state always has the upper hand, and while the citizens in a certain region may want territorial changes, this does not automatically provide a legal basis for them. Furthermore, the textbook contends that the Russian doctrine of international law does not recognize the principle of any historical right to a territory, even if that is sometimes used as a pretext for occupation and annexation.

50 Б. Р. Тузмухамедов, *Международное право* (Москва, Норма Инфра-М, 2015) (B. R. Tuzmuhamedov, *International Law*), esp. 147–50; 356–69.

The same type of legal argumentation can be found in numerous books and articles published after the Crimean annexation and Russia's interference in the eastern Ukrainian conflict. The principles of the inviolability of borders and territorial integrity as well as non-use of force can be regarded as established norms in international law, which are duly taught to students and future Russian diplomats by Russian international law professors in the best universities of the country. For instance, Galenskaya, in a 2015 textbook[51] published by the Ministry of Foreign Affairs, presents the basic principles of non-use of force, threat of violence, and peaceful resolution of conflicts; she does this in neutral terms, as mere doctrinal facts, completely neglecting to discuss why this is not the case in Russia's (or other countries') foreign policy. The same goes for the 2016 textbook by Starodubtseva et al., who declare that international law prohibits the violent transformation of state territory: "Acquisition of territory is not recognized if it is achieved by violence or by threatening it."[52]

Baranin's 2016 article[53] in turn examines how the concept of humanitarian intervention is related to state sovereignty and non-interference in other states' internal affairs. He presents the issue again in rather neutral terms but does not forget to mention that Russia belongs to the majority of countries that do not accept humanitarian intervention without a UN Security Council resolution, and that often this type of intervention is actually just a smokescreen for other than humanitarian interests. Kirilenko and Alekseev in their 2016 article,[54] to add to this "neutral" genre, admit that R2P justification for violating the sovereignty principle has become part of international law debates and practice, but they argue that its use is justified only if pursuant to a UN Security Council resolution.

The few who come under the heading of *balancers* try to refrain from blindly justifying the official Russian foreign policy. They tend to argue quite realistically that all parties, both western and Russian, sometimes fall into noncompliance for political reasons. Yet this discourse also yields to defend Russia's actions to a certain degree, and can perhaps be seen only as a subgroup under anti-westerners.

51 Л. Н. Галенская, 'Основие принципы международного права: развитие и взаимодействие (на примере принципа воздерживания от угрозы силой или её применения и мирного разрешения споров)' *Современное международное право. Теория и практика* (Дипломатическая Академия МИД России, Институт государства и права Российской Академий Наук, Москва, Оригинал-макет, 2015) (L. N. Galenskaya, 'The basic principles of International Law: development and interaction (on the example of the principle of abstention from the threat or use of force and the peaceful settlement of disputes'), *Contemporary international law. Theory and Practice*) 131–44.

52 Г. С. Стародубтсева (ред.) *Международное право* (Москва, РИОР ИНФРА-М, 2016) (G. S. Starodubtseva, *International Law*) 258.

53 Ж. Баранин, 'Гуманитарная интервенция и новые измерения концепции государственного суверенитета' (2014) *Вестник РУДН, серия Политология*, Но. 1 (Zh. Baranin, 'Humanitarian intervention and the new dimensions of the concept of state sovereignty'), esp. 61.

54 В. П. Кириленко и Г.В. Алексеев, 'Проблема государственного суверенитета в современных геополитических условиях' (2016) *Управленское консультирование*, Но. 3 (V. P. Kirilenko and G. V. Alekseev, 'The problem of state sovereignty in contemporary geopolitical conditions').

Aleksandrova's 2014 research article,[55] for example, deals directly with the Crimean issue. Western countries, the author argues, organized and financed Euromaidan and hence intervened illegally in the internal affairs of Ukraine. Representatives of the US and the EU used their external economic power with a view to exerting political pressure to make a one-sided profitable decision, which is contrary to the right of free internal self-determination, contained in sovereignty of the state. The author claims that the US spent around US$5 billion on organizing the Euromaidan protest movement. The footnote source she provides leads to a statement by US Assistant Secretary of State for Europe Victoria Nuland, where she once had said that since the declaration of Ukrainian independence in 1991, the United States had supported the Ukrainians in the development of democratic institutions and skills in promoting civil society and a good form of government, and had invested more than US$5 billion to help Ukraine achieve these goals. In this way, Aleksandrova argues, the EU and the US have consistently destabilized Ukraine's political system, depriving Ukrainians of their right to freely determine their political, economic, and social development, which is in violation of the principle of non-intervention.

Aleksandrova then turns to Russia. Russia cannot be accused of an aggressive invasion because no casualties occurred. No bombings took place, no ports were blocked (airports occupied by the Russian troops is not mentioned), no attacks by regular or irregular Russian troops against Ukrainian forces were launched. However, she states that an increase in the contingent of Russian troops in the territory of Ukraine could in principle be understood as violating the original 1997 Agreement between Ukraine and the Russian Federation on the status and conditions of the Russian Black Sea Fleet, and in which Russia promised to respect the sovereignty of Ukraine, respect its legislation, and not to interfere in its internal affairs. However, breaking the bilateral agreement under the conditions of "illegitimate Kiev authorities," the Russian Federation did not actually violate the international law principle of intervention and non-interference in the internal affairs of another state.

While there is no direct basis for claims of Russian external interference in the issue of the self-determination of Crimea, the constitutional or international legal norms for secession were still not followed. Russia, Aleksandrova argues, is not guilty but could have done better in legal terms. There was no massive violation of human rights, and there was no genocide of the Russian-speaking population that would have justified interference. Therefore, Russia could instead have appealed to the UN Security Council on the introduction of peacekeeping forces in order to prevent violence against civilians by the nationalist Ukrainian groups and to prevent a humanitarian catastrophe. In the event of the likely refusal, Russia would then have received not a legal but a political justification for holding a referendum.

Thus, the author's strategy is to blame both sides, albeit being magnanimous to Russia, and to argue that as such international law is not to be blamed, as it seems

55 Е. С. Александрова (2014) 'События на Украине и в Крыма: проблема международного права?' (2014) *Право и политика* 11 (Ye.S. Aleksandrova 'The events in Ukraine and Crimea: A problem for international law?').

to be about the political will to follow it. The solution is to make clearer rules concerning separatism and secession, and to define them clearly as distinct concepts, the latter based on the self-determination of the people.

Perhaps one could also include Trofimov's 2014 article[56] in the group of balancers. True, he follows the official line, and argues that the "reunification" of Crimea conforms to international law standards, referring to the earlier Kosovo case and the rights of the people to self-determination. At the same time, however, he concludes (in line with the liberal international relations school of thought) that Russia's actions were mainly rooted in Russian domestic politics, namely the wish to enhance President Putin's authority, rather than any legal arguments or geopolitical external conditions.

*Dissidents* here refers to Russian international law experts who criticize Russia from an international law perspective in the case of Crimea. They identify themselves most closely with the western type of legal criticism against Russia's foreign policy and military behavior. Some few Russian liberal politicians in opposition have indeed voiced their view that the reunification of Crimea with Russia was illegal. It is, however, rather difficult to find a publishing Russian legal expert of this kind.[57] While there may be more, a short 2015 article by a certain Voronezh State University lecturer Pronin,[58] published in the English-language *Russian Law Journal*, serves as a rare example. The author starts by stating that on several occasions he has heard some Russian law professor-level scholars sharing the "Crimea is ours" discourse. Pronin notes that these professors have either forgotten their knowledge in the sphere of international law or decided to use it in accordance with the proverb "little thieves are hanged but great ones escape." The author compares the logic of the legal reasoning that is used today by the Russian state and by many Russian law scholars to the ideas of the Stalinist era's tradition of Soviet international law, where fabricated referendums or invitations to invade were used to take over a territory by force. He then questions both the procedure leading up to the annexation as well as using Kosovo as justification; the International Court of Justice that confirmed Kosovo's independence in 2010 did not after all cover cases where independence had been declared in the context of an unlawful use of force by a foreign power.

## 6 Conclusions

This chapter has focused on the Russian international law expert debate in order to understand how this community and the wider Russian foreign policy elite cope with the apparent discrepancy between the deeds and the doctrine. The debate appears confused, and is highly politicized. While several discursive strategies can

56 Е. А. Трофимов, 'Кримский вопрос и будущее российского государства' (2014) *Известия Иркутского государственного университета, Серия 'Политика. Религиоведение'* Т. 8 (E. A. Trofimov, 'The Crimean question and the future of the Russian state').

57 See e.g. Mälksoo (n. 2) 192.

58 A. Pronin, 'Republic of Crimea: A Two-Day State' (2015) 3(1) *Russian Law Journal*.

be identified, for the most part Russian legal experts follow the official foreign policy line with some variations. It is difficult to know to what extent they are truly honest as opposed to merely feeling under pressure to support the official position; for instance to keep and enhance one's professional position and salary.

In any case, by using half-truths, biased information, manipulation, and pure lies in its argumentation, the Russian international law community has to a great extent separated itself from the broader international academic community and does not engage in substantive argumentation professionally. Often, the doctrinal international law debate in Russia avoids any uncomfortable discussion, opting to shift the agenda instead by starting a new debate accusing others of violations of international law. To this end, it is sometimes the factual basis rather than the interpretation of the law that is more contested and biased.

This state of affairs leads to deeper considerations. Is Putin's Russia challenging the current international legal order in general or is it intent upon creating some kind of separate post-Soviet-space legal order, thus contradicting the previously accepted universal international law approach? Most researchers that have dealt with this puzzle conclude that there is little evidence to the effect that a substantive revisionist international legal agenda lies behind Russia's actions, but rather that it is a question of legal exceptionalism within Russia's own sphere of interest.

This can be seen as purely traditional realpolitik, in the spirit of Yalta 1945, but it can also be noted that international law was not ready to cope other than in a rigid manner with the situation that emerged after the dissolution of the Soviet Union. Russia remains committed to upholding international law as an important instrument for securing international peace, but its relations with the near-abroad states form a significant exception.

This interpretation seems reasonable and supported by the available evidence. The current evidence does not confirm that Russia wants anything more. However, it raises the issue whether a more radical approach to international law in Russia is in the making. Russia has adopted an understanding of international law which in many ways harks back to the roots of traditional Soviet approaches, albeit not fully articulated. Like the Soviet Union, Russia is increasingly seeing the world in bipolar terms of two sequential systems, this time with one led by the West, and the other – although still fragmented – formed by the rising powers. Hence, the latter system rises against this dominant order and inevitably transforms it, sooner or later. In the transformed order, it is expected that Russia's role will be crucial, perhaps even leading.

In this way, Russian international law doctrine is overwhelmingly connected to ideologically or identity-driven power politics. When Russia and particularly the representatives of its international law community defend Russia and accuse others of violations of international law in the Crimean case, it is unclear whether there is any sober calculus of what the effects are, since it undermines Russia's credibility and particularly that of scholars who are internationally recognized experts in the field. It is therefore possible that self-esteem and the impossibility of acknowledging one's own violations without significant cognitive dissonance is part of the explanation of the chosen strategy. If there is calculus of influence, it is based on a rather cynical worldview, whereby legal arguments still matter as propaganda tools but not as internalized norms. Indeed, Russia is clearly invoking international law to justify unlawful military actions and territorial annexation. The dissonance between Russia's actions and the letter of international law reflects Russia's revisionist agenda to break down the western or US hegemony in international relations.

In this realpolitik world, international law is for Russia both an instrument for framing conflictual issues for one's own benefit, as well as an arena for battle, reflecting the current power balance and interests of the two systems. From Russia's point of view, the old one is declining, while the new one, where great power Russia's interests will be duly taken into account, is rising.

# Part V

# The Application of International Law and the International Economic System

# 11 Russian Banking Regulation and Supervision in Global Financial Governance

## Some Theoretical Perspectives on Soft Law Approaches to Banking Supervision

*Alexander A. Vishnevskiy*

## 1 Soft Law and Banking Supervision

### *(a) Modern Trends in Banking Regulation and Supervision*

The banking industry is the sphere of business which is traditionally heavily regulated and supervised by the competent state authorities. The underlying reason for the regulation of bank and supervision derives from the very nature of the banking business – making profit with other people's money, or, as FitzGibbon LJ put it in *Re Shields' Estate*: "the business of banking, from the banker's point of view, is to traffic with the money of others for the purpose of making profit."[1] This means that a failure of a bank is the failure of its clients as well; the bank's results and conduct of business have direct consequences for its clients, and given that "the bank clients" are in fact all the business entities as well as the majority of the population these days, banking activities have direct influence over society as a whole. Certain regulatory theories refer to this phenomenon as *negative externalities*. As Larisa Dragomir writing shortly after the 2008–9 global financial crisis puts it: "The current crisis plainly illustrates these negative externalities: the banking crisis spread into the whole financial sector and from there into the real economy, which then suffered intensively because of the credit squeeze."[2] So, it should not be a surprise that the banking industry is a heavily regulated industry.

This basic reasoning has developed into various theories of banking regulation. Sometimes the theories of banking regulation are divided along economic and social theories. The economic theories direct their attention to economic factors justifying the necessity and objectives of banking regulation. The rationale behind banking regulation in economic theory is that regulation is developed to prevent banks from obtaining excessive economic power, suppression of competition, and preventing uncontrolled money supply. Consequently, the supporters of the economic theory argue for the necessity to limit interest rates and credit ceilings to

1 [1901] 1 Ir.R 173, 198.
2 L. Dragomir, *European Prudential Banking Regulation and Supervision: The Legal Dimension* (Routledge, 2010) 44.

keep the banking industry in line with the monetary policy of the state, as well as to provide for the range of the so-called "must serve obligations" requesting banks to provide the banking services to specific industry or population segments.

The social theories deal first of all with another aspect of banking – protection of the banks' customers. According to social theories such a goal is achievable if the banks maintain the necessary level of capital and other requirements , ensure adequate levels of corporate governance in order to promote the stability of the banking system, protection, and trust of customers.[3]

It is interesting to note that all these – as well as many other theories though referring to the real aspects of banking often fall short of actual developments. The real reasons leading to the necessity of the regulation, nevertheless have been criticized and sometimes even harshly. This leads to the conclusion that the modern banking industry has to be regulated in the absence of a globally accepted theory. This is an important feature of the current "state of mind" of regulation and at the same time one of the reasons for the importance of soft law in modern global financial regulation. While soft law allows for a more flexible approach to banking regulation, there is no unanimous support for it.

At the same time, the approaches to banking regulation in relation to both regulatory objectives and tools are constantly changing. One of the inherent features of modern banking regulation is that it has become first of all *international banking regulation*, reflecting the international character of modern banking and finance.

For the purpose of this chapter we will consider the three directions of the regulation of banking activities, namely, prudential regulation, customer protection, and the discharge of public functions by banks.

For a substantial period of time the term "banking regulation and supervision" used to be synonymous with "prudential regulation and supervision." The very term "prudential" lacks not only legal or regulatory definition, but even consensus among the experts.[4] It is generally understood that prudential regulation is aimed at ensuring the adequate financial standing of banks and includes certain components or capital requirements such as:

- own funds, consisting of the core capital (basic equity) and supplementary capital, though included in own funds calculation but less qualitative; besides the relevant rules provided for the ways the calculations are to be made;
- solvency ratio understood as a proportion of own funds in proportion to the assets of the bank risk-adjusted in accordance with criteria defined in the legislation;
- limiting exposure in relation to a group of clients, and certain others.

3 See, ibid., for a comprehensive review of the various theoretical approaches to the issues of banking regulation and supervision.

4 See e.g. Lazaros I. Panourgias, *Banking Regulation and World Trade Law: GATS, EU and "Prudential" Institution Building* (Hart, 2006) 9–17.

The questions of banking prudential regulation and supervision are addressed in the banking legislation at the national and sometimes (e.g. the European Union [EU]) also at the regional level.[5]

But it is a remarkable feature of modern banking regulation that it is not limited to prudential regulation only, but includes also regulation of the conduct of business by banks and the performance of the public functions of banks.

The conduct of business rules historically started as voluntary codes of conduct and strictly speaking were not part of banking regulation. For example, in the United Kingdom the banks signed the Banking Code – later, the Lending Code – the corpus of best practices in the sphere of consumer, small business, and small non-commercial enterprises lending, elaborated jointly by the British Banking Association and the UKCARDS Association. These industry standards led to the introduction of special rules on the conduct of business by the banks' regulatory authorities. Furthermore, nowadays, the authorities pay substantial attention to the way the banks conduct themselves with their customers. This is one area where it is theoretically (and practically) possible to manipulate customers' behavior and decision-making, while at the same time keep compliance with the formal rules. The United Kingdom is a good example of this – the rules which initially appeared in the Lending Code later were incorporated into the conduct-of-business rules issued by the regulatory bodies, the Financial Conduct Authority and Prudential Regulation Authority.

Banking regulation and supervision were developed for a number of reasons. For example, the impact of consumers entering the banking market. The volume of consumer transactions reached such a level that legislators had to take measures to balance the respective positions of the banks and consumers, taking into consideration the psychology and legal illiteracy of a substantial number of consumers. These disproportions are often seen as informational, contractual, and procedural. For this reason the relevant laws and regulations have provided for the rules to be observed when providing customers with information on banking products, for terms and conditions in bank–consumer contracts, and for efficient alternative dispute resolution (ADR).

The discharging of public functions by banks is not straightforward. Banks are businesses, not public bodies, so public functions may appear at odds with the banking sector. Nevertheless, banks do have public duties: the prevention of money laundering, financing of terrorism, tax evasion; there may be other public functions the scope of which varies from country to country. I consider the discharge of public functions as not something alien to the banks or something artificially imposed on them. The discharge of public functions is inherent to the modern business of banking. Indeed, though the banks are businesses, they are doing business in the financial system – in a system which plays a very important public role in society. Therefore, the banks are "to take care" of the financial system, that is the quality of the financial system depends on how banks conduct

5 E.g. Directive 2013/36/EU, OJ L/176/338; Regulation (EU) No 575/2013, OJ L/176/1.

their business in it. As such, it is both the responsibility of the state, with the cooperation of the banks to ensure prudent regulation. In a cooperative environment, the banks are called upon to prevent abuses in the financial system.

Thus the very paradigm of banking regulation is changing. Traditionally it was seen just as prudential regulation, where the focus of the state was on the financial standing of the banks. The modern approach is not limited to this, but considers customer and public interests as inherent parts of the structure of the banking business, its regulation, and supervision. This change in the regulatory paradigm leads to changing of the paradigm of understanding of what bank and banking business is about, as well as to substantial extension and complication of the modern scope of banking regulation and supervision. For this reason, I do not endorse the approach of one of the leading authorities on financial soft law, who stated that

> the focus of bank regulation is not to protect bank customers – though national banking authorities or governments generally guarantee deposits. Instead, the purpose of banking laws is to ensure that banks are prudently run, with adequate capital and liquidity, and are involved in safe, delimited commercial activities that do not unduly jeopardize the bank's health.[6]

This may have been the case in previous times, when customers' interests were protected by banking regulation indirectly, in that so long as banks were financially stable, deposits were protected. Direct protection of customers' interests has now become one of the main targets of banking regulation and supervision, where not only deposits are protected, but the rules and principles regarding other interests of the customers as well as the banking sector's conduct vis-à-vis its customers has become one of the main focuses of modern banking law, and been developed into a body of rules for non-prudential banking regulation and supervision.

### *(b) Soft Law: Banking Regulation and Supervision*

Soft law has found its stable place in modern banking law. In general terms, soft law comprises rules that are neither strictly binding, nor completely lacking in legal significance; and when it comes to international law, soft law is understood as the guidelines, policy declarations, codes of conduct that set standards of conduct but are not legally binding.[7]

On the general theoretical level the appearance of soft law in the modern world demonstrates the shifting of a paradigm in perception of the law by modern society – change from perception of the law as *imposed* to perception of the law as *accepted*. The willingness to accept the rules and principles of law is becoming gradually the only realistic way to make the law the efficient tool for regulation of society.

6 Chris Brummer, *Soft Law and the Global Financial System Rule Making in the 21st Century* (CUP, 2012) 7.
7 *Black's Law Dictionary* (8th edn, 2004, ThomsonWest) 1426.

It may be stated that the sphere where soft law in banking supervision is applicable is mostly international banking law. Indeed, it's hardly possible to imagine that the parties to a dispute may apply soft law in the courts directly. Soft law finds its way to enforcement through the adoption of the laws and other enactments by states and their competent bodies, as well as through international treaties. Therefore, the parties to whom banking soft law might be applicable are states, and it is up to them either to implement soft law standards into national legislation and international treaties.

I would suggest that it is good to distinguish two types of soft lawmaking bodies in the sphere of banking: political and professional.

The main political soft lawmaking body today is the Financial Stability Board (FSB), established in 2009 by the heads of state and government of the G-20 countries in accordance with the Declaration on Strengthening the Financial System. It has inherited the role of the previously existing Financial Stability Forum, but with a broadened mandate. The FSB's objectives include coordination at the international level of the work of national financial authorities and international standard-setting bodies in order to develop and promote the implementation of effective regulatory and supervisory policies. The FSB mandate grew out of the vulnerabilities of the global financial system, and the need to address such vulnerabilities. Furthermore, the monitoring and advising on the best practices in meeting regulatory standards, monitoring of the implementation of agreed commitments are part of the FSB's mandate, but, at the same time, its mandate does not include any responsibility to develop soft law as such.[8]

In the course of discharging its responsibilities the FSB has approved sets of rules produced by professional soft law rule-making bodies. So far, these rules are presented like the 12 standards, relating to macroeconomic policy and data transparency, financial regulation and supervision, and institutional and market infrastructure. Among the standards directly relating to the three main spheres of banking regulation and supervision (prudential regulation, conduct-of-business regulation and discharge of public functions) are the following documents:

- Core Principles for Effective Banking Supervision, elaborated by the Basel Committee on Banking Supervision (BCBS, Basel Committee);[9]
- Core Principles for Effective Deposit Insurance Systems, elaborated by the International Association of Deposit Insurance;[10]

8 Charter of the Financial Stability Board. As amended and restated by the Heads of State and Government of the Group of Twenty at their Los Cabos Summit on June 19, 2012, arts 1, 2.

9 BCBS, *Core Principles for Effective Banking Supervision* (Bank for International Settlement, 2012).

10 BCBS, IADI, *Core Principles for Effective Deposit Insurance Systems* (Bank for International Settlement, 2014).

- Recommendations on Combating Money Laundering and the Financing of Terrorism and Proliferation,[11] elaborated by the Financial Action Task Force (FATF).

The professional soft lawmaking bodies are rather numerous. The "legislative" body for soft law on *prudential banking regulation and supervision* is the BCBS, established in 1974 following a banking crisis. The members of the Basel Committee are the central banks and other bodies with direct banking supervisory authorities (currently from 48 countries).

The Basel Committee does not have rules and procedures: the way it works remains quite obscure despite the vast literature on the subject. Perhaps the best definition of how it works is the description of this body as a "club." The documents (standards) developed by the Basel Committee are not obligatory: they do not qualify to any kind of obligatory document under modern international law, and the only way for their enforcement remains the commitments of its members, as stated in its Charter.

The starting point of the history of soft law on prudential banking regulation and supervision is the year 1994 when the so-called first Basel Accord (Basel I) – International Convergence of the Capital Measurement and Capital Standards – was adopted. Basel I has provided for the basic rules with regard to the quality of the banking capital dividing it on a more stable Tier I capital (equity, own funds, disclosed reserves), and Tier II capital, consisting of less stable items. Basel I Accord has also provided for the correlation between these two capitals, and set up the minimum standards for the amount and the calculation of own funds.

Basel II Accord appeared in 2004. This comprehensive document developed the initial comparatively simple approach of Basel I into the "three pillars" structure of the banking prudential regulation and supervision.

The first pillar was the traditional question of minimum capital requirements, but these issues have been addressed in a more sophisticated manner, insisting on a risk-based approach to banking regulation and supervision. One of the most remarkable features of the document is the admission of the internal banking systems of risk assessment for calculation of the own funds requirements, as well as more detailed analysis of the levels of risks associated with the different kinds of banking assets.

The second pillar was devoted to the supervisory review process and provided for the four underlying principles for the supervision of banks. The principles were of a rather general nature. They stated the importance of banks and supervisors being able to assess the overall capital adequacy of the banks in relation to their risk profile, as well as undertake appropriate measures to remedy the situation, including intervening at an early stage to restore capital to the required level.

Supervision of banks was further elaborated in the Basel Committee's 'Core Principles for Effective Banking Supervision.' The document lists 29 principles

11 FATF, *International Standards on Combating Money Laundering and the Financing of Terrorism & Proliferation* (FATF, 2012–18).

applicable to banking supervision, including its objectives, qualities of the supervisors, supervisory tools, control over the ownership in credit institutions, corporate governance, risk management process, items included in the scope of prudential regulation and supervision, provisions and reserves, disclosure and transparency, abuse of financial services.

The third pillars addressed the issues of market discipline which has been understood as disclosure to other parties of an adequate minimum of information, to enable them to take appropriate decisions on doing business with the relevant bank.

The financial crisis in 2008 led to adoption of the new Basel Accord known as Basel III, which provide for additional measures, such as capital buffers, to enhance bank capital.

With regard to the *soft law on the consumer protection* one of the professional rule-making bodies is the International Association of Deposit Insurers (IADI). IADI presents itself as a forum for deposit insurers from around the world for discussing, and knowledge and expertise sharing on matters related to protection of deposits.

The main relevant soft law document is the 'Core Principles for Effective Deposit Insurance Systems.' The document provides for 16 principles, covering different aspects of deposit protection systems, including their legal status, governance, mandate and powers, membership in the system, informing depositors, amount of funds.

Modern soft law on customer protection is not limited to deposit insurance. There are other examples in place. Let's consider a couple of examples at the EU level.

In 1998 the European Commission issued recommendations on ADR for consumer disputes.[12] It became obvious that consumer protection in the existing judicial systems was inefficient – in many cases the time- and cost-consuming judicial procedures were not adequate for consumer disputes involving comparatively small amounts. The document provided for the major principles for establishing ADR based on fair resolution of consumer complaints against banks. The ADR structures were supposed to meet the requirements of time and cost efficiency, fairness, and effective enforceability of the decisions of the financial ombudsman.

Another document of recommendatory nature was devoted to the provision of information for borrowers in mortgage financing.[13] The document contains rules and principles aimed at balancing the asymmetry between the banks and customers in such transactions.

This is all but one example of the development of soft law in the Russian banking sector.

One of the professional soft lawmaking bodies in the third sphere of modern banking regulation and supervision – *protection of the public interest* – in the course

12 Commission Recommendation 98/257/EC of March 30, 1998 on the principles applicable to the bodies responsible for out-of-court settlement of consumer disputes, OJ L 17/31.

13 Commission Recommendation of March 1, 2001 on pre-contractual information to be given to consumers by lenders offering home loans, OJ LL 69/25.

of banking activities is the Financial Actions Task Force (FATF). This is an intergovernmental body, established at the G-7 summit in 1989. The mandate of the FATF is to set standards and promote effective legal, regulatory, and operational measures for combating money laundering, terrorism financing and the financing of proliferation of weapons of mass destruction, and other related threats to the integrity of the international financial system.

One of the main activities of the FATF is issuing recommendations on a periodic basis. The recommendations set out essential measures to identify illegal activities in the financial system, apply preventive measures, enhance the transparency of the corporate structures and beneficial ownership, as well as to establish the competent state bodies capable of discharging these public duties.

This general picture of soft law in international banking regulation clearly shows that soft law is present in a vital and substantial sphere of modern banking. The capital requirements are the basis of the stability of the banking systems, the deposit protection is key to protecting clients' interests, while anti-money-laundering soft law forms part of the public dimension in the sector. These issues are addressed first in soft law, and only after that the relevant rules appear in national legislation, regional legislative documents (EU), and international treaties. This leads to the reasonable conclusion that soft law today, rather than international treaties and other traditional sources, is the real basis of modern international banking law.

Therefore, it is remarkable that soft law in modern international banking regulation does not remain only soft law, but finds its way into hard law provisions, both at national and international (regional) levels.

EU banking law is a clear example of that. The soft law prudential rules developed by the BCBS have been legalized in several so-called CRD (capital requirements directive) packages. Currently in force CRD IV has reflected the provisions of Basel III Standard into the relevant CRD and capital requirement regulation.[14] The Key Principles for the Effective Deposit Insurance Systems elaborated by the IADI have been clearly reflected in the directive on deposit guarantee schemes.[15] The FATF Recommendations have been incorporated in the anti-money laundering directives.[16] The Commission's recommendations on precontractual information for consumers in the housing loans sector and on ADR for consumer disputes have been incorporated into the relevant directives.[17] Moreover, the rules stated in the directives have been incorporated (or are in the process of incorporation) into EU member states' domestic law. With regard to other countries, which are not members of the EU (including the Russian Federation, as will be shown below), soft law rules have also become part of domestic law.

14 Directive 2013/36/EU, OJ L/ 176 / 338; Regulation (EU) No. 575/2013, OJ L 176 / 1.
15 Directive 2014/49/EU, OJ L 173 / 149.
16 Directive (EU) 2015/849, OJ L 141 / 73.
17 Directive 2013/11/EU, OJ L 165/ 63; Directive 2014/17/EU, OJ L 60/ 34.

Therefore, soft law exists not just as a part, important as that may be, of modern banking law, but exists as the basis for both international and domestic banking law.

What has soft law proven so "popular" in the banking sector?

The reason for this lies first in the flexibility of soft lawmaking bodies: they are not bound by the strict procedural rules of formal international public law bodies. Soft law standards are developed without formal regulations, thus soft lawmaking bodies are able to react quickly to changing environments, updating rules, principles, and standards in the process. The flexible manner in which many modern soft law standards are developed also makes for smooth implementation into domestic law.

Though there is no formal international mechanism to enforce soft law, as there is in the case of international treaties, this requires to be qualified. There are influential international bodies which are capable of putting pressure on countries to encourage them to follow soft law rules and standards. Organizations like the World Bank and IMF look at how countries comply with soft law standards when making international assessments, and this directly influences sovereign ratings. In turn, this results in more favorable terms for the financial institutions of the respective country. The FSB deploys periodic "peer review" of its members' compliance with FSB-approved standards. The FATF also deploys evaluation procedures to promote compliance of member countries with the approved standards for the prevention of money laundering and terrorism financing. Last, but not least, the "naming and shaming" technique has also proven effective in international relations.

Nevertheless, these features of soft law have not resulted in a unanimous appreciation of its advantages. Soft law has its critics, some of whom are fairer that others. As such, soft law in the banking industry sometimes appear to favor only well-developed western countries often with dubious outcomes[18]

Soft law "optimists" tend to think that "the deployment of various checks and balances to keep the use of soft law under control provides room for a pragmatically optimistic assessment of the phenomenon."[19] I do share the concerns of the critics of soft law – not in a general sense, but with regard to the failure of modern soft law to "understand" its true purpose (I will discuss this point below). Nevertheless the dynamic nature of the modern banking world forces us to accept that

> despite the various imperfections and limitations of softer methods, in the field of international financial market regulatory reform it appears to be accepted

18 Nilgun Onder, 'Global Financial Governance: "Soft" Law and Neoliberal Domination' (paper prepared for presentation at Canadian Political Science Association Congress June 2–4, 2005, London).

19 Eilis Ferran and Kern Alexander, 'Can Soft Law Bodies be Effective? Soft Systemic Risk Oversight Bodies and the Special Case of the European Systemic Risk Board' University of Cambridge, Faculty of Law, Legal Studies Research Paper Series, Paper No. 36/2011, June 2011, 8.

that no better option is realistically available in the immediate future, and that a soft law-based approach can have meaningful effect.[20]

Perhaps it is time to ask a different question: what kind of soft law is required for it to best perform its role?

Let's revert to this after considering the Russian experience in following the global financial governance of soft law standards.

## 2 The Status of Russian Domestic Legal Framework on Banking Supervision

### *(a) Russian Scholars on the Phenomenon of Soft Law in Banking Regulation*

Nowadays it is no easy task to speculate on the national obligations that a particular country has in relation to global financial governance. This is especially so when one considers the very existence of global financial governance and how *global* becomes questionable due to the so-called "sanctions regime." But this chapter does not elaborate these aspects, as they have nothing to do with the discourse developed here (indeed, they are much closer to politics and "Cold War"). Rather, it will concentrate on the scientific, technical, and theoretical aspects of banking regulation and supervision, and how they are addressed in Russian legislation and legal scholarship.

Soft law in general and in banking regulation and supervision in particular is widely discussed among Russian legal theorists and experts in banking law.[21]

Soft law in the banking industry is not questioned as such, but is accepted by Russian scholars as a reality of modern banking regulation and supervision. Russian scholars are unanimous in recognizing the non-obligatory nature of soft law in banking, including the Basel standards, considering that soft law is outside of the constitutional provisions on the priority of international law over national legislation. But this provision in the Russian Constitution covers only international agreements where the Russian Federation is a party.[22]

20 Ibid.

21 See e.g. Демин А. В. Феномен 'мягкого права': pro et contra (Alexander V. Demin, The Soft Law Phenomenon: pro et contra) (Вестник Омского университета. серия 'Право,' 2014, № 4 (41). С. 6–10); Демин А. В. К вопросу о переносе концепции 'мягкого права' на уровень национальных правовых систем (Административное право и процесс. 2016, № 3. С. 4) (Demin A. V. Regarding the transformation of the concept of soft law at the level of the national legal systems); Фогельсон Ю.Б. Фогельсон Ю.Б. Мягкое право в современном правовом дискурсе. Журнал российского права. 2013. № 5. С. 40 (Fogelson Yu.B. Soft Law in the Modern Legal Discourse); Фогельсон Ю.Б. Мягкое право и верховенство права. Журнал российского права. 2014. № 11. С. 29 (Fogelson Yu.B. Soft Law and the Supremacy of the Law).

22 Constitution of the Russian Federation, art. 15 states that if the international treaty to which the Russian Federation is a party provides for different rules than the rules of the national laws, the rules of the international treaty prevail.

Russian legal theorists differ in opinion regarding the nature of soft law. Some consider soft law not as law, but as a kind of a "precursory law," i.e. rules which are not of a legal nature, but of a political or moral nature which only later are transformed into law.[23] Some scholars also distinguish between the legal and non-legal rules within international soft law.[24] At the same time there are numerous scholars supporting the legal nature of soft law, insisting that treating soft law as "non-law" is actually a denial of the modern reality and leads to deterioration of the content of modern international law. This is even more so when one considers that in spite of the "softness" of soft law there are international tools to "enforce" it, such as economic pressure on the state, fixing the so-called "sovereign risks" leading to less favorable terms and conditions in lending, and access to financial services.[25]

This approach can be taken as a "pragmatic theory" explaining the reasons why soft law is accepted by Russian scholars as a source of law, but this is not the only approach that explains Russian pragmatism of soft law and the reasons behind its acceptance.

The acceptance of soft law as a legal, not pre-legal or moral phenomenon may find its conceptual roots in certain approaches to the general theory of legal sources developed by the Russian and even by the Soviet scholars. Gennady Muromtsev – a renowned Soviet and Russian legal theorist on the sources of law pointed out several decades ago that the formal approach to the sources of law, when they are viewed only as rules enacted or accepted officially by the state, is not enough. In fact this is and was one of the most complicated issues of the theory of law, and in his research he developed other approaches to the understanding of the nature of the sources of law based on comparative analyses of the problem.[26]

This theoretical basis allows development of further criteria for classifying soft law as a source of law, thus showing the deeper reasons of its acceptance. In this regard it is interesting to refer to those Russian scholars who put forward the other reasons for the acceptance of soft law in modern international banking regulation. For example, Alexander Demin points out the following three reasons why the rules of soft law are observed voluntarily: "trustworthiness of the creators of soft

23 Черниченко С.В. Теория международного права. Т. 2: Старые и новые теоретические проблемы. М.: НИМП 1999. С. 325 (Stanislav V. Chernichenko, The Theory of the International Law. Vol. 2: Old and New Theoretical Problems. NIMP, 1999).

24 Лукашук И.И. Международное право. Общая часть: Учебник. М.: Волтерс Клувер, 2008. С. 138 (Igor I. Lukashuk. International Law. General part: Textbook. Kluwer, 2008).

25 Гузнов А.Г. Правовые проблемы имплементации Базеля II в России (Законодательство. 2008, № 8) (Alexey G. Gouznov. Legal issues in implementing Basel II in Russia).

26 Муромцев Г.И. Источники права: теоретические аспекты проблемы (Правоведение. 1992. № 2. С. 23–30) (Gennady I. Muromtsev. The Sources of Law: theoretical aspects of the problem); Проблемы общей теории государства и права: Учебник для вузов. М.: Норма, 1999. С. 265–267) (The Problems of the General Theory of State and Law. Norma, 1999).

law, personal interest of the addressees and social pressure which follows in case of non-compliance".[27] Trustworthiness of soft lawmakers and the interest of the addressees of soft law are much deeper reasons for acceptance of soft law than just pragmatic reasons to avoid negative pressure for non-compliance; reference to the authoritativeness of lawmakers and "personal interest" of the addressees sounds more academic, than a reverence for the pragmatic side of the matter, which is just obvious.

What is the reason for such a trustworthiness and interest of the addressees? I am of the opinion that the main reason for that is the professionalism of the makers of soft law. Indeed, Basel standards, recommendations for prevention of money-laundering, principles for effective deposit insurance – all these soft law sources are developed by high-level professionals as a prompt (at least, theoretically) reaction to the issues arising in the relevant sector.

In this respect, another Russian leading scholar on soft law Yuri Fogelson considers soft law as a way to ensure legal certainty in regulation of the financial industry in a situation where traditional law has exhausted its reserves to do that. This is primarily because legislators and courts are unable to ensure the normal function of the legal system in a situation where complex financial products are constantly evolving.[28] These views of Russian scholars align the Russian doctrine with the views of western scholars supporting the idea that soft law is not a kind of a secondary law in comparison to traditional law, but a full-value alternative way of solving legal issues, with demonstrable advantages.[29]

Therefore, Russian legal doctrine has added value to the theoretical analysis of soft law as well as developed substantial grounds for acceptance of this modern phenomenon as a factor of the development of legal regulation and supervision in the banking and financial industry.

### *(b) Implementation of Soft Law Standards: Achievements*

This section looks at Russian banking legislation, and the regulatory and supervisory structure in the light of the current trends in global financial governance. We will follow the same structure – prudential regulation, customer protection, and discharge of public functions by credit institutions.

27 Демин А.В. К вопросу о переносе концепции 'мягкого права' на уровень национальных правовых систем (Административное право и процесс. 2016, № 3. С. 4) (Alexander V. Demin. Regarding the transformation of the concept of soft law at the level of the national legal systems). [All translations in the text are mine – A. V.]

28 Фогельсон Ю.Б. Мягкое право в современном правовом дискурсе. Журнал российского права. 2013. № 5. С. 40 (Yuri B. Fogelson. Soft Law in the Modern Legal Discourse); Фогельсон Ю.Б. Мягкое право и верховенство права. Журнал российского права. 2014. № 11. С. 29 (Yuri B. Fogelson. Soft Law and the Supremacy of the Law).

29 Jacob E. Gersen and Eric A. Posner, 'Soft Law: Lessons from Congressional Practice' (2008) 61 *Stanford Law Review* 626.

### *(i) Prudential Supervision*

The Russian legal system is based on the supremacy of law – the legislative acts of the supreme representative body – of the state Duma, with the subsequent approval of the Council of the Federation and signed by the president of the Russian Federation. These laws sit at the apex of all legislative sources.

Russian banking legislation is based on two main laws: the Banking Act[30] and the Central Bank Act.[31]

The current Russian domestic legal framework on banking supervision is a result of almost 30 years of historical development of the relevant legislation, which from the very beginning empowered the Bank of Russia with the responsibility and competence to oversee that credit institutions acted in compliance with the applicable legislation and regulations.

The Central Bank Act states the objective of banking regulation and supervision in the Russian Federation: this was and is to maintain stability in the banking system and to protect depositors and banks' creditors.[32]

It is noteworthy that the objectives of banking supervision in Russian legislation are not understood in a purely national dimension, but include international aspects. From the very beginning the legislation on the Bank of Russia has provided for its cooperation with the central banks and supervisory bodies of the other countries, first with regard to the exchange of information and documents for the purposes of efficient banking supervision.[33]

The scope of banking supervision includes a number of major issues such as authorization and supervision.

*Authorization* – the Bank of Russia issues licenses to banks prior to the commencement of their activities. Therefore without authorization from the Central Bank, it is not possible for banking activities to commence. This is also true of most countries with effective banking supervision. The law provides for a wide range of authorization requirements and conditions, which include inter alia initial own funds obtained from lawful sources, qualificational and reputational requirements for the management and shareholders, business plans.

*Supervision* – supervisory – or, to be more specific, *regulatory and supervisory* functions of the Bank of Russia are discharged through the Committee on Banking Supervision which is composed of leading officials of the Bank of Russia in charge of banking supervision. This is the structural body within the Bank of Russia and does not have representatives from the banking industry.

The Bank of Russia is empowered to adopt rules mandatory for the credit institutions covering all banking activities, such as:

30 Federal Law No. 395-1 On Banking and Banking Activity, December 2, 1990 (last amended 31.12.2017).

31 Federal Law No. 86-FZ, On the Central Bank of the Russian Federation (Bank of Russia), July 10, 2002 (last amended 07.03.2018).

32 Ibid., art. 56.

33 Ibid., art. 51.

- reporting and disclosure of information;
- risk management systems;
- capital requirements;
- rules on performance of banking operations;
- remuneration policies; and
- acquisitions of the shareholdings in the credit institutions.

The main tools for the supervision of the credit institutions are inspections and issuing mandatory orders for credit institutions. The law provides for the rights and obligations of the inspectors and the procedures to be followed.

In case of breach of the laws and mandatory prescriptions the Bank of Russia has a wide range of tools such as:

- imposing fines on credit institutions;
- requesting replacement of credit institutions' management;
- requesting reorganization credit institutions;
- restricting certain activities (banking transactions);
- appointing external management; and
- withdrawing the banking license.

Within the context of this chapter the following assessment is of relevance. When defining the scope and the content of banking supervision Russian legislation follows to a great extent the commonly accepted international standards, including those which are reflected in international banking soft law, as well as in the global, mainly European, approaches to banking prudential regulation and supervision. The following examples support this thesis.

First, at the time of writing (March 2018) Russia is in the process of adjusting its banking legislation to bring it in the line with the Basel III standards. In this respect Russia has been favorably viewed as making good progress.[34]

Second, the structure of modern banking regulatory and supervisory authorities has followed the modern approach to integral regulation both with regard to the integrity of the financial market and with regard to micro- and macro-prudential regulation.

There is a consensus that a financial market consists of three main segments: banking, securities, and insurance. For a long time many countries assigned regulatory supervisory responsibilities to different authorities, on the bases of these segments.

By the end of the twentieth century another approach started to dominate: as the financial market requires integral regulation and supervision, regulatory and supervisory functions should not be dispersed between separate bodies, but aggregated in the body responsible for all three segments of the financial market.

As a result, the financial markets' unified supervisory bodies have taken different shape in different countries: the Financial Markets Authority (FMA) in the United Kingdom, BaFin in Germany.

34 BCBS, *Thirteenth Progress Report on Adoption of the Basel Regulatory Framework*. Bank for International Settlements. October 2017, 19–21.

Another issue in banking regulation and supervision addressed in the discussions and reforms recently is the role of the central banks in this process. For a long time central banks were excluded from the administrative side of banking regulation and supervision. Under this model the central banks were responsible for macro-prudential regulation of the sector, while micro-prudential regulation was left to designated state bodies. Central banks were to be spared administrative burdens, as there were other regulatory tools available to them, such as economic regulation, ability to alter base rates.

On the other hand, in the course of time, the shortcomings of such an approach became evident. The upshot was that, on the one hand there were the central banks as the bodies with economic strength but no administrative powers; on one other hand, were the supervisory bodies with administrative powers but no any economic capabilities (e.g. FMA, BaFin). Over time this situation has been evaluated as inefficient. Mervyn King, former Governor of the Bank of England, compared the role of the Bank of England in such a supervisory structure to the church: able to provide sermons, but to a congregation that does not heed them when it sees alternative conduct, which is highly profitable.[35]

Russian banking legislation traditionally entrusted to the Central Bank the regulatory and supervisory powers at both macro- and micro-prudential levels, so it is long-established practice in the Russian Federation.

The three segments of the financial market – banking, securities, and insurance – are now regulated by a single supervisory body. In this respect the Russian banking system has made a choice in favor of the mega-regulator model of financial regulation and supervision. Since 2013 the Bank of Russia is entrusted with responsibility for regulation and supervision of the whole financial market.[36]

The evidence discussed in this chapter clearly shows that both prudential regulation and supervision as well as the regulatory and supervisory structures in the Russian banking system develop in line with modern trends in the financial world, following the standards which initially appeared as soft law. But on the other hand, following these trends has resulted in certain asymmetries between the structural elements in the banking system.

### *(ii) Deposit Protection*

Though deposit protection is just one aspect of customer protection in modern banking law, this discussion is limited to deposit protection, as an area that is not so well covered by contemporary international soft law.

The body entrusted with deposit protection in the Russian banking system is the Deposit Insurance System (DIS), established in 2004 by the Deposit

35 Speech by Mervyn King, Governor of the Bank of England at Lord Mayor's Banquet for Bankers and Merchants of the City of London, Mansion House, June 17, 2009. The text is available at: https://publications.parliament.uk/pa/cm200809/cmselect/cmtreasy/767/767.pdf

36 Central Bank Act, ch. X.1,

Insurance Act.[37] The key basic points of the deposit protection system can be summarized as follows.

Under the IADI classification Russian DIS is a "government legislated and administered" system of deposit insurance. The basic rules for the deposit protection are provided for at the level of federal laws. The body in charge of the deposit protection is the Deposit Insurance Agency (DIA, the Agency) which is a state corporation with statutory functions, including maintenance of the DIS, maintenance of the register of the banks, DIS members, calculation and collection of insurance premiums, keeping depositor records, and controlling payments to them.[38]

The Agency is governed by a board, headed by the chairman of the Bank of Russia.

The daily activities of the Agency and performance of its functions, including those vis-à-vis depositors and members (banks) are maintained by the management board and the general director.

The protected deposits under Russian legislation include all deposits of natural persons, save for deposits for professional purposes (notaries, advocates), bearer deposits, e-money deposits, and nominal accounts deposits.[39]

If deposits become unavailable, due to withdrawal of the banking license or moratorium for payments to the creditors imposed by the Bank of Russia, they are subject to cover by the special fund.[40]

Cover is calculated on the basis of all unavailable deposits of one depositor placed with one bank. The maximum coverage is the full amount of all such unavailable deposits but not more than 1,400,000 rubles.[41]

Cover is to be paid within three days following the presentation to the depositors of all the documents listed in the law, but not earlier than 14 days following the default.

The participation of the banks in the DIS is obligatory. The contribution of the banks to the fund for protection of the deposits is calculated based on the amount of the deposits and varies depending on the criteria provided by law.[42]

These features of the DIS in the Russian Federation in essence follow the Key Principles for the Effective Deposit Insurance Systems, that kind of assessment has also been expressed by the IADI.

Under a generally accepted classification deposit insurers worldwide are divided into three main categories depending on the scope of their mandates:

- paybox, when the DIS powers are limited to collection of the participating banks premium and payment of insurance coverage to the depositors;

37 Federal Law No. 177-FZ, On the Insurance of the Deposits of the Natural Persons in the Banks of the Russian Federation, December 23, 2003.
38 Deposit Insurance Act, ch. 3.
39 Ibid., art. 5.
40 Ibid., art. 8.
41 Ibid., art. 11.
42 Ibid., ch. 6.

- paybox with extended powers mandate allows the DIS to participate in the bank resolution process; and
- risk minimizer – according to the IADI this is the most advanced type of DIS, able to manage its own risks (ability to exert supervisory authority).[43]

This comparative analysis was undertaken by the IADI in 2012, after which Russian banking legislation reshaped the responsibilities of the DIA. Nevertheless the conclusion of the IADI experts, that deposit insurance in Russia has a wider mandate than a "paybox" system[44] is still valid. Indeed, the DIA may participate in the prevention of the bankruptcy of the banks in various ways, including financial support to investors purchasing not less than 75 percent of shares in the bank, financial support to the bank if the approved investor or the DIA has purchased not less than 75 percent of the shares in the bank.[45]

As of March 1, 2017 the DIA was participating in the financial recovery of 25 banks.[46]

The advanced techniques used for the recovery of problematic banks have both advantages and disadvantages. For example, with regard to purchasing of 75 percent of the bank's shares there is some criticism: by injecting capital into the equity the DIA undertakes responsibility for the bank's management; besides, if a significant amount of capital is injected it may lead to a substantial imbalance between the value of the bank's assets and the Agency's contribution, causing difficulties for the further sale of the Agency's shares to potential investors.

Nevertheless, these advanced techniques provide substantial flexibility in resolving the problem banks' issues. The main advantage of the advanced techniques is the ability to take into consideration the interests of all the elements of the banking system and the financial system as a whole, while the "paybox" technique is limited only to a passive reaction in case of a default of the banks. I am a supporter of the approach, that the most efficient way of protection of the interests of the different stockholders in the banking system is to protect their interests as different elements of the same system, but not in isolation. This means, inter alia, that an attempt to protect the interests of one of the elements in a financial system *against or ignoring* the interests of other elements of the system will sooner or later lead to the system's crashing. In this respect, the possibility to use the deposit protection fund for the purposes of recovery of a bank serves the interests of the banking

43 IADI, *Problem Bank Resolution Methods and Payouts of Insurance Coverage to Depositors of Forcibly Liquidated Banks: Comparative Analysis of Deposit Insurance Systems in CIS Countries. Research Paper Prepared by the Eurasia Regional Committee* (IADI, 2012) 5.

44 Ibid.

45 Federal Law No. 127-FZ, On Insolvency (Bankruptcy), October 26, 2002, art. 189.49.

46 Data from DIA official website: www.asv.org.ru/sanation. It should be borne in mind that only Russian legal entities are allowed to be registered/licensed as banks, so no grounds for a foreign law application, even if they have foreign shareholders. So far Russian law does not allow foreign banks or their branches to operate in Russia. Only offices are allowed.

system as a whole and as a main consequence of it the interests of depositors will be protected in a more balanced and efficient manner. Indeed, to save a bank in difficulty simply means that the depositors will get their deposits in full amount, instead of limited payment under the insurance case.

### *(iii) Public Functions (Prevention of Money Laundering)*

Russia has adopted special legislation on prevention of money laundering and terrorism financing at the level of the federal law. The main legislative act on this matter is the Anti Money Laundering Act (AML Act).[47] The special law is a good illustration of the fact that Russia follows the recommendations of the FATF in the process of development of its national laws on prevention of abuse of the financial system. Some examples are:

- credit institutions are obliged to conduct due diligence with regard to potential clients (including verifying personal data). Credit institutions are also obliged to undertake reasonable steps to clarify the beneficial owners of the clients, and keep all such information updated on a regular basis;[48]
- provisions relating to certain transactions considered suspicious or prohibited under international standards, as well as for the criteria to identify transactions as suspicious;[49]
- record-keeping and reporting requirements imposed on the credit institutions with regard to suspicious transactions in accordance with the applicable legislation.

The AML Act also provides for the competent body for the prevention of money laundering and terrorism financing and defines the legal status of that body, its authorities in the process of discharging of its public functions.[50] All these legislative provisions correspond to the relevant sections of the 40 FATF recommendations.

It is also remarkable that the AML Act provides for extensive international cooperation in this field, cooperation between the competent authorities of different countries – members of the FATF, which includes exchange of information, cooperation in preliminary investigations, as well as judicial and enforcement procedures.[51]

This list is not exhaustive, but for the purposes of this chapter these examples suffice to show that the Russian Federation follows international anti-money-laundering and terrorism prevention standards in the development of its national legislation.

47 Federal Law No. 115-FZ, On Prevention of the Legalization (Laundering) of the Incomes Obtained in an Illegal Manner and of the Terrorism Financing, August 7, 2001.
48 Anti-Money Laundering Act, art. 7.
49 Ibid., art. 6.
50 Ibid., art. 8.
51 Ibid., art. 10.

## 3 Implementation of Soft Law Standards: Challenges

Reviewing national experiences in following the rules of global financial governance, including soft law standards, is a useful exercise as it reveals not only "success stories," but also the imbalances in implementing modern soft law. In this respect it serves as constructive feedback for soft lawmakers of the modern banking world.

In this respect Russian experience shows a number of "good-to-learn" paradoxes. On one hand, compliance with soft law standards definitely helps to improve Russia's national financial system, thus strengthening global financial governance and promoting the prevention of abuse of the global financial system. But on the other hand in implementing soft law standards Russia faced substantial and even sensitive asymmetries with regard to the interests – lawful interests – of different stakeholders in the financial system.

This is relevant to all three spheres of the implementation of soft law which this chapter has explored: prudential regulation, consumer protection, public functions.

Let's start with prudential regulation and supervision.

It has been demonstrated in this chapter that Russia is in the process – positively assessed by international supervisors – of implementing modern standards, both with regard to soft law financial requirement for banks' financial standing and the regulatory and supervisory structure, where all three financial market segments are controlled by a unified supervisory body.

On the other hand in the Russian legal and legal-policy context it has led to the development of the Bank of Russia as a regulatory and supervisory "superpower" with no efficient way to challenge its decision by vested stakeholders.

For example, one of the well-established prudential requirements in modern banking law is the necessity for the shareholders and managers of the banks (including potential acquirers) to meet the financial and reputational criteria. One of the tools entrusted to the Bank of Russia for these purposes is the maintenance of the "blacklist" – a database of people whose reputation is not sufficient to become a shareholder in or manager of a bank. Bank managers and shareholders who have filed for bankruptcy are blacklisted. The law is rather specific on this matter, stating that the ground for inclusion in the "blacklist" database for a shareholder is to possess more than 10 percent of the shares, and – an additional requirement – to be able to influence the decision-making of the bank. In other words, the law is clear that mere possession of more than 10 percent of the shares does not automatically lead to a situation where the respective shareholder is able to influence or define the decision-making in the bank.

But practice shows that the Bank of Russia is reluctant to analyze the particular cases in a detailed manner, tending to consider all cases when a shareholder has more than 10 percent of the shares as ground for blacklisting.[52] Given such an

52 In this respect a remarkable case has been recently reported (though the case has been reported and addressed by the media, I will avoid stating in this chapter the names of the legal entities and natural persons involved). A reputable investment firm from western Europe acquired more than 10 percent but less than 20 percent of the shares in a Russian bank. The amount of shares for acquisition was calculated based on the

approach has led to the blacklisting of individuals, including western bankers that had supervisory roles in the sector, this is not to be considered as a problem for domestic legislators to solve. The consequences of such an asymmetry go beyond national borders.

The asymmetry in the field of prudential regulation and supervision has also been addressed in Russian legal studies, specifically the right of the Bank of Russia to use professional judgment. This has led to the Bank of Russia gaining further competence with respect to the development of a risk-oriented approach to banking supervision, which has been one of the key features of the Basel II standards.[53]

The use of professional judgment by the Bank of Russia caught the attention of the Russian High Court of Arbitration,[54] plus the term "professional judgment" appeared in the Banking Act suggest the legalization of soft law. But the use of professional judgment is not as a general power of the Bank of Russia, but resides with the Committee on Banking Supervision.

Thus following the modern trends, advanced standards in the banking supervision, allowing the integrated supervision of all the three segments of the financial market, has become asymmetrical with the uncontrolled powers of the supervisory body. The judicial control proved to be ineffective when the case concerns the specifics of the financial industry. Indeed, judges are not trained as financiers, and, for example, the complex activities of investment funds often present a challenge to those on the bench who are not trained in banking and financial law.

usual approach of investment funds – to avoid acquisition of the shares leading to the management capacity, as far as the task of an investment fund is a profit, not management. In this particular case more than 75 percent of the shares were in the possession of one beneficiary, thus the fund, as well as any other shareholder has been left without any possibilities to influence the decision-making of the bank. The bank got into trouble, and the position of the Bank of Russia with regard to the blacklisting of the shareholders was pretty formal – it blacklisted the managers of the fund based on the fact that the fund possessed more than 10 percent of the shares, thus ignoring the clear approach of the law, that just possession of more than 10 percent is not enough per se to be treated as a person with undue reputation. The sadness of the story comes not just from the position of the Bank of Russia, but from the position of the courts. The judges ignored the clear arguments of the fund's advocates, who provided the reasonable evidences that in this particular situation the fund had not been able to influence the decision-making, and accepted the position of the Bank of Russia. As a result several leading professionals of the European banking world (some of them even used to hold official positions in international banking authorities) have been blacklisted in the Bank of Russia register.

53 Гузнов А. Г. Правовые проблемы имплементации Базеля II в России. Законодательство. 2008. № 8 (Alexey G. Gouznov, Legal issues in implementing of the Basel II in Russia); Гузнов А. Г., Чистюхин В.В. Профессиональное суждение как основополагающий элемент банковского надзора и правовая проблема // Аналитический банковский журнал. 2008. N 4 (Alexey G. Gouznov and Victor V. Chistukhin, Professional Judgment as a Basis for the Banking Supervision and as the Legal Issue).

54 Resolution of the Presidium of the Highest Arbitration Court of June 19, 2007 N 1583/07.

Modern best practices in the banking sphere provide ADR mechanisms to address disputes arising between the supervisory body and financial institutions. For example, in the United Kingdom under the Financial Services and Markets Act the Financial Services and Market Tribunal was established.

I am not arguing here that Russia is to follow the UK example in this respect – as it would be unreasonable to insist on a mirror approach in countries with different legal traditions and cultures. Nevertheless, the very idea of an ADR body in the highly professional financial sphere could be a solution to the real problem existing in Russia. That is, that the Bank of Russia exists as a "superpower" in the financial system, with complainants having no recourse to effectively challenge its decisions. This issue has also been addressed by scholars from the Bank of Russia, but the proposed solution is discouraging: to entrust the Committee on Banking Supervision of the Bank of Russia with dispute resolution functions,[55] which would make the Bank of Russia judge in its own case.

This asymmetry is not the only example. A similar issue arose in the prevention of abuse of the financial system (prevention of money laundering and terrorism financing).

On one hand, the development of the Russian efforts has been positively assessed by the FATF. In 2002 Russia was removed from the FATF blacklist and in 2003 became a full member. Moreover in 2013–14 the Russian representative was appointed chairman of the FATF, and the activities of the Russian Federation in this sphere have been favorably assessed by the international community.

On the other hand, there is another "blacklist" – a blacklist of legal entities and natural persons who have had their attempted transactions rejected on grounds that banks deemed them to be suspicious. It appeared that a substantial number of such refusals have not been adequately grounded, and sometimes such refusal resulted from technical mistakes. The list was reported by the banks to the Russian Financial Monitoring Service[56] and the Bank of Russia. The list was circulated to all banks, resulting in those so listed being automatically refused banking services.

It has been recognized, even by officials, that there is no efficient way to remedy the situation with regard to bona fide clients who have been erroneously blacklisted. The attempts to remedy the situation through the courts proved ineffective; procedures are lengthy and the approaches of courts are contradictory and sometimes even prone to mistakes.[57]

55 Гузнов А.Г. Правовые проблемы имплементации Базеля II в России. Законодательство. 2008. № 8 (Alexey G. Gouznov A.G. Legal issues in implementing of the Basel II in Russia).

56 The body in charge of prevention of money laundering and terrorism financing.

57 These considerations are based on the issues exposed during the round table in the Institute of State and Law of the Russian Academy of Science on the problems of applications of the provisions of the Anti-Money Laundering Act in the banking practice in February 2018. The data on the round table is available at: https://arb.ru/arb/press-on-arb/problemy_primeneniya_bankami_zakonodatelstva_pod_ft-10184830/?sphrase_id=306943

Another example of asymmetry comes from the protection of the deposit system.

Under Russian bankruptcy law the transactions entered by the bankrupt company prior to the start of bankruptcy proceedings might be challenged on the ground that such transactions has worsened the financial state of the bankrupt to the detriment of the interests of its creditors. The official source for publications on bankruptcy proceedings has reported[58] that several courts have issued decisions holding invalid the transactions under which the depositors have withdrawn their money from the bankrupt banks prior to bankruptcy proceedings, initiated against such a bank, thus requesting depositors to repay the money to the bankrupt bank with subsequent repayment from the DIA within the limits prescribed by the law. And the initiative to nullify such withdrawals has come from the DIA – the very body in charge of the protection of the interests of the depositors. These cases undermine public trust in the banking system, especially when ordinary depositors were honestly unaware of the poor financial standing of a bank.

But let's take a look at this situation from a wider perspective.

Russian law provides for a number of tools for the protection of the interests of the depositors. One of the relevant rules states that in case the deposit is placed with a bank for a specified period (not on call, but time-tenure deposit), still the depositor – if the depositor is a natural person – is entitled to withdraw the deposit at any time. The only consequence is that the interest on such deposit will be paid by the bank under the lower interest rate (in default – under the interest rate applicable to the on-call deposits).

On one hand, such a rule looks positive in the light of the depositors' protection policy. But, on the other hand, the interests of the depositors are protected *against the interests of the banking system* as a whole. Indeed, the banks cannot rely on such "long" money because they can be requested by the depositors at any time. This creates instability with regard to treatment of such money, while the soundness of the system – the financial system requires stability pursued both on macro and micro levels. It's interesting that premature withdrawal of the funds from such deposits were treated as bad faith transactions by the courts if this took place prior to the bank's insolvency.

These cases can be taken as an illustration of the law of the functioning of a system. If an element of the system is protected against the interest of the system as a whole, it will sooner or later result in a situation detrimental to the interests of the initially protected element. Indeed, initially depositors' interests were protected, ignoring the interest of the system as a whole, but at the final stage it resulted in ignoring the interests of the depositors, because ultimately the interests of the financial system as a whole might be more important to the state than the interests of certain depositors. An asymmetry with the similar undesired consequences appears when the interests of the good faith clients are ignored in favor

58 АСВ востребовало вклады: с граждан взыскивают средства, снятые со счетов перед крахом банков: www.kommersant.ru/doc/3535344

of the prevention of abuse of the financial system in a legal environment where no effective dispute resolution structure exists.

It is interesting to note that the issue of asymmetries with regard to soft law have been addressed by experts, though in a different respect – as an asymmetry between the global rules of soft law, on the one hand, and the national interests, on the other. This issue has been specifically addressed with regard to emerging market countries (EMCs). As Onder puts it:

> despite the G-7's recent efforts to better include the EMCs in the decision-making organs of the global financial system, such standards and codes are made without adequate representation and participation of the EMCs. Furthermore, as these standards and codes are modeled on the institutions and practices prevailing in the developed countries, they fail to address the specific problems and needs of the less developed countries, besides, lack of transparency of the rule-making process and representation and participation "works against the weak and enhances the power of the strong."[59]

One may argue, that it is necessary to distinguish between the two situations. The first situation is when the EMCs are not participating in the development of soft law rules. As a result the rules are not taking into consideration the realities of the less developed countries which nevertheless are supposed to follow them. Another situation is when Russia is participating in the soft lawmaking process, being a member of soft lawmaking bodies, including the BCBS, so if the asymmetries arise in the process of the implementation of soft law rules, this is already a problem of the respective country; the asymmetry is not created by soft law as such.

My approach to this issue is a different one. In order for soft law to be *soft* law in *global* financial governance, soft law, soft lawmaking bodies are supposed to be alert to the possible negative outcomes of soft law rules, and provide counter-balances to avoid such negative consequences.

## 4 Conclusions

I am of the opinion that the time has come to take further steps in assessing the very phenomena of modern soft law in global financial governance in the light of the quality of its content.

The main issue, the main problem of the efficiency of modern soft law in global financial governance lies not in the willingness or unwillingness of the countries to follow its standards, but to a certain degree, in the quality of the content of soft law itself.

In fact, modern global soft law in global financial governance is not global in the deepest sense of the word. It is global in that it is developed by the leading industrialized countries, and it is being expanded around the world. But the true globality comes from a different approach – from elaborating the standards which

59 Onder (n. 18) 2–3.

take into consideration not only the desired outcomes, but legal realities of countries, cultural differences between different jurisdictions, with an understanding that the same rules may easily lead to different and sometimes, unfortunately, negative outcomes in different legal cultures.

Russian legal culture has always focused on public interests as opposed to private interests. For that reason, for example, the FATF recommendations which end with the provision that "countries should adopt effective measures which protect the rights of *bona fide* third parties acting in good faith when implementing the obligations",[60] is generally seen in Russian legal culture contexts like the protection of private interests is secondary to public interests.

The same consequences are visible when following the Basel Committee standards regarding effective banking supervision – strengthening the powers of the Bank of Russia as effective supervisory body without developing effective systems for the protection of the good faith banks led in some cases to neglecting their interests to the detriment of the interests of the financial system as a whole.

The time has come for the law of global financial governance to take into consideration not just the technical aspects of the industry, but legal and cultural differences between the countries to develop a set of standards, which not just pursue some important targets, but provide for a *balanced* financial system, where interests of the parties are balanced when pursuing this important public law objective. Recent developments in banking law have provided examples that balance is not achieved if the law pursues the public objectives and protection of the consumer as a "weak party." The fair balance of the interests of all stakeholders in the financial system has to be at the heart of regulation, and this target is not achievable if global law is developed ignoring the peculiarities of national legal cultures.

Without such an approach soft law in global financial governance will not develop into an efficient system of regulation, but will develop into another tool of international pressure.

At the same time I don't want this approach to be overinterpreted in that national jurisdictions may consider this to be exclusively a problem for international soft lawmaking bodies. This is also the responsibility of national legislators and responsible state and non-state bodies to detect the asymmetries resulting from the implementation of soft law standards and articulate them to the international soft lawmaking bodies. The time has come that the social goals of banking regulation and supervision (and, needless to say, that in our times social goals take precedence over purely economic goals, as nobody wants rich bankers and unhappy customers) may not be achieved without that kind of cooperation. The only way to avoid such undesired consequences is to take into consideration the interests of other elements and the system as a whole while making any decision in the course of pursuing one's own interests. The regulator, which by its nature is the most "aware" element of the system, should heed this and encourage others to do likewise.

60 FATF (n. 11) recommendations 6, 7.

As I've made clear, modern banking soft law is the law of the professionals, and a professional approach requires the ability of the professional soft lawmakers to be able to see, assess, and take into consideration not only the desired economic and political targets, but the social consequences of implementing soft law in national jurisdictions.

# Index

www.ingramcontent.com/pod-product-compliance
Ingram Content Group UK Ltd.
Pitfield, Milton Keynes, MK11 3LW, UK
UKHW010955180926
475701UK00004B/383

* 9 7 8 0 3 6 7 5 8 6 0 2 7 *